Praise for *The Age of Acquiescence*

"Delivered with real verve. . . . Like Marx in the *Communist Manifesto* and Thomas Piketty's *Capital*, but from an American perspective, Fraser writes majestically if not almost poetically about the making of capitalism."
—Harvey J. Kaye, *Daily Beast*

"Vivid . . . brilliantly document[s] . . . the long-term undermining of popular sovereignty and its replacement by the sovereignty of organized money over an atomized, impotent populace . . . stellar . . . packs a punch . . . unlike most of his academic and Marxist predecessors, he writes lively prose and furnishes much colorful detail. . . . Fraser's narrative is fast-paced and broad-gauged." —George Scialabba, *Nation*

"Fraser's cultural critique is refreshingly unfashionable. For decades, American historians have emphasized the agency of consumers, their alleged ability to transform consumption into an autonomous, maybe even resistant gesture. Fraser refuses to play this game. . . . Fraser challenges the discourse of inevitability by reminding us that things were different once, and might be again."
—Jackson Lears, *London Review of Books*

"Fraser's chapter on 'the political economy of auto-cannibalism,' with its relentless, horrifying litany of statistical evidence of the wreckage, is alone worth the price of the book. . . . Fraser provocatively suggests that the last vestiges of nineteenth-century reactionary radicalism are to be found in the Tea Party . . . rich scholarship . . . persuasive. . . . He has admirably made accessible to a wide readership a narrative that would not meet with the approval of most local school boards." —*Christian Century*

"[An] important new book. . . . Fraser is one of the great historians of both American capital and labor over the past thirty years. He has written foundational books on both the labor movement during the first half of the twentieth century and Wall Street. . . . *The Age of Acquiescence* is an arresting and sobering account of what must be called the rise and fall of class struggle in the United States. . . . His writing is also often beautiful, a combination of compressed aphoristic power and soaring imagery. . . . Fraser thrillingly tells this story of exploitation and resistance." —*Dissent*

"Fraser leads the reader on a fascinating and relevant journey."
—Brian Tanguay, *Santa Barbara Independent*

"A cutting study of how American workers lost the will to battle for their well-being. It took decades to get ourselves into this mess. It's going to take decades to get out of it. Fraser makes that all too clear in a book that deserves to spark a national conversation."
—Michael Causey, *Washington Independent Review of Books*

"*The Age of Acquiescence* is an engaging, thoughtful, and, at times, inspirational read. Through past examples of resistance, Fraser demonstrates that other avenues are available to us, even though they might be relics of the past. It's not inconsequential that this past wave of resistance came at a time of the American frontier's closing. Now, when it seems that all other horizons are off limits, that there is no other choice but what's before us, Fraser reminds us that it wasn't always so, nor should it be."
—Bookslut.com

"Important. . . . [H]as spurred a useful discussion." —laprogressive.com

"The great strength of the book is its detailed accounts of levels of both working class resistance and acquiescence to an aggressive capitalist class before and after the 1930s and 1940s. . . . Fraser's reconstruction of the myriad forms of opposition in the period before the 1930s is a welcome alternative to the all too common notion that the US working class lacked a tradition of class warfare." —NewSocialist.org

"A sharp-edged, completely fascinating look at American history and the contemporary politics of the haves and have-nots."
—Vanessa Bush, *Booklist*

"Fraser's work shines as an angry but cogent denouncement of America's growing wealth disparity. Highly recommended." —*Library Journal*

"An absorbing, vigorous account of class politics. . . . an excellent, very readable recreation of an authentically American form of working-class militancy and its eclipse." —*Publishers Weekly*

"No one writing history today does it with the power, passion, insight, and rigor of Steve Fraser. In *The Age of Acquiescence*, Fraser reaches back a century to the first Gilded Age and then pushes forward into our own Gilded Age, providing his readers with a history that matters, that informs, and that, most critically, raises essential questions we should all be asking about wealth, power, and inequalities in America today."
—David Nasaw, author of *The Patriarch: The Remarkable Life and Turbulent Times of Joseph P. Kennedy*

"Steve Fraser is that rare writer who combines a deep knowledge of history with a penetrating analysis of our current political and social condition. Here, in the lively prose that marks all his writing, he probes the similarities and differences between America's two gilded ages—the late nineteenth century and today—offering provocative observations about why the first produced massive popular resistance and the second resigned acquiescence."
—Eric Foner, the Pulitzer Prize–winning author of *The Fiery Trial: Abraham Lincoln and American Slavery*

"Over the last few years, there's been a wealth of books describing our new gilded age and bemoaning the extreme economic inequality that now defines modern America. Steve Fraser's fascinating *The Age of Acquiescence* is indispensable because it explains how that happened, how America's long standing opposition to concentrated wealth was defeated. Steve Fraser, in other words, is Thomas Piketty with politics, providing a crucial guide in helping the ninety-nine percent understand the terms of their defeat and, more importantly, how it can once again go on the offensive."
—Greg Grandin, author of *The Empire of Necessity: Slavery, Freedom, and Deception in the New World* and *Fordlandia: The Rise and Fall of Henry Ford's Forgotten Jungle City*

"A splendid and illuminating book. Fraser's writing is clear-headed and free of cant. I know of no better an accounting for the division of America over the last forty years into a minority of the terrified rich and a majority of the humiliated poor."
—Lewis Lapham, editor of *Lapham's Quarterly* and author of *Pretensions to Empire: Notes on the Criminal Folly of the Bush Administration*

"Steve Fraser has given us a sweeping account of the economic and cultural changes in American society that combined to create an earlier era of working class struggle and hope, and then in our present moment have generated quiescence and despair. Read this book for its synoptic account of the ways that cultural manipulation has accompanied intensifying economic exploitation. But read it also to snatch glimmers of a better future from the past."
—Frances Fox Piven, author of *Challenging Authority: How Ordinary People Change America*

THE AGE OF
ACQUIESCENCE

Also by Steve Fraser

Labor Will Rule

Every Man a Speculator

Wall Street

THE AGE OF ACQUIESCENCE

THE LIFE AND DEATH OF
AMERICAN RESISTANCE TO
ORGANIZED WEALTH AND POWER

STEVE FRASER

BASIC BOOKS
A Member of the Perseus Books Group
New York

The Library of Congress has cataloged the hardcover edition as follows:
Fraser, Steve.
The age of acquiescence : the life and death of American resistance to
organized wealth and power / Steve Fraser.
pages cm
ISBN 978-0-316-18543-1 (hardback)
1. United States—Politics and government—1945–2. Social conflict—
United States—History. 3. Protest movements—United States—History.
4. Income distribution—United States—History. 5. Elite (Social
sciences)—United States—History. 6. Power (Social sciences)—United
States—History. 7. Acquiescence (Psychology)—History. 8. Social
psychology—United States—History. I . Title.

E 169.Z8F73 2015
973.91—dc23 2014020466

ISBN 978-0-465-09779-1 (paperback)

10 9 8 7 6 5 4 3 2 1

In memory of Mohawk

Contents

Contents

THE
AGE OF
ACQUIESCENCE

Introduction

Occupy Wall Street, a movement that began as a small encampment of young people in lower Manhattan, became a riveting public spectacle in the fall of 2011. A mere month after the first sleeping bags were unrolled in Zuccotti Park, a stone's throw away from the New York Stock Exchange on Wall Street, millions of "occupiers" in a thousand cities around the world all on the same day echoed the plaint of those New York rebels that the whole planet had been hijacked and then ruined by a financial elite and its political enablers. "The 99%" who were its victims had had enough. Nothing of this scope and speed had ever happened before, ever. It was testimony not only to the magical powers of the internet, but more important to the profound revulsion inspired by institutions that just a few short years earlier had commanded great authority and respect. Now they seemed illegitimate and disgraced.

Peering back into the past at a largely forgotten terrain of struggle against "the Street" and the domination of empowered economic elites of all sorts, a historian feels compelled to ask a simple question: Why didn't Occupy Wall Street (OWS) happen much sooner than it did? During those three years after the global financial meltdown and Great Recession, an eerie silence blanketed the country. Stories accumulated of Wall Street greed and arrogance, astonishing tales of incompetence and larceny. People lost their homes and jobs. Poverty reached levels not seen for a generation. The political system proved as bankrupt as the big banks. Bipartisan consensus emerged, but only around the effort to save "too big to fail" goliaths—not the legions left destitute in the wake of their financial wilding. The political class prescribed what people already had enough of: yet another dose of austerity, plus a faith-based belief in a "recovery" that for the 99% of Americans would never be much more than an optical illusion. In those years, the hopes of ordinary people for a chance at a decent future waned and bitterness set in.

Strangely, however, popular resistance was hard to find. Or rather it was invisible where it had always been most conspicuous: on the left. Right-wing populism, the Tea Party especially, flourished, excoriating "limousine liberals" and know-it-all government bureaucrats. Establishments in both parties ran from or tried to curry favor with this upwelling of hot political emotions. But the animus of the Tea Party was mainly aimed at big government and social liberalism. To be sure, it wasn't fond of financial titans collecting handouts from the Federal Reserve. Still, Tea Party partisans were waging war on behalf of capitalism, not against it. That mission had always belonged to the left.

What left? In the light of American history, its vanishing, or at least its frailty and passivity, was surpassingly odd. From decades before the Gilded Age of the late nineteenth century through the Great Depression, again and again landed gentry, slave owners, industrial robber barons, monopolists, Wall Street, the Establishment, and assorted other oligarchs had found themselves in the crosshairs of an outraged citizenry. After all, from the outset Americans had displayed an easily irritated edginess toward any sign of political, social, or economic pretension. Aristocrats had never been welcome here. No plutocrats or oligarchs need apply either. Hierarchies of bloodlines, entitled wealth, or political preferment were alien and obnoxious—in theory at least, not part of the DNA of the New World. Elitism, wherever and whenever it showed itself, had always been greeted with a truculent contempt, what guardians of the ancien régime in the Old World would have condemned as insufferable insolence.

Is this a misreading of the American past, a kind of consoling fairy tale of the way we never were? If today's bankers, corporate chiefs, and their political enablers managed to perpetrate wrack and ruin yet emerged pretty much unscathed, at least until OWS erupted—and even then all the sound and fury spent itself quickly—what else is new? Arguably, America is and always has been a business civilization through and through, ready to tolerate high degrees of inequality, exploitation, and lopsided distributions of social and political influence. The famously taciturn president Calvin Coolidge ("Silent Cal" was so mute that when social critic Dorothy Parker got word he had passed away, she waspishly asked, "How could they tell?") once pointedly and bluntly pronounced that "the business of America is business." Isn't that the hard truth? So long as people have believed the country still offered them a credible shot at "the main chance"—an equal right to become unequal—the rest would take care of itself.

One version of the American story has it that the abrasions of class inequities get regularly soothed away in the bathwater of abundance. Rancorous conflicts, which anybody would acknowledge there have been plenty of, are, in this telling, more often about cultural and social animosities than about "class struggle."

Class warfare, however—something that became virtually unspeakable during the last generation—was a commonplace of everyday life during what might be called the long nineteenth century. It was part of our lingua franca from the days when Jefferson and his democratic followers denounced counterrevolutionary "moneycrats" through the grim decade of the 1930s, when Franklin Roosevelt excoriated "economic royalists," "Tories of industry," and pillagers of "other people's money."

Presidents once felt entirely comfortable using this vocabulary. Andrew Jackson waged war against "the Monster Bank" (the second Bank of the United States, which he and his Democratic Party supporters drove to extinction, claiming in a fit of demagoguery that it was an aristocratic monopoly of the country's credit resources run by the politically privileged). Abraham Lincoln, when informed that Wall Street traders in government bonds were bearing the market, hoping for Union Army defeats, suggested these speculators be shot. Theodore Roosevelt interdicted "malefactors of great wealth" in one of his frequent moods of moral high dudgeon, not shy about voicing his disdain for those plutocrats who thought they deserved the deference of their fellow citizens because of the size of their bank accounts. When Woodrow Wilson ran for president in 1912, he campaigned against "the Money Trust," arguing that small circle of white-shoe investment banking houses headed up by J. P. Morgan not only controlled the capital wherewithal of the nation's economy, its chief industries, its lines of credit, and its access to technological innovation—in sum, the pathways to economic opportunity—but used that enormous economic throw weight to subvert the democratic institutions of the republic.

Were these men—not to mention FDR, whose enemies insinuated he was a Communist fellow traveler—closet Marxists? To think so would do a disservice to both Karl Marx and these presidents. It is rather their use of the class-inflected, emotionally charged language of a bygone America that is noteworthy. It is hard to imagine any president of the last half century or so having resort to such rhetoric.

Marx once described high finance as "the Vatican of capitalism," its diktat to be obeyed without question. Several decades have come and gone during which we've learned not to mention Marx in polite company. Our vocabulary went through a kind of linguistic cleansing, exiling suspect and nasty phrases like "class warfare" or "the reserve army of labor" or even something as apparently innocuous as "working class." In times past, however, such language and the ideas they conjured up struck our forebears as useful, even sometimes as accurate depictions of reality. They used them regularly along with words and phrases like "plutocracy," "robber baron," and "ruling class" to identify the sources of economic exploitation and inequality that oppressed them, as well as to describe the political disenfranchisement they suffered and the subversion of democracy they experienced. Never before, however, has the Vatican of capitalism captured quite so perfectly the specific nature of the oligarchy that recently ran the country for a long generation and ended up running it into the ground. Even political consultant and pundit James Carville (no Marxist he), confessed as much during the Clinton years, when he said the bond market "intimidates everybody."[1]

Occupy Wall Street, even bereft of strategy, program, and specific demands as many lamented when it was a newborn, nonetheless opened up space again for our political imagination by confronting this elemental, determining feature of our society's predicament. It rediscovered something that, beneath thickets of political verbiage about tax this and cut that, about end-of-the-world deficits and missionary-minded "job creators," had been hiding in plain sight: namely, what our ancestors once called "the street of torments." It achieved a giant leap backward, so to speak, summoning up a history of opposition that had mysteriously withered away.

True turning points in American political history are rare. This might seem counterintuitive once we recognize that for so long society was in a constant uproar. Arguably the country was formed and re-formed in serial acts of violent expropriation. Like the market it has been (and remains) infinitely fungible, living in the perpetually changing present, panting after the future, the next big thing. The demographics of American society are and have always been in permanent upheaval, its racial and ethnic complexion mutating from one generation to the next. Its economic hierarchies exist in a fluid state of dissolution and recrystallization. Social classes go in and out of existence.

Nonetheless, in the face of this all-sided liquefaction, American politics have tended to flow within very narrow banks from one generation to the next. The capacious, sometimes stultifying embrace of the two-party system has absorbed most of the heat generated by this or that hot-button issue, leaving the fundamentals intact.

Only under the most trying circumstances has the political system ruptured or come close. Then the prevailing balance of power and wealth between classes and regions has been called into question; then the political geography and demography of the nation have been reconfigured, sometimes for decades to come; only then have axiomatic beliefs about wealth and work, democracy and elitism, equality and individualism, government and the free market been reformulated or at least opened to serious debate, however briefly.

A double mystery then is the subject of this book. Speaking generally, one might ask why people submit for so long to various forms of exploitation, oppression, and domination. And then, equally mysterious, why they ever stop giving in. Why acquiesce? Why resist? Looking backward, the indignities and injustices, the hypocrisies and lies, the corruption and cruelty may seem insupportable. Yet they are tolerated. Looking backward, the dangers to life, limb, and livelihood entailed in rebelling may seem too dire to contemplate. Yet in the teeth of all that, rebellion happens. The world is full of recent and long-ago examples of both.

America's history is mysterious in just this way. This book is an attempt to explore the enigma of resistance and acquiescence as those experiences unfolded in the late nineteenth and again in the late twentieth century.

We have grown accustomed for some years now to referring to America's two gilded ages. The first one was baptized by Mark Twain in his novel of that same name and has forever after been used to capture the era's exhibitionist material excess and political corruption. The second, our own, which began sometime during the Reagan era and lasted though the financial meltdown of 2008, like the original, earned a reputation for extravagant self-indulgence by the rich and famous and for a similar political system of, by, and for the moneyed. So it has been natural to assume that these two gilded ages, however much they have differed in their particulars, were essentially the same. Clearly there is truth in that claim. However, they were fundamentally dissimilar.

Mark Twain's Gilded Age has always fascinated and continues to fascinate. The American vernacular is full of references to that era: the "Gay Nineties," "robber barons," "how the other half lives," "cross of gold," "acres of diamonds," "conspicuous consumption," "the leisure class," "the sweatshop," "other people's money," "social Darwinism and the survival of the fittest," "the nouveau riche," "the trust." What a remarkable cluster of metaphors, so redolent with the era's social tensions they have become permanent deposits in the national memory bank.

We think of the last third of the nineteenth century as a time of great

8

accomplishment, especially of stunning economic growth and technological transformation and the amassing of stupendous wealth. This is
the age of the steam engine and transcontinental railroads, of the
mechanical reaper and the telephone, of cities of more than a million and
steel mills larger than any on earth, of America's full immersion in the
Industrial Revolution. A once underdeveloped, infant nation became a
power to be reckoned with.

For people living back then, however much they were aware of and
took pride in these marvels, the Gilded Age was also a time of profound
social unease and chronic confrontations. Citizens were worried about
how the nation seemed to be verging on cataclysmic divisions of wealth
and power. The trauma of the Civil War, so recently concluded, was
fresh in everyone's mind. The abiding fear, spoken aloud again and
again, was that a second civil war loomed. Bloody encounters on railroads, in coal mines and steel mills, in city streets and out on the Great
Plains made this premonition palpable. This time the war to the death
would be between the haves and have-nots, a war of class against class.
American society was becoming dangerously, ominously unequal, frac-
turing into what many at the time called "two nations."

Until OWS came along, all of this would have seemed utterly strange
to those living through America's second Gilded Age. But why? After
all, years before the financial meltdown plenty of observers had noted
how unequal American society had become. They compared the skewed
distribution of income and wealth at the turn of the twenty-first century
with the original Gilded Age and found it as stark or even starker than at
any time in American history. Stories about penthouse helipads, McMan-
sions roomy enough to house a regiment, and private island getaways
kept whole magazines and TV shows buzzing. "Crony capitalism,"
which Twain had great fun skewering in his novel, was very much still
alive and well in the age of Jack Abramoff. Substitute those Fifth Avenue
castles, Newport beachfront behemoths, and Boss Tweed's infamous
courthouse of a century before and nothing much had changed.

Or so it might seem. But in fact times had changed profoundly. Gone missing were the insurrections and all those utopian longings for a world put together differently so as to escape the ravages of industrial capitalism. It was this social chemistry of apocalyptic doom mixed with visionary expectation that had lent the first Gilded Age its distinctive frisson. The absence of all that during the second Gilded Age, despite the obvious similarities it shares with the original, is a reminder that the past is indeed, at least in some respects, a foreign country. Why, until the sudden eruption of OWS—a flare-up that died down rather quickly—was the second Gilded Age one of acquiescence rather than resistance?

If the first Gilded Age was full of sound and fury, the second seemed to take place in a padded cell. Might that striking contrast originate in the fact that the capitalist society of the Gay Nineties was nothing like the capitalism of our own time? Or to put it another way: Did the utter strangeness of capitalism when it was first taking shape in America— beginning decades before the Gay Nineties—so deeply disturb traditional ways of life that for several generations it seemed intolerable to many of those violently uprooted by its onrush? Did that shattering experience elicit responses, radical yet proportionate to the life-or-death threat to earlier, cherished ways of life and customary beliefs?

And on the contrary, did a society like our own long ago grow accustomed to all the fundamentals of capitalism, not merely as a way of conducting economic affairs, but as a way of being in the world? Did we come to treat those fundamentals as part of the natural order of things, beyond real challenge, like the weather? What were the mechanisms at work in our own distinctive political economy, in the quotidian experiences of work and family life, in the interior of our imaginations, that produced a sensibility of irony and even cynical disengagement rather than a morally charged universe of utopian yearnings and dystopian forebodings?

Gilded ages are, by definition, hiding something; what sparkles like gold is not. But what they're hiding may differ, fundamentally. Industrial capitalism constituted the understructure of the first Gilded Age. The second rested on finance capitalism. Late-nineteenth-century American capitalism gave birth to the "trust" and other forms of corporate consolidation at the expense of smaller businesses. Late-twentieth-century capitalism, notwithstanding its mania for mergers and acquisitions, is known for its "flexibility," meaning its penchant for off-loading corporate functions to a world of freelancers, contractors, subcontractors, and numberless petty enterprises. The first Gilded Age, despite its glaring inequities, was accompanied by a gradual rise in the standard of living; the second by a gradual erosion.

During the first Gilded Age millions of farmers, handicraftsmen, shopkeepers, fishermen, and other small property-owners—not to mention millions of ex-slaves and dispossessed peasants from the steppes and parched fields of eastern and southern Europe—became the country's original working class. They were swept up, often enough against their will or with little other choice, into the process of capital accumulation happening at the forges and foundries and engine houses and packing plants and mills and mines and bridges and tunnels and wharves and the factories in the fields that were transforming the face of America. This reprocessing of human raw material into wage labor extended well beyond the Gay Nineties and was still going on when the whole economy fell to its knees in 1929. By the late twentieth century, however, the descendants of these industrial pioneers were being expelled from that same industrial heartland as it underwent a reverse process of disaccumulation and deindustrialization.

Profitability during the first Gilded Age rested first of all on transforming the resources of preindustrial societies—their lands, minerals, animals, foodstuffs, fisheries, rivers, workshops, stores, tools, muscle, and brainpower—into marketable commodities produced by wage laborers who had lost or were losing their access to alternative means of staying alive. Profitability during the second Gilded Age relied instead on cannibalizing the industrial edifice erected during the first, and on exporting the results of that capital liquidation to the four corners of the earth—everywhere from Nicaragua to Bangladesh—where deep reservoirs of untapped labor, like newly discovered oil reserves, gave industrial capital accumulation a fresh start. Prosperity, once driven by cost-cutting mechanization and technological breakthroughs, came instead to rest uneasily on oceans of consumer and corporate debt. Poverty during the first Gilded Age originated in and indicted exploitation at work. Poverty in the second Gilded Age was more commonly associated in the public mind with exclusion from work.

We can once again, like our Gilded Age forebears, speak of "two nations," geographically the same, separated by a century, one on the rise, a developing country, one in decay, becoming an underdeveloped country.

Stark contrasts in emotions, behavior, and moral sanctions grew up alongside these two divergent ways of making a living, amassing money, and organizing the economy. During the first Gilded Age the work ethic constituted the nuclear core of American cultural belief and practice. That era's emphasis on capital accumulation presumed frugality, saving, and delayed gratification as well as disciplined, methodical labor. That ethos frowned on self-indulgence, was wary of debt, denounced wealth not transparently connected to useful, tangible outputs, and feared libidinal excess whether that took the form of gambling, sumptuary display, leisured indolence, or uninhibited sexuality.

How at odds that all is with the moral and psychic economy of our own second Gilded Age. An economy kept aloft by finance and mass consumption has for a long time rested on an ethos of immediate gratification, enjoyed a love affair with debt, speculation, and risk, erased the distinction between productive labor and pursuits once upon a time judged parasitic, and became endlessly inventive about ways to supercharge with libido even the homeliest of household wares.

Can these two diverging political economies—one resting on industry, the other on finance—and these two polarized sensibilities—one fearing God, the other living in an impromptu moment to moment—explain the Great Noise of the first Gilded Age and the Great Silence of the second? So too, is it possible that people still attached by custom and belief to ways of subsisting that had originated outside the orbit of capital accumulation were for that very reason both psychologically and politically more existentially desperate, more capable, and more audacious in envisioning a noncapitalist future than those who had come of age knowing nothing else?

And does the global explosion of OWS mark the end of the Age of Acquiescence? Is it a turning point in our country's history? Have we reached the limits of auto-cannibalism? Is capitalism any longer compatible with democracy? Was it ever? During the first Gilded Age millions were convinced it was not. During the second Gilded Age, conventional wisdom had it that they went together like love and marriage. Indeed, it became an imperial boast as the United States assumed the burden of tutoring other nations on how they too might confect this perfect union. But then OWS articulated what many had long since concluded: that the 99% have for all practical purposes been banned from any effective say-so when it comes to determining how the resources of the country are to be deployed and distributed. Is there then a future for democracy beyond capitalism? An old question is being asked anew.

To take the measure of how we are now entails first getting a sense of how we once were. Part I will examine the "long nineteenth century," when capitalism "red in tooth and claw" met fierce enemies from every walk of life. Part II will probe for the sources of our remarkable silence in the modern era.

This book hardly pretends to be a new history of the United States. The American Revolution, the Civil War, presidential elections, wars, and much else show up briefly, indirectly, or not at all. But it is nonetheless an attempt to say something essential about the nature and evolution of American society. How well we manage the grave dilemmas confronting us now and in the future may depend on how well we grasp the buried truths of our past.

PART I

CLASS WARFARE IN AMERICA: THE LONG NINETEENTH CENTURY

Dead bodies hardly in the ground, memories of the Civil War's carnage still raw, millions of Americans woke up one summer's day in 1877 to discover the nation verging on fatal division all over again. In July of that year a countrywide railroad strike—soon to become infamous as the "Great Uprising"—left commerce paralyzed, millions of dollars of wrecked and incinerated railroad property, and scores dead and wounded as the uprising spread from West Virginia to Baltimore and Pittsburgh then on to Chicago, St. Louis, and points west. One observer, a St. Louis journalist, summed up the mood of apocalyptic dread that would hover over the country from then on into the next century. The spectacle "made one feel as though it was a tearful witnessing in perspective of the last day, when secrets of life, more loathsome than those of death, shall be laid bare in their hideous deformity and ghastly shame." He added that "the whole country seemed stricken by a profound dread of impending ruin." When he later compiled his reportage in a book, its table of contents constituted an inventory of ominous forebodings. Chapter titles suggested a serial nightmare: "A Day of Dread," "A Night of Terror," "A Sea of Fire," "The Spirit of Desolation Lighting the Torch of Destruction," "Demoniac Satisfaction." Profoundly shocked, he had to contemplate that "even in America, the proletariat is becoming great in numbers and dangerous in disposition."[1]

For people alive during America's Gilded Age, 1877 was a year to remember, impossible to forget. That was not because the Great Uprising was unique. Rather it was because it was the first in a series of times just like it—1884–85, 1886, 1892, 1896, 1905, 1914—marked by pitiless social confrontations between what some called "the classes and the masses" or the haves and have-nots. Farmers faced off against bankers, workers against robber barons. Harriet Beecher Stowe's earlier justification for the War Between the States as "the war for the rights of the working classes of mankind as against the usurpations of privileged aristocracies" seemed now like a premonition. Dread of a second civil war became a pervasive journalistic commonplace, echoed by prominent businessmen. In Chicago at the height of the '77 insurrection, the city's industrial elders—men like George Pullman, Philip Armour, and Marshall Field—were convinced that "the communists were in their second heaven, the canaille was at the very summit of its glory," that like Paris a few years earlier during the Commune, Chicago now was in the hands of "the revolutionary element." They lent horses, wagons, and Gatling guns to the police, formed vigilante groups and the Law and Order League, armed for battle.

Less minatory voices, like that of the preacher Lyman Abbott, noted that "the low growl of thunder is already to be heard in great cities" where the working class harbored "a great discontent in its heart which a great disaster might easily convert into bitter wrath." In the panic that followed the Chicago Haymarket bombing in 1886, the *Chicago Tribune* and other metropolitan papers likened the moment to the firing on Fort Sumter, observing that although the Republic seemed on firmer foundations than it had been in 1861, still the specter of anarchy was "menacing law, property, government, the pulpit, the home, and public and private rights." E. L. Godkin, founder of *The Nation* magazine, a patrician abolitionist but no friend of the workingman, congratulated the governor of Wisconsin for calling out the troops in Milwaukee to put down the 1886 demonstrations for the eight-hour day: "Unlike Illinois, Wisconsin has a government to be proud of....A single volley at long-range showed the mob that the troops 'meant business' and broke the backbone of the insurrection against authority." Again and again the mortal threat to the Republic recalled for many, no matter which side they were on, the fratricidal war still so fresh to memory.

If the forces of law and order, the arbiters of public opinion and bourgeois propriety, deployed a vocabulary that belied their own customary composure, their foes perceived the world in just the same way, but inside out. So for working-class militants who sometimes marched through the streets in armed militias or irate farmers prepared to warn off the sheriff from enforcing foreclosures, it was the police who were criminals, the law that was lawless, order actually disorder, "civilization" a form of barbarism. Even middle-class intellectuals could see it like that: Henry Demarest Lloyd, a journalist and spokesman for the antitrust movement, who was appalled by the violent response of the railroad barons in 1877, concluded that "if our civilization is destroyed as [Thomas Babington] Macaulay predicted, it will not be by his barbarians from below. Our barbarians come from above."

Authorities of the criminal justice system might compare anarchists to "savages" and "hyenas" hovering over "the corpses of the dead," but were themselves analogized as "police Apaches," the functionaries of "slave-holders" and "factory lords." Working-class rebels memorialized John Brown as their hero and they reminded their enemies that they too once honored the abolitionist for doing what they now wanted to hang anarchists for: namely, putting his life on the line to emancipate labor.[2]

Indeed, alongside these nightmarish premonitions of apocalyptic disaster, exultant visions of emancipation and transcendent social harmony lit up the nation's dreamscape. Some foresaw a limitless Progress powered by science and technology. Embattled farmers and handicraftsmen imagined a cooperative commonwealth triumphing over the ferocious hatreds and resentments of class against class. Voluble ranks of labor radicals prophesied the imminent end of capitalism and the dawning of a socialist republic. Appalled by the epidemic of greed and callousness that seemed to be poisoning the country's moral atmosphere, Christian divines proselytized on behalf of the Social Gospel: What would Jesus do, they asked, and began erecting the institutional sinews of the brotherhood of man. The intellectual classes together with enlightened industrialists set to work designing model cities, factories, and great public exhibitions, avatars (they hoped) of a world without acrimony. Supreme Court Justice John Marshall Harlan remembered the 1880s as a period of "deep feelings of unrest. The conviction was universal that the country was in real danger from the aggregation of capital in the hands of a few individuals controlling for their profit and advantage exclusively the entire business of the country." Even the most privileged—the gilded "400"—spied a retro utopian escape hatch. They hunkered down inside their imported castles and reimagined themselves as some New World feudal aristocracy, rather than the nouveau riche they really were.[3]

Back when the first Gilded Age was just picking up steam in the late 1870s, a wayfaring journalist named Henry George prophesied that the great American republic was headed to hell, that like Rome, "so powerful in arms, so advanced in the arts," it might too be done in by the forces of economic and social division and moral decline at loose in the land. *Progress and Poverty,* George's famous book, was in part inspired by the astonishing railroad insurrection of 1877. It electrified the country (there were one hundred printings in twenty years and it had sold two million copies by 1905) and became the bible of a reform movement that lasted for decades. "Strong as it may seem," he warned, "our civilization is evolving destructive forces. Not desert and forest, but city and slum and country roadside are nursing their barbarians who may be to the new what Hun and Vandal were to the old."

George asked a fundamental question: What exactly was the relationship between progress and poverty? Under the conditions of late-nineteenth-century industrial capitalism, he concluded, the relationship was toxic; progress spawned poverty. All the mammoth factories, miraculous machines, and soaring metropolises, every landmark of Progress with a capital P, incubated poverty, ignorance, morally asphyxiating materialism, and a looming social Armageddon. His peculiar answer to the paradoxical dilemma he worried about—a single tax on landed wealth—went down a political dead end, winding up as little more than a historical curiosity. But it is the question he asked, not his answer, that endures.[4]

Long before Henry George entered the scene, his question already had. It was there at the creation of the Republic. Ferocious arguments between Hamilton and Jefferson and their legions of followers broke out immediately after the adoption of the Constitution. They didn't come to blows over industrial capitalism, which in an underdeveloped country like the United States was at most a faint proposition. But Progress and what it might entail were very much at issue.

Alexander Hamilton envisioned a vigorous commercial civilization, urban-centered, absorbing the latest scientific and technological discoveries, resting on an extensive division of labor and expansive international trade, steered by private/public elites of merchant princes and statesmen who were deferred to by ordinary workaday folk. We recognize this world instantly: it has banks and manufactories, delights its inhabitants with a kaleidoscope of novelties and amusements, uproots settled ways of doing things, allures country people to pack up and head for the city, assigns pride of place to the wealthiest, feeds cravings for social status, and is in love with money. England, more than any other place on earth at the end of the eighteenth century, exemplified such a society. It was Hamilton's model, a rich, fashionable, culturally sophisticated paragon of Progress.

For Thomas Jefferson, England was the example to be avoided at all costs. He imagined instead an agrarian republic of smallholding farmers and handicraftsmen integrated into local economies, engaged in but not dependent on domestic and international trade, and enjoying some measure of economic and therefore political independence thanks to their proprietary self-sufficiency. A world like that, made up of self-possessed individuals of roughly the same social rank, would be the foundation of a stable, egalitarian social order and a democratic one. It cultivated a robust suspicion of money, debt, and speculation, was leery of the city as a sinkhole of vice, and frowned on the race for social preferment. And it had a good chance of lasting for generations, Jefferson believed, thanks to the vast "unsettled" wilderness he went about acquiring as president from Napoleon through the Louisiana Purchase. Thanks to what then seemed an inexhaustible landscape, America enjoyed a unique reprieve from history, a blessed exemption from the English fate Hamilton yearned for.

In Jefferson's eyes, English-style progress generated, inevitably, an ever-widening chasm between the wealthy and the destitute. Cities spawned luxury and cultural refinement, but also poverty, disease, beg-gary, and crime. The slavish dependency of people cut off from their own means of self-support, demoralized, prey to the power-hungry designs of their social and economic superiors, would soon enough sour the promise of democracy if Progress were allowed to infect America.

Anxieties about the latent immorality of commercial society articu-lated by Jefferson were shared even by such paladins of the free market as Adam Smith. He recognized that poverty and inequality were inevitable outcomes of the growth of the market, arguing that the market could not by itself relieve those "who by the products of their labor feed, clothe, and lodge the whole body of the people should have such a share of the product of their own labor as to be themselves tolerably well fed, clothed, and lodged." Nor, he believed, could one depend on the powers that be because "civil government...so far as it is instituted for the secu-rity of property, is in reality instituted for the defense of the rich against the poor, or all those who have some property against those who have none at all."[5]

Hamilton instead feared the leveling instincts aroused by the Jefferso-nians. They might threaten the property holdings of the rich and well-born (Hamilton, although not hailing from those rarefied precincts, nonetheless felt a powerful affinity for what passed for a native aristoc-racy in the New World). And by frightening those circles who were, he believed, the distinctive bearers of economic and cultural improvement, Progress would come to a dead stop, leaving the new country stagnant and at the mercy of European designs. These were the primordial differ-ences that turned founding fatherhood into political fratricide at the dawn of the country's history.

Arguably then, all the issues raised to a fever pitch during the first Gilded Age, the same ones that hibernated during our own second Gilded Age and have recently leapt from the shadows to ambush us now, bedeviled the country from the outset.

We should then conceive of a "long nineteenth century" lasting from postrevolutionary days through to the Great Depression of the 1930s.

Not every year or decade for that matter was as fraught as 1877, to be sure. But the epoch that encompassed the transformation of a sliver of coastal villages, small farms, slave plantations, and a few port cities into a transcontinental commercial, agricultural, and industrial preeminence was a wrenching one. For those generations that lived through it, it often called forth a cri de coeur, recurring waves of resistance to the inexorable, a stubborn, multifarious insistence that the march of Progress was too spendthrift in human lives, that there were alternatives. That long nineteenth century of class against class climaxed in the labor insurgency that followed in the wake of the system's Great Crash of 1929. It seemed to resolve itself in the New Deal. But the questions it raised have endured, resurfaced, and grown more pressing of late.

Economic and moral questions were, for our Gilded Age forebears, joined at the hip. In our own day, the antiseptic, mathematical language of risk assessment and probability analysis made that seem overly sentimental. For well more than a century, however, anxious Americans asked if the panting after money and social distinction might corrupt the country's soul. For our Victorian ancestors, "parasite" was both a moral category and an economic one. Did wealth carry with it a moral dilemma, a confrontation with God? Or was it the royal road to social harmony? Or was it both? Was amassing wealth the touchstone of Progress, but also its fatal flaw?

Aristocracy and democracy, slavery and freedom, equality and individualism, labor and capital, god and mammon, progress and poverty: these are the antinomies that helped define the contours of the long nineteenth century, and especially the decades between the Civil War and the Great Depression. That is why this book begins there.

1

Progress

When the railroad threatened to come to Lancaster, Ohio, back in the mid-1840s, the local school board greeted the prospect as a looming moral disaster. The board refused to make its building available to discuss the coming of the iron horse. Citizens, these officials decided, might use the schoolhouse to debate "all proper questions," but railroads and telegraphs were beyond the pale, examples of "rank infidelity." Concluded the board, "If God had designed that his intelligent creatures should travel at the frightful speed of 15 miles per hour, by steam," he would have said so, or had one of his prophets approve it. Clearly, the railroad was "a device of Satan to lead immortal souls down to Hell."[1]

Soon after that, people coming of age around the time of the Civil War felt and saw things differently, still awestruck but not afraid. The 1876 Centennial Exposition in Philadelphia celebrating the country's birth elicited a national love affair with Progress, not just with the iron horse but with all the manifestations of American industrial genius and its promise of unimaginable abundance. (Indeed, the Exposition's theme was "A Century of Progress.") Covering 236 acres in the city's Fairmount Park, the exposition was full of delights. Ten million people came to marvel at the young republic's accomplishments.

Breathtaking above all was the display of sheer power. The giant Double Walking-Beam Corliss Steam Engine, which supplied the energy for all the other thirteen acres of machines housed at Machinery Hall, captured the most attention. It was 45 feet high, equipped with two 10-foot pistons and a flywheel weighing 56 tons rotating at the astonishing rate of six times a minute. Massive, silent yet emanating an unearthly force, the engine struck the writer William Dean Howells as "an athlete of steel and iron with not a superfluous ounce of metal on it." A journalist from Wisconsin was there when it sprang to life, manned by only a single attendant:

> In obedience to the simple touch of a wheel and a lever, the cross-beam rocked high and low; the crank revolved; the pistons shot in and out of their cylinders, and nearly eight miles of steel shafting gave motive power to 13 acres of machinery simultaneously! A thousand different noises assailed the ear, some in short, staccato notes; others in a dull, draining hum; others still in the brisk rattle of musketry; and many in a spiteful hiss and splutter. Long bands of leather writhed and crackled over fly-wheels.... Man's power over matter never received so complete an exemplification before. The terrific force adapted by his hand to his will, the fertility of his inventions, the delicacy of his touch, and his inexhaustible muscularity, appeared at once in cohesion and in contrast.

Beside the engine itself, a multitude of other mechanical marvels dazzled the hundreds of thousands who visited the exhibit (numbers that grew especially after a hellish July heat wave cooled). On view were a prototype of the first automatic screw-making machine, power looms, lathes, sewing machines, toolmaking machines, pumps of assorted kinds and purposes, an Otis elevator, Westinghouse air brakes for railroads, Pullman cars, farm machinery of great variety, a typewriter, a precursor of the electric light, a slice of steel cable that not many years later would be used by the Roebling brothers to support the monumental Brooklyn Bridge, and of course locomotives. Alexander Graham Bell's telephone was on display as well and so shocked the Emperor Dom Pedro of Brazil that, startled, he dropped it exclaiming, "My god! It talks." New consumer devices and delicacies were also exhibited including refrigerators and the first bottles of Heinz ketchup and Hires root beer.

Howells, who would later go on to become a coruscating critic of American industrial capitalism, was reverential. He noted the Corliss engine's "vast and almost silent grandeur," its "unerring intelligence." Something immaterial, something exalted, lodged deep within the animated mass of energized iron and steel. For many the notion of Progress had become a kind of rapture. Or to put things the other way around, the metaphysical had become physical, spirit had transmogrified into tangible nuts and bolts, pulleys and screws, steam and smoke and fiery furnaces. Taking in the exposition's whole spectacle, swelling with patriotic pride at this "glorious triumph of skill and invention," Howells declaimed: "Yes, it is still in these things of iron and steel that the national genius most freely speaks."[2]

Once upon a time the meaning of Progress had been less focused, both homelier yet more mind-expanding. The term might have suggested something as simple as moving from one place to another; or might have inflated to embrace the nation's manifest destiny as the birthplace and haven of liberty and democracy. Indeed, before there was a nation, the New World had beckoned as the last frontier of spiritual progress, a teleological mission or Pilgrim's Progress at the end of which waited a safe harbor for the saved. It was, even in secular form (and for all social classes, although not in the same way), the defining utopian conceit of an age given over to utopian anticipations. Only during the Gilded Age did Progress first take on its overriding, singular attachment to industry, science, technological innovation, economic development, material abundance, and private capital accumulation.

Progress became earthbound, enmeshed in a network of axles and gears, coal mines and iron rails, steel plows, coke ovens and telegraph wires. But even as it took on this material density, it reached for the infinite. If the country was destined to be a city on a hill, promising a fresh chance for humanity as its Puritan forebears had believed, it was because the hand of Providence was manifest in the "silent grandeur" of creations such as the Corliss engine. The wonders of scientific discovery, the amazing acrobatics of the machine, the calling forth of the stupendous energies locked away in a fossilized underground or somewhere in the invisible ether, the cornucopia pouring out of the factories and fields— all this was evidence of some more profound truth about man's fate.

Faith in economic growth soon enveloped and embodied all other airborne hopes for freedom and equality. It was not only providential, but inevitable. Gilded Age Americans, a lot of them anyway, fervently believed in economic progress and abundance as the pathway to freedom; indeed its champions conflated the metaphysics of freedom with the mechanics of material abundance, believing that was how the New World would escape the sorry fate of the Old, weighed down as it was by those scarcities and inequities that left it plagued with bitter social jealousies, resentments, and incipient violence.

Ever since the days of the Corliss engine, America has worshipped at the altar of Progress and Abundance. At the height of the Cold War, Vice President Richard Nixon visited Russia, where he faced off against Soviet premier Nikita Khrushchev in what thereafter became known as the "kitchen debate." Standing in the middle of a model kitchen on display at the American National Exhibition in Moscow, Nixon extolled American freedom and the American way of life by pointing to the exhibit's array of electric ranges, washing machines, and television sets. If a bellicose Khrushchev had once prophesied that communism would inevitably "bury" capitalism, the vice president retorted by promising that an avalanche of American consumables would do the same to the Soviet Union. Even now this amalgam of freedom, free enterprise, and material plenty constitutes the axiomatic hard core of the American credo.

Yet discontent so profound it would shake the foundations of American life rose up alongside this miracle of Progress, like a countermiracle. To grasp how astonishing that was we must first reckon with just how stupendous were the accomplishments of the American triumph.

There at the Creation

All this first took shape during the Gilded Age. No nation in history (now with the possible exception of China) industrialized as rapidly as the United States. In a historical eye-blink America went from being an underdeveloped country to an industrial goliath mightier than the chief economies of Europe combined. Measured in carloads of wheat, tons of coal, ingots of steel, kilowatts of electricity, locomotive and machine engine horsepower, miles of railroad and trolley track and telegraph wire, acreage under cultivation, patents per capita, numbers of new cities, bridges, tunnels, dockyards, and sewage and water treatment plants, evidence of Progress in post–Civil War America mounted up year by year at a dizzying pace. People born in 1860 when Abraham Lincoln was elected would have felt more at home in late-twentieth-century America—at least with respect to their material surroundings—than the world their parents grew up in, Lincoln's world.

Every era has had its signature industry: big box retailing, information technology, and finance today, cars in the mid-twentieth century, steel before the Great Depression. Railroads first assumed that position in post–Civil War America. They were the engine house of the economy, knitting together from ocean to ocean the first national marketplace, thereby spurring the growth of factory-based mass production, speeding up communications and the transfer of information between far-flung regions, midwifing new towns, populating the wilderness, and opening up its natural resources to economic exploitation. No terrain—no matter how mountainous, arid, or remote—and no weather—no matter how hot, freezing, windswept, or snowy—could stop the iron horse.

Already in the decades before the Civil War, the transportation revolution had cut a trip from the East Coast to the Ohio valley from fifty days by wagon to twenty-five days by steamboat. Thirty years later it took a week by train. By the turn of the century a trip from New York to San Francisco, which before the Civil War took months, could be done in three and a half days. Moreover, the railroad fueled a nearly insatiable demand for the output of basic industries like coal, iron, and steel, as well as machine making of various sorts. Shipping costs plummeted first, thanks to canals and then the iron horse, from thirty to seventy cents a ton/mile to seven cents or much less. And this is not to mention the way this transformation inspired ancillary technological innovations and the growth and complexity of trade and finance. One observer from the 1860s described the iron horse as "the most tremendous and far-reaching engine of social revolution which has ever either blessed or cursed the earth."[3]

By 1891, the Pennsylvania Railroad (the U.S. Steel or General Motors or WalMart of its day) employed 110,000 people, more than the combined armed services of the United States. Although America accounted for a mere 6 percent of the earth's land mass (and an even tinier percentage of its population), by the end of the century its rail network accounted for 42 percent of the world's total trackage, or nearly 200,000 miles. The railroads employed nearly a million people and spent more than all governments—local, state, and federal—put together. Between 1880 and 1900, freight and passenger traffic nearly quadrupled.

Thanks in part to the impetus provided by the railways, steel production expanded exponentially. By 1880 three-fourths of all steel manufactured in the United States was consumed by the railroads. A good portion of the remainder found its way into the I beam skyscraper, steel ships, steel cable and piping, and all varieties of machinery and armaments.[4]

Everywhere one might look the iron horse had left its imprint. Along with the telegraph whose wires paralleled the tracks, it became the information superhighway of the nineteenth century. It accelerated transactions and communications—first commercial and then private ones—so rapidly as to constitute a triumph over time and space at least as dramatic as the one we now associate with computers, the internet, and the telecommunications industry. Moreover, the relationship between new ways of traveling and communicating was symbiotic: the telegraph facilitated the railroad revolution by making instantaneously available information about train times, expediting the safe shipment of products and people. As a consequence the costs of production and transportation for all kinds of goods and services fell dramatically.

Rural America would never be the same. The railroad commercialized Jefferson's "empire for liberty" to an extent that would have unnerved the Virginia visionary. It swept the farthest reaches of frontier settlement into the orbit of global commodity production and trade, and once and for all put an end to the world of yeoman self-sufficiency.

Industrialization often implies rural depopulation; certainly the proportions of the labor force living on the land did shrink in comparison with town and city dwellers. But the expansion of American agriculture during the Gilded Age was so outsized that the number of farmers and farms, sheep, and cattle ranches also grew considerably. More land was settled or occupied by farmers, cattle herders, and speculators after the Civil War than in the three centuries preceding it. In the 1880s alone grain plantings of all kinds (wheat, corn, oats, rye, etc.) covered the Great Plains as the federal government sold off public lands twice the size of California, three times the area of Missouri. And this vast domestication of the landscape became itself the country's core primary production and at the same time a market for the richly diversified output of national industry.[5]

During the 1870s an area the size of France was put to the plow. Over the next two decades planted acreage exceeded the size of France, Germany, and Wales combined. Southern cotton production also doubled during the same period. "Bonanza farms" encompassing thousands of acres of the flat, fertile land of Minnesota and the Red River valley of the Dakotas, usually owned by capitalist investors from back east, were run like highly mechanized food factories. The Cass-Cheney farm founded near Fargo, North Dakota, in 1874 was the prototype; by 1880 it cultivated 30,000 acres, employed 2000 people, and every day loaded 30,000 bushels of wheat onto waiting freight cars. Longhorn cattle ranchers (in Texas the XIT Ranch, organized in the mid-1870s and spread over 3 million acres surrounded by 600 miles of barbed wire, was the largest) and sheepherders joined grain farmers in turning the "Middle Border"—all that newly opened land west of the Mississippi and north of Missouri—into a food machine.

Miraculous is a fair way to characterize this makeover of the American landmass. Total acreage under cultivation more than doubled from 408 million acres to 841 million between 1870 and 1900. And indeed, without all the new machinery that transformed farming— threshers, binders, reapers, harvesters, the steel plow, corn huskers, sugar mills, cotton presses, and more—and without the railroad which connected the agricultural backcountry to domestic and worldwide urban markets, that agrarian miracle was inconceivable. So, for example, one man using a machine to harvest wheat in 1900 could do the work that not long before required twenty. An acre of wheat that in antebellum America took sixty hours to cultivate required only four by the end of the century. The Scott and Chisolm pea sheller could remove as many peas from a pod as it once took 600 workers to do by hand. In 1881 a new machine turned out 70,000 cigarettes every day, compared with the 3000 a skilled worker could manage. The telegraph (or "lightening wire") trimmed the time to transmit information from weeks or months to days or hours. "What has become of space?" an astonished *New York Herald* asked.[6]

Summoning powers once undreamed of made all this happen. From time immemorial human and animal muscle, wind, the tides, waterfalls, and wood provided the energy making settled society possible. New godlike sources of energy suddenly changed all that. Steam, coal, oil, gas, and electricity revolutionized everyday life and vastly expanded productive capacity. Coal, for example, was the principal energy source for the steam engine. No steam engine would mean no mechanized factories, no steamboats plying the rivers and oceans, no locomotives, smelters, or agricultural machinery like those harvesters, threshers, binders, and tractors, and so on.

An official in the U.S. Patent Office put the case for the steam engine as the summa of industrial life: "It speeds the locomotive across the continent . . . [and] the mighty steamship on the seas; it grinds our grain; it weaves our cloth; it prints our books; it forges our steel, and in every department of life it is the ubiquitous, tireless, potent agency of our civilization." In 1882 most city streetcars were pulled by horses; by 1900, thanks to the advent of electrical power generation, 99 percent were racing down boulevards as if driven by hundreds and hundreds of horses, whipped along by the conversion of coal to steam and steam into the galvanic magic of an electric current. While wood accounted for 73 percent of energy consumption in 1870, by 1920 it had fallen below 8 percent; meanwhile the coal that had supplied 17 percent of the nation's energy sources accounted for 73 percent by the end of World War I.[7]

And then there were those great urban conurbations that seemed to spring out of nowhere and which made the rapid transit of masses of people essential. No fossil fuels, no high-rising elevators, no skyscrapers would mean no Chicago or New York, those exemplars of the new city. Powers so extraordinary, whether embodied in the first incandescent lightbulbs, telephones, refrigerators, sewing machines, or streetcars, conveyed an awe-inspiring sense of power in general, of limitless human capacities. Progress indeed.[8]

Gadgets like the telephone or even items like the modern bicycle or ready-made clothes or packaged cereals, meats and ready-to-eat canned foods, central heating, indoor plumbing, and the electrified home full of new appliances and utensils (not to mention the first prototypes of the horseless carriage and, soon to emerge, the phonograph and first motion pictures) testified to the inventive genius that seemed to inspire this unparalleled Progress. More than that, they became the desired paraphernalia of a new consumer economy and culture: brand names, national advertising, chain stores, the whole spectacle that began redefining people by what they consumed, not by what they did. Soon enough consumer delectables would supplant the machine as the quintessence of Progress and the Abundant Society. At first this shift was largely confined to an upwardly mobile middle class, but its growth was spectacular. The director of the 1890 Census estimated private consumer debt at $11 trillion, three hundred times more than any economist or social observer had predicted.[9]

Whether or not you were among the fortunate able to afford a phone or some other modern gizmo, there could be little doubt that the more basic measures of national economic growth and the standard of living were tracking upward. Between 1860 and 1890 national wealth increased almost sixfold, from $16 billion to $90 billion. Per capita income rose from $514 to $1165—a greater and faster increase than in any other nation in the world. Output per capita in 1899 was 250 percent greater than a half century earlier. Extraordinary productivity and intense competition lowered prices for all goods, agricultural and industrial, so that real wages improved and average hours of work declined from eleven a day to nine and a half.

Together with the agricultural revolution, this made city life possible for millions; the country's urban population tripled between 1870 and 1900. Public education became widely accessible. Thanks to improved nutrition, modern medicine's assault on bacterial disease, and innovations in public sanitation—especially as piped water began to replace cisterns, and incinerators, sewers, and paved roads became more common features of urban living—life expectancy rose by six years as the Gilded Age drew to a close.[10]

Soon enough this cornucopia became the envy of the world and a favorite American boast. Why not? Triumphalism like this was abetted by the remarkable and growing differential between the pace of industrial progress in the United States as compared with Europe's. Already by 1886 America turned out more steel than Britain; by the end of the century its steel output exceeded that of the United Kingdom and Germany combined. Broader comparisons were even more striking. The value of what American manufacturers produced was twice that of the United Kingdom and half as great as that of the whole European continent. Between 1850 and 1880 factory output in Britain rose by 100 percent; in America by 600 percent. There were more miles of railroads and telegraph lines than in all of Europe. The United States led the world in the production of virtually every strategic industrial commodity, including steel, coal, gold, timber, silver, oil, telephone, telegraph, electric lighting, machine tools, hardware, and locomotives. One historian sums up this extraordinary ascent: "American industrialization created the infrastructure for what became the richest and most influential material civilization in history."[11]

Providence and Property

How did this happen? Conventional explanations have long emphasized the New World's perfect combination of the factors of production—land, labor, and capital—that together created the skeletal structure of the modern world. A nation stretching from ocean to ocean offered up inexhaustible natural resources (at least they seemed inexhaustible back then). Portions of the labor force were remarkably literate and skilled. To the degree that workers were in short supply, their numbers were periodically refreshed from abroad by immigrants who either were equally adept or, if less so, bore the burden of brute manual labor that factory production, digging up coal, laying the tracks, chopping down the forests, and harvesting the crops demanded in ever-increasing quantities. If relative shortages of labor could sometimes be a problem, they were also a blessing in disguise that encouraged technological innovation so machines could substitute for humans.

Critical too, the country's political and legal environment was emphatically supportive of private property and private capital accumulation, which further encouraged this audacious entrepreneurial ingenuity. True since the days of Benjamin Franklin, it became truer still during the Gilded Age. First of all, the pervasive atmosphere of liberty, democracy, and individualism acted as a tonic exciting the imagination of those enterprising adventurers and inventors. Local, state, and federal governments provided all sorts of incentives to private businesses, including tax exemptions, subsidies, land grants, mineral rights, franchises, scientific research, and, when necessary, force of arms to assure the sanctity of private property. Meanwhile, the federal judiciary warded off efforts by local authorities to encumber business with rules and regulations regarding their pricing, labor, and competitive practices. Nothing was allowed to dull the appetite for private capital accumulation; the rate of personal savings and reinvestment of company profits was higher in the United States than anywhere else, behavior encouraged by the government's rigid adherence to the gold standard that helped stabilize the currency and attract foreign capital.

America emerged like some exquisitely designed (some thought divinely inspired) hothouse of Progress in sync with universal laws of nature, including especially the law of evolution. But it might have remained barren, or so standard interpretations suggest, had this American scene not nurtured, above all, the country's fearless embrace of change. Alexis de Tocqueville had already captured this unique zeitgeist decades before the Civil War: "America is a land of wonders in which everything is in constant motion and every change seems an improvement.... [They] all consider...humanity as a changing scene in which nothing is, or ought to be permanent; and they admit that what appears to them today to be good, may be superseded by something better tomorrow." From this hot-blooded zest for the new a lot followed. Above all, it invited the emergence of the restless, driven, far-seeing hero of the story of Progress: the American Entrepreneur.[12]

Railroad, coal, steel, iron, meatpacking, and oil barons like Cornelius Vanderbilt, E. H. Harriman, Henry Clay Frick, Andrew Carnegie, Philip Armour, and John D. Rockefeller (and numerous others less famous than they) made their mark not as inventors or managers but as inspired organizers and risk takers. First of all, they extended and deepened the division of labor and specialization of tasks without which the miracle of mass production was inconceivable. Then they erected complex administrative structures to supervise and coordinate this vast, highly integrated labor process. More than that, these managerial dynamos mastered those intricate connections between production on the one hand and transportation, distribution, marketing, and finance on the other, an ensemble of functions that together created the national marketplace. And they did this in the teeth of a mercilessly competitive economy that drove many of their commercial rivals under.

The modern corporation, which emerged as the economy's dominant institution by the end of the Gilded Age, was born out of this fierce struggle to survive killing panics and depressions. Such economic disruptions occurred every fifteen years or so, beginning in 1837 and continuing through to the end of the century. For example, Frick (he of the often noted riveting "grey-eyed gaze") fished in troubled waters, like others of his ruthless disposition. In a pitiless pattern characteristic of this age of hypercapitalism, the Lilliputian titan (he was five feet tall) fashioned an empire by buying up coke lands and ovens and railroads bankrupted by the brutal depression of 1873.

One historian has described the dynamic at work:

> The competitive market, left to itself, yielded not the harmonies...not the equilibrium...not the steady investment and accumulation of capital, not the balancing of supply and demand at high levels of employment of labor and resources, but market disorganization, "wastes of competition," business failures, recurrent depressions, strikes and lockouts, social distemper and political upheaval....By the mid-1890s, in the midst of the third long depression in three successive decades, a revulsion against the unregulated market spread among the bourgeoisie of all sectors of the economy.[13]

By the time this economy of marvels imploded in the Great Depression, what had begun as the handiwork of entrepreneurial patriarchs had morphed into the impersonal domain of the "men in suits." Corporate America as we have come to know it had arrived.

Out of these rites of passage, demanding nerve, gamesmanship, moral amnesia, and the will to power, dynastic capitalists transformed entrepreneurial into corporate capitalism of a peculiarly dynastic kind. Bourgeois society is by its very nature matter-of-fact, sober and businesslike, peaceable and modest, methodical, calculating, and prudential—in a word, unromantic to the bone. Its true and only hero is the acquisitive individual writ large: the businessman as warrior. The larger-than-life financial titans, coal and steel barons, and railroad Napoleons who lit up the stage of Gilded Age industrialism were the heroes of middle-class society. As the architects of Progress, they absorbed into their otherwise unprepossessing lives all the honorariums that once attached to the soldier, the aristocrat, the knight errant, the conquistador, the adventurer, the explorer—the doers who turned a society's most cherished dream, its most valued value, into reality, a reality so grand and transformative it takes the breath away.

Yet a question remains. If Progress was, as this account would have it, a benign outcome of indigenous talents and natural endowments, a perfect union of temperament, institutional genius, and felicitous political invention, then why all the deep misgivings and uproar it incited? Where was the devil hiding in the weeds that would dim for millions the infatuation with Progress everlasting?

2

Progress, Poverty, and Primitive Accumulation

"The 'tramp' comes with the locomotive, and alms-houses and prisons are as surely the marks of 'material progress' as are costly dwellings, rich warehouses, and magnificent churches."[1]

—*Henry George*

No one better embodied the romance of bourgeois heroism than Andrew Carnegie. So it is sobering to hear the famous steelmaker say this: "As I know them, there are few millionaires, very few indeed, who are clear of the sin of having made beggars." Carnegie's verb sense is strikingly apt: it is not merely the unfortunate fact that poverty coexisted alongside plenty, but that progress actually produced beggars where there had been none before. So while it is true that life expectancy rose by six years during the Gilded Age, it is also the fact that the life expectancy of white males born during or after the Civil War was ten years less than it had been a century earlier. What can explain this paradox?[2]

Our Gilded Age ancestors were well aware—sometimes painfully aware—that Progress begat poverty. Since then, the triumphant story of the American Industrial Revolution has always acknowledged that Progress was not cost-free. Abuses occurred. The New World's natural endowment was drawn down without regard to the future and the environment bore the scars. Farmers lost their homesteads. Handicraft workers lost their trades. Industrial workers lost some of their humanity. Cities developed slums, as well as sweatshops that were staffed by children. Businesses went belly-up in the competitive maelstrom. Social unrest boiled over now and then.

However lamentable this dark side of Progress may be, it does not alter the underlying assumption: Gilded Age industrialism was the irresistible and empyrean story of the orchestration of the forces of production at the hands of great men. Joseph Schumpeter, the renowned Harvard economist, would later call this period one of "creative destruction."

Dispossession, however, should not be treated as an ancillary subplot to the principal drama. Instead the whole industrializing enterprise may be seen to rest on the systematic cannibalizing of various forms of precapitalist economies and the societies they supported. Capital accumulation at the expense of these "others"—a process that has been characterized as "primitive accumulation"—constitutes the underground history of Gilded Age Progress. It is what accounts for the gross inequalities of income and wealth that emerged alongside a rise in the standard of living for some. It is why it is possible to speak of those days as the best of times and the worst of times. More profoundly than that, primitive accumulation fostered an abiding sense of loss felt by all sorts of ordinary people. It inspired them to resist their own social extinction, to form counter-dreams to the official romance of Progress. Indeed, resisting what some chose to call, both at the time and in hindsight, the inevitable did not seem that way to those living through the agonies of primitive accumulation back then.

Capitalism did not emerge de novo out of the ether. Native pastoralists and buffalo hunters, slaves and ex-slaves, artisans, homesteaders, European peasants and peddlers, small-town shopkeepers, Southern hillbillies, New England fishermen, prairie sodbusters, and subsistence agrarians were the raw material of the miracle of Progress. Wealth once embedded in these societies was absorbed by fair means and foul into the musculature of the new economy. The mechanisms included conquest, legerdemain, and theft. Slavery depended on all that and more, transforming the flesh and blood of whole African civilizations into the liquid capital of Atlantic commerce. Funds accumulated that way later became the foundation of industrial investment.

More peaceable, orderly, everyday means were also at work. Trade, for example, could function less innocuously than mere trucking and bartering might suggest. Export of factory-made goods swamped local, self-contained economies not involved in accumulating capital but rather in the reproduction of ancient ways of life. Here and abroad cheaper goods drove under peasants, husbandmen, and handicraftsmen, detaching men and women from traditional occupations, "freeing" them to join the founding generations of wage labor. Banks built up their resources by similarly digesting alien life forms silently and most of the time lawfully. Farmers who might have been content to maintain the family homestead were inexorably caught up in the web of international commerce, making them ever more dependent on lines of credit to survive. Depending on creditors until they couldn't bear the load anymore also afflicted handicraftsmen and local merchants, corroding away their independence until they too joined the new ranks of the proletariat. Something as homely as taxes could function as a kind of forced savings, extracted from people involved in small-scale farming or artisanal pursuits, the revenue then used to subsidize capitalist enterprises like railroads.

Nor did primitive accumulation entail strictly an economic uprooting, which ended once the ex-peasant, homesteader, artisan, slave, or shopkeeper walked through a factory gate or descended down some mine shaft or found herself picking strawberries on someone else's plantation. Slavic or Italian immigrants stoking furnaces in Pittsburgh or threading a needle in a New York City sweatshop had not all of a sudden become acclimated to capitalism's brave new world simply by virtue of pocketing a weekly paycheck. It would take decades, more than a single generation, before primitive accumulation as a social undertaking had extinguished the last vestiges of older ways of life.

From Aboriginal to Hip

Take Native Americans. They were subject to the whole repertoire of primitive accumulation. In a generation millions of bison that had supported communities for centuries—providing their food, clothing, shelter, and tools—were reduced to hundreds, their hides filling up the arteries of domestic and international trade. Buffalo skins morphed into leather belts for millions of industrial machines so that the nomadic way of life became insupportable. Cross-country trains traveled the Great Plains, stopping to allow armed passengers to slaughter whole herds as part of a deliberate policy to coerce tribal resettlement on reservations. Even the Dawes Act of 1887, ostensibly designed to convert Native American communalists into private farmers and tradesmen, ended finishing off the bloodier story of mass Indian removal: under the act's allotment system, most tribes suffered catastrophic losses of land and resources that reduced their members to a state of woeful dependency.[3]

Collateral damage up to and including social extinction had been the market price paid by native cultures even before the advent of industrialism, beginning with the first New England settlers. The Montauketts of eastern Long Island, for example, did not think of their lands as privately owned and alienable but rather as, like them, part of the natural order of things, to be used, not possessed in perpetuity. Europeans thought otherwise. They treated parcels as if they were commodities like any other, to be bought and sold whether or not the "owner" maintained any other active connection to that land.

For some generations during and after the colonial era, Dutch and British settlers negotiated deeds of "sale." The Montauketts might get manufactured goods in return—hatchets, pots, knives, coats. The deeds included clauses allowing Montauketts to continue to live and hunt, fish, and collect shells for wampum on portions of the land. They could as well salvage the fins and tails of beached whales, which—before the Europeans drove them far offshore—had supplied a regular part of the Montauketts' livelihood, had been hunted from oceangoing coastal canoes, and had been featured as items in ceremonial rituals. Meanwhile, the colonists could use the same territory to graze their cattle and hunt and trap animals for the marketplaces of New York and New England. They regularly renewed the deeds, anticipating that eventually the Indian population would die out or get killed in some war among indigenous tribes or by getting inveigled in intracolonial conflicts or both.

That was a sound speculation. And it was hurried along by the inexorable ecological rhythms of the market economy. As they grew more accustomed to using English finished goods, the Montauketts became less able to make their own. Meanwhile, livestock owned by colonists flourished so well that the animals put enormous pressure on lands still in some sense possessed and used by the native population. So, for example, the Montauketts normally hunted wild hogs for immediate consumption. But the British planned on fattening the quarry for slaughter and sale later on. And for that they increasingly wanted access to those common lands, feeding their animals on cornfields in areas the Indians were presumably entitled to live on. As for the English hogs, "The poor brutes were drove without any respect or mercy, driving off the sows that had young pigs leaving the pigs to starve in the swamp."

Conflict erupted inevitably. In 1657, for instance, several members of the Shinnecock tribe and a group of African American women conspired to burn down buildings in Southampton. But it was the demographic and economic drift of events that was most fatal. During the last four decades of the seventeenth century the Montaukett population drastically declined and its cultural cohesion withered away, due to European-borne disease, military defeats, and the relentless dwindling and expropriation of their material wherewithal. One after another customary right—for example, sovereignty over grazing meadows or wood rights for fuel—was ignored. Modern technologies like scythes and axes

43

felled trees and cut grasses so that deer, an Indian staple, disappeared. Commercial herds of foraging horses, goats, and hogs devoured what grass was left and hogs particularly spoiled vital clam banks.

Soon enough dispossessed Montauketts were absorbed into East Hampton households as domestics, day laborers, and indentured servants... or were not absorbed at all, but instead became "vagabonds upon the face of the earth," as one Montaukett put it. By the eighteenth century they were tenant farmers or proletarians working as cattle keepers, whalers, fence menders, and casual migratory laborers. Most of their land was gone: "They take our land away every day, a little and a little," mourned a local sachem.

Moreover, the English had managed as well to undermine what had once been a thriving local coastal economy hunting right whales as they migrated south in the fall. By taking over Montaukett skills and organizational savvy, and reducing the native population to the status of deeply indebted aquatic sharecroppers, colonial enterprises moved large volumes of whale oil to the ports of New York, Boston, and London. By the mid-eighteenth century, onshore whaling was practically over with. So too was the world of the Montaukett people—by the twentieth century the remnants of that tribe no longer even had the legal right to call themselves by that name.[4]

Before letting the Montauketts vanish into the maw of the market, one other landmark on their road to extinction is worth noting because of its implications for the larger story. In *Captains Courageous*, his tale of rough and tough adventuring, Rudyard Kipling featured a railroad baron and his wastrel son. Kipling selected Austin Corbin as his real-life model for the railroad king. Corbin had made his fortune during the Gilded Age, first out in the Midwest buying up the land of homesteaders who couldn't meet their mortgages. He founded a bank in Iowa and ran a plantation in Arkansas that used convict labor. Then he headed east, founded another bank, and started investing in railroads. He became president of the Reading line.

By the 1890s he had hooked up with Arthur Benson, another fabulously wealthy New York tycoon. Benson was busy buying up large chunks of Montauk. This entailed closing off or simply ignoring what remained of the Montauketts' customary and legal access to their common lands. It was done. After all, Benson and Corbin had big plans, which included extending Corbin's Long Island Rail Road from Bridgehampton to Montauk so as to turn the whole region into a resort for the rich, including the leisure classes from Europe who could disembark, so Corbin hoped, at the new deepwater port he also had in mind to build at Montauk. It was done. Today Montauk is the capital of summertime hip. So it was that an obscure tribal society was finally swallowed up by the inexorable mechanisms of global capitalism.[5]

"Redskin" Nation

Lost in the mists of history (if it ever got into the textbooks at all), this general dynamic was once well-known and commented on, first of all by Karl Marx: "The expropriation of the direct producers was accomplished by means of the most merciless barbarism, and under the stimulus of the most infamous, the most sordid, the most petty, and the most odious of passions." Certainly the Montauketts could testify to that. But so too might John Locke, who called for children to be put to work at the age of three, or Jeremy Bentham, who preferred four-year-olds. About that and bearing on the miracle of American Progress, Marx noted that "a great deal of capital, which appears today in the U.S. without any birth certificate, was yesterday in England, the capitalized blood of children."[6]

Although he didn't call it primitive accumulation, that specter haunted Jefferson's mind (an irony to be sure for someone whose on-again, off-again fortunes rested on slavery) when offering up what he saw as the best available alternative: "...A manufacturer [by which Jefferson meant an industrial worker] from Europe will turn to labour of other kinds if he finds more can be got by it, and he finds some employment [*sic*] so profitable that he can lay up enough money to buy fifty acres of land to the culture of which he is irresistibly tempted by the independence in which it places him." Some were fortunate enough to gain or retrieve that way of life. Many more were not.[7]

If Indians ended up on reservations or scattered to the winds, all those other refugees from preindustrial capitalist ways of life and of making a living ended up as proletarians of factory and field. Or sometimes worse, driven into lives of semipeonage, toiling away as convict laborers, indebted tenant farmers and sharecroppers, and contract workers, making up a whole menagerie of unfree or semifree labor.

The miracle of capital accumulation in the Gilded Age depended on a second miracle of disaccumulation taking place beyond the borders of capitalism proper. The new order depended on creating proletarians where there had been none or too few. By expanding the market for capitalist-produced goods, the process of primitive accumulation also worked its magic by absorbing and eliminating all those preexisting forms of household and craft production that until then had supplied those markets.

Appetite in this instance is insatiable, inexorable, and systemic, not a function of personal greed. As the revolutionary and political theorist Rosa Luxemburg noted, "Capital must begin by planning for the systematic destruction and annihilation of the non-capitalist social units which obstruct its development..." so that it "ransacks the whole world...all corners of the earth, seizing them, if necessary by force, from all levels of civilization and all forms of society."[8]

Industrial capitalism did not invent cruelty and exploitation. But its advent set in motion wholesale social transfigurations never seen before. Once there had been many slave, subsistence, and petty forms of production and social reproduction: plantation monocultures, smallholder agriculture in America and seigniorial village cultivation across southeastern and central Europe, handicraft production on both sides of the Atlantic, mercantile activities serving local markets, and an enormous variety of small businesses filling up the arteries of production and distribution. It isn't the advent of the market that placed them in jeopardy. Most were quite accustomed to engaging in exchange and regularly made use of credit and carried on private production alongside and in harmony with common holdings. They were even used to price fluctuations as long as they didn't go so far as to threaten honest livelihoods, the "just prices" that protected them, and the ways of life that depended on them. Capital did precisely that to all of these customary societies.

Most of this was disappeared—that is, was caused to vanish, in one way or another. Early on in colonial Virginia, for example, people clung to traditional forms of subsistence farming, even enduring bouts of periodic hunger, preferring it to working for others. The harshest measures had to be taken by colonial authorities to force the change, including various forms of corporal punishment.

Later, war ended the slave system. Yet in the course of a single generation ex-slaves—freedmen—were reduced to various forms of agricultural peonage, thanks to the failure of the Republican Party to provide them the landed wherewithal to become freeholders. If slaves were abandoned, so too were those millions who took Horace Greeley seriously and thought they would reinvent themselves out west.

Particularly galling was the way the Homestead Act was abused. Passed during the Civil War, it was supposed to make a reality out of Lincoln's version of the free labor, free soil dream. But fewer than half a million people actually set up viable farms over nearly half a century. Most public lands were taken over by the railroads, thanks to the government's beneficent land-grant policy (another form of primitive accumulation); by land speculators backed by eastern bankers, who sometimes hired pretend "homesteaders" in acts of outright fraud; or by giant cattle ranches and timber companies and the like who worked hand in glove with government land agents. As early as 1862 two-thirds of Iowa (or ten million acres) was owned by speculators. Railroads closed off one-third of Kansas to homesteading and that was the best land available. Mushrooming cities back east became, in a kind of historical inversion, the safety valve for overpopulated areas in the west. At least the city held out the prospect of remunerative wage labor if no longer a life of propertied independence. Few city workers had the capital to migrate west anyway; when one Pennsylvania legislator suggested that the state subsidize such moves, he was denounced as "the Pennsylvania Communist" for his trouble.

During the last land boom of the nineteenth century (from about 1883 to 1887), 16 million acres underwent that conversion every year. Railroads doubled down by selling off or mortgaging portions of the public domain they had just been gifted to finance construction or to speculate with. But land-grant roads were built at costs 100 percent greater than warranted and badly built at that, needing to be rebuilt just fifteen years later.

Cattle companies, often financed from abroad, used newly invented barbed wire to fence in millions of acres of land once depended on by small farmers and ranchers to water and graze their animals in common. This American version of the British enclosure acts of the seventeenth century (which turned British landlords into commercialized land barons and British yeomen into wayfaring, itinerant laborers) left in its wake dead cattle and bankrupted homesteads.[9]

Nature conspired with global commodity capitalism to ramp up the rate of dispossession from the land. A punishing drought in the mid-1880s was by itself enough to drive thousands of farmers under. Then, as the Russian and Canadian steppes, the Australian outback, and the Argentine pampas added to the tidal wave of grain and meat flooding world markets, prices collapsed: corn that cost $8.60 an acre to grow could be sold for only $6.60; $9-an-acre wheat for $5.53. Prices for staples declined by two-thirds after 1870 and by two-fifths for all products coming off the farm: barley was worth 20 percent less in 1900, wool 30 percent less, and wheat 29 percent less than it had been in 1860. As the mechanization of American and worldwide agriculture overwhelmed the markets, prices tended to fall off a cliff. In 1889 corn fell to 10 cents a bushel in Kansas (it had been 46 cents in 1870). Between 1889 and 1893, eleven thousand farms were foreclosed on in Kansas alone. A mass exodus of farmers from western Kansas and elsewhere followed.[10]

Impoverished Southern tenants and sharecroppers turned to large planters or local "furnishing agents" to borrow what they needed for essentials; collateral consisted of a pledged portion of their next year's crop. Their creditors charged usurious rates of interest, ranging from 25 to 80 percent; such creditors in Louisiana were charging 60 percent in the late 1880s. Usury laws, which once existed in most states, were systematically attacked and often modified or eliminated entirely as "barbaric relics" to please investment institutions back east. Nor were eastern farms exempt. In a surpassing irony, bankrupted farmers there sold off small pieces of land to industrial workers who were themselves trying to produce enough to subsist through the merciless uncertainties of the market.[11]

To survive this mercantile cyclone, farmers hooked themselves up to long lines of credit that stretched circuitously back to the financial centers of the east. These lifelines provided the wherewithal to buy the seeds and fertilizers and machines, to pay for storage and freight charges, to keep house and home together while the plants ripened and hogs fattened. When market day finally arrived, the farmer found out what all his backbreaking work was really worth. If the news was bad, then those life-support systems of credit were turned off and became the means of his own dispossession.

In the South, hard-pressed growers found themselves embroiled in a crop-lien system, dependent on the local furnishing agent to supply everything needed, from seed to clothing to machinery, to get through the growing season. In such situations, no money changed hands, just a note scribbled in the agent's ledger, with payment due at "settling up" time. This granted the lender a lien, or title, to the crop, a lien that never went away.

In this fashion, the South became "a great pawn shop," with farmers perpetually in debt. In Alabama, Georgia, and Mississippi, 90 percent of farmers lived on credit. The first lien you signed was essentially a life sentence. Either that or you became a tenant farmer or you simply left your land.[12]

This was primitive accumulation with a vengeance. In the South the furnishing agent was often enough himself in debt to financiers up north. Frequently what sharecroppers or tenants owed exceeded the value of the crops just harvested; an endless cycle of debt dependency ensued.

And because cotton was the most liquid of all commodities, planters and merchants and northern banks insisted on its exclusive cultivation, inhibiting any diversification, leaving Southern farmers, black and white, singularly vulnerable to the world cotton market. The emergence of Egypt and India as major cotton producers only exacerbated the plight of Dixie agriculturalists by exerting further downward pressure on prices.

Just as barbed wire out west had fenced in what was once common grazing land, so too in the South the planter oligarchy passed laws excluding self-sufficient, up-country hog farmers from pastures and water sources once available to all. Nearly one-half of all Southern farms were run by various species of non-owners. The human runoff from this systematic undermining of small-scale producers, cut off from any other legitimate means of support and compelled to survive one way or another, even outside the law, became itself a crop to be harvested by enterprising capital.

The convict lease system—the renting of prisoners (overwhelmingly African American) to planters and private industry—boomed and was symptomatic of a regional system of primitive accumulation that blanketed the post–Civil War South. In fact, prison labor as a lucrative form of capital accumulation was ubiquitous in the north and among white prisoners in the antebellum years. Convicts were worked either inside prisons by outside contractors or in all sorts of manufacturing facilities outside prison walls, ranging from small-scale carpentry shops to very large textile and shoe factories. New York State led the way, but there was virtually no state in the union that didn't provide this kind of coerced and very cheap labor.[13]

In the South, convict leases provided workers for cotton plantations, mining, lumbering, and turpentine camps as well as for quarries, dockyards, and road-building projects; Alabama derived 73 percent of its state revenue from leasing convicts. Nor was this flow of unfree labor restricted to regional industries and agribusinesses. Large, northern-headquartered banks and corporations were complicit. So, for example, the Tennessee Coal and Iron and Railway Company, the leading coal, iron, and steel producer in the rich fields surrounding Birmingham, Alabama, was a heavy user of prison labor; by the early twentieth century it had become an affiliate of the J. P. Morgan–run U.S. Steel, and by 1907 it had become the largest user and profiteer of this slave-labor system.

Making sure the supply of coerced workers was ample became a function of the region's policing and judicial systems. Wholesale arrests among black men in Georgia and throughout the South for disobeying a boss, being impudent, gambling, partying, talking to white women, having lascivious sex, riding freight cars without a ticket, vagrancy, or even for just being out of work produced a robust supply of convict labor at harvesttime or when railroad track needed to be laid or phosphate mined. Some didn't survive the ordeal, having been worked to death: 44 percent of the 285 convicts building the South Carolina Greenwood and Augusta Railroad died. The mortality rate among convict laborers in Alabama was 45 percent. At the Pratt mines in the Appalachian foothills of northern Alabama, among the largest in the South, the mortality rate was 18 percent. At Tennessee Coal and Iron, workers were shackled together in underground pits, lived in fetid, disease-ridden barracks, worked to exhaustion from sunup to sundown, were regularly whipped and sometimes tortured (water torture was commonly resorted to) for every imagined infraction, and were hunted down by dogs if daring enough to attempt escape. If they didn't die of whipping, disease, near starvation, or a bullet in the brain, they committed suicide at alarming rates, their bodies tossed into nameless roadside graves. A rare government investigation in Alabama in 1882 concluded these prisons "were totally unfit for use, without ventilation, without water supplies, crowded to excess, filthy beyond description," where the prisoners were "excessively and sometimes cruelly punished." An equally rare ex-Confederate plantation owner appalled by what was going on described these prison mining operations as "nurseries of death."

Unlike slave masters of old, those overseeing the process in this way had no stake in, nor did they offer any paternal pretense about caring for, the health, well-being, or reproductive potential of their unfree workers. Those more candid among them admitted they thought of these peons as mere "clever mules." Moreover, the whole judicial system of the South, from the lowliest country sheriff and justice of the peace to the highest reaches of state capitals, conspired to replenish the supply of convict labor as a lucrative source of self-enrichment and government revenue. In effect the legal apparatus became a mechanism of primitive accumulation by monetizing criminal behavior (if it could even be called that) of the most trivial or contrived nature through a web of debt. Labor in this arrangement became a kind of currency used to pay off judicial fines and accumulate capital in the private sector.

A regional economy rooted in the production of foodstuffs and primary raw materials rested to some considerable degree on these related forms of unfree labor. And soon enough a regional market in convict labor emerged in which agents scoured the countryside to fill positions in coal mines, lumber and turpentine camps, and numerous other enterprises. In this venture into primitive modernism there was even ample opportunity for speculators to buy up discounted script for prisoner debt only redeemable when the convict had worked off his fine (a day that for the least fortunate never came, in which case the speculator lost his shirt).

Three generations after the Civil War the system was still ensnaring hundreds of thousands. Extreme in its flagrant disregard of the 13th Amendment abolishing involuntary servitude and laws against peonage, this fixing of the human body so it could be milked until dry was, after all, part of the broader scheme implemented in the South after the war to restrict the mobility of the newly emancipated so that they would remain an ever-ready labor force.[14]

Most Dixie labor contracts—when they existed at all—contained all sorts of obligations coercing workers to stay put for a year or more (even sometimes including lifetime contracts). In Mississippi if you hadn't entered into a contract by January 1, you were subject to arrest. In Alabama, North Carolina, and Florida, it was a crime to change employers without permission. Together with all the other disabling features of post–Reconstruction life and labor, the network of debt peonage functioned to forestall or destroy independent farming and other forms of economic self-reliance, reducing a whole population to a state of abject dependency. At the turn of the twentieth century, a young black man in the South (and some poor whites as well) faced three options: "free labor camps that functioned like prisons, cotton tenancy that equated to serfdom, or prison mines filled with slaves." Resistance when it miraculously surfaced was met with violence and, not infrequently, consignment to forced labor. And while young African American males languished in industrial and agricultural prison camps, black women (if they weren't also working in prisons, sometimes as unpaid prostitutes), once the helpmates of their husbands on small family plots, found work instead as wage earners in canning and tobacco factories, as domestics, in mechanized laundries and textile mills, and in the fields.

Inundated by debt, Jefferson's independent farmer was becoming an endangered species. By the turn of the century, two-thirds of all agricultural work, north and south, was performed by tenants, sharecroppers, or wage laborers. In South Carolina plow hands earned as little as twenty cents a day, paid partly in cornmeal and tobacco.[15]

Debt-based capital formation, which may or may not be reinvested in industry, has been a classic mode of primitive accumulation around the world. Here in the United States, it was enforced by adherence to the gold standard, which offered debtors no relief, safeguarded creditors, and kept foreign investment capital — British funds especially — flowing into what was after all still a developing country and a risky one. Creditors and investors were reassured by the gold standard that they could always redeem their paper assets in a fixed amount of gold. For debtors, however, this meant their obligations became ever more onerous as prices for agricultural commodities and other goods declined. It was because so many independent proprietors, especially on the land, but also in small towns and cities, found themselves entangled in webs of credit and debt which threatened their social existence that Gilded Age politics often seemed obsessed with the money question, with greenbacks and the gold standard, with cries for the free coinage of silver and fiat money.

The Disinherited

Globalized capitalist agriculture also wiped out or imperiled peasant proprietors and other small producers in Sicily and southern Italy and all across the Balkans, Germany, Austro-Hungary, Poland, and Scandinavia. As miraculous as the rapidity and scope of American industrialization (and as enmeshed in its triumph) was the overnight uprooting of millions of people from their ancestral villages and from traditional ways of life that could no longer be sustained. If local populations managed to hang on, they did so only by a process of social amputation, exporting their young (and not so young) men, and eventually whole kin networks, to work in the New World, there to remit back what they could to those left behind. A century before industrial ghost towns haunted the American Midwest, ghost villages made their spectral appearances across the underbelly of Europe.

Nearly seven million migrated to America from Europe between 1881 and 1894, increasing numbers of them from the continent's rural hinterland. In 1907 five thousand immigrants arrived at Ellis Island each day. By 1910, immigrant working-class women from the old country constituted the core of the workforce in textiles and garment manufacturing, and in mechanical laundries and domestic service. Human chains of sojourning labor migrated back and forth across the Atlantic in rhythm with the business cycle, returning home when the economy went south. Once in the United States they joined their efforts with home-grown superannuated farmers along with native handicraftsmen displaced by the machine and the factory's exquisitely refined division and specialization of labor. These legions of displaced immigrants became charter members of an American proletariat. By 1870 the foreign-born accounted for one-third of the industrial workforce; soon enough in some cities, like Chicago, they would constitute the majority.[16]

Expatriated peasants were not the only river flowing into the sea of wage labor. Mass-production, factory-based, machine-driven industry grew robust at the expense of home-grown handicraft economies and the knowledge, skills, and traditions embedded in those ways of life. They weakened, were debased in a futile effort to compete with the factory, and then vanished. Craftsmen—woodworkers and printers, barrel makers and bakers, butchers and iron molders, tailors and shoemakers, glassblowers and brass workers, masons and smithies, weavers and bookbinders—were swept up into the process of industrial capital accumulation. Once they had been small-shop proprietors in their own right. Or, even after losing that independence, they had clustered together inside factory gates as groups of invaluable industrial craftsmen, enjoying a functional quasi-independence thanks to their secret knowledge, experience, and self-directed control of what went on in their specialized precincts; iron puddlers, rollers, boilers, and heaters, for example, for a time exercised decisive control over production in the iron and steel mills; skilled butchers did the same in the new meatpacking plants of Chicago.

Soon enough, however, these industrial artisans became "nothing more than parts of the machinery that they work." Capital accumulated at the expense of their social existence; they took up new lives, became part of that larger waged labor force which modern capitalism produces and depends on—its chief commodity and natural resource. Indeed, the stupendous rate of mechanization in America was in part driven by the need to reduce the high costs associated with those forms of handicraft, skilled, and highly valued labor that for a while continued on into the factory age. They not only were expensive but, given their leverage over vital aspects of the manufacturing process, slowed the pace of production on the shop floor. New machines promised to wipe out those remnants that resisted. After a while the machines, aided by the efforts of determined managements, won.[17]

Victory, however, emerged only gradually. In the early decades of the nineteenth century, farmers, handicraftsmen, and various tradespeople swept into the new textile or shoe factories or the farm women set to work out in the countryside spinning and weaving for merchant-capitalists still held on to some semblance of their old ways of life. They maintained vegetable gardens, continued to hunt and fish, and perhaps kept a few domestic animals. When the first commercial panics erupted and business came to a standstill, many could fall back on precapitalist ways of making a living, even if a bare one. When industrial capitalism exploded after the Civil War, unemployment suddenly became a chronic and frightening aspect of modern life affecting millions. Crushing helplessness in the face of unemployment was also a devastating new experience for those great waves of immigrants landing on American shores, many of them peasants accustomed to falling back on their own meager resources in fields and forests when times were bad.

Inexorably, or so it seemed, capital prevailed, and its triumph could assume a somber shape. During this formative phase of industrialization, 35,000 workers died each year in industrial accidents, many of them key skilled mechanics. In 1910, one-quarter of all workers in the iron and steel industries were injured at least once, partly because of management's failure to install safety devices or shorten the hours of work. Two thousand coal miners died each year on the job. Every day, around that same time, there were one hundred industrial accidents somewhere in the country.

Especially for various skilled occupations, the railroads, for example, became a killing ground. Between 1890 and 1917, 158,000 mechanics and laborers were killed in railroad repair shops and roundhouses. In 1888–89 alone, of 704,000 railroad employees, 20,000 were injured and nearly 2000 killed. On the Illinois Central between 1874 and 1884, one of every twenty trainmen died or was disabled; among brakemen—railroaders who did the most dangerous work—the ratio was one in seven (and among railroad switchmen, another skilled position, the number was almost as alarming). Part of the reason for this appalling record of disfigurement and death was management's relentless drive to increase the workload; brakemen, for example, were required to brake four or five cars rather than the two or three that had been the custom earlier. The bones of thousands of workmen were encased in the concrete of dams and bridges, bodies interred by the thousands in underground caverns, limbs shattered and sheared off by gears, wheels, lathes, chains, pulleys, spindles, cables, and flywheels; mountains of fingers, forearms, legs, ears, and even heads made up the human geography of industrial Progress.[18]

High death, injury, and unemployment rates; precipitous deterioration in diet as well as in the size and comforts of home; abandoned backyard vegetable gardens; common hunting grounds and fisheries privatized; urban squalor; obsolescent skills and forsaken traditions; exhausting, high-speed work routines lasting twelve hours or more unlike anything experienced before; a daily life cycle consisting of work, punctuated by shorts bouts of eating and sleeping; chained to the inorganic respiration of machines and the befouled climate of "dark Satanic mills"; chronic insecurity and dread, of work, of no work, of the foreman, of the poorhouse; periodic or permanent excommunication as vagabonds and tramps; social disgrace, demoralization, dependency.

Loss. A typical coal mining family in Pennsylvania during the 1870s lived like this: in a two-room "black coated shack," dining on potatoes, soda crackers, and water, forced to buy their paltry groceries with company scrip exchangeable only at a "truck store" (also known as "pluck me" stores) run by the colliery. When one of their two daughters got sick, there was no way to pay a doctor. Nor was there any money to bury her when she died.

Childhood itself became a resource for capital accumulation. In Pennsylvania late in the nineteenth century, children contributed 25 percent of family earnings, 40 percent among the unskilled. These kids ranged in age from ten to fifteen. Already by 1880, 69 percent of boys and

20 percent of girls aged fifteen to nineteen were working, and 18 percent of children between the ages of ten and fourteen were working at non-agricultural pursuits in 1890. At the turn of the century, one-fifth of all children in the country under the age of fifteen worked for wages, and this doesn't count the millions who worked on farms. In the Carolinas toddlers picked strawberries.

These children toiled especially down in the mines, in the meatpacking plants, in textile mills north and south, and in the tenement warrens of garment and cigar-making shops. One-third of those between ten and fifteen worked twelve-hour days in the Carolina and Georgia textile mills, in Virginia tobacco sheds, and all over the country in toy and candy factories, in coal mines and glass and food-packing plants. There were four-year-old button sewers and basting pullers in the garment industry. There were pea shellers not much more than infants. When the Triangle Shirtwaist Factory went up in smoke in 1911, many of those killed were not really women yet, but young teenage girls. And then there was that sizable population of abandoned children, cast off and barely surviving in urban underground economies.[19]

Falling and Failing

Downward mobility—more precisely, the descent into social oblivion—is the arc inscribed by primitive accumulation. It is the underground, invisible story of industrial Progress, the counterpoint to that widely celebrated tale of upward mobility at the heart of the American mythos. And it left its mark not only among the "lower orders"—struggling farmers, peasant immigrants, dispossessed, déclassé handicraftsmen—but also among middling merchants, storekeepers, and petty producers in towns and small cities across the nation. They succumbed to the relentless pressures of the giant corporation. Often enough, that corporation was erected on their remains, sometimes absorbing their facilities, their equipment, their personnel, or else leaving all that bankrupt and inert by the side of the road. Or just as frequently those small businessmen devoured one another or effectively committed suicide, driven to compete close to and then past the point of economic survival. Their death cleared the market, opened up the way for enormous industrial combines, raw materials producers, mass market distributors, nationwide transportation and communications corporations, the champions of consolidated capital accumulation and the integrated national marketplace — all the purveyors of Progress.

Winning was definitely better than losing in this Darwinian war to the death. However, one central irony of this era is that the same competitive strains that produced a relentless downward pressure on prices and that helped account for the rising standard of living enjoyed by many, also generated a pervasive unease among even the biggest capitalists. Their profit margins were under constant assault, their mood oscillating between surly and gloomy, always anxious, often lacking in confidence except when periodic but short-lived booms temporarily restored their good spirits. Matters improved dramatically around the turn of the century, when the publicly traded corporation began to occupy vast stretches of the economic landscape and brought with it oligopolistic powers to restrain competition and raise prices and profits. But for decades during the long nineteenth century, even the new bourgeois elite harbored doubts about the course of Progress. Still, those who survived did thrive, often at the expense of what was once an ocean of petty entrepreneurs.

Stepping beyond the boundaries of the Gilded Age for a moment, it is worth noting that 80 percent of Americans were self-employed in 1820; by 1940 that number had shrunk to 20 percent. Was it all a matter of the inexorable, impersonal workings of the free market? Sometimes it was, but sometimes not.[20]

The most famous conspiracy to bring about that kind of social extinction was authored by John D. Rockefeller and Tom Scott, who ran the Pennsylvania Railroad (the nation's largest). Together they cobbled together a cartel of oil refiners and oil transporters (including William Vanderbilt's New York Central and Jay Gould's Erie). Calling their new enterprise the South Improvement Company (SIC), they divided up the market among themselves, fixed the rates, provided SIC members a 40 to 50 percent discount, and drove a host of independent refiners out of business. SIC's basic mechanisms for digesting or obliterating once freestanding enterprises were duplicated many times across broad stretches of the economy, from raw materials to retailing, and from the beginning to the end of the Gilded Age and beyond.

A menagerie of comparable trusts loomed over the economic landscape. There was a jute or bagging trust, a cottonseed oil trust, a fertilizer trust, a binding twine trust, a tobacco trust, a beef trust, trusts in leather, salt, rope, sugar, lead, lumber, and so on, all of which represented mortal threats to free enterprisers. All sorts of small-scale businesses, from local merchants to neighborhood butchers, were placed in harm's way.

Insofar as Progress was strongly associated, as it was perceived to be back in the Gilded Age, with gigantic concentrations of both dynastic and corporate capitalism, this was the metabolism responsible, petty businesses its waste material. Entrepreneurs and would-be entrepreneurs struggled and often failed to get off the ground, thanks to the choke hold on entering the market exercised by trusts or monopolies. Nor were they the only unwilling contributors to capital accumulation. Towns were tithed for tax subventions and rural and urban consumers of industrial goods, foodstuffs, transit services, and other necessities were gouged at the cash register by those predatory oligopolies no longer subject to the rival competitive pressures.

Yet it is also undeniable that even without the conscious connivance by trust builders and their political enablers, the ground-level remorseless logic of the free market worked to destroy the free market.

Some economic historians have described the whole last third of the century as one long depression, worldwide in scope, characterized by price deflation, mass bankruptcies, and declining rates of profit, interrupted by spasms of meteoric growth. Occurring with increasing frequency and ferocity, depressions—there were major ones beginning in 1837 and recurring in 1857, 1873, 1882, 1893, and 1907—became the killing fields for legions of small and medium-sized enterprises. The Darwinian struggle to survive was succinctly described by Karl Marx: "No sooner has the capitalist fairly adopted an improved machine, than it must be thrown away for a still later and better invention which must be purchased at dear cost if the manufacturer would not see himself eclipsed by his rival." The process elicited merciless cost-cutting (labor costs especially), overproduction, saturated markets, devaluing of existing means of production by newer, more productive ones, and overall commercial chaos, a war of all against all. Depressions were the free market's solution to its own dilemmas. But their consequences were often worse than the disease they were meant to cure. Even the victors, not to mention the vanquished, were disturbed.[21]

Corporate consolidation emerged as a way out of this maelstrom, suspending (permanently some hoped) the laws of the free market, replacing them instead with conscious centralized control—of pricing, output, and technological innovation, as well as of costs of raw materials, marketing, transportation, and distribution—by a singularly powerful corporation or by secret alliances of a tiny handful of such goliaths. Rockefeller, for one, had nothing but contempt for free market competition, scorning "academic Know-Nothings about business" who prated on about its virtues. "What a blessing it was that the idea of cooperation, with railroads, with telegraph lines, with steel companies, with oil companies, came in and prevailed." He was a believer in the genius of monopoly and managerial control, not shy about pronouncing that "the individual has gone, never to return." Rockefeller's oil combine, Armour's meatpacking supremacy, Carnegie's steel dominion, Frick's coke and coal mine empire, among others, all emerged first out of the ruins of the catastrophic depression that lasted through the heart of the 1870s.[22]

Six thousand firms went under in 1874 alone. Similarly, business activity plummeted by 25 percent in the downturn of the early 1880s, dragging down railroad revenues, pig iron and coal production, domestic cotton consumption, imports, and multitudes of petty businesses that depended on their patronage. During the depression that began in

1893—the worst of them all until 1929—the nation's output imploded, dropping by 64 percent. The rate of business failures nearly tripled over the previous bust. In just a few years, farm income dropped by 18 percent. Freight cars stood empty, factory chimneys remained smokeless, steel furnaces were banked. The economy as a whole operated at 25 percent below capacity.[23]

Calamity for many, however, was a boon for a fortunate few. During the collapse of the 1870s, for example, the Mellon family banking and real estate empire swallowed up liquidated businesses auctioned off at sheriff sales and evictions. A decade later the Mellons used the capital accumulated in this way to fund investments in natural gas, plate glass, western land development, and more.[24]

The Reserve Army of the Unemployed

Pain from a spasmodic economy like this one penetrated deep into the tissues of American society, way below the level of the family business. Casualties accumulated among the country's growing population of invisibles. When Jay Cooke, the country's most famous financier, went under in 1873 along with his recklessly overextended and highly speculative Northern Pacific Railroad, the bottom also fell out for millions of working people. Between then and 1877, when the Great Uprising shocked the nation, wages fell by as much as 60 percent and 3 million out of a total population of 45 million were without work of any kind (this was nearly one-fifth of the workforce).

We have long since grown accustomed to treating unemployment as a normal and natural part of the economic order of things. But during a good part of the long nineteenth century, unemployment struck people as shocking, unnatural, and traumatic. This strange new calamity had already surfaced in the colonial era. The first manufactories were public enterprises created in the 1760s and '70s to relieve the larger eastern cities of what had been unthinkable before—namely, a growing population of unemployed, idling laborers no longer able to find work in settled areas of the coastal colonies. People feared they would breed crime, dissipation, and disorder, transplanting to the New World vices already rife in the Old one.[25]

Unemployment as a recurring feature of social life really caught American attention, however, only with the rise of capitalism, first in the pre–Civil War era. Before that, even if the rhythms of agricultural and village life included seasonal oscillations between periods of intense labor and downtime, farmers and handicraftsmen generally retained the ability to sustain their families. Hard times were common enough, but except *in extremis* most people retained land and tools, not to speak of common rights to woodlands and grazing areas, and the ability to hunt and fish. They were—we would say today— "self-employed." Only when such means of subsistence and production became concentrated in the hands of merchant-capitalists, manufacturers, and large landowners did the situation change fundamentally. "Unemployment" was not even invented as a census category until the 1870s. Then a proletariat—those without property of any kind except their own labor power—began to appear, dependent on the propertied for employment. If, for whatever reason, the market for their labor power dried up, they were set adrift.

What soon came to be called "the reserve army of labor"—able-bodied but destitute workers—stunned onlookers. The "tramp" became a ubiquitous figure, traveling the roads and rails, sometimes carrying his tools with him, desperate for employment. For villagers and city people alike, he was a foreboding specter. "Tramp acts" were passed to "check or exterminate" the tramp. In 1877 one million vagrants were arrested, double the number of the year before. Their punishment often enough was forced work. Missouri, for instance, auctioned such prisoners off to the highest bidders.

Whether working or not, fifteen million people lived in poverty; the cost of food took up three-fifths of a worker's pay. And legions of the homeless also tramped the roads. During the "milder" downturn of the mid-1880s, unemployment exceeded 13 percent and wages fell by more than one-quarter. "Soup houses" and "societies for the Improvement of the

Conditions of the Poor" provided some food and sponsored laundries, woodyards, workrooms, and wayfarer lodges for the homeless, but couldn't keep up with the need. The Johns Hopkins economist Richard Ely noted that "never before had there been seen in America such contrasts between fabulous wealth and absolute penury." Fetid slums that were often dark, airless, and wintry cold; filthy streets and alleys; people scouring in ash cans for rotten vegetables; epidemic disease—all of this social ugliness and more shocked observers like Ely.[26]

Matters only became grimmer during the great depression of the 1890s. Real earnings declined by 18 percent during the first two years of the collapse as wages were slashed. The consumption of items like clothing, canned corn, coffee, shoes, and dry goods of all kinds shriveled. In Boston more than a third of the city's craftsmen were out of work. Millions more across the nation were fired (only during the 1930s would unemployment levels exceed those of the 1890s), the homeless took shelter in empty school classrooms, and "armies" of tramps (sometimes known as "industrials") demanding work or relief converged on Washington, D.C., from all over the country—Boston, St. Louis, Seattle, Spokane, Chicago, San Francisco, Portland, as well as Massillon, Ohio, and the hinterlands of Colorado, Montana, and Utah.

Twenty thousand vagrants huddled in the streets of New York, where for two months Joseph Pulitzer's *New York World* handed out 5000 loaves of bread. Desperate, some hurled stones through store windows hoping to be arrested and so sheltered in a jail cell for the night. At least 100,000—some estimated close to 200,000—were workless in Chicago during the bitter winter of 1893–94. Accounts appeared of people "living from the ash barrels where they found half rotten vegetables and from offal they were given by local butchers." From Buffalo came reports of 5000 Polish immigrants in "imminent danger of starvation"; the city's postmaster, who moonlighted as a baker, distributed free bread. In Washington, D.C., a scene of "greater destitution than before known," especially among the city's always hard-pressed African Americans, included "a vast army of unemployed and men pleading for food who have never before been compelled to seek aid." Trainloads of out-of-work silver miners in Colorado were shipped eastward for free to get them out of the state. Zones of rural devastation in Kansas, Nebraska, and the Dakotas were depopulated virtually overnight. Kansas governor Lorenzo Lewelling declared the state's vagrancy law unconstitutional, ordered police not to harass the state's swelling population of the homeless, and made a personal observation: "It is no crime to be without visible means of support. I was in that condition once, in 1865, in Chicago. I was no thief, but I was a tramp."[27]

Prosperity and Primitive Accumulation: History's Paradox

Primitive accumulation thus helped generate the stupendous economic inequality that the Gilded Age is famous for. But the picture is more mixed than that. Capital was indeed piling up in factories, mills, pipelines, railroads, granaries, shipyards, stores, and of course banks. Owners naturally benefited. So too did a new species of middle managers and clerical and administrative employees. That white-collar population of managers, technicians, clerks, and sales and other personnel rose from under 400,000 in 1870 to more than three million by 1910. Moreover, the standard of living of skilled industrial workers also measurably improved. Their precious forms of know-how, so long as they lasted, were rewarded by managements with little choice in the matter.

Fierce competition drove prices down through the whole era, so that even if nominal wages fell (in severe downturns, for example) real wages did not; indeed, the division of spoils between labor and capital tended to favor the former, especially among the skilled, as internecine competition drove down not only costs but profits as well. The purchasing power of skilled workers doubled between 1865 and the end of the century.

For some then, and by no means only an elite few, Progress, measured at least in material terms, was real. Per capita income doubled between the end of the Civil War and the turn of the century. Health and nutrition got dramatically better for multitudes, thanks to the advent of bacterial biology and the technologies of canning and refrigeration. Technological innovation could and did both intensify and ease toil. But the rate of productivity slowed each decade beginning in the 1870s. So that for others—many, many others—inequality was stark and growing starker.[28]

By the midpoint of the Gilded Age about 4000 families owned as much wealth as the remaining 11.6 million. Two hundred thousand individuals controlled between 70 and 80 percent of the nation's property. The arithmetic of dispossession and of the descent into the new American proletariat went like this: while 87 percent of private wealth belonged to a privileged fifth of the population and 11 percent to the next luckiest fifth, the bottom 40 percent had none at all. Multimillionaires (another invention of the Gilded Age) accounted for 0.33 percent of the population but owned one-sixth of the country's wealth. The richest 1 percent owned 51 percent of all real and personal property, while the bottom 44 percent came away with 1.1 percent. Most workers earned less than $800 annually, which wasn't enough to keep them out of poverty. And most of them had to toil for nearly sixty hours a week to make even that much.

Progress—that is, capital accumulation—had created a nation of haves and have-nots. Whether pleased with the result or not, all were astonished at its strangeness. The shock reverberated up and down the ranks of this new world, now pockmarked by a steep hierarchy once thought alien to the American experiment. Nor did the lower orders, those living on the edge of social if not physical extinction, think they'd ended up there by accident. On the contrary, they were convinced they had been driven down by an overweening aristocracy, presumptuous beyond measure, a noxious import from the Old World.[29]

Observing this in the Old World, Marx was struck by something that prefigured, at least in part, one answer to the mystery this book wrestles with: "The class struggles here in England, too, were more turbulent during the period of development of large-scale industry, and died down just in the period of England's undisputed industrial domination of the world . . . and it will be no different probably in America. It is the revolutionizing of all traditional relations by industry as it develops that also revolutionizes people's minds." Decades before he issued this forecast, Americans were already experiencing similar premonitions of stormy weather ahead.[30]

3

Premonitions

"Are we a plutocracy?"[1]
— *William Dean Howells*

Howells's question, by the time he articulated it in 1894, was for him and for many other observers of the American scene largely a rhetorical one. The answer was all too obvious: a tiny yet conspicuous elite of industrialists and financiers exercised inordinate power over economic affairs, over all three branches of the federal government, over the criminal justice system, over the nation's institutions of higher education, over many of the most important metropolitan newspapers, and over the country's mainline religious denominations. Its social preeminence was everywhere on display in how it dressed, where it lived, how it educated and entertained itself. Millions marveled at its splendor. In the realm of ideas, how the plutocracy justified its great wealth and its own heroic conception of what it had accomplished became America's reigning ideas—not its only ones, not unchallenged ones, but the ones carrying the greatest cultural heft.

Plutocracy was cause enough for worry. But a dreadful, kindred apparition was even more frightening. Because of its overweening power, its wildly pretentious behavior, and the utterly bizarre nature of its appearance on a native landscape so saturated in homespun, everyman customs and beliefs, aristocracy even more than plutocracy set off alarm bells in the American political psyche.

From a contemporary vantage point, sightings of aristocrats can't help but strike us as at best exaggerated, cartoonish, and a paranoid anachronism born of an overheated political imagination. After all, today, no matter how rich, influential, and self-involved in acts of conspicuous social preening members of our corporate and financial elite may be, we don't seriously mistake them for real aristocrats. The whole idea of an actual aristocracy in the land of the free seems outlandish.

That was not the case for those alive during the long nineteenth century. People like Howells were only two or three generations removed from the American Revolution. Memories of their ancestors' war against monarchists and Tory aristocrats had been refreshed again and again. Jefferson had waged a tooth-and-claw fight against what he and his followers believed to be counterrevolutionary conspiracies hatched by Hamilton's moneycrats. A generation later, Andrew Jackson declared war on the second Bank of the United States, an institution he anointed "the Monster Bank," which was run by a bewigged Philadelphia aristocrat, Nicholas Biddle, in the interests—so the president alleged—of a politically privileged elite monopolizing the country's capital resources. Jackson's triumph over the "Monster Bank" was followed by Lincoln's far grander victory over the country's most powerful, indigenous aristocracy, the Southern "slaveocracy."

Irish and German immigrants streaming into the country in the decades before the Civil War (and afterward) brought with them their own rough experiences with British and Junker titled gentry. Peasants from eastern and southern Europe arriving later in the century were in some cases not even a generation removed from serfdom or less formal systems of peonage and dependency. In the Old World all the structures of hierarchical social and political life—clerical, landed, and military castes endowed with distinct political and economic powers, privileges, and exemptions—were under assault but still very much a part of everyday affairs and still in charge. Suspicions, resentment, and anger directed at aristocrats were therefore not only a homegrown temperament, but were being regularly replenished from abroad.

The American Revolution, in that respect, turned out to be a permanent one. It was always on guard, under assault, and in danger of being overthrown. The specter of the aristocrat haunted the corridors of the nation's political imagination for generations, so much so that at the end of the long nineteenth century Franklin Roosevelt could still inveigh with great energy and effect against "economic royalists" and "Tories of industry."

Were these moneycrats, robber barons, factory lords, and economic royalists misidentified? Were they really no more and no less than over-sized capitalists of one variety or another? Were they, as Howells asked, mere plutocrats? Strictly speaking, yes. They enjoyed no heritable status, often came by their wealth quite recently, accumulated it far more often in commerce and industry than on the land, and rested their elevated social position on mountains of cash, not on family lineage, breeding, education, or statutory prerogatives. Still this apparent confusion—the conflation of the aristocrat and the capitalist—is a telltale sign of a political culture of resistance. It was invoked and reinvoked when people steeped in precapitalist ways of life first confronted the new order of things. Premonitions that this encounter would be a harsh one originated early on.

Paradise Lost

John Smith of the Virginia colony in Jamestown had a vision of the New World as a special place where "every man may be a master and owner of his own labour and land; or the greatest part in a small time." This hope was shared by many at the time and with a sense of urgency. Back home in seventeenth-century England, new forms of semifree labor—people involuntarily cut loose from the land, hirelings dependent on the propertied to give them work, or "masterless men" compelled to roam the countryside or London as vagabonds—alarmed people like Smith. America, they thought, might provide an escape from that descent into dependency and all the moral, political, and social consequences that they dreaded would follow.[2]

To this day, that seductive promise to "be a master and owner of his own labour" remains a cherished part of the American mythos. How real or fantastical it's become over the centuries is debatable. Certainly from the time John Smith conceived it through to the time Abraham Lincoln articulated a more or less identical outlook on the kind of society he expected once the country rid itself of slavery, this anticipated reprieve from the slavish subordinations of the Old World enlivened the American imagination. But so too did the creeping fear that time was all too quickly running out; older and newer hierarchies of labor were cropping up in towns and in the countryside, putting in jeopardy that prospective haven of self-reliant men of roughly equal social station.

Even during the colonial era various forms of unfree labor—slaves, indentured servants, journeymen, and apprentices—defined the social contours of port cities. But wage labor (or, as it was often called, "wage slavery") was also becoming more and more common, especially in the lesser crafts among tailors, cordwainers, and mariners and in the construction and shipbuilding trades. Already by the end of the eighteenth century, the notion of class had made its presence felt in a society more accustomed to thinking about its social anatomy in terms of ranks, sorts, orders, stations, and estates. It would take generations for a world defined by relations of deference and networks of patronage to give way to the more strictly impersonal and arms-length ones dictated by the market. During that long interregnum, ambiguously configured "middling sorts" populated the economic and political landscape. They were handworkers of various kinds, artisans, and mere mechanics; a smaller percentage were storekeepers or clerks, respectable all of them, but they were experiencing a creeping erosion of their social standing and a fear of falling further. Friction points accumulated.

Resistance emerged here and there, emphatically among sailors so vital to the transatlantic commercial economy that kept the colonial seaboard towns humming. Repercussions from the Glorious Revolution in England of 1688 (the installation of the dual monarchy of William and Mary ended decades of civil war, military dictatorship, and counter-revolution) were felt in colonial America as working people voiced their resentment of those politically privileged to whom they'd been taught to defer; there were even attacks on merchant property in New York.[3]

Soon enough skilled artisans—carpenters, printers, and shipwrights, particularly—were organizing into fraternal societies and even embryonic unions. Even before the American Revolution, these rebels were identifying themselves politically by their social class in broadsides signed by "A Tradesman," "A Carpenter," "Mechanic." In Philadelphia they called for a wider suffrage, lower property qualifications to vote, and the opening up of public offices to hoi polloi; and they excoriated rapacious master capitalists, demanding that "all ranks and conditions would come in for their just share of the wealth." The upper registers of New York were hardly shy about replying, swearing their enmity "to Cobblers and Tailors so long as they take upon their everlasting and immeasurable shoulders the power of directing the loyal and sensible inhabitants of the city." Mercantile elites worried about the "many-headed monster," the "Hydra" of lower-class rebellion showing itself on both sides of the Atlantic.[4]

Founders of the new nation were hardly caught unawares by these intimations of social fracture. Legend treats Ben Franklin, for example, as an eighteenth-century avatar of free market capitalism, a fountain of folk wisdom about how to succeed in business. Actually, he was a good bit more skeptical about how the New World was evolving. If manufacturing loomed on the horizon, it was arising out of the dependency of multitudes no longer able to support themselves on the land. He wrote, "Manufactures are founded on poverty," because "it is the multitude of the poor without land in a country and who must work for others at low wages or starve that enables undertakers to carry on a manufacture." The Old World's mercantile economy, Franklin averred, rested on exporting the products of cheap labor, on an economy of subsistence wages and grinding poverty, and on workhouses designed to impose discipline on those recalcitrant about knuckling under to the new order of things. Progress in incubating commercial-manufacturing enterprise here in the New World would carry with it a similar inventory of "poverty, inequality, dependency, and misery."[5]

Like Franklin, Thomas Jefferson, James Madison, and other architects of the new nation—although not Alexander Hamilton and his circle, who looked forward happily to the gestation of a prosperous and inevitably stratified commercial order—clung to the possibility of a society of morally vigilant, independent small property holders, agriculturalists, artisans, and petty tradesmen. The New World would become a new "Land of Labour" where all enjoyed access to their own means of production and produced useful articles of consumption, not items of luxury that would conduce to vice and frivolity. But apprehensively they often foretold the opposite.

Even John Adams, who certainly did not share the agrarian fantasies of Jefferson, nonetheless somberly observed, "The Great Question will forever remain who will work." In many ways distrusting the instincts of the masses, he nonetheless inveighed against "the dons, the beshaws, the grandees, patricians, the sachems, the nabobs, call them what name you please." He considered it an "infallible maxim" that "power follows property." Madison, in one of the most enduring passages of *Federalist Paper No. 10*, dwelled on the social abrasiveness that surely lay ahead in a society where "various and unequal distributions of property" would become the "most common and durable source of faction." As this Virginia planter saw it, "Those who hold and those who are without property have ever formed distinct interests in society."[6]

Certainly some Federalists who helped fashion the new constitution were motivated, at least in part, by a fear of the leveling mob, "the lower classes of our motley vulgar," which they believed a more empowered federal government might be better able to hold at bay. Undergirding Hamilton's distinctly wary approach to democracy was his sociological conviction that communities "divide themselves into the few and the many. The first are the rich and well-born, the other the mass of the people . . . turbulent and changing, they seldom judge or determine right. Give therefore to the first class a distinct, permanent share in the Government." He issued terrifying alarms about "mobocracy," as did his enemies; Madison for one prophesied that as the population grew, so too would "the proportion of those who will labour under all the hardships of life and secretly sigh for a more equal distribution of its blessings."[7]

An Un-manifest Destiny

Madison turned out to be perhaps more right than he anticipated. Antebellum America went through an enormous commercial expansion, especially in the north and west. New lands were "opened up" forcibly or otherwise to settled agriculture, town and urban life spread westward into the hinterland, and new means of transportation and communication—including canals, the railroad, steamships, and the telegraph—widened the orbit of the marketplace. All of this expanded the possibilities John Smith had dreamed of for each person to become the "master and owner of his own labour." But at the same time, it accelerated for many others the descent into unfree labor. And those who suffered this fall, or worried they might, did more than "secretly sigh" for a more just arrangement.

Jacksonian America was alive with a great multitude of democratic impulses, from antislavery and communal utopias to women's rights and universal free public education. A considerable portion of those egalitarian energies originated among artisans and "mechanics," who in one way or another found their existence as skilled, self-reliant producers slipping away or already out of their grasp. Manufactories in a variety of trades from textiles to shoe-making, selling their wares into the widening marketplace, began to supplant older forms of handicraft, in which customized production had served a local clientele.

As time went on, this became even truer of skilled trades like cabinet-making, printing, and house construction. Some of these enterprises were mechanized, some not. Other trades introduced the "sweating system," which gathered together large numbers of workers in one place, simplified their tasks, accelerated the pace of work, and subjected once self-directed journeymen to factory management supervision. Some new enterprises merely consisted of merchant-capitalists "outsourcing" the work of weaving or spinning or shoe-making to farm women in their homes. All, however, greatly extended the division of labor Adam Smith had paid so much attention to and which brought in its wake stunning cost efficiencies. Yet they also fatally undermined the skills, know-how, customary work routines, rules governing the pace and duration of labor, material well-being, and social identity long associated with the traditional handicraft economy.[8]

On one side, an act of creation was under way. The emerging capitalist system of production was bringing into being its most essential resource; namely, a pool of men and women less and less able to survive without offering their services for wages. Opportunities for journeymen to rise and become masters steadily declined. In the printing trade, for example, the number of journeymen grew along with the mechanization and subdivision of tasks; this in turn eroded away their distinctive talents and capacities to comprehend and direct the whole work experience. A skilled shoemaker lamented the psychological toll exacted by the new industrial regimen, "the strain on a man doing just one thing over and over again must necessarily have a wearying effect on him; his ideals, I believe, must be lowered."

No wonder this experience of displacement and loss set off shock waves of resistance and rebellion aimed at restoring older ways of life or at softening the impact of the "stark utopia" of the free market, or somehow aimed at doing both. Opposition to the new order of things might be silent and subtle. Onetime artisans, finding themselves in alien work-places whose rules and rhythms of work violated customary practices, simply ignored those strictures, took off when they needed to help back on the family farm or to hunt and fish, or while at work broke off (as they always had) to drink, talk, and read. This was widely the case and especially so among a great many emerging industrial enterprises that were, before the advent of the steam engine, necessarily based in the countryside, in small villages close to falling water. Iron making and metal and implement fabrication were commonly rural-based industries in these years, their workers still closely attached to country ways of life and the rhythms of labor dictated by the passage of the seasons, not the methodical ticking of the time clock or the blowing of the factory whistle.

Artisan-based insurgencies, both economic and political ones, recurred all through the antebellum decades, especially during the 1820s and '30s, and then again after the economy recovered from a long depression set off by the panic of 1837. Journeymen faced off against a new breed of master-capitalists and merchant capitalists. Proto-unions were formed. A movement for the ten-hour day enlisted thousands because merchant capitalists exerted a relentless downward pressure on piece rates, which in turn inexorably lengthened the workday far beyond traditional and natural limits, leaving people angry, "enervated, dependent, and slav-ish." Strikes shut down some of the newly opened shoe and textile factories.[9]

Political clubs and local political parties agitated for an end to debtor's prisons and property qualifications restricting the suffrage. Often enough they denounced land speculators and raised the cry for land reform to keep alive the hope of some future smallholder independence (a wish later fulfilled, at least in theory, by the passage of the Homestead Act in 1862). Many workingmen's movements rallied behind President Andrew Jackson's war to abolish the second Bank of the United States. In part this was because of the animosity they felt toward its blue-blooded head, the bewigged Philadelphian Nicholas Biddle. But they also suspected the motives of politically privileged financiers and other merchants and business elites enjoying special access to government franchises and corporate charters that aspiring smallholders didn't.

Radical-minded weavers and other skilled craftsmen, more and more at odds with their employers, likened them to slave owners, denouncing "lord of the loom and lords of the lash." In Lowell, Massachusetts, in 1834 the "daughters of free men" working in the new textile mills struck out against their "Tory" employers whose draconian work rules were turning them into "factory slaves." Journeymen strikes in New York in 1850 were particularly menacing as gangs of militants ruled over whole sections of the city. Subject to the periodic and unpredictable oscillations of the business cycle, confronted for the first time by the desperate helplessness of being unemployed during the 1830s and thereafter, dispossessed people in Massachusetts occupied the state house and seized vacant lands. They wanted the government to deed them titles so they might support themselves by farming. Some demanded the government put them to work or provide relief.[10]

Farmers struggling under a growing burden of debt to East Coast merchant banks began clamoring for the government to issue paper currency to inflate the money supply and make it easier for them to hold on to their ancestral farms and the lives that had been grown there. In 1848 Edward Kellogg, a self-made merchant ruined by the panic of 1837, published what would become known as "The Bible of Currency Reformers," which would still be read decades later by populists and other radicals. Its formal title, practically book-length itself as was the custom, said a mouthful: *Labor and Other Capital, The Rights of Each Secured and the Wrongs of Both Eradicated. Or, an Exposition of the Cause of Why Few are Wealthy and Many are Poor, and the Delineation of a System Which, Without Infringing on the Rights of Property, will Give Labor its Just Reward.*[11]

A distinct workingmen's newspaper and pamphlet literature vented resentments about exploitation and also about the humiliations that had begun to accumulate around the status of manual labor. In words and pictures middle-class magazines conveyed an under-text of tattered clothes, darkened skins, and visible mental slowness, stereotypes of lower-order inferiority. With growing frequency, working-class women were depicted as morally deficient, prey to the city's "boiling, seething caldron of licentiousness that rages forever here." All of this was naturally infuriating.[12]

Warfare broke out elsewhere on the cultural front, most famously in the Astor Place riot of 1849 in New York. The occasion was an odd sort of theatrical jacquerie. In a city grown increasingly self-conscious about its class stratifications, Irish and other working-class youth frequented their own playhouses on the Bowery, while status-conscious middle-class theatergoers went to Broadway. When the new Astor Place Opera House opened to entertain the "upper ten thousand," the "baser sort" showed up to contest the space, which was in fact provocatively close to their own warrens. The opera house was intended to be an edifice of refinement, good taste, and educational uplift, a literate barricade against the onslaught of the tawdry sensationalism purportedly preferred by the lower orders.

William Charles Macready, a famous British Shakespearean actor of that time, embodied this studiously genteel bourgeois aesthetic. Edwin Forrest was his American opposite. Also a celebrated Shakespearean, Forrest was extravagant in gesture and overheated passion, decidedly physical in his style of acting. When not performing Shakespeare, he often portrayed Jacksonian popular heroes struggling against imposed authority. Those multitudes who flocked to his performances especially loved his mockery of the "codfish aristocracy," "grasping nabobs" in "kid gloves," preening in the front pews of their exclusive churches, at their by-invitation-only fancy dress balls, clubs, and soirees. Macready and Forrest were fierce rivals.

In the aftermath of the 1848 revolution in Europe, tempers were high, anti-aristocratic sentiment was on the boil, fear of the "mob" raging. Ten thousand partisans of Forrest filled the streets around the opera house, where Macready was performing in *Macbeth*. Dozens of others had managed to purchase upper-tier seats from which they bombarded the stage with rotten eggs, tomatoes, lemons, and a foul-smelling liquid, origins unclear. As the crowd outside grew more boisterous, the city militia was ordered to disperse them and ended up killing at least twenty-five and injuring over a hundred people.

Delighted, the conservative press crowed that the clash was hard evidence to "the capitalists of the old world that they might send their property to New York and rely upon the certainty that it would be safe from the clutches of red republicanism, or Chartists, or communionists [*sic*] of any description." In the eyes of the haute bourgeoisie, this was the rabble, a ragtag group of the unemployed, loafers, criminals, and transients. But as a matter of fact the people filling the streets outside the opera house were mainly members of the city's artisanal working class: butchers, jewelers, sail-makers, painters, carpenters, and others from the middling ranks of this decomposing handicraft economy. They were no more hardened outlaws and anarchists than their social superiors among the city's mercantile and manufacturing elite were true blue-blooded aristocrats.[13]

East of Eden

Lines were being drawn nonetheless. Antebellum America was to be sure electric with a kind of bumptious optimism, a sense of manifest destiny, and get-up-and-go entrepreneurial individualism—a mythic land of limitless possibility. After all, this was an American's singular indigenous birthright. In the mid-twentieth century, the esteemed historian Louis Hartz explained that America had enjoyed a kind of immaculate conception, free of the infection of class animosity that so disturbed the peace of the Old World because of our near universal commitment to property-holding independence. Hartz had a lot of predecessors who had made that same observation a century before.

Among the most widely read was the Frenchman J. Hector St. John de Crèvecoeur, who eventually settled here. In writing about his new homeland in 1782 he identified "the bright idea of property" that infused the countryside with an egalitarianism and belief in social mobility at odds with the society he hailed from. A generation later, his fellow countryman Alexis de Tocqueville would make essentially the same point.

Still, some close observers like Herman Melville detected the canker in the worm. Melville's short story "Tartarus of Maids" is a chilling portrait of women slaving away in a paper mill in an isolated gulag high in the Berkshire Mountains of Massachusetts. Young, virginal and deathly white, wraithlike, nearly inanimate, subject to the despotism of machinery and male superintendents, these women stood like a barely living reproach to those early utopian hopes associated with the first textile mills farther east in Lowell and Waltham. There, back in the 1820s, young farm girls came to work and were treated like family by the proprietors, who showed concern for everything from their literary tastes to their housing; they were sheltered in well-kept dormitories, supplied with nourishing food, looked after by matronly housekeepers charged with maintaining a "tranquil scene of moral deportment and mutual good will." A mere twenty years later Lowell had become Lawrence, the site of the New World's own version of Blake's "dark satanic mills," staffed now not by American girls from the countryside, but by a despised class of Irish immigrant women.

Other Melville creations were populated by deeply angry, often inscrutable workingmen, burning with rage or stubborn impassivity or a sense of wounded dignity, as in Bartleby's famous "I prefer not to" or Redburn's mordant observation that "there are classes of men in the world who bear the same relation to society at large that the wheels do to a coach," and that such men are "shunned by the better class of people and cut off from all access to respectable and improving society." In this world, work maims, kills, ruins, and is fatal to desire. Yet it ought to be hallowed. Ishmael from *Moby Dick* celebrates the democratic dignity that regardless of rank "shines in the arm that wields a pick or drives a spike; that democratic dignity which on all hands, radiates without end from God; Himself...His omnipresence, our divine equality," which, however, was being poisoned at its source by the sharklike competitiveness of the new commercial order, "mean and meager."[14]

Melville had intellectual compatriots who together formed an evolving culture of opposition. Boston mechanics rallying for the ten-hour day in the mid-1830s heard Theophilus Fisk deliver an address on "Capital Against Labor" in which the radical theologian and fervent Jacksonian "Young Democrat" issued a "warning to the parasitical classes" that "beneath their feet an earthquake slumbers." These lawyers and quill pushers, "monopolists, the professional men," collect what they haven't earned. They don't cultivate fields, fell forests, or build houses, bridges, and canals, but are "indolent drones...clothed in purple and fine linen." Fisk called for "the immediate emancipation of the white slaves of the North" from those "heathen idolaters of the worshippers of Mammon." That something as matter-of-fact as the length of the working day could arouse such deep emotion was evidence, as Fisk put it, that "the creation of a normal working day is therefore the product of a protracted civil war, more or less dissembled, between the capitalist class and the working class."[15]

Like Fisk, Orestes Brownson, a maverick Universalist and Unitarian minister and champion of the Workingman's Party in New York (who later converted to a conservative version of Roman Catholicism), warned of an impending war between great wealth and wage slavery, "a war the likes of which the world" had never witnessed and which he considered "irresistible." For Brownson the issue spanned time and geography, whenever "man has approximated a state of civilization," found "in every nation in Christendom": "Where is the spot on earth in which the actual producer of wealth is not one of the lower class, shut out from what are looked upon as the main advantages of the social state?" The new employing class, he suggested, whether "master mechanic" or "owner of a factory," was the fiercest enemy of the "proletarii," which Brownson defined as those who no longer owned "the funds of production, neither houses, shops, nor lands, nor implements of labor, being therefore solely dependent on their hands." Still a theologian, this radical minister who in this phase of his career anticipated the Social Gospel movement that would divide Protestantism a half century later, saw the wages system as "a cunning device of the devil for the benefit of tender consciences who would retain all the advantages of the slave system without the expense, trouble, and odium of being a slaveholder." In keeping with John Smith's original vision, Brownson called on America to "emancipate the proletaries" so that all might become "independent laborers [each] on his own capital, on his own farm or in his own shop. Here is our work."[16]

Ideological defenders of Southern slavery were quick to zero in on the emerging new order of "free labor" as a hypocritical sham, far worse than their own labor system. However commercially active they actually were, Southern planters and their media denounced the mercenary mean-spiritedness of northern capitalism. Slave owners' paternalism, their chivalry, their love of the land—the whole self-deluded romance that allowed the slaveocracy to look down their noses at northern self-seeking and moneygrubbing—would shield them against the commercial dark arts that lured people away from the "wholesome labors of the field and the enjoyment of modern independence."

It was a grand delusion, but a telling one. Profits north of the Mason-Dixon line were based on the "increased suffering of labourers and the hardworking mass." Senator John C. Calhoun of South Carolina, the South's leading political defender, chastised the Whig Party for mortgaging the people's inheritance to parasitic circles that "look to debts, stocks, banks, distributions, and taxes as the choicest of blessings. The greater the debt—the more abundantly the Stock Market is supplied."

For Southerners it was naturally tempting to condemn the new system outright: there was no escape from this charnel house. It bred demoralization and social insurrection, and was ultimately doomed. The "only check on its diffusion is the existence of slavery; for the institution, and the social system determined by it, have hitherto repelled its ravages, and even its extensive admission in the Southern States." Southern spokesmen declaimed against abolition, arguing that emancipation would end only in the creation of a class of "white slaves," people abandoned to the merciless ravages of the marketplace and lacking the paternal protections enjoyed by black bondsmen. Proletarians, unlike chattel to be protected and preserved, were instead to be used, then disposed of. What happened to them after hours was a matter of indifference to Yankee manufacturers and abolitionists alike.[17]

Personal experience confirmed this prospect of fatal descent for some northern observers. William Leggett, a radical journalist in New York, became a coruscating critic of what one historian has called the "capitalist sublime," the exalted view of Progress that raised its technological wonders and promise of abundance and commercial grandeur to some empyrean plane where risk and the control of risk, adventure and order, conjoined. Leggett grew up in a family and a world of downwardly mobile urban artisans. His father had started and lost several businesses before a temporary success as a blacksmith. Then the family property was seized by creditors in the 1819 panic. Next the Leggetts migrated to the Illinois prairie and failed again. Now the son peered below the surface shimmer of Progress, recognized the political and social as well as the cultural horrors of the new world coming, and forecast a great moral war pitting everyone against the banks.

Champions of a more egalitarian entrepreneurial capitalism waged war against financial capitalism on behalf of capitalism. Somehow a middle zone of simple commodity exchange needed to be rescued from the predatory urges of the new order. Some could take this all in and still foresee a more pacific future. Ralph Waldo Emerson, for example, hypothesized that the new work discipline would, in the end, tame the passions it began by inflaming: "Fear haunts the building of the railroad, but it will be American power and beauty when it is done. And these peaceful shovels are better, dull as they are, than pikes in the hands of the Kearns [Irish] and the stern days of work of 15–16 hours, though

83

deplored by the humanity of the neighborhood...is a better police than the sheriff and his deputies to let off the peccant humors." Emerson worried about a growing social distemper and hoped the new methodical routines of industrial work might act as a sedative.[18]

Prophecies like this turned out to be premature. Trouble lay ahead.

Before the Deluge

On the eve of the Civil War, American society was still in many regards a precapitalist and preindustrial one in which wage labor and market relations were limited, one in which household economies, handicraft production, and self-sufficient agriculture remained deeply rooted. "Machinofacture" and factory production generally were still unusual features of the country's economic geography. In 1860 more people worked in small workshops and farmhouses and used hand tools than worked in factories. Even in most cities, only 10 percent of the population was employed in manufacturing. "Dark satanic mills" were the exception, as most manufactured products were fabricated in homes, small shops, or through the "out-work" or "putting out" system in rural farmhouses.

Farms were where most people still lived—80 percent of them, in fact. And they were even less affected by the emerging industrial order, unless they were farm women caught up in the "putting out" arrangements common in some New England and mid-Atlantic states. But even in that case, sustaining the farm and the customs of rural life were what all efforts aimed at. While such households did engage in trade for items like tea, some metal goods, and articles of clothing, often enough they bartered with itinerant handicraftsmen for shoes and boots and hats rather than using coin or paper money. Conversion to cash-crop farming was still not very common in the 1830s and was slow to develop because the opportunities to carry on in the old ways were so relatively abundant. In many ways households remained self-reliant, maintaining vegetable gardens, small herds for meat and dairy needs, pastureland and woodlots for fuel and timber, commonly used forests and streams in which they hunted and fished. The kind of independent household economy that John Smith envisioned inspired the imagination and anchored the lives of many.[19]

Abraham Lincoln and elements of the Republican Party certainly saw things that way. In a speech before the Wisconsin Agricultural Society in 1859 and again in his first annual message to Congress after the outbreak of war, Lincoln stuck to that view. "The world is agreed that labor is the source from which human wants are mainly supplied." This was a "labor theory of value" that celebrated the middling sorts and their aspirations, whether on the land or household enterprises in towns and cities, for a "competency." Here the urge to achieve a competency was not an acquisitive one; the object was not social mobility in the way we think of that now, nor even a desire to escape from manual labor. Indeed, on the contrary, a competency implied a modest degree of propertied independence built up through honorable work, a set of economic relations governed by social and moral limits established by tradition and sometimes religious sanction, designed to ensure a stable, approximate equality of condition and to avoid any permanent subordinate status of the sort wage slavery implied.

While acknowledging the existence of hired labor, Lincoln denied, as so many before had, that anyone need be "fatally fixed in that condition for life; and that thence again that his condition is as bad as, or worse than that of a slave." And while it might be true that labor and capital did indeed enter into relations of super- and subordination, that was more exceptional than commonplace. The much larger part of society was and would continue to be composed of neither class, "neither work for others, nor have others work for them."

Like John Smith, Lincoln conceived America as a land of families working for themselves, "taking the whole product to themselves, and asking no favors of capital on the one hand, nor of hirelings or slaves on the other." If "the prudent penniless beginner in the world labors for wages a while, saves a surplus with which to buy tools or land for himself...then labors on his own account another while...and at length hires another new beginner to help him," then all might enjoy that competency which ensured their independence. Put more concretely and through the eyes of a Philadelphia printer, for example, a competency entailed a whole way of life and culture that included a decent-sized house, an education in the arts and sciences, enough to afford a newspaper, some recreation, and the wherewithal to live with dignity in old age. Or put more poetically by Walt Whitman:

> Neither a servant nor a master I...
> I shall be even with you and you shall be even with me.[20]

Ironically the war Lincoln's election precipitated would vastly accelerate the industrial and financial upheaval so fatal to those household economies in town and country, as well as the rough egalitarianism they sustained and that the new president cherished. But even before the bloodshed, the drift in this direction was apparent. By the 1850s commercial, cash-crop agriculture had already made significant strides in the Midwest, where farmers had begun using harrows instead of hoes, steel instead of iron plows, and automatic drills for sowing grain, and started adopting the new mechanical mowers and reapers on the Great Plains. The growing leverage exercised by merchants and bankers functioning as intermediaries increasingly compelled farmers to intensify their cultivation of cash crops or else face the loss of their farms and a life as a rural proletarian or in some other dependent status.

Decomposition of the handicraft economy sped up as well. While in 1840 one in five craftsmen owned his own shop, by 1860 only one in ten did. The percentage of home owners among mechanics fell in the same way. Just to get by, more and more had to rely on home gardens and on hunting and fishing in common fields, forests, and bays and streams in their spare time...and those resources were becoming scarcer. So too, children and women in growing numbers were offered up to the abusive "sweating system," but not paid enough to lift their families out of poverty. The future looked grimmer than Lincoln contemplated.[21]

Assaults on these traditional ways of life and labor had produced their share of economic, political, and cultural outbursts in antebellum America. But they would seem mild compared to the massive and often violent eruptions in countryside and city set off by the relentless workings of primitive accumulation once the country settled its original labor question—the slave question—and left everyone free. The question then would become "free" to do what?

4

The Second Civil War: In the Countryside

All the highways of global capitalism found their way into the track-less vastness of rural America during the last third of the nineteenth century. Farmers were in dire straits not because they suffered the privations of their own backwater isolation. On the contrary, they lived at ground zero, where the incendiary energies of industrial, financial, and commercial modernity detonated.

American agriculturalists were by no means unfamiliar with the market. At least part of their output had been bartered or traded for a long time, if only locally. That did not make them capitalists but rather petty producers of foodstuffs who did not trade in the market for labor, or if they did then only marginally or under extraordinary circumstances. The land they tilled might have been theirs by virtue of earlier acts of violent expropriation of indigenous pastoral or nomadic hunting societies. But even if so, those original means of primitive accumulation left behind family farms, not agribusinesses.

However, with the vast geographic expansion of the market, these ordinary farmers became both the beneficiaries and the victims of finance—of mortgage finance, in particular. On the one hand, the mortgage offered the chance of independent proprietorship; on the other hand, it undermined that freedom.

Mortgage-backed securities are no recent invention. Their capacity to wreak havoc long predated the subprime lending business. A global market in such securities was already well developed by the 1870s. It was centered on the East Coast, focused particularly on mortgages in the Plains states and out west (one-half of all Kansas farmers owed mortgages in 1886), and generated an intricate network of financial intermediaries. Homesteaders were often market-oriented farmers enmeshed with finance capital—that is, with investors concerned not with the agricultural value of the land but with its financial worth. And the railroads these settlers depended on were themselves so often submerged under a sea of bonded indebtedness, deposited there by rapacious Wall Street speculators, that they had the strongest incentive to seek out every way of squeezing their agrarian clients and customers.[1]

Farmers were notoriously cash poor anyway and regularly indebted to eastern banks for land, supplies, and machinery. Mortgage debt increased 71 percent in five years during the 1880s. Liquid capital (cash or assets readily converted into cash) consequently accumulated on Wall Street, piped there from the prairies. While railroads opened up new markets for agriculturalists here and abroad, they charged discriminatory rates for hauling farm goods long distances to urban markets. This accelerated the rate of capital accumulation for the roads by eating away at the spare resources sustaining the independent homesteader. Tariffs, levied mainly on industrial goods from abroad, exacerbated this cannibalizing of rural America; the west and South were compelled to buy their manufactured goods from high-priced domestic suppliers while selling their wares into low-priced global free markets. Growers were dependent on storage facilities—such as grain elevators for cereals—that were usually controlled by eastern business interests and exacerbated the precarious position of freeholders.[2]

To make matters worse, new commodity exchanges allowed for well-organized speculation in the value of agricultural goods. Paradoxically, those exchanges could regularize the flow of capital and credit into and

out of wheat and corn and sorghum and cotton or pig and sheep raising...but they could also leave Nebraska wheat growers and Alabama
cotton farmers at the mercy of wildly fluctuating prices that could turn
all their careful husbandry to dust in a moment.

Any downturn in prices or any disaster (flood, insects, drought, plant
disease) produced a new crop of foreclosures, tax sales, and evictions. So,
for example, there was a great grasshopper plague in 1874; a blizzard out
west in 1886 that devastated homesteaders, leaving behind absentee
investor-owned ranches in the Dakotas and Montana; a drought in Kansas in 1893; a grasshopper infestation there and in eastern Colorado in
1894; flooding of the Mississippi three years in a row (1893–1895); a
punishing blizzard on the prairies in 1895; and, in the South, a boll wee-
vil invasion beginning in 1892, aggravated by a freeze in Florida in 1894
and a scorching heat wave enveloping the whole region in 1895. One
might accept all these as acts of God and leave it at that. But these natural
afflictions victimized farmers whose entanglement in the international
web of finance and trade left them living on a razor's edge, producing
single cash crops only, at the mercy of the vagaries of the market, lacking
either stockpiles of other edibles or cash to keep them afloat. They went
under instead.[3]

Going under followed various routes. Those foreclosed upon might
become tenant farmers, farm laborers, or migratory workers. The 1880
Census revealed that one-quarter of all farmers were tenants. As the factory came to the field, the number of migratory laborers, sometimes
recruited seasonally among the unemployed in the cities (including children) soared. In the Midwest, 40 percent of those living off the land
were wage workers. Bonanza farms owned by absentee investors extended
the division of labor common in the factory to the fields, where specialized tasks like loading bound sheaves of wheat or running twine-binding
machines were a premonition of the future. Three million people
worked as farmhands, six hundred thousand of them women.[4]

In no way was this restricted to the Midwest: colonial dependency became the fate of the southland. The former Confederacy relied on the capital accumulation going on in the industrializing north. Not only did high tariffs compel the region (as they did the agrarian west) to absorb the higher cost and high-priced output of America's "infant industries," they relegated the region to a condition of permanent underdevelopment. Primitive accumulation as a regional relationship mimicked imperial economic dynamics generally. What development that did take place was skewed, so that, for example, railroads made forays into the outback to extract raw materials, but otherwise contributed next to nothing to all-around industrial, commercial, and urban growth.

Large portions of the South were frozen in time, left poor and growing poorer. Ex-slaves as well as much of the white yeomanry fell into penury. Landless whites in the up-country South were driven off by the enclosing of common lands by plantation monoculturalists, landing in company textile towns springing up in the piedmont.

In a sense, the farmer was the looniest speculator in a nation overrun with them. He was wagering he would master this fathomlessly intricate global game, pay off his many debts, and come out with enough extra to play another round. On top of that, he was betting on the kindness of Mother Nature, always supremely risky. But the farmer had no choice if he hoped to sustain himself and a way of life, the family farm. Instead, he was drawn into a kind of social suicide. The family farm and the whole network of small-town life that it patronized were being washed away into the rivers of capital and credit that flowed toward the railroads, banks, and commodity exchanges, toward the granaries, wholesalers, and numerous other intermediaries that stood between the farmer and the world market. Disappearing into all the reservoirs of capital accumulation, the family farm increasingly remained a privileged way of life only in sentimental memory.

Perversely the dynamic Lincoln had described as the pathway out of dependency—spending a few years earning wages, saving up, buying a competency, and finally hiring others—now operated in reverse.

Starting out as independent farmers, families then slipped inexorably downward, first mortgaging the homestead, then failing under intense pressure to support that mortgage (they called themselves "mortgage slaves") and falling into tenancy—or into sharecropping if in the South—and finally ending where Lincoln's story began, as dispossessed farm and migrant laborers.

On the "sod house" frontier, poverty was a "badge of honor which decorated all." In his *Devil's Dictionary* the acid-tongued humorist Ambrose Bierce defined the dilemma this way: "Debt. n. An ingenious substitute for the chain and whip of the slave-driver."

"The Tramp's Story," an 1880 poem by Will Carleton, caught the bitter pathos of what today we might call the financialization of the land:

> We worked through spring and winter—through summer and
>   through fall—
> But the mortgage worked the hardest and the steadiest of us all;
> It worked on nights and Sundays—it worked each holiday—
> It settled down among us, and never went away.
> Whatever we kept from it seemed almost as bad as theft;
> It watched us every minute and ruled us right and left.
> The rust and blight were with us sometimes, and sometimes not;
> The dark-browed, scowling mortgage was forever on the spot.
> The weevil and the cut-worm, they went as well as came;
> The mortgage staid forever, eating hearty all the same.
> It nailed up every window—stood guard at every door—
> And happiness and sunshine made their home with us no more.[5]

Less Corn, More Hell

Malcontented farmers spread blame for their predicament far and wide. Mortgage holders, grain-elevator operators, absentee landlords, railroad monopolists, farm-machinery manufacturers, local provisioners, commodity and land speculators, and creditors were singly or all together targeted for censure. However, while none of these villains were ever let off the hook, agrarian anger tended to pool around the strangulating systems of currency and credit run out of the great banking centers of the east, especially Wall Street.

Rural hostility to the "money power" was an entrenched tradition, its roots extending as far back as Jackson's war against the Bank of the United States. Actually the role of finance in determining the shape of the economy was a preoccupation of politics from the beginning to the end of the nineteenth century. Nor was it confined to the countryside.

Smallholders, shopkeepers, handicraftsmen, local and regional merchants, aspiring entrepreneurs, cooperatives, and the whole universe of debtors were in a chronic uproar over the paucity of currency and credit and the price deflation that the government's and Wall Street's strict adherence to the gold standard imposed on the economy. For that reason, calls to print greenbacks or coin silver gripped the imagination of not only the farm population but also much of middling America. A whole range of protest movements concerned in one way or another with the drying up of entrepreneurial opportunity—including the National Labor Union and Knights of Labor in the cities, along with the Grange and rural-based cooperatives—fixated on the interest rate and the dearth of credit, uncovering linkages between "interest, bonds, and the whole speculating power that now owns and runs the government."[6]

It also led to the creation of the Greenback and various labor-related parties during the 1870s and '80s. Like these populist precursors, the People's Party (commonly known as the Populist Party), which formed in 1890, tried to appeal to all those crucified on "the cross of gold," not only to beleaguered farmers. Moreover, to nourish its roots in the South, the border states, and the far west, the Democratic Party too became a medium bearing the message of debt relief, although in this case it was always at war with its eastern wing of bankers and merchants. That stress would cause the party to fracture down the middle in the presidential election of 1896. So it was that calls for the free coinage of silver or for the use of both gold and silver as measures of value, by promising to open up the sluice gates of commercial credit, appealed way beyond the immediate zones of rural misery.

Critical Mass

Arguably, primitive accumulation breeds a politics focused on finance. Debt, in a multitude of forms, has often been the mechanism through which the centers of international trade and finance have absorbed the wealth created by societies not themselves capitalist or even engaged in the regular production of commodities for the market. Finance and trade may grow prosperous in this way without actually invading the realm of production itself. During the long nineteenth century, this older form of debt-based primitive accumulation coexisted alongside the new realm of capital accumulation based on wage labor.

Eventually, financial capital internalized and dominated the processes of wealth production directly by investing in and managing new enterprises, especially the railroads and publicly traded industrial corporations that Wall Street helped midwife around the turn of the century. The convergence of these two systems of capital accumulation—finance and factory—and the resistances they gave rise to is one way of explaining why the long nineteenth century was so tumultuous.[7]

Combined and happening at the same moment, the immanent extinction of the family farm and the descent into the dependency of wage slavery in the city provided the critical mass for the unparalleled explosion of anticapitalist resistance that distinguished the long nineteenth century. America has experienced nothing like it since.

By the mid-1880s, the last of the great western trunk lines opened up millions of acres on the Great Plains and in the southwest to settlement and to a frenzy of speculation. Inflated farm prices, overextended loans, overbuilt towns, and mountains of insupportable commercial paper rested on these rickety foundations. It all came crashing to earth amid the biblical afflictions of grasshoppers, blizzards, and the devastating drought of 1889–90. Mass bankruptcies and evictions followed. Throughout the South everyone knew that a sign posted on an evacuated homestead reading G.T.T. meant "Gone to Texas," which in fact 100,000 beleaguered farmers did every year of the 1870s, and in similar numbers thereafter.

Brooding over the debacle in the countryside, a farmer concluded in 1892 that "few Reading, thinking men in America, Deny the Slavery of the Masses, to the Money Power of our Country." The axiom of agrarian rage was bracingly blunt: "the agricultural masses" were being "robbed by an infamous system of finance." The language of rural revolt carried with it the same end-of-days foreboding and menace then running through the factories, mines, and mills of industrial America. Populist-inspired economic language was simultaneously a vocabulary and grammar of political and moral anathema. Words like "robbed," "enslaved," "plunder," "virtue," and "parasite"—the lingua franca of farm protest and of the whole family of antimonopoly movements—conveyed both analytic economic meaning as well as thunderous condemnations and benedictions. Populist cosmology consigned bankers and speculators to their own distinctive hellish ecological niche. They were, in a word, economic deadwood.[8]

Fused together were the moral, religious, and economic condemnations of the new system. One North Carolina insurgent denounced a financial system

> concocted in Hades, and transplanted to earth, and it has made a pandemonium of a garden of Eden.... The father of lies, the incubator of all meanness, it has damned more souls, committed more perjury, it has made a hell of heaven, banished God from earth, and set up the devil's kingdom, it has debauched our elections, established the reign of political thieves, it has brought the cause of Christ into disrepute and shut the minister's mouth, and it is the quintessence of all that is mean.[9]

James H. Davis, a charismatic orator from Texas, condemned bondholders of railroads, state governments, and corporations. Led by "private greed alone," they were guilty of taxing "the unborn generations" to pay their bonds. Another North Carolina activist asked: "Who are these bankers anyway? What do they produce? What do they distribute? What moral right do they have to cumber the earth?" The money power was not merely unproductive, it was counterproductive, like an incubus sucking away at the economic vitality of households and businesses.

When critics of the money power talked of "fictitious value," they meant not only to judge but to explain. Economic practices originating in Wall Street were fictitious because they were deceptive and unreal, resting on deliberate falsifications—watered stock, for example. But they were fictitious in another impersonal, morally neutral sense as well. Fictitious value was the systemic outcome of the mechanisms of trustification. Without anyone's conscious connivance, it produced a parallel universe of paper values increasingly at variance with and greater than the underlying wealth-generating capacity of the tangible properties that made up the foundation of that house of paper. Small-town editors, local preachers and politicians, itinerant writers and traveling lecturers— the whole populist, antimonopoly intelligentsia—busied themselves showing how this second, phantom economy exacted its heavy tribute.[10]

One acid-tongued observer did a postmortem on the heavily hyped and extravagantly financed new railroad ventures and found that at the end of the day "the road was unballasted, the ties are rotting, the station-houses are tumble-down shanties, the trestles and culverts and bridges are dangerous, the quarries and mines and forests have not been discovered." The only real beneficiaries were Wall Street figures doing a heavy business in foreclosing on railroad mortgages, canceling old securities, organizing new companies, issuing new securities, and floating them out into the world on rafts of fraudulent reports—the cycle then primed to repeat itself without end. Rural critics of commodity speculation, regularly derided by orthodox economists as backward-gazing rustic yahoos, were often fully aware of the inner workings of international trade, but in their eyes "phantom cotton," "spectral hogs," and "wind wheat" subverted rather than sustained commerce.[11]

Political Apocalypse

Whatever the merits or demerits of populist economics, it was in the political realm that the issue would be settled once and for all. In a refrain heard again and again, the movement demanded not merely an economy but a society that raised "man over money." As the farmers' plight grew more desperate and "man" remained mudsill, many looked ahead to a political Armageddon.

Entering the presidential race for the first time in 1892, the People's Party whipped up enthusiasm with a campaign book authored by Georgia congressman and flamboyant orator Tom Watson. It bore the incendiary subtitle *Not a Revolt; It Is a Revolution*. Watson depicted what was happening in 1892 as a replay of the historic confrontation between Hamilton and Jefferson in 1792 over whether the country was to be governed by "a moneyed aristocracy supported by special privilege." The division between the forces of privilege and those ready to take up arms on behalf of egalitarian democracy was a primordial one, and the Populists were hardly shy about tracing their lineage back to the Revolution's early days. When the party assembled in Omaha, Nebraska, to formulate its platform, the delegates cheered a fire-and-brimstone preamble that reviewed the "thirty year war" against monopoly and vowed to carry on the ageless struggle against "the oppression of the usurers."

However, the party's populism was not a species of antimodernism. The Omaha platform itself showed none of the aversion to big government that had once been an axiom of the Jeffersonian persuasion. On the contrary, Populists proposed government control of the money supply and credit so as to benefit all the "producing classes." A "sub-treasury" would function like a purchasing and marketing cooperative run by the government, making low-interest loans to farmers in legal-tender notes in return for their crops. The sub-treasury would then warehouse that agricultural output, releasing or holding back supplies from the market so as to maintain stable prices—prices that would ensure loan repayment as well as the farmers' material well-being. Ultimately, the goal was to wrest control of the monetary system from the Wall Street banking elite and vest it in the hands of the U.S. Treasury.

Although the sub-treasury plan (and the free coinage of silver) constituted the heavy artillery for breaking Wall Street's choke hold on credit, it was by no means the movement's only foray into the economic future. The party advocated a graduated income tax. It demanded strict regulation or even public ownership of the means of transportation and communication (the railroads and telegraph and also public utilities). Along with notions of a government-run or heavily monitored banking system, these were radical departures from the ancestral suspicion of the state.[12]

Yet if Populist politics can't be dismissed as an antediluvian rejection of the modern world, it is undeniable that the movement owed its fervor and sense of political and moral peril to the republican, smallholder mentality of the Revolution. Passionate attachments to immemorial traditions and ancient creeds—one might say to a useable or empowering past—were conjoined to creative methods of reconfiguring the future, all as a way of escaping the torments of an intolerable or even fatal present.

Government itself wasn't inherently bad then, but democratic government was a fragile creature. For the Populists it depended on a broadly even distribution of wealth and property, as had been more or less the case before the new order of things. Upon that rough egalitarian competence rested civic independence and vigilance against the usurpations of a self-aggrandizing elite. But these would-be aristocrats qua moneycrats moved stealthily. They used their wealth to seduce and demoralize institutions of popular government until those instruments were weakened beyond repair—or even worse, until those instruments became the means of disinheriting and disempowering the people, stripping them of the economic self-reliance and political wherewithal to stand up to the forces of counterrevolution.

The great banking houses of the east now gathered in all these tributaries of counterrevolution, concentrating their force. Populists were aware of that shift in the political center of gravity, mindful that the nation was no longer put together as it had been. Nonetheless they grounded their condemnation of the new financial-industrial dispensation on the enduring insights of an ancestral faith. Stump orators on the prairie were fond of reminding their listeners that in Jefferson's time moneyed corporations and financiers were often "tories," that "a man was not considered a sound man to fill a government office if he was a banker or 'stockbroker' or corporate man." An Alabama Populist congressman likened the arrogance and insolence of the Wall Street plutocracy to the French monarchy, the Stuart king Charles I, and of course England in 1776, all instances of aristocracies "intoxicated by power," "surfeited with a redundancy of money," and intent on making slaves of their subjects. In a speech to a gathering of Populists in Chicago, Henry Demarest Lloyd, the country's most celebrated journalistic warrior against the trusts, echoed a widely shared conviction about the two major parties: they were done for, their best work behind them. "The Republican Party took the black man off the auction block of the Slave Power, but it has put the white man on the auction block of the Money Power."[13]

Fear of enslavement—the recurring under-theme of so much of what made the long nineteenth century so apocalyptic in mood—sounds strange in our ears today. For Lloyd and so many others, however, it was a reference not only to economic exploitation, but to the theft of their political birthright. The money power cast its chilling shadow over the courts, the legislature, and all the branches of the state along with all the vital institutions of civic and educational life.

In 1892, Populist presidential candidate James Weaver (a brigadier general in the Union Army and the Greenback Party congressman from Iowa) captured the pervasiveness of baleful influence of the money power:

You meet it in every walk of life. It speaks through the press, gives zeal and eloquence to the bar, engrosses the attention of the bench, organizes the influences which surround our legislative bodies and courts of justice...determines who shall be our Senators, how our legislatures shall be organized, who shall preside over them.... It is imperial in political caucuses... is expert in political intrigue and pervades every community from the center to the circumference of the Republic.

For its part the People's Party campaign book included a biopsy of a sickened two-party system. The chairman of the Democratic Party, Calvin Brice, accumulated his fortune as a railroad speculator, the book reported, then bought himself a Senate seat in Ohio and went on to become a "Wall Street operator; an ally of Jay Gould in corporate combines; a part owner of a convict camp in Tennessee." Former president Grover Cleveland, running for another term, seemed to have "imbibed the financial views of Wall Street." Nor were the Republicans any different. Both parties were predators: "Under the Banking and Bonding System all the Roads of Produce lead to the Rome of Imperial Plutocracy."[14]

Populist insurgents meant to block those roads. Leading up to the final conflict in 1896, their political effectiveness and savvy steadily increased. When General Weaver had run for president on the Greenback Party ticket in 1876, he won only a handful of votes. In 1880, the handful was larger, but still a handful. By 1892, as the People's Party candidate, he garnered over a million votes and carried the states of Kansas, Nebraska, and North Dakota.

Enmity directed at the whole expanding universe of financial middlemen — financiers, railroad promoters, purveyors of watered stock, bankers and mortgage holders, organizers of trusts and "combines" — was raising the temperature of political life. The preamble to the People's Party platform put things starkly:

> We meet in the midst of a nation brought to the verge of moral, political, and material ruin... our homes are covered with mortgages; labor impoverished; and the land concentrating in the hands of the capitalists.... The fruits of the toil of millions are boldly stolen to build up colossal fortunes for the few, unprecedented in the history of mankind;

and the possessors of these, in turn, despise the republic and endanger liberty. From the same prolific womb of governmental injustice we breed the two great classes...tramps and millionaires.[15]

Vitriol tossed Wall Street's way grew more acidic each passing year. Defenders of the gold standard were prone to treat such talk as the ravings of lunatics and cranks—"border ruffians," "Cossacks," and "bandits" out of step with the march of Progress. But what is most striking is how widespread this verbal violence was.

Bewhiskered William A. Peffer, for example, looked like some eastern newspaper's caricature of a hayseed radical. Actually, he was a sober-minded judge, newspaper editor, and successful Populist candidate for the U.S. Senate from Kansas in 1890. But Wall Street shenanigans made him irate. A year after his election, he published "The Farmers Side: His Troubles and Their Remedy." Wall Street boasted— without warrant, according to Peffer—that it deserved credit for the country's industrial and commercial development. What Wall Street apologists got right was that the power of the men assembled on the Street "to catch the driftwood of trade is greater than that of monarchies." They were despicable hypocrites parading their "patriotism in lending a few millions of their ill-gotten gains to the government of their imperiled country at 12% interest, when thousands of farmers and wage workers...were voluntarily in the army at risk of life and home."

Armageddon came finally and inevitably in 1896. The People's Party split apart. Millions flooded back into the Democratic Party, drawn by William Jennings Bryan's eloquence, his solemn vow that "mankind shall not be crucified on a cross of gold," and to the alluring panacea of freely coined silver. They were prepared to give up all those other demands and desires that fired populism from the outset. Legions, however, remained faithful to populism's daring and its programmatic independence. Together agrarian-minded Democrats and Populists joined battle with the "money kings of Wall Street." In his electrifying peroration at the Democratic Party convention in Chicago, Bryan quoted John Carlisle to challenge the delegates: "Upon which side will the Democratic party fight; upon the side of the 'idle holders of idle capital' or upon the side of the struggling masses?"[16]

War of the Worlds

Which side indeed. It was a war of the worlds. Populist politics took on the world of J. P. Morgan by looking backward and forward at the same time. It anticipated the modern regulatory-state way in advance of the urban upper-middle classes, which after all stayed wedded to the outmoded shibboleths of laissez-faire for some time to come.

But the money power's offenses aroused enduring cultural anxieties and predilections about religion and sex, nature and the city, trust and infidelity. These were not, first of all, political emotions. The glare of Wall Street lit up an antique nightscape in the Populist imagination. It was populated by the oversexed and the emasculated, by urban tricksters and sybarites, by hook-nosed Shylocks and moral prostitutes, alien conspirators and apocalyptic demons. It was a despoiled landscape robbed of its natural vigor and hard-earned virtue. To redeem it called upon a reservoir of profound discontent, stoking a resistance of salvationist intensity. This was the cultural understructure of the politics of primitive accumulation as it unfolded in the countryside.

Whatever else one might think about this culture of opposition—expressed in utopian and dystopian fantasies, hellfire sermons, realist novels, and cartoon allegories, as well as in poetry—it was an undeniably luxuriant world, allusively dense and dramaturgically alive. It presumed a familiarity with biblical, Shakespearean, and pastoral themes and images. Together they composed a psychic armature with which to defend a sense of sacred honor and fend off the specter of social oblivion.

This was "culture war" *avant la lettre*. No terrain was spared. But there were hot zones of the most concentrated fire. The money power was an impiety and a pollutant that threatened above all the purity of the land, the family, and the nation.

Populism made serious if intermittent attempts to include the urban proletarian poor within its embrace, but it remained ambivalent about the city. It viewed the exfoliating financial network, no matter how far into the outback it extended its reach, as an irreducibly urban phenomenon. And it sometimes recoiled from the visage of proletarian squalor and demoralization.

Instead, proximity to the land was inherently salubrious, the natural soil nourishing manly independence and honest dealing upon which in turn a healthy society rested. The spirit of Wall Street was its antithesis. Wall Street ravaged the countryside by converting the land into a medium of commercial exchange and speculation, tearing it up by the roots, so to speak, from its preordained role as a giver of life.

This social drainage system headquartered in lower Manhattan could be displayed with graphic earthiness as in a cartoon sketch of a cow feeding in the west, then getting milked in New York. Or it might inspire sublime meditations. In this age full of looming premonitions of social cataclysm, the virgin land carried sacred meaning; its deflowering at the hands of alien financial interests amounted to a national calamity. Henry George's *Progress and Poverty* fixated on ground rent in part because it expressed a more general cultural preoccupation with parasitism that set the stakes high indeed:

> The general intelligence, the general comfort, active intervention, the power of adaptation and assimilation, the free, independent spirit, and energy and hopefulness that have marked our people are not causes, but results—they have sprung from the unfenced land. This public domain has been the transmuting force which turned the thriftless, unambitious European peasant into the self-reliant farmer; it has given a consciousness of freedom even to the dweller in crowded cities, and has been the well-spring of hope even to those who have never thought of taking refuge upon it.[17]

Agrarian suspicion of and repugnance for city life had of course been a deeply rooted tradition in Western civilization for centuries before the settlement of the New World renewed its momentum. Wall Street was a city institution through and through, marked by all of urban life's most dangerous proclivities, both old ones and new ones. Even its geography was suggestive, tucked away at the intestinal end of New York, conducting its business in the shadows of its serpentine alleyways.

Financial oligarchs wallowed in the immoralities of city life and threatened the moral fiber of the rest of the country. Sexual mores and family integrity were especially in jeopardy. The Sioux Falls *Daily Argus*, which concluded that J. P. Morgan had done more harm in the world than "any man who ever lived in it," singled out for special censure his contribution to "the blighting of womanhood" and the "premature aging of children." Angry farmers itemizing, often in capital letters, the most repugnant traits and abuses of the money power invariably raised the specter of "Debased Manhood."

The populist brief against Wall Street's sexual impropriety and subversion was part of a broader indictment of its sensual abandon and descent into a kind of overcivilized barbarism. Morgan's world seemed morally pathological, the Street a boulevard of ravenous appetite. Millions were wasted there on outlandish feasts while "gaunt starvation walked the streets." There men posed as "missionaries conquering deserts and building republics," feigning piety and wisdom, soaking up the adulation and honorifics of the credulous, while "living in luxury and ease, renting costly pews in splendid churches and hiring their worshipping done; men petted and feasted by the rich everywhere." Adversarial politicians and jaundiced-eyed journalists kept a scorecard of the Social Register's monumental castles, their yachts "ready at the wharf," their "private cars at the depot," their private chapels and private priests," and their fancy dress soirees, all the stigmata of a "libidinous plutocracy."[18]

Wall Street wasted the soul. Populists likened the contemporary economic inequalities to the impassable scriptural divide between Dives and Lazarus: the rich Dives cast into hellfire, while the beggar Lazarus reposed in the bosom of Abraham. To stay loyal to republicanism and equality was to defend the battlements of a Christian way of life, its spiritually invigorating attachment to hard work and abstemious restraint in the face of iniquitous temptation. What the money power defiled was an essential innocence, a core conviction that "honorable labor in every walk of existence...will be counted Monarch among men." Somehow there needed to be a return to the "principles and practices of primitive Christianity," a restoration of that millennial community of human sympathy and fellowship. Unless this rather etherealized form of the labor theory of value prevailed against the corrosive logic of a leisure-infatuated commercial civilization, there would be hell to pay.

Hell was familiar territory: in the populist view of the world, the final conflict with the money power would inevitably take place on its borders. There the enemy would appear in all its ghastly viciousness, a fearsome, brutal figure of ancient lineage and apocalyptic import. A Populist congressman called trusts "institutional vampires." Wall Street machinations were a "devil's dance...an orgy of fiduciary harlotry." Sometimes a primordial octopus, sometimes a "great Devil Fish" or vampire, the money power engaged not so much in acts of commerce as in acts of "necromancy." Strip away Wall Street's veneer of urbane sophistication and what stared you in the face was a demon—horrifically violent or unendurably seductive, but a demon nonetheless. The "trust" was "soulless"; beneath its avaricious, power-mad exterior beat a heart of pure nihilism, driving the whole human community down and backward into some dark age. Populist eschatology thought in terms of an "irrepressible conflict" joined generations earlier. Bred in the bone, it was a war over the soul of man with an uncertain outcome.[19]

Often enough, Populist insurgents on the western prairies and Southern cotton fields had arrived there only recently. Their homesteads might be just a generation old, two or three at the most. For these husbandmen, their fortunes had always been tied to the coming of the railroad and eastern banks—that is, to the infrastructure of modernity. Yet they cherished beliefs far older than that, a sacerdotal commitment to rural and small-town virtues that went back to Jefferson's day. The money power and its voracious appetite for the wealth generated outside its immediate orbit of operation threatened a way of life as much as a way of making a living. For that reason, the populist uprising, whether it resisted in ways perspicacious or retrograde, lent the whole era a certain gravitas, an undercurrent of apocalyptic finality so foreign to our sense of things today.

End Days

With William McKinley's triumph in 1896, heavily fortified by the biggest guns of industry and finance, one species of anticapitalism went extinct. Agrarian reform would remain an important feature of American politics through the Great Depression. But the revolution invoked by Tom Watson was over with. It died along with the frontier, as the eminent historian Frederick Jackson Turner intimated at just this time. Turner's address to the American Historical Association at the Chicago world's fair in 1893, "The Significance of the Frontier in American History," has been thoroughly criticized, revised, and rejected in the generations since then. But his notions—that "American social development has been continually beginning over again on the frontier," that "so long as free land exists, the opportunity for a competency exists, and economic power secures political power," and that each new frontier furnished, at least psychologically and sometimes in actuality, "a gate of escape from the bondage of the past"—were clearly alive and well within the ranks of agrarian unrest. The vanishing that Turner detected in the findings of the 1890 Census imparted a sense of imminent loss that inspired a paradoxical revolutionary nostalgia.

Moreover, this same vanishing was felt back east. By the time Turner composed his "frontier thesis," the "dignity of labor" had become a hollowed out homily, a cruel joke in the face of the looming specter of a fixed and despised class of proletarians that, Turner noted, gave new urgency to the "social question." Far from the cornfields and cotton farms of the heartland, root and branch challenges to the new order of things gathered steam.[20]

5

The Second Civil War:
On the Industrial Frontier

Far from the homesteads of the Middle Border and cotton fields of the Old Confederacy, a mood also verging on the apocalyptic shadowed the country's mines and mills and tenements of urban America. Slavery had just recently drowned in a sea of blood, or so it seemed. Yet within practically no time at all, not even a decade after Appomattox, the nation was preoccupied with a new version of human bondage.

Slavery was actually the ultimate form of primitive accumulation. The greatest fortunes of the era were amassed because slaves were forcibly dispossessed of everything they had or were born into that state of dispossession. So long as the perpetual enslavement of four million human beings lasted, conflicts over the real nature of "free labor" remained marginal if heated, a premonition, not an overriding reality.

Emancipation emancipated the labor question. It became the principal interrogative of American public life for the next seventy-five years. As late as 1919, President Woodrow Wilson cabled Congress from the World War I peace conference in Versailles to confirm precisely that: "The question which stands at the front of all others amidst the present great awakening is the question of labor...how are the men and women who do the daily labor of the world to obtain progressive improvement in the conditions of their labor, to be made happier, and to be served better by the communities and the industries which their labor sustains and advances?" And this was a decidedly genteel formulation of the way the labor question was often posed.[1]

Nor was the labor question confined to life in the coal mines, steel mills, railroads, and sweatshops of the industrial heartland. Instead it embraced multitudes, exposing the machinations of the new slavery here, there, and everywhere: in the countryside, where self-reliant farmers were being reduced to some form of debt peonage or migratory wage labor; in small towns and cities, where once independent businessmen were being driven into bankruptcy and down into the ranks of the property-less; in the ateliers of craftsmen compelled to surrender their cherished skills and work to the dronelike regimen of shoe and textile factories; in Southern lumber and turpentine camps, coal mines, iron forges, and cotton plantations, where convict laborers, overwhelmingly African American, descended into an invisible world of coerced labor hard to differentiate from legal slavery. Bondage had died at the hands of the sword. Long live the new slavery.

Language as strong as that seems overwrought to our ears. How could it not? It has been at least another three-quarters of a century since people regularly talked or thought about working for wages as a kind of slavery. The whole notion strikes us as odd. Yet for a long time references to wage slavery were a journalistic commonplace. That doesn't mean everyone back then agreed that working for wages entailed enslavement. Nor is it the case that most people in those days concurred that the money power was subverting the freedoms fought for in the Revolution—far from it. But it does mean that these claims, which now appear so alien, were once upon a time treated with great seriousness and hotly debated. A society that feels it may be living on the precipice of slavery is a society living on the precipice, on the edge of some final confrontation, pregnant with violent emotion. Violent language and the language of violence did indeed characterize this era to a degree hard to imagine today. Thoughts of this sort, moreover, emanated from all quarters, not from oddball eccentrics and fringe elements.

Old World or New World

"Bread or Blood," for example, was a common slogan at working-class demonstrations during the economic depression of the mid-1870s. The cry was stunning for its starkness, but also because it signaled a level of outraged militancy that hard times often discourage. The 1870s, however, were marked by more bad years than good ones. This was true through the mid-1880s, which suffered their own periodic slumps. Nevertheless, these decades witnessed a crescendo of strikes, shoot-outs, and labor-oriented political movements.

When thousands of destitute unemployed, many of them homeless, including women and children, gathered in Tompkins Square Park in New York City in 1874, "Bread or Blood" is what they cried. They were demanding work or relief in what one labor activist called "a folk movement of primitive need." Plans were to march on City Hall to ask the city to distribute food and funds, and to suspend evictions (some may have talked of marching on Wall Street as well; a similar gathering at the park had done that during the panic of 1857). Barricades were erected. Then the police, on horseback, dispersed the protesters in a spasm of brutality—the police commissioner later described the assault as "the most glorious sight I ever saw." The local press applauded, damning the protesters as "communards." Wild claims were made that these "Communists" had smuggled diamonds and jewels stolen from the churches of Paris with which to buy ammunition and bombs.[2]

"Communards" was a word needing little definition, since the Paris Commune three years earlier conjured up memories of barricades and blood in the streets, rioting and pillage, and primitive nightmares about "petroleuses"—Amazonian women, their hair streaming wantonly behind them in the wind, armed with the nineteenth century's version of the Molotov cocktail, setting Paris aflame. *Harper's Weekly* rejoiced at the mob's suppression because it taught the lesson that "follies and ferocities of the Commune are alien to American thought and methods." Glad that the "American Commune" had met its master, the *Philadelphia Inquirer* advised that in the future, should it rear its head again, public authority should "club it to death at the hands of the police or shoot it to death at the hands of the militia."[3]

If the peaceable Tompkins Square rally could ignite this level of hysteria, imagine the reaction to the land seizures and state capitol occupations that others, newly recruited into capitalism's "reserve army of the unemployed," engaged in elsewhere. A great fear of the unemployed pervaded the country and lasted a long time, rising into panic with each serious dip in the economy. "Some communities when the hard times came this winter," wrote the *Charity Review* in 1894, " and the army of unemployed swept through the streets were panic-stricken, the inhabitants fortified themselves behind soup-houses and threw loaves of bread out upon the besiegers; naturally the siege continued." Tompkins Square set a precedent. In big cities like Chicago similar demonstrations were met with force and the participants were stigmatized by the press and officialdom as "heavily armed German revolutionaries," "atheists," believers in "free love," and potential assassins.[4]

Fearmongering of this sort about "un-American," often foreign-born agitators stirring up trouble where there had been none became commonplace soon after the Civil War and remained so all through the Gilded Age and well beyond. In Chicago where by 1890, 80 percent of the population was foreign-born or of "non-American" parentage, talk about "Slavic wolves," of filthy freaks, foreign in an excremental sense, needing evacuation, was not unusual among local officials. And "foreign" didn't necessarily mean from abroad; any ominous "other" would do. By the end of the Civil War, urban business elites had already soured on the Jacksonian infatuation with universal suffrage. Instead they treated the "commercial classes" as the backbone of society, holding the fort against "an ignorant proletariat" too easily manipulated by urban demagogues like Boss Tweed, head of New York's Democratic Party machine. They acknowledged class differences and welcomed the advent of a proletariat so long as it remained docile.[5]

Docility could not be counted on. In that event, malcontents were to be treated as savages, likened to Native American hostiles on the frontier and requiring the same kind of ruthless suppression. Two could play at that deadly game, however.

Take, for example, the Molly Maguires. Irish immigrant coal-mining militants, they hailed often from rural parts of Ireland, where rough and ready peasant revenge against enclosing and rent-gouging landlords was an established if unofficial ritual of village justice, carried out by local secret societies. Transplanted to America, they worked the anthracite fields of Pennsylvania — mine labor was a kind of industrial agriculture — alongside thousands of other hard-pressed miners from Ireland, Wales, and Germany.

Here, during the long depression of the 1870s, "day after day men, women, and children went to the adjoining woods to dig roots and pick up herbs to keep body and soul together." Here, 5500 children aged seven to sixteen worked down in the pits alongside their fathers. Here, when 110 men were killed in a mine fire, John Siney — not a Molly, but a more mild-tempered head of the Workingmen's Benevolent Association — implored his members: "Men, if you must die with your boots on, die for your families, your homes, your country, but no longer consent to die like rats in a trap for those who have no more interest in you than in the pick you dig with." As tempers boiled over, a fatal duet played itself out as bodies of mine superintendents and union activists and Mollys, mauled, mutilated, and crucified, showed up in the streams and woods of Schuylkill County and elsewhere. Trains were derailed, a telegraph office burned to the ground, and vigilantes roamed the countryside. After a strike against Francis B. Gowen, the wealthiest anthracite mine owner in the world, was crushed by Gowen's Coal and Iron Police with the help of Pinkerton spies, twenty Molly Maguires were hurriedly shuffled off to the gallows between 1876 and 1878 on suspect charges of murder, kidnapping, and arson. Big metropolitan dailies helped produce that terminal resolution by drawing a straight line between Molly resistance to the coal barons and "Indian savagery." As the county district attorney put it, "The name of Molly Maguire being attached to a man's name is sufficient to hang him."[6]

As these cries for "Bread or Blood" and acts of mutual terrorism suggested, strong emotions were hardly confined to one side of this great and widening divide. William Sylvis, who led the Iron Molders International Union and who had founded the country's first national labor federation (the National Labor Union) soon after the Civil War ended, declared that the classes were locked in "an irrepressible conflict" which had "commenced with the world, and will only end with it." Edwin M. Chamberlain, a onetime candidate for governor of Massachusetts and labor reformer, took note that the ownership of "surplus wealth" by one class created poverty, inequality, and crime, and that these fatal maladies could not be cured within the "profit system" and private property. He shuddered at what he concluded was the looming and inevitable outbreak of class bloodshed.[7]

Even those who earnestly wanted to damp down and ameliorate these high-temperature conflicts nonetheless were influenced by a similar under-text of barbarism versus civilization. Three years before Tompkins Square, when Paris was burning, former abolitionist Wendell Phillips, aware of these same volcanic tensions building at home, suggested that if one were to "scratch the surface of New York society...you will find the Paris Commune." Phillips was disgusted by the callous indifference of official society to the epidemic impoverishment of its laboring classes. Tompkins Square insurgents went further, denouncing monarchic despotism, and comparing the police with the men who had dragged William Lloyd Garrison, the nation's most famous abolitionist, through the streets of Boston or with the Virginia governor who had executed John Brown. Back in slavery days, they aptly pointed out, "every anti-slavery man would have been denounced as a Communist."

Charles Loring Brace, who founded the Children's Aid Society, warned in 1872, even before that decade's depression hit, of "the Proletaries of New York." These were the people many described as "the dangerous classes" composed of the American-born sons of German and Irish immigrants who were, Brace concluded, "far more brutal than the peasantry from whom they descend." He added that this group made up "just the same explosive social elements beneath the surface of New York as of Paris," and that "Capital to them is a tyrant," so that if the law relaxed its vigilance for a moment, "we should see an explosion from this class which might leave the city in ashes and blood." And this sense of imminent danger came from someone in many respects sympathetic to the plight of the urban, immigrant poor.

Preachy and superior but not without insight, Brace sensed that "the breaking of the ties with one's country has a bad moral effect, especially on a laboring class," loosening ties to the church, weakening the informal mechanisms of communal surveillance, and fraying sexual inhibitions ("the fruits of 'Free Love' are a weak marriage bond"). It also eroded self-esteem for those with "want of a trade" and accelerated the descent into dependency "on manual labor or chance means of living."[8]

People less inclined to help (if just as inclined as Brace to pass judgment) could be ferocious. From the outset, the Great Uprising of 1877 (the national railroad strike set off by drastic wage cuts in the depth of the decade's depression) was treated by that era's mainstream media as "a war against society." The *National Republican* in Washington called it an "American Commune," "a poison introduced into our social system by European laborers." The *New Orleans Times* announced that "the war between labor and capital has begun in earnest." Railroad barons like Jay Gould, giving up on the republican form of government, ruminated about recruiting some savior on horseback, a Napoleonic figure like former president Ulysses S. Grant, to ride to the rescue. Eminent figures, including future president James Garfield and Wall Street banker Jacob Schiff, pushed hard for measures to suppress the suffrage. Judge Walter Gresham, who would later become Grover Cleveland's secretary of state, declared that "democracy is now the enemy of law and order and society itself, and as such should be denounced."

If that wasn't sanguinary enough, *The Independent,* a Congregationalist journal, had this to recommend: "If the clubs of the policemen, knocking out the brains of the rioters, will answer, then well and good; but if it does not promptly meet the exigency, the bullets and bayonets, canister and grape...constitute the one remedy....Napoleon was right when he said the way to deal with a mob is to exterminate it."

Primitive imaginings, some with racial and sexual undertones, rose to the surface of public rhetoric as journalists likened what they were witnessing to the Jacobin terror of the previous century and described "mighty masses of strange, grimy men, excited by passion, dark and fearful, surging along the streets," incited by women "frenzied with rage...who played the part of petroleuses boldly urging the men on to acts of outrage and bloodshed."

These newspapers or this particular ministry did not by any means represent universal opinion. But no matter where one's sympathies lay, the sense of utter estrangement was common. A reform-minded minister observed that "we now have intrepid men and women who plunge for a time into the life of the lower classes and return to write about this unknown race." Less in doubt, a New Jersey educator summed up this "race": "They eat, drink, breed, work, and die."[9]

When the Great Uprising reached Chicago, in an act of counterterror, businessmen patrolled the streets with rifles and demanded that the militia suppress "the ragged commune wretches." In Pennsylvania and elsewhere, when local militiamen proved unreliable, not willing to fire on neighbors and friends, railroad executives like Thomas A. Scott of the Pennsylvania Railroad and John W. Garrett of the Baltimore and Ohio called on President Rutherford B. Hayes to send in federal troops instead. They urged that the army deal with the strikers as if the latter were waging war on the United States. Hayes did as he was asked—he even sent ironclads and other naval vessels and mobilized the whole War

Department—something he'd done before as governor of Ohio, when he ordered in the state militia to suppress a coal mine strike.

As the uprising spread into the Midwest, another future president, Benjamin Harrison, led the state militia of Indiana against the strikers and their allies. In Pittsburgh armed clashes between strikers—aided by their friends, family, and neighbors—on the one side and state and federal militiamen on the other punctuated a chaos already marked by burning locomotives, freight cars, and railroad roundhouses, not to mention scores of wounded and killed. In the end the railroads would prevail.[10]

Official society blamed it all on a vast crime wave perpetrated by that newly menacing figure of industrial capitalism, the tramp. Brigades of these workless paupers were alleged to have descended on the cities, adding their criminal intentions to the cataclysm. Vigilante antitramp committees soon formed in metropolises and smaller towns everywhere to deal with this particular species of "savage." The Western Gun Works ran a booming business selling a specialty item known as the "Tramp Terror," a kind of primitive machine gun. The "savages," however, were not shy about talking back. A Pittsburgh paper sympathetic to those "savages" declared, "This may be the beginning of a great civil war in this country, between labor and capital.... The laboring people, who mostly constitute the militia, will not take up arms to put down their brethren. Even if so-called law and order should beat them down in blood...we would, at least, have our revenge on the men who coined our sweat and muscles into millions for themselves." Pittsburgh became an armed camp, under curfew, patrolled by militiamen.[11]

Farther west, in St. Louis, the stakes were raised even higher when what began as a railroad strike became a citywide general strike (Toledo and Chicago came close to experiencing the same). A local Workingmen's Party with a considerable following set up an executive committee to run the city, keep order, distribute food, and provide medical assistance. The very sight of men "who had hitherto been buried in the depths of obscurity, possessing neither social, financial, or political importance in the community" suddenly reigning "as princes" was to say the least shocking to the city's establishment. It retaliated by setting up a committee of public safety equipped with a cavalry and artillery to put down the rising. The city fathers of St. Louis—judges, politicians, army officers, police officials—mobilized private troops of white-collar clerks, tradespeople, and others to fight a local civil war. They likened the executive committee running the strike to "Robespierre and his brace of fellow conspirators," who "sit in darkness and plot." Some local newspapers scared the citizenry with headlines like "The Reign of the Canaille" and "Glutted with Gore." But others, just as bellicose, lined up on the other side; the *St. Louis Journal,* for one, declared that "if the laboring men of this country must choose between revolution and abject submission to the heartless demands of capital, they will certainly not be condemned by the *Journal* if they prefer war to starvation."[12]

The intransigence of the railroad barons further enflamed sentiment far beyond the ranks of the striking workers themselves. By this time the phrase "soulless corporation" had become part of the American idiom. It didn't help matters when the country's most celebrated clergyman, Henry Ward Beecher, offered up this bit of pious cruelty: "God has intended the great to be great and the little to be little.... I do not say that a dollar a day is enough to support a workingman," not "if he insist[s] on smoking and drinking beer.... But the man who cannot live on bread and water is not fit to live." All the stigmata of class contempt were meticulously noted down by the press and the inquisitive guardians of law and order; every hat brim askew, dirty shirt, or missing collar was duly cited as a telltale sign of lower-class contempt for civility and good order.[13]

After the 1877 insurrection, fortresses armed with Gatling guns were erected in major cities, financed and sometimes even manned by leading manufacturers, merchants, and financiers (or their male offspring). Calls went out for the harshest punishments to deal summarily with the threatening "mobocracy." In response, worker militias paraded through the streets, rifles at the ready, prepared to defend themselves should they be attacked by hostile armies, public or private. Having witnessed a near Armageddon, a St. Louis journalist concluded that "even in America the proletariat is becoming great in numbers and dangerous in disposition." However, for the moment at least, the St. Louis establishment, like urban elites elsewhere, managed to restore the old order.[14]

The Mass Strike

Tempers stayed white-hot. The decade running from the Great Uprising of 1877 through the original May Day demonstrations of 1886 was remarkable for the frequency, intensity, and violence that marked the standoffs between labor and capital. More profoundly, it also witnessed the birth of a kind of strike—the mass strike—and the explosive growth of a kind of organization—the Knights of Labor—that embodied an inherent challenge to the new industrial order.

A rally in Chicago of three thousand people early in May of 1886 in Haymarket Square assembled to condemn a brutal attack the previous day by police on striking workers at the McCormick Harvesting Machine Company. Six workers had been killed at McCormick. During the Haymarket protest a bomb exploded, killing a police officer. Police unleashed a fusillade. In the crossfire six more officers and four workers died while hundreds more were injured in the panic and melee that followed. With little and mainly fabricated evidence, including perjured and coerced testimony, and a judge partial to the prosecution, the ensuing trial seemed to many at the time to border on travesty, and the bombing was successfully blamed on the city's anarchist movement. (Recently a dispute has developed among historians about how irregular the trial really was, given the standards of the time; at the time legions of people around the world had no such doubts.) Leading Protestant clergy denounced the workers as communists and urged they be hunted down like "mad dogs." State Attorney Francis Walker likened the accused to "hyenas" feasting "over the corpses of the dead." Others in authority, invoking the arche-typical fears of their ancestors, denounced them as "savages," compared the women in their ranks to "squaws" and their gatherings to "war dances."

Primitive accumulation in America has again and again found justifi-cation in the psychic netherworld of racial phobia. More was at stake than material desires and needs. Anxieties about a threatened manhood infused both camps. Each accused the enemy of being unmanly. Leaflets circulated during the McCormick conflict compared the workers' lot to the humiliations suffered by Southern blacks compelled to surrender their children to "factory lords": "If you are men, if you are the sons of your grand sires, then you will rise in your might." But their opponents knew, on the contrary, that in standing up to this savagery they were "the true and noble men" waging a war on behalf of order; they were steadfast and fearless in the face of terrorists who were the real cowards, doing their poisonous work in the dark when they weren't drinking themselves into a debauched oblivion. Metaphors of sexual violation sig-naled how deep down into the psychic interior the class struggle could seep. Workers denounced their bosses as sexually depraved, corrupted by their power to give free rein to their lust. McCormick's depravity was "only common among people who have exhausted their vitality and manhood by unbounded licentiousness." Capitalism itself was a voluptu-ary. The moral integrity of the working-class family was at risk. On the other side of the barricades, the city's elite imagined itself the knightly protectors of a virgin community under assault by rapists and seducers.

The trial that led to the hanging of four anarchist leaders became a national and global disgrace, leaving people like William Dean Howells, a leader of the movement to save the condemned, grief-stricken and despairing about the future of American democracy. Edward Bellamy, whose utopian novel *Looking Backward* would soon captivate the nation, wrote to Howells to say that so much was on the line at Haymarket that "socialism smells to the average American of petroleum, suggests the red flag and all manner of sexual novelties and an abusive tone about God and religion." Hysteria about racial pollution, moral depravity, alien conspiracy, and sexual inversion made for an emotional firestorm hard to counter.

At the end of the day, the outcome pleased the powers that be—men like Philip Armour, George Pullman, and Cyrus McCormick—who thought of their working-class opponents as depraved riffraff and urged on the forces of law and order to round them up and shutter their meeting places and newspapers as if in a police state. As John Swinton, the country's most widely read labor journalist, noted, the death sentences were a form of judicial murder intended to "gratify the frightened bourgeoisie."[15]

Anarchists and their sympathizers lived in a world turned upside down. For them the real conspirators and the real terrorists were the bourgeoisie. Louis Lingg, a German-born carpenter and at twenty-one the youngest of the convicted anarchists, proclaimed after the verdict was pronounced: "I despise you. I despise your order, your laws, your force-propped authority. Hang me for it!" As it turned out, he didn't allow them that final pleasure. Lingg blew himself up in jail rather than suffer the indignity of state execution.[16]

Haymarket was the culminating if unintended event of a nationwide movement for the eight-hour day that had begun two years earlier with the formation of Eight Hour Leagues. How pedestrian that demand for an eight-hour day may sound today (although fewer and fewer of us enjoy it now), but just as it had during the insurrection of 1877, this movement took on the form of a mass strike.

A mass strike is something akin to but much rarer than an ordinary strike and one that comes much closer to turning the world upside down. The relative frequency with which such events happened during the long nineteenth century is itself perhaps the best evidence of just how fragile and provisional the new order of things remained.

What came to be known as the Great Upheaval, the movement for the eight-hour day, elicited what one historian has called "a strange enthusiasm." The normal trade union strike is a finite event joining two parties contesting over limited if sometimes intractable issues. The mass strike in 1886 or before that in 1877—all the many localized mass strikes that erupted in towns and small industrial cities after the Civil War and through into the new century—was open-ended and ecumenical in reach. Its desires, however exalted, were always tethered to the needs of the most abused and exploited.

So, for example, in Baltimore when the skilled and better paid railroad brakemen on the Baltimore and Ohio Railroad first struck in 1877 so too did less well off "box-makers, sawyers, and can-makers, engaged in the shops and factories of that city, [who] abandoned their places and swarmed into the streets." This in turn "stimulated the railroad men to commit bolder acts." When the governor of West Virginia sent out the Berkeley Light Guard and Infantry to confront the strikers at Martinsburg at the request of the railroad's vice president, the militia retreated and "the citizens of the town, the disbanded militia and the rural population of the surrounding country fraternized," encouraging the strikers.

This centrifugal dynamic of the mass strike, widening the orbit of its influence and engagement so long as it was in the ascendancy, was characteristic of this extraordinary phenomenon. By the third day in Martinsburg the strikers had been "reinforced during the night at all points by accessions of working men engaged in other avocations than railroading," which, by the way, made it virtually impossible for federal troops by then on the scene to recruit scabs to run the trains. By the fourth day, "mechanics, artisans, and laborers in every department of human industry began to show symptoms of restlessness and discontent." Seeping deeper and deeper into the subsoil of proletarian life, down below the "respectable" working class of miners and mechanics and canal boatmen, frightened observers reported a "mighty current of passion and hate" sweeping up a "vast swarm of vicious idlers, vagrants, and tramps." And so it went.[17]

Smaller cities and towns like Martinsburg were often more likely than the biggest urban centers to experience this sweeping sense of social solidarity (what today we might call a massing of the 99%). During the

1877 Great Uprising, the social transmission of the mass strike moved first along the great trunk lines of the struck railroads, but quickly flowed into the small villages and towns along dozens of tributary lines and into local factories, workshops, and coal mines as squads of strikers moved from settlement, to settlement mobilizing the populace.

In these locales face-to-face relations still prevailed. It was by no means taken for granted that antagonism between labor and capital was fated to be the way of the world. Aversion to the new industrial order and a "democratic feeling" brought workers, storekeepers, lawyers, and businessmen of all sorts together, appalled by the behavior of large industrialists who often enough didn't live in those communities and so were the more easily seen as alien beings.

It was not uncommon for local officials, like the mayor of Cumberland, Maryland, to take the side of the mass strikers. The federal postmaster in Indianapolis wired Washington, "Our mayor is too weak, and our Governor will do nothing. He is believed to sympathize with the strikers." In Fort Wayne, like many other towns its size, the police and militia simply could not be counted on to put down the insurrectionists. In this world, corporate property was not accorded the same sanctified status still deferred to when it came to personal property. Sometimes company assets were burned to the ground or disabled; at other times they were seized, but not damaged.[18]

Metropolises also witnessed their own less frequent social earthquakes. Anonymous relations were more common there, the gulf separating social classes was much wider, and the largest employers could count on the new managerial and professional middle classes for support and a political establishment they could more often rely on. Still, the big city hardly constituted a DMZ. During the mass strike of 1877 in Pittsburgh, when sixteen citizens were killed, the city erupted and "the whole population seemed to have joined the rioters." "Strange to say," noted one journalist, elements of the population who had a "reputation for being respectable people—tradesmen, householders, well-to-do mechanics and such... openly mingled with the [turbulent mob] and encouraged them to commit further deeds of violence." Here too, as in smaller locales, enraged as they clearly were, mass strikers still drew a distinction between railroad property and the private property of individuals, which they scrupulously avoided attacking.[19]

In Chicago in 1886 and in other cities as well, the mass strike exploded at a thousand points at once, leaping across boundaries of skill, gender, nativity, ethnicity, and race, winning the support of many people whose immediate economic interests did not depend on the outcome, including farmers, neighborhood merchants, and whole ethnic neighborhoods, from schoolkids to the aged and unemployed. Often enough the momentum of the mass strike was enough to win concessions on wages, hours, or on other conditions of work—although they might be provisional, not inscribed in contracts, and subject to being violated or ignored when law and order was restored.

Brickyard and packinghouse workers, dry goods clerks and iron molders, unskilled Jewish female shoe sewers and skilled telegraphers, German craftsmen from the bookbinding trade and unlettered Bohemian freight handlers, all assembled together under the banner of the Knights of Labor or less formal, impromptu assemblies. The full name of the Knights was actually the Noble and Holy Order of the Knights of Labor, a peculiar name that like so much of the electric language of the long nineteenth century sounds so dissonant and oddly exotic—in this case even quaint—to modern ears. With one foot in the handicraft past and the other trying to step beyond the proletarian servitude waiting ominously off in the future, the Knights was itself the main organizational expression of the mass strike. It was part trade union, part guild, part political protest, part an aspiring alternate cooperative economy.

At all times and especially in smaller industrial towns, the Knights relied on ties to the larger community—kin, neighbors, local tradespeople—not merely the fellowship of the workplace. Like the Populist movement it practically constituted an alternative social universe of reading rooms, newspapers, lecture societies, libraries, clubs, and producer cooperatives. Infused with a sense of the heroic and the "secular sacred," the Knights envisioned themselves as if on a mission, appealing to the broad middling ranks of local communities to rescue the nation and preserve its heritage of republicanism and the dignity of productive labor. This "Holy Order," ambiguous and ambivalent in ultimate purpose (as it no doubt was), nevertheless mustered a profound resistance to the whole way of life represented by industrial capitalism even while wrestling with ways of surviving within it. So it offered everyday remedies—abolishing child and convict labor, establishing an income tax and public ownership of land for settlement not speculation, among others. Above all, however, it conveyed a yearning for an alternative, a "cooperative commonwealth" in place of the Hobbesian nightmare that Progress had become.[20]

Transgressive by its nature, this "strange enthusiasm" shattered and then recombined dozens of more parochial attachments. The intense heat of the mass strike fused these shards into something more daring and generous-minded. Everything about it was unscripted. The mass strike had a rhythm all its own, syncopated and unpredictable as it spread like an epidemic from worksite to marketplace to slum. It had no command central, unlike a conventional strike, but neither was it some mysterious instance of spontaneous combustion. Rather, it had dozens of choreographers who directed local uprisings that nevertheless remained elastic enough to cohere with one another while remaining distinct. Its program defied easy codification. At one moment and place it was about free speech, at another about a foreman's chronic abuse, here about the presence of scabs and armed thugs, there about a wage cut.

It ranged effortlessly from something as prosaic as a change in the piece rate to something as portentous as the nationalization of the country's transportation and communication infrastructure, but at its core stood the demand for the eight-hour day. Blunt yet profound, it defined for that historical moment both the irreducible minimum of a just and humane civilization and what the prevailing order of things seemingly could not, or would not, grant. The "Eight Hour Day Song," which became the movement's anthem, captured that intermixing of the quotidian and the transcendent:

> We want to feel the sunshine
> We want to smell the flowers;
> We're sure God has willed it.
> And we mean to have eight hours.
> We're summoning our forces from
> shipyard, shop, and mill;
> Eight hours for work, eight hours for rest
> Eight hours for what we will.[21]

When half a million workers struck on May 1, 1886—the original "May Day," (although not memorialized until the next year to honor the executed Haymarket anarchists), still celebrated now most places in the world except in the United States, where it began—the strikers called it Emancipation Day. How archaic that sounds. Such hortatory rhetoric has gone out of fashion. The eight-hour day movement of 1886 and the mass strikes that preceded, accompanied, and followed it were a freedom movement in the land of the free directed against a form of slavery no one would recognize or credit today.

Insofar as the mass strike had an ideology and a political vision, it was ecumenical and apocalyptic yet hard to pin down. Was it the embryo of the cooperative commonwealth dreamed of by the Knights of Labor, or the rebirth or salvation of the Producers Republic, which for at least two generations had excited the imagination of farmers, smallholders, and handicraftsmen in town and on the land? Was it some variant of socialism or anticapitalist anarchism? Was it an experimental living collage of Marx and Jefferson, Thomas Paine and Mikhail Bakunin?

The "Secular Sacred"

Insurgent labor was most often secular and anticlerical. Still Jesus could be a comrade. Ministers from the Social Gospel movement informed their congregants that "the carpenter's son taught what socialism teaches," and "labor temples" were common sights in cities and towns, their labor-accented religiosity a wake-up call to those unaware of the new hellish realities of proletarian life. Christian Socialist Jesse Jones alerted those myopic enough to believe that wage labor was an "un-American institution"; instead he insisted "a fixed, hopeless proletariat" did indeed exist and was "the very foundation of our industrial system." The "single-tax movement" inspired by Henry George's electrifying treatise *Progress and Poverty* (the single tax on land rent was designed to flush out idling pools of parasitical capital so they might flow into more productive uses) was touched deeply by an ethical yearning for a millennial community of sympathy and fellowship akin to the Social Gospel. For some of its followers, resolving the labor question was the secular equivalent of a final reckoning.

Similar quasi-religious, millennial urges to restore a lost spiritual coherence and the imagined harmonies, customary rights, and fraternity of preindustrial society also informed other middle-class reform movements of the late nineteenth century. This was even true of the so-called Nationalist clubs that coalesced after the publication of Edward Bellamy's didactic and wildly popular utopian novel *Looking Backward*. Bellamy himself was the son of deviant clerics and was driven to write his book out of a sense of Christian moral outrage at the Haymarket events. *Looking Backward* is often remembered for its futuristic and rather modernist depiction of technological marvels and its faintly ominous scenario for state-managed material well-being. But what Bellamy stressed was the moral revolution that was the prerequisite to solving the labor question, that "Sphinx's riddle of the nineteenth century... threatening to devour society."[22]

Like-minded preoccupations even permeated the ranks of the otherwise more prosaically oriented antimonopoly movement that swept into its orbit multitudes of small tradespeople and entrepreneurs as well as working- and middle-class consumers in towns and cities everywhere. Breaking up the trusts that had grown to dominate whole spheres of production and distribution—or, conversely, regulating or nationalizing them, which many in the movement favored (especially when it came to vital infrastructure industries in transportation, communication, and power generation)—became equally compelling alternatives to the hierarchies of the new economic order. Alliances formed naturally with the Populists and Knights. Antimonopoly became for many an enveloping creed, a way of life, and a call to arms to restore some revised version of Jeffersonianism for the modern age.

Moreover, all of these movements—the Knights, Nationalist clubs, populism, antimonopoly organizations, local labor, and Greenback Labor parties—frequently interacted, drew energy from the mass strike, and together formed a culture of opposition. As a persuasion, that culture concerned itself with more than economic organization, extending its reach into ethical matters, the built environment, and the art of virtuous government, all in one way or another tethered back to the labor question. Henry Demarest Lloyd, the journalist whose book *Wealth Against Commonwealth* would become the bible of the antimonopoly crusade, pronounced the "religion of labor," insisting that the sacred categories of an older moral economy needed to take precedence over the chillingly inhuman calculations of the free market and its monopolistic offspring.[23]

Even nineteenth-century socialism could speak this language. Eugene V. Debs, a railroad unionist who would later become the charismatic leader of the American Socialist Party, inspired multitudes with what he described as the "religion of socialism." Socialism in the American southwest, for example, embraced independent farmers facing the prospect of becoming tenants. It had room as well for miners, lumbermen, and migratory workers together with local businessmen threatened with extinction by mercantile, landed, and industrial elites. It brought together religious and secular hostilities. The amalgam became a prophetic movement that spread across the region's small towns and rural outback. The enmity felt for the new corporate order penetrated deep into cultural bedrock. There people were accustomed to the fluidity of roughly egalitarian social relationships and the immemorial assurances of masculine dignity and paternal authority so typical of the western frontier. They felt the sharp sting of proletarian emasculation and the wounding degradations of hardening distinctions in dress, schooling, and what we might today call lifestyle. In communities like this, "socialism" could become a placeholder for a patriotic and religious universe under duress.[24]

It is hard to say precisely just what this heterodoxy of desires and imaginings added up to, what blueprint if any it formed. Yet it unmistakably opened up the prospect of a new society founded on principles at odds with the tooth-and-claw struggle for self-advancement so celebrated in many precincts of social Darwinian America.

That yearning for an alternative was best expressed not in some formalized credo, but in the mass strike's tactical repertoire. Its two principal weapons were the boycott and the sympathy strike. And indeed what else was to be expected from a movement whose social character and capacious programmatic embrace made it the living embodiment of sympathy? The boycott drew on a long rural tradition of resistance to landlords. It was the perfect tactical expression of communal mobilization, which perhaps is why *Harper's Weekly* decried it as "a new form of terrorism" and "an outrage upon the American principle" because it violated the market and property rights. Used so frequently, the boycott was declared here and there a violation of the statutes against conspiracy.[25]

Sympathy strikes and boycotts expressed solidarity as an organized social emotion, not merely a piece of inspiring rhetoric, but as palpable reality, the spirit come to life, discovering all the exfoliating networks of its social nervous system. The form of the mass strike was its content, the medium the message.

For the legions who participated, or for those perhaps greater in number who looked on in vicarious empathy, the experience excited the imagination just because it was so fluid, its purpose and outcome uncertain yet pregnant with possibilities. Depending on one's location along the social hierarchy, it could also be deeply alarming. What was at stake, many believed, was nothing less than the future of the good society.

Would the patriarchal family survive or give way to something scarily unknown? Would the social order be hard-wired by ethnicity and race, or would it surmount those purportedly natural divisions? Was wealth compatible with democracy? Could concentrated power coexist with freedom? How could hierarchy coexist with equality? No wonder that when hunger marchers paraded solemnly past the mansions, gentlemen's clubs, and luxury department stores of Chicago's "better half," hallucinations about "unwashed gutter snipes" from Paris disturbed the equanimity of those accustomed to their prerogatives. The mass strike, precisely because it seemed to place everything about the prevailing social order on the agenda all at the same time, infused the atmosphere with a mounting readiness to settle accounts once and for all and in terms not reducible to dollars and cents.

Chicago may have been its epicenter, but the shock waves of the Great Upheaval were felt in many places. In Missouri, the Knights of Labor shut down Jay Gould's Southwestern Railroad in both 1885 and 1886, the first time victoriously, the second in defeat. Farmers from the surrounding region, members of the Farmers Alliance, blocked the tracks, blood flowed, and Gould, in an outburst of belligerent cynicism, declared he could hire one-half of the working class to shoot down the other half. But the social reach of the Knights was great enough that just a few years later, in 1890, they shut down New Orleans in a general strike.

In New York, relations between "the classes and the masses" had been bitter for a while; that spring of 1886 a rolling series of strikes preceded and followed May 1. And Henry George was running for mayor. His United Labor Party campaign attracted the support of the city's Central Labor Union, the Knights of Labor, socialists, antimonopolists, and others. In addition to the single tax, the campaign proposed public works, a municipally owned transit system, and the end of "class legislation" and police intimidation of demonstrators.

George's campaign presented the political face of the mass strike's "strange enthusiasm." As election day neared, thirty thousand marched in an evening rainstorm past the landmarks of working-class fortitude, including Tompkins Square and Cooper Union. The gathering resembled a great artisanal festival of olden times, with signs held aloft ("We are striving to elevate our craft"), fireworks, Chinese lanterns, and chants like "Hi-ho—the leeches must go." Talk of a "Gettysburg of labor" filled the air. There were hundreds of street-corner rallies spilling out of saloons and union halls. African Americans and immigrant workers joined in. A version of Catholic radicalism was preached by Father Edward McGlynn; it was rooted in the Irish war against landlordism at home and here in America.

No ordinary political assemblage, the coalition crossed boundaries of race, class, ethnicity, religion, craft, ideology, and politics. "Ecumenical and militant," noted one historian, it extended an open invitation to all those threatened by the onrush of primitive accumulation and wage slavery: dispossessed craft workers and unskilled immigrant industrial peasants, land reformers, conventional trade unionists and Knights from the Holy Order, Irish radicals and German socialists, neighborhood businessmen and tenement dwellers, advocates of the eight-hour day as well as proponents of greenback currency. The mayoral campaign was enveloped in a wave of strikes—twelve hundred of them, involving 180,000 workers—with plenty of victories along the way. It culminated in a citywide streetcar strike of great violence—many workers were beaten, tracks and streetcars were destroyed, and there were three fatalities at the hands of the police—about which William Dean Howells would write with tragic pathos in *A Hazard of New Fortunes*.

In the end, George did quite well, finishing second to Democrat Abram Hewitt, himself a reformer and onetime defender of trade unions.

The charismatic single-taxer polled more votes than the Republican nominee, Theodore Roosevelt. George prophesied "a new division of parties...soon to take place which would for the question of industrial slavery do what the Republican Party did for the question of chattel slavery."

George was far from a revolutionary; indeed, he felt uncomfortable with the collectivist sentiments that ran through the labor and radical movements and would soon enough draw back from these associations. He saw himself as a conciliatory figure and feared the bestiality of proletarian life, seeking instead a pathway to social concord. But his campaign was nonetheless vilified by the city's patricians as an anarchist agency of revolution. His Democratic rival called these political rebels "enemies of civilization and social order." Local government, the press, the judiciary, and clergymen let loose a torrent of abuse. The Brahmin editor of *The Nation* attacked "the securing of impunity for the use of violence and coercion in support of strikes." And more damaging than the nasty verbiage, injunctions rained down against striking and boycotting. Similar treatment was handed out to the like-minded labor tickets running that year in 189 municipalities and thirty-four states (out of a total of thirty-eight).[26]

After the Knights

Matters grew only more bloody-minded by the 1890s. But there was also a discernible shift in the balance of power. The antimonopoly movement reached its apogee during the new decade and into the new century. But the Knights of Labor, whose rise in the 1880s was meteoric and often triumphant, were in decline and disarray even before the new decade began. They were coerced into submission by the police, militia, and judiciary, especially following the Great Upheaval of 1886. One sign that concentrated industry wielded an overweening power was its ability to manipulate the legal system to thwart labor resistance to its will. That included the ability to keep public authority on the sidelines of these disputes, as well as to call on its coercive intervention when necessary. Legal nullification of wage and hour laws, boycotts, and sympathy strikes hurt the mass strike where it lived.[27]

Knights were overwhelmed as well by the devolution of skilled labor introduced by factory production, which intruded into all the main arteries of economic life. Divisions—ethnic, ideological, and occupational—reasserted themselves. Trade unionism of the sort we are familiar with today—devoted more or less strictly to matters of collective bargaining—emerged under the auspices of the newly created American Federation of Labor. It competed with Knight assemblies for members. Still great confrontations lay ahead.

> But, oh, there was a weeping last night at the Homestead!
> The river ran red on its way to the sea,
> And curses were muttered and bullets whistling,
> And Riot was King of the land of the free

So an anonymous poet lamented in the wake of the strike against Andrew Carnegie's steel plants in Homestead, Pennsylvania, in the summer of 1892. Determined for years to destroy the Amalgamated Association of Iron and Steel Workers, management locked out its employees. These were largely skilled workers who thanks to their organization had maintained a decent standard of living, and, just as meaningfully, real control over their work, a kind of "propertied independence" in its own right. The lockout precipitated a pitched battle along the Monongahela River, first between a bargeload of armed Pinkerton detectives and steelworkers firing on the barge from the shore, and then pitting the workers, their families, and neighbors against the Pennsylvania militia sent in to shepherd scab laborers into the steelworks.

Here too, hostilities and mutual suspicions had accumulated for years and penetrated well beneath the surface of the work-for-hire relationship. Homestead, like so many other mining and steel locales, was a company town where nearly everything—stores, houses, transport—was run by the company, pay was often in company script redeemable only at such establishments, and the town was arranged more like military barracks than anything else. Yet the Amalgamated enjoyed real political influence there as well, one feature of this transitional moment. Many of the other, nonunion workers in the coke ovens and furnaces in Homestead and throughout the country's iron and steel belt were Hungarians, Poles, and other unskilled Slavic immigrants who were often treated with a kind of racially inflected contempt. In a *Harper's* article appearing months before the blowup in Homestead, they were depicted as naturally prone to violence and drink: "These Hungarians are the most difficult class of laborers to manage when they are peaceful, or to pacify when they are enraged.... They know nothing of American life or manners."

Others, however, felt differently. Some of the first wood-engraving illustrations of mill workers in Pittsburgh portrayed the dignity and danger of the work, and the pride shown by puddlers and iron molders in their skills and the control they exercised over the small-batch production operations. But it was precisely those skills and that competence and power to direct operations on the shop floor which Carnegie and other steelmakers were determined to eviscerate.

Plenty of newspaper coverage in the days preceding the lockout evinced a basic sympathy for the workers and an underlying skepticism about the company's real intentions. However dependent they were on the corporation, or precisely because of that overweening dependency, townspeople viewed the company as an alien body, a chronic threat to communal integrity. One Carnegie employee and town burgess explained, "We have our homes in the town, we have our churches here, our societies and our cemeteries. We are bound to Homestead by all the ties that men hold dearest and most sacred." A worker told the novelist Hamlin Garland, who came to visit two years after the confrontation, "The worst part of the whole business is this. It brutalizes a man."

While some clergymen, especially from upper-crust Presbyterian congregations, condemned the workers because "property rights are sacred," others weighed good and evil differently. From his pulpit at the Church of the Carpenter in Boston, W. D. P. Bliss condemned the Pinkertons as the "desperado hirelings of capital," and he wasn't the only man of the cloth to say so or worse. The Reverend Thomas Dixon Jr.— who would later go on to infamy as the author of a trilogy of racist novels, the most celebrated of which, *The Clansman,* was the source for D. W. Griffith's celebrated film *Birth of a Nation*—concluded that "if every man of them [the Pinkertons] were taken out and hanged the only loss to the nation would be the wear and tear on the rope."[28]

This was war, and mentalities on both sides fit the occasion. Recounting the fierce battle between the Pinkertons on the barge and their shore-bound enemies, one major newspaper described an elderly woman combatant: "This was Mrs. Finch, the leader of the Amazons whenever this dark dahomney land of labor goes to war. High and shrill and strong for her years as the voice of the lustiest fisherwoman who marched on Versailles..." The people had gone mad, "wild with warlike delight."

That sanguinary appraisal seemed confirmed shortly thereafter. Henry Clay Frick, a coal baron in his own right, had been put in charge of the day-to-day operations of the company (Carnegie was off vacationing at his castle in Scotland, although he had fully approved beforehand of everything Frick did in confronting the union). Not long after the company's victory, Alexander Berkman, a twenty-one-year-old anarchist, burst into Frick's office and severely wounded him, nearly killing the corporate chieftain. The young man would serve fourteen years in jail for the deed.

In fact, "propaganda of the deed"—acts of terrorism directed at royalty, prime ministers, titans of finance, heads of state, and industrial moguls of which the attempt on Frick's life was exemplary—remained an abiding if infrequently used component of the anarchist tactical arsenal both in Europe and America all through this period. This included the fatal shooting of President McKinley by a crazed admirer of Emma

Goldman in 1901 and culminated in the bombing outside the Wall Street headquarters of the J. P. Morgan bank in 1920. But however deranged and politically misguided Berkman's act undoubtedly was, it happened amid an atmosphere of widespread loathing for people like Frick; as a result, even an eminently respectable newspaper like the *St. Louis Post-Dispatch* or *The New York Times* condemned the "cold-blooded principles of supply and demand" that justified the Fricks of this new world in treating their employees "as a soulless factor in processes of manufacturing, like capital or raw material." The editors of the *Post-Dispatch* judged that while "three months ago Andrew Carnegie was a man to be envied..., today he is an object of mingled pity and contempt. In the estimation of nine-tenths of the thinking people on both sides of the ocean he has confessed himself a moral coward." Ultimately, however, the victory was Carnegie's. The union was destroyed. It would be nearly another half century before the industry's workers managed to stand up again.[29]

Andrew Carnegie would go on to become a generous-hearted philanthropist. He always professed his solicitous regard for the workingman (his father after all had himself suffered the indignity and material hardship of dispossession as a skilled weaver back in Scotland). Later in life, he depicted himself a wise and disinterested steward, holding his great wealth in trust, using it for the general interest as defined by his sagacity. While not particularly religious, he no doubt thought he had a "soul" of some sort or another.

So too did George Pullman, who, like Carnegie, thought he knew best how to ensure social concord. What a shock awaited him then just two years after the "river ran red" at Homestead and spoiled forever the delusions he shared with Carnegie.

The Pullman strike of 1894 began as a rebellion of employees in his carefully constructed model company town. Of all places, raw class conflict wasn't supposed to break out there. Pullman, Illinois, was conceived precisely to forestall that possibility. It was the country's best known example of how, by meticulous design, benevolent corporate authority might create an environment of industrial comity, insulated from the pernicious influences of urban depravity.

Trouble was brewing in paradise nonetheless. The town was overrun with company spies ferreting out any sign of unionization. Many residents considered themselves to be "camping out," with no sense of belonging or ownership in homes whose leases could be canceled on ten days' notice and for no reason. No one dared criticize Pullman or his company, nor was there any vehicle like an independent newspaper for doing so. "One feels that one is mingling with a dependent servile people" inhabiting a "benevolent, well-wishing feudalism," remarked one visitor. Then, provoked by the patriarch's decision to cut wages, lay off people, and reduce hours while holding steady on rents for company housing, all amid a punishing depression that had begun the year before, the town descended into the bitterest animosity.

By itself, that was shocking enough to incite press hysteria. More was at stake, however. The Pullman strike did not remain confined to the town of Pullman for long. Instead it became a gigantic sympathy strike conducted by the American Railway Union (ARU), led by Eugene Debs, against every railroad line that dared hitch a Pullman car to its line—or at least all those lines headed west from Chicago, since the conservative-minded railroad union brotherhoods kept the movement from spreading back east. Strictly speaking, the ARU organized a boycott, not a strike, one that nonetheless showed every sign of spilling over into local general strikes throughout the sympathetic hinterlands of the Midwest and west. President Cleveland, at the behest of the railroad trunk lines, ordered out federal troops to break it, ostensibly to ensure the mail got through. Ruling he had the right to do this, the Supreme Court made its own contribution to the era's minatory language: "The gigantic conspiracy of the ARU staggers the imagination...neither the torch of the incendiary, nor the weapon of the insurrectionist, nor the informed tongue of him who incites to fire and sword is the instrument to bring about reform." Mayhem followed, the boycott was broken, and Debs jailed.

For the future leader of the American Socialist Party, these events accelerated his ideological evolution. Once, during the ARU's earlier triumph over James Hill's Great Northern Railway, when the union won substantial improvements, he could still imagine an "era of close relationship between Capital and Labor...dawning"; afterward, "abolishing the wages system" became his ne plus ultra. As for the ARU, one of the first industrial unions that encompassed all workers regardless of craft, it became, briefly, the rightful heir of the Knights of Labor, a group that embodied the sentiment of social "sympathy" so characteristic of the long nineteenth century's tradition of resistance. But it could not stand up against this all-sided assault and died.

So, not long thereafter, did George Pullman. During the strike and afterward he had put his house under guard, evacuated the servants, and locked up the family's best dishes in a vault. After he passed, his family was so afraid that his corpse would be desecrated by enraged workers, they had it buried at night in Chicago's Graceland Cemetery in a pit eight feet deep, encased in floors and walls of steel-reinforced concrete in a lead-lined casket covered in layers of asphalt and steel rails soldered together and topped by a Corinthian column.[30]

Buried but not forgotten. The Pullman strike had been a spectacle of such fearsome gravity that it gave people like Henry Demarest Lloyd and Jane Addams cause to reflect. During the standoff, Lloyd told Samuel Gompers (head of the American Federation of Labor, who studiously and strategically kept his distance), "This crisis is greater than that of 1776 or 1861." Echoes of the Civil War would not go away. Jane Addams, a founder of the settlement-house movement, later remembered "the shocking experience of that summer, the barbaric instinct to kill, roused on both sides, and the sharp division into class lines with the resultant distrust and bitterness." What George Pullman failed to realize, Addams thought, was "that the social passion of the age is directed toward the emancipation of the wage-worker; that a great accumulation of moral force is overmastering men and making for the emancipation of the slave."

Maybe so, but others drew diametrically opposite conclusions. Welcoming the return of Admiral George Dewey from his triumph in the Philippines during the Spanish-American War in 1898, a New York corporate lawyer cheered the creation of a large standing army, seeing it as the best way to "show these anarchists and socialists that there is an armed force in this country able to defend property against the rabble."[31]

Before, during, and after the depression of the 1890s (which lasted four miserable years beginning in 1893), events like the face-off at Homestead recurred elsewhere with stunning frequency, lending the era an air of foreboding. And this was so without even taking account of the Populist insurgency rolling across the Great Plains and cotton South that climaxed in 1896, nor does it encompass the massing of armies of the unemployed.

Demonstrations of the unemployed resurfaced with each major economic downturn. In the winter of 1893–94, for example, ragged "armies" of the desperate gathered in various parts of the country, forty of them in all. (Eighteen-year-old future novelist Jack London joined one in California.) The largest commandeered a train in an effort to get to Washington, D.C., and was chased for three hundred miles across Montana by federal troops.

The most famous of these armies was led by Jacob Coxey, a self-made Ohio businessman. When "Coxey's Army" (more formally known as the Commonwealers or the Commonwealth of Christ Army) reached Iowa, the Northwestern Railroad banned the marchers from its line and threatened that if they seized a train the company would send a riderless engine down the track to collide with it. In the end, the army made it all the way to Washington, a "living petition" to Congress. It was led by Coxey's seventeen-year-old daughter as "the Goddess of Peace" riding a white horse.

In the nation's capital, the army lodged its plea for relief, work, and an increase in the money supply. (Jacob's son was called Legal Tender Cox.) President Cleveland wasn't hearing any of it, having already made his views known in 1889, during his first term in office: "The lessons of paternalism ought to be unlearned and the better lesson taught that while the people should patriotically and cheerfully support their government, its functions do not include support of the people." The army demobilized and left emptyhanded.[32]

The Blunt Instrument

Eventually, a double dose of corporate and state repression—including court injunctions, troops, police raids, union-busting lockouts, spies and saboteurs—wore down resistance. Between 1886 and 1893 state governors would call out the National Guard more than one hundred times to deal with labor turmoil; some called it "government by injunction." However, recurrent economic calamity, state repression, and the passing of the Knights of Labor notwithstanding, the labor question would not die.[33]

In 1892, just as Carnegie was locking out his workers in Homestead, a lockout of miners in Coeur d'Alene, Idaho, produced a similar bloody confrontation, as the silver miners confronted scabs, company guards, and federal troops rushed to the scene by President Benjamin Harrison.

Embattled mining towns were a common feature on the social landscape well past the turn of the century. Indeed, less than a decade later, Coeur d'Alene itself would once again be ripped apart as mine owners called on Idaho's governor to quash yet another strike by the Western Federation of Miners, this time carrying with it aftershocks that would resonate for the next decade. What happened in these obscure places— dreary, forlorn industrial towns like Colorado City or Cripple Creek— often went unnoticed except by those living nearby or when things got really out of hand.

Ludlow, Colorado, was such a place. The site was essentially a feudal demesne of the Colorado Fuel and Iron Company, which was owned by the Rockefellers. Stores, homes, churches, and schools, the teachers, ministers, and doctors, as well as the whole law enforcement apparatus, were run and employed by the company, according to rules no federal or state legislature had any role in formulating. There, in 1914, twenty out of twelve hundred striking coal miners and their families, living in a tent colony when they were evicted from their company homes, were massacred (some of them burned to death or asphyxiated) by the Colorado National Guard and private security forces (the Guard was in part made up of Colorado Fuel and Iron mine guards). The killings outraged the nation. President Wilson ordered federal troops to the scene. Congress set up a committee to investigate—it would condemn the company's "industrial feudalism"—and Rockefeller scurried to repair his damaged public reputation. But Ludlow was actually the culmination of an intermittent civil war in the coal fields of southern Colorado that had begun a decade earlier at Cripple Creek and continued for weeks after Ludlow (during which another one hundred people perished), a long conflict that was little noticed and soon forgotten.[34]

From the 1890s through to the First World War, the west seethed with social animosities chronically verging on violence. Those profiting from the extraction of the primary raw materials of capital accumulation to which the Rocky Mountains and southwest were especially suited treated its human capital the way it did the natural world: it was to be exploited until exhausted. Capital calculations didn't need to pay attention to the family, craft, and community ties that soldered together mining villages—not to mention their lost lives as independent farmers, prospectors, and ranchers, which made pit labor that much more insulting. The rough-and-ready renegade spiritedness of the mountain west and Pacific northwest made it ripe organizing ground for the syndicalist Industrial Workers of the World (the "Wobblies," formed in 1905). The Wobblies were active throughout the region, organizing miners (coal, copper, silver, and gold), migratory field hands, lumberjacks, teamsters, dockworkers, and others.

The group's insouciance, its readiness to jettison conventional contractual labor obligations, its on-again, off-again flirtation with industrial sabotage, its penchant for direct action tactics, and its contempt for the bourgeoisie's tort court mightily alarmed private corporations and public officials. After all, Wobbly leaders instructed members to "disobey and treat with contempt all judicial injunctions." (Indeed, the era was so pregnant with this rebellious spirit that even the far more prudent American Federation of Labor believed court injunctions against strikes unconstitutional—a violation of the Thirteenth Amendment's prohibition of "involuntary servitude"—and so considered it a worker's duty to "refuse obedience and take action whatever the consequences.") In turn, elites resorted to the most extreme measures of repression. These included vigilante killings, beatings, deportations out of state, and of course repeated arrests. In one notorious case in 1905, government authorities from Idaho conspired to kidnap three Wobbly leaders, including the IWW's charismatic founder, "Big Bill" Haywood, and transport them across state lines from Colorado. Their intent was to convict Haywood and his comrades for the murder of the former governor of Idaho in the aftermath of the Coeur d'Alene strike of 1899.

While the men were ultimately found not guilty, the case exemplified how overwrought class relations had become out on the industrial frontier. About the assassinated ex-governor, Frank Steunenberg, Eugene Debs had this to say: that the ex-governor, had "reaped what he had sown" in using force to quash the strike by the Wobbly-run Western Federation of Miners, and that American capitalists had shown themselves to be "gray-beaked vultures" out "to pluck out the heart of resistance to their tyranny" so that labor "may be stark naked at their mercy." During the trial the Socialist leader vowed that if the authorities dared hang these men a "million revolutionists" would descend on the state. President Theodore Roosevelt declared Debs "an undesirable citizen," part of what he considered the "lunatic fringe." Meanwhile forty thousand Yiddish-speaking garment workers marched through the streets of New York to protest the framing of the three Wobblies. Upton Sinclair, recently become famous for his exposé of the meatpacking industry in

The Jungle, predicted a revolution to "displace capitalism" would happen immediately after the 1912 elections.[35]

The Industrial Peasantry

Sinclair was right about the timing if not about the revolution. Between 1909 and 1913, a series of immigrant worker uprisings back east sometimes assumed the character of peasant jacqueries. This was almost literally the case among Slavic and Italian miners and steelworkers, fresh from their desiccated plots back home. Once here, they made up a despised underclass who vented at their new overlords just as their ancestors had done in furious fits and starts for generations.

Likewise, convulsive eruptions throughout broad stretches of the garment industry in New York, Boston, Chicago, and in smaller cities periodically paralyzed production. These flare-ups were already common before the turn of the century. Often these risings seemed to emerge spontaneously, set off by anything: a change in the piece rate or some abusive act by a foreman, a command to work longer than humanly tolerable or a preventable accident—or by general refusal to allow the relentless tedium, exploitation, and indignity of daily life in the dark and dreary warrens of garment manufacturing to go on any longer. Erupting for an hour, a day, or a week, these spontaneous strikes almost automatically enlisted the sympathies of neighbors, whole neighborhoods, and large segments of the ethnic barrios where the strikers lived (Jewish most frequently, but also Italian and various eastern Europeans as well). Often enough, they achieved improvements in the piece rate or some change in the pace of work or even something as elementary as a bathroom break. But these flare-ups proved ephemeral. When they died down, they left few if any permanent organizational residues behind. Time and again women, often young women and teenagers, constituted the vanguard of these outbursts.

In hindsight these mobilizations might seem to have aimed, intentionally or not, at regularizing labor relations through the creation of a trade union, sometimes industrial in nature, sometimes restricted to a particular craft. But these upsurges were both more personal and more universal in their desires, simultaneously about settling some immediate grievance and expressing millennial yearnings, religious or secular, to be free. So it was just as likely for strikers to quote scripture and swear biblical oaths of fealty to the cause as it was for them to sing choruses of "The International." The shtetl was dying, the peasant village collapsing, petty traders and peddlers sinking out of sight, but in part for just those reasons millennial moods could get a grip.

The Era of Anticapitalism

A culture of anticapitalism defined the horizon of what was then conceivable; it had become a common element of the atmosphere. An "uprising of the twenty thousand" in New York in 1909, which shut down the production of women's clothing for weeks, was explicitly conceived of by its mainly female participants as an emancipation movement. Like earlier mass and general strikes, it ignited the active sympathy and participation of other social milieus and movements: conscience-stricken middle-class consumers, social workers, the women's movement, and political reformers. If the final distillate of this explosive social chemistry ended up as labor unions — the International Ladies Garment Workers Union and Amalgamated Clothing Workers of America, most notably — that does not efface their origins as antislavery rebellions.

Anticapitalism nourished the fiery rebellions of 1912 and 1913 among kindred immigrant workers (mainly women and girls) in the textile industry, especially the operatives in Lawrence, Massachusetts (who won), and the silk workers of Paterson, New Jersey (who lost). They survived, if they could, on an average pay of six dollars a week, and could be expected to die twenty-two years before their employers did. Meanwhile, William Wood, who owned the American Woolen Company in Lawrence, traveled about in yachts and private trains and summered on his private 600-acre island not far from Martha's Vineyard. Even President Woodrow Wilson, otherwise deeply hostile to organized labor, was moved to note, "The truth is, we are all caught in a great economic system which is heartless."[36]

No doubt, all the insults and hardships nourished a profound skepticism about the good intentions of capitalism. It left these uprooted peasants and villagers adrift. Some still harbored dreams of returning to native villages and an older way of life. (In fact, among Italians, for example, about half of those who immigrated to America eventually returned home or made multiple round trips.) Open to the calls of the IWW to strike en masse, they preferred anarchists and syndicalists and other assorted radicals to their official union leaders. That is also why, as had been the case in 1877, 1886, and at other moments in the long nineteenth century, brittle barriers of ethnic estrangement and suspicion (there were sixty nationalities at work in Lawrence) dissolved in the heat of battle, why the cry for "bread and roses too" became emblematic of a movement whose desires could not be yet contained within the confines of "normal" trade unionism.

Here again, these rebellions aroused broad patches of the middling classes and bohemian intellectuals and artists to identify with and come to the aid of that era's "undocumented." These allies marched in the streets, cared for the children of the beleaguered strikers, opened soup kitchens as well as food and fuel banks and medical clinics, staged great public pageants to dramatize the strikers' plight, shared with them their own misgivings about "really existing capitalism." This counterculture was defined by its all-purpose assault on bourgeois order, drawing on Marx and Freud, Wobbly irreverence and anarchist audacity, ancient Greek pastoral and the criminal underworld, myths of African American paganism and ethnic spontaneity, as if they were all more or less exotic versions of the class struggle.[37]

A few years later, in 1919, just after the war to "make the world safe for democracy" ended, a war to bring democracy to the steel industry— the epitome of American industrial autocracy—again bloodied the steel towns of Pennsylvania, Ohio, and elsewhere. Slavs and Italians, Poles and Lithuanians, African Americans and Irishmen, in one of those extraordinary acts of social creation, momentarily transcended long-lived racial and ethnic prejudices and hatreds to shut down the nation's signature corporation, U.S. Steel. They defied its panoply of security guards, compliant sheriffs, mayors, and judges, its dependent newspapers and cowed churches, not to mention its overwhelming economic heft. And so again, as they often had before, employing classes relied on the mailed fist: thugs and police to shepherd scabs through the lines, rough-necks to intimidate and beat up strikers, court injunctions, blacklists, spies and provocateurs, the whole arsenal of rule by blunt instrument that helped make the long nineteenth century so extraordinarily fractious.

6

Myth and History

Eighty-five, bent, and nearly blind, as poor as the day she arrived there more than a half century earlier, Lucy Parsons addressed a rally in Chicago on November 11, 1937. It was the fiftieth anniversary of the day her husband, Albert Parsons, and three other anarchists were hanged by the State of Illinois for the Haymarket Square bombing. She was there to memorialize the Haymarket anarchists and to cry out against a more recent act of deadly violence, the "Memorial Day massacre" that spring, when Chicago police shot ten men in the back who had gathered, along with thousands of others, to demand union recognition at Republic Steel, a bitterly antiunion corporation. For Lucy nothing had changed. Such savagery would continue, she told her listeners, until capitalism was overthrown.

Lucy Parsons embodied William Faulkner's adage: that the past is not dead, it's not even past. In a country otherwise renowned for its historical amnesia, deep wounds kept memories fresh.

With each passing year, this atmosphere of hardening suspicions and conspiratorial paranoia grew more enveloping. The material and cultural abyss separating the "dangerous classes" from their social betters severed all communication, except the exchange of metaphorical artillery: incendiary hallucinations about "crazed offal" and "Slavic wolves" and "ungrateful hyenas" alongside fulminating denunciations of the

145

"Property Beast" and wits'-end anarchist hallelujahs for dynamite as the proletariat's best friend.[1] Tensions pitched this high reverberated from one end of the social order to the other. Was there no exit? Desires to overcome, to escape, to find resolution inflamed the imagination. Utopias and dystopias lit up the intellectual landscape of the long nineteenth century. Businessmen and bohemians, proletarian intellectuals and theologians, novelists and statesmen, agrarian radicals and Social Register aristocrats pondered, prophesied, and panicked. Taken together, they forecast some terminal blowup. How could society continue on in this state?

America the Exceptional

For generations historians and social scientists have asked a quite different question about the American experience: Why has there been no socialism in America? The question implies that there is something singular about American history. Something exceptional about the way capitalism took hold here, as opposed to in the rest of the Western world, seemingly immunized the nation against any substantial socialist-minded political movement of the sorts so common in Europe.

This is a worthwhile question. It has given rise over the years to many important insights: about the fissiparous impact of mass immigration, the way race relations have overridden class antagonisms, about how the early onset of electoral democracy in America made political parties grounded on class divisions seem unnecessary, and most enduringly how the extraordinary productivity of the American capitalist economy (partly a blessing of the continent's natural endowments, partly credited to the ingenuity of its businessmen) dissolved potentially abrasive social encounters in the bathwater of near universal abundance. Werner Sombart, a renowned early-twentieth-century German sociologist, observed that the American worker consumed three times the amount of bread his German counterpart did and four times the amount of sugar. On these caloric facts of the matter, he rested his conclusion: "On the shoals of roast beef and apple pie socialistic Utopias of every sort are sent to their doom."

Nor, many have observed, should we make too much of what everyone acknowledges was the exceptionally harsh face-off between capital
and labor on the shop floor. While legions of madder-than-hell farmers
managed to create a political party of national stature with numerous
victories to its credit, their industrial counterparts did not. True, local
labor parties or labor-backed candidates sprang up here and there and
now and then won elections; often the Knights of Labor were involved
politically, as in the attempt to elect Henry George mayor of New York
in 1886. Remarkable as it might seem today, in the early 1890s, the
mayor of Selma, Alabama, was a Knight. There was plenty of talk about
forming an alliance between the Populists and elements of the labor
movement, including the American Federation of Labor. But little came
of that. Even in its heyday the People's Party didn't do well in working-
class wards.

Generally speaking, the civil war on the industrial frontier never managed to rise to the level of a sustained, national political confrontation.
Crosscutting religious and ethnic divisions within working-class America
splintered the proletarian vote. The winner-take-all two-party system
discouraged mobilization along class lines into third or labor parties. Nor
did the trade union leadership want to strain the loyalties of its members by
raising partisan differences. Urban machines offered working-class constituents jobs and services essential to negotiating the hazards of the new economy. The Socialist Party did grow substantially during the first decade of
the twentieth century but remained confined to niche constituencies
among professional and small-town middle classes, mining communities, and certain immigrant working-class enclaves, especially Jews, but
also among Finns, some eastern Europeans, and Italians. The Wobblies
showered sparks everywhere, in the years leading up to and during the
First World War. Government raids, arrests, and deportations made sure
the IWW left few organizational residues behind by the time the war
ended. And many immigrant workers had little stake anyway as they were
planning or hoping to go home.[2]

Some issues — most notably the protective tariff, which industrial workers tended to support (along with their employers)—kept the urban proletariat apart from agrarian insurgents, who had to foot the bill when they bought finished goods from the east. In turn, agrarian calls to inflate the currency struck a discordant note among city folk, who worried that food prices would inevitably go up. The decline of the Knights and the fissuring and defeat of the People's Party didn't help either. So too, the onslaught in the courts and in the streets by the forces of law and order was devastating. What survived was a trade union movement struggling to establish a toehold within the framework of wage labor, one no longer inspired to abolish it. Ways of talking about labor shifted accordingly. What once was considered an all-inclusive category of "productive labor" (or something very close to that sort of nineteenth-century version of the 99%) came to be thought of as one among many organized social bodies.

Even minus the repression, some would maintain that inexorable mechanisms were at work foretelling all this. Progress, or so its believers from all points on the spectrum—from Marxists to ideologues of the free market—have argued, ordained the dying away of all these resistance movements. Populists, antimonopolists, and the Knights of Labor (even in some respects the syndicalists of the Wobblies), each in their own way sought not to abolish capitalism but to find room within it for the survival of petty forms of enterprise: farms, ranches, prospecting, small businesses, handicraft shops, shop-floor havens of self-regulation, cooperatives. Sometimes they managed to hang on or even triumph. But capitalism's tidal drift was in the direction of the large, complex corporate form best suited to engage in mass production and mass distribution. It changed the economic ecology, crowding out earlier species.

In the long view of things, so argue those who adopt a rather Olympian historical perspective that tends to extend across multiple life cycles, there were far more winners than losers thanks to this capitalist dynamo of economic development. Nor was this merely a material achievement: for millions swept up in the global flow of people and goods, the process was uprooting and emancipating at the same time. The road may have been a rough one, but it was an exit away from traditional forms of patriarchal servitude, indenture, slavery, guild hierarchies, feudal seigniorialism, and religious and ethnic stigmata and exclusion. Loss plus liberation: What is the sum?

A new slavery, a new freedom: that was the dilemma of the long nineteenth century. It created anomalies. So it is striking, for instance, that just a year before the Great Uprising of 1877, the Centennial Exposition in Philadelphia drew thousands upon thousands to celebrate the country's marvelous industrial achievements—the railroad especially—and its new cornucopia of consumer delectables. Amid all the tumult that would ensue for the next half century, people would also remain absorbed in enjoying, if they could, the new world as it grew up in front of them. They got by or they did better than that, which can help account for the country's exceptional immunity: namely, its remarkable political stability and so its missing socialism.

Persuasive as all of this might be, it does not quite capture the paradox of an allegedly orderly society living chronically on the razor's edge, where virtually every social stratum from the highest to the lowest dreamed of ways to escape the chaos.

Law and Disorder

Stable as the American political experience no doubt was compared with the European one, there were nonetheless decisive breaks in that equipoise. Three such moments stand out and they punctuate the long nineteenth century: 1860, 1896, and 1932. The first abolished slavery, the second promised but failed to replace tooth-and-claw industrial capitalism with a vision of the cooperative commonwealth, and the third succeeded in supplanting laissez-faire industrial autocracy with an American version of social democracy, or what might be called the Keynesian commonwealth.

Visions of a new order—one of "free soil, free labor, free men" in the case of Lincoln's victory; one in which mankind would no longer be "crucified on a cross of gold" had William Jennings Bryan defeated

William McKinley for the presidency; one that would chase "the money-changers from the temples of our civilization," as FDR vowed— are what made these elections so thrilling, so fraught, so feared by some, and so passionately welcomed by others. In all three cases, a general crisis of the ancien régime—disunion, a revolt of the producing classes, and the Great Depression—turned great expectations into real political flesh and blood.

So it might be worthwhile to reconceive the question about why there has been no socialism in America. On the one hand, compared with the class-inflected political upheavals that preoccupied much of western Europe and Russia throughout this period, culminating in the continentwide near revolutions of 1917–1919, the United States seems remarkably even-keeled. No land seizures disturbed life in the countryside. No soviets were set up here. Although a general strike did paralyze Seattle near the beginning of 1919, it stayed there rather than spread across the country, as happened a few years later in Britain. No Socialist, Social Democratic, Communist, or labor parties ran the government or won significant representation in the halls of Congress or even further down the political food chain. And while the Populists did get elected to hundreds of local and state offices, including governorships, and to the House and Senate, their triumphs were fleeting. Should we conclude then that America was indeed exceptional? Is that story of a long century of anticapitalist resistance in rural and industrial America, one fired by the existential trials and tribulations of primitive accumulation, more mythic than real?

Not if we take the reaction of Jane Addams to the Pullman strike as emblematic. Her anxiety about the imminence of civil war was echoed again and again all through this period by people from all walks of life— high and low, artists and farmers, preachers and presidents, Fifth Avenue matrons and denizens of the Lower East Side's "rag-pickers alley," anarcho-terrorists and Wall Street bankers, coal miners and steel magnates, hard-boiled journalists and utopian dreamers. Plaintive, angry, despairing, outraged, and frightened, this chorus suggests a different set of questions:

Why for such a long time was the country so infected with anticapitalism? Why did this contagion embrace both the countryside and the city? How could it be that a vast population of petty commodity producers, whose conditions of life normally left them in a state of localized, isolated competition—if they summoned up resistance to their victimization, they usually did so informally, tacitly, without programmatic or ideological clarity in prepolitical hidden acts of everyday self-advancement and resistance—managed to mount a sustained collective political alternative? How could they hold that together during the severest years of economic depression when "devil take the hindmost" was an instinct hard to resist? Why did social emotions rage so violently that armed confrontations between workers and employers in the United States were far more common than anywhere else in the Western world? Why did people feel obliged to characterize their social enemies in the most apocalyptic terms, such as Wall Street "devil fish" or anarchist "offal"?

Why did others—theologians, manufacturers, novelists, architects, social workers, engineers, handicraftsmen, and poets—feel driven to devise ways around the social conflagration they all saw headed their way, schemes that sometimes were and sometimes were emphatically not socialist, but were decidedly averse to capitalism as it actually existed then?

When we look back at that time and note its striking contrast to our last half century—during which the labor question and all the tributary questions it once gave rise to have dropped beneath the horizon of public life—it is hard to deny the profound transformation. To point out that back then most people went along to get along is not a refutation that nonetheless society was at a boil. After all, it is always the case that societies set off in some new direction—when those rare moments arise—largely through the catalytic behavior of minorities, whether they are elites or insurgents.

Utopias, Dystopias, and the Anticapitalist Imagination

The long nineteenth century witnessed the convergence of three ecological extinctions or near extinctions—handicraft production; the family farm and peasant agriculture; and a kind of urban family enterprise as familiar to fifteenth-century mercantile Italy as it still was in 1840 America, but which feared for its life just a half century or so later. That this multidimensional existential crisis happened alongside the promise of infinite Progress forced a reckoning with a future of which no one could be certain. It aroused premonitions both exalted and dreadful. Utopias and dystopias—literary, political, and social—marked the era and emerged from all levels of the country's crystallizing hierarchy. They were impassioned evidence of how disturbing and deeply unsettled matters had become.

Americans shared this hunger for utopias, political panaceas, and gloomy previsions with others in the West undergoing similar wrenching dispossession. Tolstoy romanced the peasant village, and *narodniks*, young revolutionary offspring of the Russian gentry, fancied it a pathway to communal living. William Morris revered the world of the artisan, seeking in its rekindling an end run around the dehumanization of Adam Smith's pin factory. The first half of the nineteenth century witnessed journeys of intellectuals and the pietistic to self-contained communal laboratories of the disaffected—Brook Farm, the Shakers, Oneida, the Moravians, New Lanark, and many other utopian communities. During the urbanizing/industrializing century's second half, the instinct to withdraw was supplanted by the urge to overthrow the new order of things, to replace it with something old and something new.

Mother Earth

In 1880, a decade before the Census Bureau announced the closing of the frontier, Henry George warned that the "fencing in" of the American domain was the most important event since Columbus. Losing access to the land, even if only in theory and in some future time, was profoundly disturbing, the termination of Jefferson's "empire for liberty" prematurely, generations before anyone had anticipated.

An antiurban animus pervaded George's work, a dread of the city's new impoverished "underclass" that threatened civilization. For just that reason, a single tax on land rent would allow for the resettlement of these dangerous classes out into the countryside, in harmonious, cultured communities of small-scale producers. Colonization, once the bane of the New World, would become its salvation.[3]

Even a down-to-earth institution like the Senate Committee on Labor and Capital was inundated with colonization proposals in 1883. Indeed Congressional investigations (as well as many held by state legislatures) convened to examine the fraught relations between capital and labor were held with regularity beginning in the 1870s and continued through to the eve of World War I. Such inquiries today would seem weird, but they serve as evidence of the incendiary state of the labor question during the long nineteenth century. These investigations contained much testimony and documentary evidence about mundane matters like hours, wages, and unionization. But they also became an arena for more far-reaching propositions and declamations, such as the land colonization idea, denunciations of the entire wages system, and calls for public ownership of the arteries of transportation, communication, and power.

This fusion of the utopian with the pragmatics of legislation supplied much of the era's moral and political energy. Marx, no fan of utopias, scoffed at George's single-tax panacea but still thought of it as a "first though unsuccessful effort at emancipation from orthodox political economy." In a society as protean as America still was, where what passed for the orthodox had only shallow roots, breaking through to the other side and not just in the intellectual realm became common if not commonplace.[4]

A range of working-class-based movements advocated land reform— meaning the redistribution or confiscation of concentrated holdings, as well as measures to forestall their future engrossment—as a core feature of a new political economy. The idea was not to resurrect some agrarian arcadia, but rather to invent a balanced economy of the industrial arts and farming, resting on a latticework of independent producers. As the Knights of Labor grew meteorically in the 1880s, this attachment to the land remained part of its outlook. Moreover, the Knights' ardor for establishing cooperatives was both a quite practical undertaking in dozens of towns and cities, and more than that. As the molecular substructure of the cooperative commonwealth to come, it was a form of tangible economic and social utopianism in the here and now.

Dyspepsia on the Right

A river of theocratic, humanist, academic, and technocratic literature, all of it carrying heterodox desires for a future at odds with the present, washed over the country during the 1880s. According to one report, "hardly a novel is published without its little contribution to the literature of the social problem, hardly an issue of a newspaper but has its leader on some phase of what, as the world is coming to feel, is the greatest of all questions, or some lamentations over the threatening revolution." Even the sober-minded American Economic Association proclaimed that "we hold that the doctrine of laissez-faire is unsafe in politics and unsound in morals."[5]

As verdicts went, that was tame, given the dyspeptic mood and urge to repudiate the new order of things before it had a chance to crystallize. Harsher fare was always on offer. And it did not necessarily come from the usual suspects.

From the pen of an outraged clergyman, Josiah Strong, came *Our Country,* a plea to "Christianize the money power." Strong was an avowed imperial racialist who thought there was "no more serious menace to our civilization than our rabble-ruled cities." He worried about "volcanic forces of deep discontent" and spared no invective in denouncing every species of satanic radicalism: "their god is their belly, free love, in all social arrangements...in other words anarchy—Away with private property! Away with all authority! Away with the state! Away with the family! Away with religion!" However, Reverend Strong acknowledged that all the conditions of the modern division of labor were debasing and impoverishing. They conduced to ensure a permanent class of demoralized operatives, so that America would soon mimic Europe, both as a sinkhole of moral degradation and as incubator of the anarcho-socialist contagion. Monopoly, Strong argued, was "one of the darkest clouds on our industrial and social horizon," which if not addressed would give rise to a "modern and republican feudalism." Nor did he hold much faith in democracy as a solvent of class antagonisms: "It is useless for us to protest that we are democratic.... There is among us an aristocracy of recognized power and that aristocracy is one of wealth.... Our laws and customs recognize no noble titles; but men can forgo the husk of a title who possesses the fat ears of power." Hope, if there was any, lay in the return of a cultured Anglo-Saxon, Protestant dominion over America and the world.[6]

Prognostications could get worse than that among Strong's conservative fraternity brothers. John Hay, once Lincoln's private secretary, went on to become one of the grand old men of national politics; during his stint as secretary of state for Presidents McKinley and Roosevelt, he is credited with conceiving the Open Door policy and pronouncing the Spanish-American War "a splendid little war." But imperial ambitions, he shuddered, might be spoiled by domestic unrest among the "dangerous classes," so Hay took time off from politics in 1883 to write a cautionary, dystopian novel called *The Bread-winners*, which forecast a nightmare of communist destruction. Around the same time, a less well-known author named Joaquin Miller published *The Destruction of Gotham*, in which a city is burned to the ground by a mob overcome with a kind of erotic madness. The eponymous metropolis had "a gorgeous shell... outwardly beautiful... but inwardly full of dead men's bones and uncleanliness." This novel sold a quarter of a million copies.[7]

The Dreamscape of the Left

From the other shore came a literature that was part exposé, part reform-minded, and part jeremiad about the fateful choices facing the nation. The Danish immigrant Laurence Gronlund's *Cooperative Commonwealth*, a piece of utopian socialist fortune-telling, still made room for a reconnection with the land. With a tincture of the anti-Semitism not uncommon in this genre, Gronlund promised his new commonwealth's "greatest gain" would be "the suppression of that talent, so peculiar to our Plutocrats and seemingly acquired by them with their mother's milk: the faculty of speculation.... The New Regime will, like the Man of the New Testament, lash the howling lunatics, the brokerers and the cornerers.... Cooperation and Speculation are strangers." The book was published in 1884, and its influence was still being felt a decade later, when Debs read it while doing time in jail for leading the Pullman strike. What the future Socialist Party leader liked in particular was Gronlund's emphasis on the need to depopulate the great cities and colonize the countryside as a way to restore the moral health and harmony of the social order.[8]

Far and away the two most famous literary expressions of the utopian imagination appeared as the 1880s drew to a close, taking the country by storm. Edward Bellamy's *Looking Backward* was published in 1888 and was soon challenging *Uncle Tom's Cabin* and *Ben-Hur* as the most popular book of the century (it quickly sold one million copies). Two years later readers were devouring *Caesar's Column* by Ignatius Donnelly (sales of a quarter million). Profoundly similar and profoundly different—Bellamy's a utopia, Donnelly's a bloody dystopia—both conformed to the moral didacticism that inspired so much nineteenth-century fiction. Both cried out against the gross social inequities, economic chaos, and raw class antagonisms that marked the age. Both floated on a sea of ethical certitudes and imagined a future of social harmonies resting on the values of small-town and rural America.

Yet in spirit *Looking Backward* and *Caesar's Column* were utterly at odds. Bellamy's was an upbeat book with a happy ending. His utopia, set in the year 2000, is a place of material abundance, universal enlightenment, and perfect peace, an urban idyll of technical wonders. It got to be that way not by rejecting Gilded Age industrialism, but by extracting and reorganizing its most promising features—that is, its scientific and technological achievements, its rationalism, and above all its aptitude for highly sophisticated and centralized forms of industrial and social organization. It was only necessary for the community as a whole (the nation)

to take over direction of all the great productive and distributive enterprises, at present irrationally left in the hands of selfish plutocrats. Then
the spirit of Christian fraternity, a living part of Bellamy's clerical background, would soon enough overwhelm the base instinct of individual
greed.

Caesar's Column was an infinitely darker book, whose vision of the
future was almost, if not entirely, hopeless. A degraded and brutish proletariat faced off against an oligarchy of suppurating perversions. One
side's horrific sadism was matched by the other's murderous fury in an
Armageddon of fire and ash—an Armageddon, however, in which it
was impossible to tell who represented the forces of good, who the
armies of evil. Indeed, that was precisely Donnelly's point: America's
urban and industrial civilization, organized under the auspices of a soulless financial cabal, had turned into an anticivilization, a moral disaster,
an organism so pathological it was doomed to a horrible death. The New
World was finished. It was like the Old World, only worse, having
achieved a demonic perfection in the technical means of its own immo-
lation. A saving remnant, escaped to a verdant island off the coast of
Africa, represented the novel's frail and solitary hope for a second chance,
a rebirth of the human family in the salubrious soil of mother earth.[9]

Because they were so anchored in the era's hybrid culture of utopian
pragmatism, both novels inspired political activism. As mentioned earlier, Nationalist clubs formed themselves in towns and cities all around
the country soon after *Looking Backward* appeared. Members felt inspired
by its vision to work toward an efficient and equitable metropolitan
order, one resting on the highest technical and organizational discoveries inspired by the industrial zeitgeist, but freed of the fatal distortions
introduced by the concentration of financial and productive resources
among a tiny handful of men. Bellamy's fundamental premise—that
industrialism represented the royal road to social well-being—was
shared by a whole family of reformers and revolutionaries around the
turn of the century.

Seen from the parched prairies of the west and the exhausted cotton fields of the South, however, the empires of Rockefeller and Morgan seemed infinitely more alien and forbidding. Ignatius Donnelly was a veteran of agrarian politics. Long before he wrote *Caesar's Column*, he'd served as a congressman from Minnesota, migrating among the Republican, Democrat, and various Greenback, Greenback-Labor, and Populist parties and movements. He was known far and wide as the "Prince of Cranks" and the "Apostle of Discontent." Soon after his dystopia became a sensation, Donnelly wrote the preamble to the People's Party, declaring war on the great satan back east.

Caesar's Column captured an end-of-days mood that a world was verging on extinction, that if the new order of finance and industrial capitalism was allowed to complete its work, a whole way of life—small in scale, robustly self-reliant, modest, literate, egalitarian, full of neighborly good fellowship, intimate with nature, civic-minded and pious— would vanish from the face of the earth.

The crushing depression of the 1890s—the worst of the century— unleashed an avalanche of utopian and dystopian literature of all kinds. Over one hundred novels of that genre were published during the decade. New worlds showed up in the bowels of the earth, at the poles, in the past—what if Revolutionary War soldier and agrarian rebel Daniel Shays had won? was the counterfactual premise of one, and in another the White House was the site of populist fable, where President John Smith leads the country to a socialist nirvana. Frank Baum began his series of Oz novels, which allegorized the titanic confrontation between Wall Street and the ordinary folk of town and country, reserving his hope not for the chimera of free silver but rather for the good common sense of heartland America.

These utopian writers were simultaneously attracted to the Populist movement. Henry Olerich's *Cityless and Countryless World* prophesied an extraterrestrial rescuer visiting a small prairie community and teaching its residents how his fellow Martians had built a paradise of "big houses" that contained classless "families" of a thousand people, along with a strict quota of factories, mines, warehouses, and cultural institutions. Trade without profit took place between these settlements. And Charles W. Caryl, a Colorado investor and mining promoter, described in *The New Era*, a play about a gigantic model city, the New Era Union of one million souls, a "city beautiful" comprised of seven class divisions, from common laborers to the generals who directed this utopia. Class lines were to be fluid; each class ministered to its own needs and adhered to its own obligations. Caryl went on to set up a real colony of the New Era Union in the mountains northwest of Denver. It lasted a year.

Caryl's was not the only "real" utopia. Cooperative colonies, neither communal ones like the pre–Civil War variety nor religious, cropped up here and there. Often enough they were sponsored by local Populist parties, as in Kansas, and aimed particularly at the unemployed. There were about a dozen in California, Arizona, Alabama, and Washington where ex-miners, farmers, and cast-off workers gathered. All fizzled.

William Dean Howells joined the utopian chorus. He was known, somewhat unjustly, for the decorum and gentility of his fiction. But amid the trauma of the depression and after the heartbreaking tragedies of Haymarket, Homestead, and Pullman and the futility of Coxey's quixotic march on Washington for jobs and relief, Howells published *A Traveler from Altruria*. It was a stupefying, abstract, didactic exercise, but a heartfelt one, in which the author barely concealed his bitterness beneath the cloying language. Prophesying a society descending into two armed camps, Howells had the novel's Russian revolutionary, of all people, invoke its ghastliness: "I had never seen anywhere such a want of kindness or sympathy between rich and poor.... There was no respect from high to low...as there [was] in countries with traditional ties and old associations." The new society of Altruria that emerges out of this holocaust does so gradually, moving through the ballot and methodical government takeover of the functions of transportation, communication, mining, and industry. The reign of "the Accumulator" is supplanted by the "era of Cooperation," in which the world of mass industrial sham and shoddy gives way to products of utility and beauty. Work once again becomes self-fulfilling and joyful. The natural rhythms and health-giving routines of small-town life replace the old world's great urban conurbations, pestilential holes of misery, disease, and piles of money. Altruria's simplicity of manners, dress, and possessions becomes the outward sign of an inner moral chastity.

Altruria was a land of perpetual sunshine. But fiction more in Donnelly's dystopian mood, matching the decade's ghastly events, also left its mark on what has otherwise come down to us as a fin de siècle costume ball. The same apprehension of irreconcilable differences, the same message of retribution and catastrophe, echoed from novels like Alexander Fuller's *A.D. 2000,* Ames Fiske's *Beyond the Bourne*, and Alexander Craig's *Ionia*. Premonitions of oligarchic capitalism mutating into a vicious totalitarianism continued to surface after the turn of the century, in particular in Jack London's *Iron Heel*.[10]

The Left Wing of the Possible or the Right Wing of the Impossible

Powerful undercurrents that mingled together the visionary and the practical also seeped into the era's nonfiction, as it first had done in George's *Progress and Poverty*. Henry Demarest Lloyd, the Chicago journalist whose reporting eventually led to his full immersion in the resistance movement against corporate capitalism, wrote *Wealth Against Commonwealth* in 1894.

Lloyd's father was a Calvinist moralizer and Lloyd himself remained under the influence of Christian socialism his whole life. Similarly inflamed by the Great Uprising of 1877, Lloyd did not share Henry George's night sweats about the lower orders. He wrote, thinking of George's anxieties, that "if our civilization is destroyed as Macauley predicted, it will not be by his barbarians from below. Our barbarians come from above." Like Howells a defender of the Haymarket anarchists, Lloyd was a zealous champion of the labor and cooperative movements; he ran unsuccessfully for Congress on the Populist ticket and sought to establish a utopian colony out west.

Convinced that "liberty produces wealth and that wealth destroys liberty," Lloyd anchored his faith in the mythos of the American Revolution. The commonwealth he fought to reestablish would restore those lost liberties, but do so by embracing the notion of public ownership of those essentials of everyday life whose possession by private interests was the foundation of a new tyranny. His book, full of the facts and figures of ordinary journalism, also evoked a promise of redemption:

> Nature is rich; but everywhere man, heir of nature, is poor. Never in this happy country or elsewhere — except in the Land of Miracle, where "they did all eat and were filled" — has there been enough of anything for the people. Never since time began have all the sons and daughters of men been all warm, and all filled, and all shod and roofed. Never yet have all the virgins, wise or foolish, been able to fill their lamps with oil.

But now finally the world "has reached a fertility which can give every human being a plenty undreamed of even in the Utopias." What stood in the way was "the 'corners,' the syndicates, trusts, combinations.... Holding back the riches of the earth, sea, and sky from their fellows who famish and freeze in the dark.... They assert the right, for their private profit, to regulate the consumption by the people of the necessities of life." The nation's democratic heritage was put at forfeit by this "gluttonous" elite: "The locomotive has more man-power than all the ballot boxes.... Beyond the deep is another deep. This era is but a passing phase in the evolution of industrial Caesars, and these Caesars will be of a new type — Corporate Caesars."

Monopoly for Lloyd, and for those thousands and thousands who mobilized against it, was the form in which all restraints of culture, fellow feeling, learning, honor, and tradition came to ruin, a world where "to get it is...the chief end of man." Monopolists had sprung "in one generation into seats of power kings do not know.... Power has intoxicated and hardened its possessors, and Pharaohs are bred in counting rooms as they were in palaces." To vanquish this new system was a moral challenge because it entailed attacking its central principle, "that strength gives the strong in the market the right to destroy its neighbor. Only as we have denied that right to the strong elsewhere have we made ourselves as civilized as we are." Only a restoration of ancient truths, that "the interest of all being the rule of all," that the strong should serve the weak, and above all that "the first being the last—'I am among you as one that serves,'" can bring back "the republic in which all join their labor that the poorest may be fed, the weakest defended.... Not until then can the forces be reversed which generate those obnoxious persons— our fittest."[11]

Elevated, redemptive language of this sort, ringing so oddly in our ears today, composed the sentimental sea on which the mass resistance to the trusts floated. Trust-busting for many became, in the words of historian Richard Hofstadter, "a way of life and a creed," in which the trust took on a satanic majesty. For just that reason the antimonopoly movement became one of a family of oppositional currents—the Knights of Labor, the Populists, the Greenback-Labor parties, the socialists, and the anarchists—fired up against the new orthodoxy, commingling their images of the good life. However different their social profiles and forms of protest, all were freedom movements inspired by visions of a paradise lost.[12]

Capitalism, Christianity, and the Church

Family members are not all alike of course. Some believed in a moral physics capable of reversing the fissioning of the social order. Circles of Protestant theologians evangelized on behalf of the new Social Gospel, a Christianity that would transcend classes and restore the communal concord of the ancient faith. They were prepared to stand up against the conventional views of mainstream ministers and theologians.

And such orthodoxy could be harsh indeed. Minister William Slocum's message to the National Conference on Charities and Corrections warned, "Indiscriminate alms giving is a crime against society. It saps the very foundations of the self-respecting home." Poverty researcher and charity reformer Robert Hunter noted, "The sins of men should bring their own punishment, and poverty which punishes the vicious and the sinful is good and necessary." In fact much of the religiously inspired charity reform of the Gilded Age aimed not at providing charity but denying it, finding most applicants wholly "undeserving."[13]

Washington Gladden, a leader of the dissenting socially conscious Christianity, felt otherwise. He indicted a way of life that reproduced a "vile, debauched...impure and besotted mass of humanity." Appalled by the slums spreading like an epidemic across urban America, he, like Donnelly, warned that "a horror of great darkness rests upon our cities." The Reverend Heber Newton foresaw in this social pathology a political danger, noting that it "won't take many panics for property to cry aloud for some strong man to come forth as a savior of society."[14]

Bleak forebodings demanded active intervention in worldly affairs to prepare for the final coming of the Kingdom of God. Walter Rauschenbusch, a Baptist seminary professor, urged that the "spiritual force of Christianity" take on "the materialism and Mammonism of our industrial and social order." How hard it is to imagine today in a country otherwise so preoccupied with its own piety and spiritual rebirth, churchmen exclaiming, in overtones of Marxism hard to miss, that "our industrial order...makes property the end, and man the means to produce it," as Rauschenbusch did. And he was by no means the most fiery and unforgiving of Social Gospel ministers. The millennial ambitions of the Social Gospel could carry its adherents a long way. Some, like George Herron, so emphasized the "social" part of the Social Gospel that they in effect became partisans of the class struggle rather than Christian utopians seeking a sacerdotal reconciliation.[15]

The border between theological and secular millennialism was porous. Anticlericalism, for example, ran through the bloodstream of the IWW. But even the Wobblies evinced a kind of religious devotion to the cause, what today might be called "liberation theology," whose core consisted of a transcendental valuation of the laboring human. Its kinship with the whole universe of anticapitalism was apparent at the IWW's founding gathering in 1905, where delegates called for the "working class administration of the Cooperative Commonwealth"; nor were they shy about invoking the "Hobo carpenter from Nazareth" whose dream "clothed in the original garb of communism and brotherhood continues to sound intermittently across the ages." Wobbly songs—their "Little Red Songbook" was widely disseminated and used—reworked well-known religious hymns, including "Solidarity Forever." Likewise, the eschatology of Jewish socialism amounted, at least in some instances, to a transliteration of the faith's messianic convictions.[16]

Still alive at the twilight of the long nineteenth century, in the 1930s, religious desires mingled with the labor upsurge of that decade, most notably in the Catholic Worker movement led by Dorothy Day. She believed that "the poor and the oppressed were going to rise up, they were collectively the new Messiah, and they would release the captives." Catholic workers were concentrated in the industrial Midwest and northeast, but Southern workers in that same era, mainly Protestant, were also up in arms. Here too, especially in textile towns, there was an organic connection between evangelical religion and labor insurgency, especially a Pentecostal movement that wanted nothing to do with the local church establishment, which invariably sided with the bosses.[17]

The Utopian Ambitions of the Bourgeoisie

Reform theologians and their following among the working and middling classes sought a postcapitalist form of Christian fraternity. There were others, however, among the haute bourgeoisie who envisioned such reconciliation occurring within the framework of industrial capitalism, and they were not merely hypocrites or dissemblers. Theirs too was a kind of utopianism, though of a distinctly bourgeois kind. It drew on the same apprehension of a society living on the edge that motivated their foes.

Urban life was a quintessential bourgeois experience. Naturally enough, these haute bourgeois forays into the future were often set in real cities or their simulacra by those who were both most invested in the city yet frightened and affronted by its raw abrasiveness. The most famous attempt at its fanciful domestication took shape at the World's Columbian Exposition in Chicago in 1893. The city's civic and business elite, along with its leading architects, engineers, and artists, deliberately set out to construct a "fairy city" of no practical import but of great didactic purpose. In a way, their product was not unlike Bellamy's futuristic Boston in the year 2000. Full of technological marvels, its core—what came to be known as the White City because of its stunning alabaster buildings—displayed an orderly elegance, shimmering white, illuminated by thousands of the marvelous new electric lights.

It was enormously popular. William Dean Howells thought that was "because the place is so little American in the accepted sense." Even Eugene Debs found it a healthful influence on the national character. In a utopian talk, "No Mean City," Henry Lloyd elegized the soul of the "Dream City," forecasting a real one that would liberate mankind from money madness and competition, and holding up the prospect of a Christian democracy of self-regulating harmony without violence, hatred, and sexual inequality—a safe haven for human labor conducted cooperatively, no longer despised but honored. The White City was a pastoral, yet it was surrounded on all sides by commercial exhibits, suggesting the peaceful coexistence of market society and its idealized antithesis. Among its showcases was a small-scale replica of the model town of Pullman.[18]

A fantasy, the White City was soon dismantled, its glittering memory mocking the suffering that descended over Chicago and the whole country almost the moment the world's fair ended and the century's worst depression began. And although the town of Pullman was no fantasy, it expressed, in starkly different form than the White City, the wish of an ascendant bourgeoisie to escape the consequences of its own triumph.

Pullman was one outgrowth of the hysteria provoked by the Haymarket affair, hysteria George Pullman along with his peers among Chicago's manufacturing and civic elite had helped incite. (Indeed, Pullman had first become active as a vice president of the Law and Order League during the insurrection of 1877.) The model municipality was designed to sustain the underlying values and social hierarchies of the new industrial order in a way that would appeal to its working-class subjects. There parks, lakes, museums, schools, and banks; a theater seating eight hundred and a library housing six thousand volumes; paved, tree-lined streets and company-landscaped lawns; a company church, sanitation services, indoor plumbing, and adult education classes; and, above all, decent housing together constituted an industrial arcadia. The town might be rightly considered a bourgeois utopia: a place that would combine social harmony, profit making, efficiency, and moral uplift; no booze or gambling allowed. Pullman confidently predicted that "thus a new era will be introduced into the history of labor." All the antinomies between labor and capital, man and machine, utility and beauty, wealth and commonwealth that had bedeviled American life for a generation and more would find their resolution out on the prairie fourteen miles south of Chicago.

However preposterous that might strike people now, it was widely believed, or believed in. Pullman became a tourist destination. A Boston newspaper called it "a Western Utopia." *Leslie's Illustrated*, a mainstream magazine, predicted that "all great employing corporations will realize . . . that the true solution of all troubles of Labor and Capital lies in the application of the principle upon which Pullman is built." The town's principle of planning from the top was celebrated as a kind of "benevolent despotism," a stewardship of the fittest. Even labor "experts" employed by the growing number of state government labor departments came to the town and applauded what they saw. One recommended it be "held up to the manufacturing employers of men throughout the country as worthy of emulation." The town of Pullman became the pride of Chicago. Not long before it all collapsed into rancorous chaos, a historian of Chicago boasted that "if the path in front of Pullman proves fair to the foot as its vista appears to the eye, then the enterprise sounds the keynote for the full and final chorus of concord between labor and capital. In that case its founder has, single-handed, built the enduring monument of the passing nineteenth century."

No one took the trouble to ask the workers and citizens of Pullman their opinion. But after all, that was part of this peculiar utopian conceit. Their habits and values were assumed inferior; they were not competent to judge—not yet anyway, not until they were transformed by the meticulously controlled environment installed at Pullman. The community's patriarch and his lieutenants would educate and uplift, making that human raw material more tractable and productive. A company vice president put the case succinctly, noting that the whole design and operation of the town "would improve their character as citizens and the quality of their work." Everything and everybody would be cleaner, thriftier, more orderly, refined, and dignified; in a word, more middle class, the class that is no class. The "fallen" would be "saved."[19]

Pullman was to function as a social inoculation, providing immunity there and eventually everywhere, against the squalor, ugliness, depravity, and acrimony of the industrial city. Soon enough similar satellite model cities were springing up elsewhere, established by manufacturers similar to the Pullman Company. Gary, Indiana, was in part conceived that way early in the new century by contemporary observers, although the fact that Elbert Gary, head of U.S. Steel, made sure a moat separated the town from the steelworks suggests he was hedging his bets. Of all places on earth, outside of Buffalo, Love Canal of later toxic infamy started out as a model city.[20]

Living utopias, these settlements also had about them the air of heroic romance so fitting in this age when titans of industry and finance supplanted generals and presidents and men of the cloth as proper objects of outsized admiration. Each such town was a display of dynastic preeminence. Here, in the guise of the meticulously planned settlement run from on high, the natural totalitarianism evolving out of the mechanics of the free market took shape. The tycoon, Napoleonic in ambition and self-regard, felt empowered by his own mighty presence to reorder and heal the world under his personal diktat.

Under ordinary circumstances, bourgeois society is not given to heroics; it's more comfortable with the pedestrian workaday spirit of the countinghouse. The era was not ordinary, however. Rather it was the birthing time of a new social universe. So, for example, a figure like George Pullman could emerge, not only in his own mind, but in the mind's eye of legions of worshipers as a kind of Supreme Being: one who seemed to combine the qualities of the engineer, the aristocrat, and the redeemer. He was after all called "the Duke."

Precisely this kind of industrial paternalism was the inverse of a society that purported to rely on the impersonal operations of the market rather than active human agency to resolve its social tensions. The quid pro quo in this frictionless invention is that the patron will care for his charges only if they are docile, leaving to him all power and rights to decide. But, inexorably, such a figure arouses a sense of irritating dependency, shame, fear, and in the end a growing sense that the authority is illegitimate. After the Pullman strike, Jane Addams would characterize the company founder as a "modern Lear," an out-of-touch dictator, blinded by his own pride.

Pullman and his ilk, men like Armour and Carnegie, practiced a philanthropic benevolence that bred in them a taste for submission and dependency, as well as a practiced arrogance and condescension. On rare occasions they might see this in their peers. Richard Crane, the Chicago elevator manufacturer, hated Carnegie, whom he called "the Dr. Jekyll of library building and the Mr. Hyde of Homestead rioting and destruction." His "paltry thousands" bestowed on libraries his employees would never have the time or energy to use were as nothing when measured against the vast wealth Carnegie's works devoted to producing armaments and the ocean of poverty washing up on the banks of the Monongahela. "If we would be sure of the permanency of our social institutions," Crane observed, something would have to be done about that, including an acknowledgment that often "the wealth of the rich has been wrung from the poor. They have been robbed of their rights."

Generally speaking, the long nineteenth century would end by ignoring this injunction. Exercising a control over affairs greater than German chancellor Otto von Bismarck's, according to Richard Ely, Pullman stood at the vanguard of a "benevolent well-wishing feudalism," a new order that promised to quell the distemper of an "Awful Democracy."[21]

The Potemkin Village of the Nouveau Riche

Feudalism, of a distinctly theatrical kind, was the utopian refuge of the upper classes. Mostly that consisted of a retreat from an active engagement with the tumult around them. Some, like Pullman or J. P. Morgan, were, on the contrary, deeply implicated in running things; Morgan functioned as the nation's unofficial central banker, but from a distinctly feudal point of view, famously declaring, "I owe the public nothing." Other corporate chieftains, like Mark Hanna, a kingmaker within the Republican Party, or August Belmont, who performed a similar role for the Democrats, became increasingly involved in political affairs. (Hanna once mordantly remarked, "There are only two things that are important in politics. The first is money and I can't remember what the second one is.") The two party machines had exercised some independence immediately after the Civil War, demanding tribute from the business classes. As the century ran down, however, they were domesticated, becoming water carriers for those they once tithed. Legislative bodies during this era, including the Senate, otherwise known as "the Millionaires Club," filled up with the factotums of corporate America.[22]

Far larger numbers of the nouveau riche, a rentier class of landlords and coupon clippers, however, were gun-shy about embroiling themselves. Instead, they confected a hermetically sealed-off Potemkin village in which they pretended they were aristocrats with all the entitlements and deference and legitimacy that comes with that station. Looking back a century and more, all that dressing up—the masquerade balls where the Social Register elite (the "Patriarchs" of the 1870s, the "400" by the 1890s) paraded about as Henry VIII and Marie Antoinette, the liveried servants, the castles disassembled in France or Italy or England and shipped stone by stone to be reassembled on Fifth Avenue, the fake genealogies and coats of arms, hunting to hounds and polo playing, raising pedigreed livestock for decorative purposes, the helter-skelter piling up of heirloom jewelry, Old Masters, and oriental rugs, the marrying off of American "dollar princesses" to the hard-up offspring of Europe's decaying nobility, the exclusive watering holes in Newport and Bar Harbor, the prep schools, and gentlemen's clubs fencing them off from hoi polloi, the preoccupation with social preferment that turned prized parterre boxes at opera houses and concert halls into deadly serious tournament jousts—seems silly. Or, more to the point, it all appears as incongruously weird behavior in the homeland of the democratic revolution. And in some sense it was.[23]

Yet this spectacle had a purpose, or multiple purposes. First of all, it is a time-tested way of displaying power for all to see—what today's academics might call "performing power." More than that was going on, however. It constituted the infrastructure of a utopian cultural fantasy by a risen class so raw and unsure of its place and mission in the world it needed all these borrowed credentials as protective coloring. An elaborate camouflage, it might serve to legitimate them both in the eyes of those over whom they were suddenly exercising or seeking to exercise enormous power, and in their own eyes as well.

After all, many of these first- and second-generation bourgeois potentates had just sprung from social obscurity and the homeliest economic pursuits. Their native crudity was in plain sight, mocked by many. Herman Melville remarked, "The class of wealthy people are, in aggregate, such a mob of gilded dunces, that not to be wealthy carries with it a certain distinction and nobility." As their social prominence and economic throw weight increased at an extraordinary rate—and, along with it, the most furious challenges to their sudden preeminence—so too did the need to fabricate delusions of stability and tradition, to feel rooted somehow even in the shallowest of soils, to thicken the borders of their social insulation.[24]

Mrs. Astor, the doyenne of this world, whose grandfather-in-law had started out as a butcher, wrestled to express how such tensions might be resolved. Her aristocratic pretensions scoffed at, she was accused of being an admirer of the French royalist cause, of deploying her drawing room's huge red damask divan on a raised platform like a throne. Her family's life was described by one observer this way: "The livery of their foot-men was a close copy of that familiar at Windsor Castle and their linen was marked with emblems of royalty. At the opera they wore tiaras, and when they dined the plates were in keeping with imperial pretensions." To all this, Mrs. Astor made this riposte: "I believe in a republic and I believe in a republic in which money has a great deal to say, as in ours. Money represents with us energy and character.... It were well if Europe were imbued more with the American ideas of money and power—I do not say ideals—that is another thing.... I have no sympa-thy with the establishment of a monarchy in France.... I am an Ameri-can...and opposed to the overthrow of any republic." This was pretty confusing.

Similar portraits could be and were painted of many of the great dynastic families and their offspring; the Goulds, Harry Payne Whitney, the Vanderbilts, and others were depicted in ways that made them highly improbable candidates to form a socially conscious aristocracy. Mrs. Astor herself was once described as a "walking chandelier" because so many diamonds and pearls were pinned to every available empty space on her body. Her relative John Jacob Astor IV, a notorious playboy, was chastised, along with his peers, by an Episcopal minister: "Mr. Astor and his crowd of New York and Newport associates have for years not paid the slightest attention to the laws of the church and state which have seemed to contravene their personal pleasures or sensual delights. But you can't defy God all the time. The day of reckoning comes and comes in our own way." Some years later Astor went down with the *Titanic*. Another member of the clan declined an invitation by President Hayes to serve as ambassador to England on the grounds that it violated the family credo: "Work hard, but never work after dinner."[25]

Ward McAllister, the majordomo of the Social Register's "400," took a stab at coherence from another angle. The problem was to somehow devalue exactly what it was that underpinned this whole social enter-prise to begin with: namely, money. How, without it, to define "society," especially as with each passing year there was more money sloshing about in great pools than ever before? "But now with the rapid growth of riches, millionaires are too common to receive much deference; a fortune of a million is only respectable poverty," McAllister said. "So we have to draw social boundaries on another basis: old connections, gentle breeding, perfection in all the requisite accomplishments of a gentleman, elegant leisure and an unstained private reputation count for more than newly gotten riches."[26]

Maybe so in theory, but the "old connections" were as new and ephemeral as yesterday's business negotiation, and "gentle breeding" for some didn't even include full literacy or numeracy but did include copious spitting; the "accomplishments of a gentleman" would have to embrace every kind of shrewd dealing in the marketplace, or else the pickings would be scarce. And the tides of America's volatile economy meant that no matter how high the sand dunes were built around the redoubts of "old money," they could never resist for long the onrush of new money.

It was all, as one historian noted, a "pageant and fairy tale," a peculiar arcadia of castles and servants, a homage to the "beau ideal" by a newly hatched social universe trying but failing to "live down its mercantile origins." But this dream life was ill suited to the arts and crafts of ruling over a society that at best was apt to find this charade amusing, at worst an insult. What was missing was an actual aristocracy. Commenting on that absence, the British poet and critic Matthew Arnold noted, "The refinement of an aristocracy may be precious and educative to a raw nation." He was particularly worried about getting past the vulgarity of middle-class life. The point, however, was a telling one also with regard to taking up a more disinterested responsibility for public affairs.[27]

Wall Street Brahmin Henry Lee Higginson, fearing "Awful Democracy"—that whole menagerie of radicalisms—urgently appealed to his fellows to take up the task of mastery, "more wisely and more humanely than the kings and nobles have done. Our chance is now—before the country is full and the struggle for bread becomes intense. I would have the gentlemen of the country lead the new men who are trying to become gentlemen." The appeal fell mainly on deaf ears. Many in this set were sea-dog capitalists, dynasty builders, for whom accumulation was a singular, all-consuming obsession. They reckoned with outside authority if they had to, manipulated it if they could, but just as often went about their business as if it didn't exist.

Bred to hold politics in contempt, one Social Register memoirist recalled growing up during the "great barbeque." He was taught to think of politics as something "remote, disreputable, and infamous, like slave-trading or brothel-keeping." It was a world there to serve a broader "economism" whose "god was its belly." Free market ideology justified, indeed demanded, this kind of behavior. "It had the morale of the looter, the plunderer.... 'Go and get it' was the sum of the practical philosophy presented to American young manhood." William Graham Sumner, a Yale professor and the proselytizer for social Darwinism in America, made matters bluntly clear. Asking in a book *What Social Classes Owe to Each Other*, he answered, bluntly, nothing. He insisted churchmen and others stop making the rich feel guilty for not alleviating the suffering of the poor. On the contrary, "It is not at all the function of the State to make men happy." The authority that counted in this new world was no longer attached to living personages like a king; instead it adhered in the purported lawfulness of the system of market exchanges. Political abstinence (except to take care of immediate company business) grew logically enough out of the ineluctable nature of the new order of things.[28]

This flight from the public arena struck many observers of the American scene. An English visitor, James Bryce, in a chapter of his travelogue *The American Commonwealth* called "Why the Best Men Do Not Go into Politics," noted "a certain apathy among the luxurious classes and fastidious minds, who...are disgusted by the superficial vulgarities of public life." Indeed, as the economist Thorstein Veblen, who used a slightly different term than Bryce's "luxurious class," pointed out, the whole raison d'être of the leisure class was to separate itself off from any form of work, manual or otherwise.

Some who gingerly ventured into the electoral political arena quickly scampered away disgusted by "a fine roll in the mire—unfamiliar streets, outlandish slums, villainous drinking saloons, Negroes trying to be white, speeches inane, humorous, half mad." Most belonging to this privileged caste kept their distance. Either they decamped abroad or kept to the counting house, where "business is religion and religion is business," leaving little space for the wider concerns that ruling classes need to take into account in order to rule.[29]

E. L. Godkin of *The Nation* was a perfect specimen of nineteenth-century liberalism—a believer in the free market, xenophobic, and hostile to unions and uppity African Americans. But he was a through and through political man. He sought in vain for an elite educated and cultured enough to function as social stewards, but instead found himself immersed in what he called a "chromo civilization." The rise of democracy had divorced political ambition from social success; Washington was a dull place and no passage led from there to Society.

Older mercantile and landed establishments from earlier in the century had given way to or merged with capitalism's new upper classes. In St. Louis, for example, the amalgam was aptly described as "one with grandfathers and no dollars and the other with dollars and no grandfathers." Together, although not without intramural squabbling, they concocted a world set apart from the commercial, political, sexual, ethnic, and religious chaos threatening to envelop them. An upper-class "white city" of chivalry, honor codes, and fraternal loyalties, mannered, care-free, and self-regarding, it was a laboratory of narcissistic self-indulgence, an ostensible repudiation of those distinctly bourgeois character traits of prudence, thrift, and moneygrubbing.[30]

Born into an age defined by steam, steel, and electricity, they attempted to wall themselves off from modernity in an alternate universe, part medieval, part Renaissance Europe, part ancient Greece and Rome, a pastiche of golden ages. The long nineteenth century had given birth to a plutocracy unschooled and indisposed to win the trust and preside over a society it feared. Instead, the plutocracy preferred playacting at aristocracy, simultaneously confirming all the popular suspicions about its real intentions and forming a Society that had forsaken society.

Brute Force

The self-imposed aloofness and feudal pretentiousness of the upper classes left the institutions and cultural wherewithal of the commonwealth thin on the ground. An indigenous suspicion of overbearing government born out of the nation's founding left the apparatus of the state strikingly weak and underdeveloped well past the turn of the twentieth century. All of its resources, that is, except one: force, rule by blunt instrument. The frequent resort to violence that so marked the period was thus the default position of a ruling elite not really prepared to rule. And of course it only aggravated the dilemma of consent. Those suffering from the callousness of the dominant classes were only too ready to treat them as they depicted themselves—that is, as aristocrats but usurping ones lacking even a scintilla of legitimate authority.

But what about Horatio Alger? one might ask. Didn't the universal faith in pluck and luck keep society sedated? The most famous intellectual defense of that position was offered fifty years ago by Louis Hartz, the Columbia University scholar, in his seminal work *The Liberal Tradition in America*. He argued that thanks to the lack of any serious aristocratic tradition in American society and politics, the country had always been locked inside a Lockean liberalism in which everyone more or less subscribed to the virtues of propertied independence and material acquisition.

No doubt the plebeian origins of a fair number of first-generation robber barons—men like Cornelius Vanderbilt, Jay Gould, and Jim Fisk, who bore their humble upbringings, rugged individualism, and readiness to defy convention as a badge of honor—encouraged heroic dreams of the same kind among a broad population of strivers. For Hartz, this discovery bred a kind of Marxist-inflected ennui about the prospects for social and political alternatives in an America given over to the pursuit of democratic capitalism. However, Hartz's view has greater traction in explaining mid-twentieth-century America (when Hartz wrote) than it does in accounting for the rolling earthquakes of the long nineteenth century. It was just then, when Hartz claimed that democratic capitalism achieved its stranglehold, inscribing a kind of capitalist homunculus inside every red-blooded citizen, that the country entered the era of the mass strike.

Yet in a way, Hartz was right. The American upper classes did not constitute a seasoned aristocracy, but could only mimic one. They lacked the former's sense of social obligation, of noblesse oblige, of what in the Old World emerged as a politically coherent "Tory socialism" that worked to quiet class antagonisms. But neither did they absorb the democratic ethos that today allows the country's gilded elite to act as if they were just plain folks: a credible enough charade of plutocratic populism. Instead, faced with mass social disaffection, they turned to the "tramp terror" and other innovations in machine-gun technology, to private corporate armies and government militias, to suffrage restrictions, judicial injunctions, and lynchings. Why behave otherwise in dealing with working-class "scum," a community of "mongrel firebugs"?

One historian has described what went on during the Great Uprising as an "interlocking directorate of railroad executives, military officers, and political officials which constituted the apex of the country's new power elite." After Haymarket, the haute bourgeoisie went into the fort-building business; Fort Sheridan in Chicago, for example, was erected to defend against "internal insurrection." New York City's armories, which have long since been turned into sites for indoor tennis, concerts, and theatergoing, were originally erected after the 1877 insurrection to deal with the working-class canaille. During the anthracite coal strike of 1902, George Baer, president of the Philadelphia and Reading Railroad and leader of the mine owners, sent a letter to the press: "The rights and interests of the laboring man will be protected and cared for...not by the labor agitators, but by the Christian men of property to whom God has given control of the property rights of the country." To the Anthracite Coal Commission investigating the uproar, Baer proclaimed, "These men don't suffer. Why hell, half of them don't even speak English."[31]

Despite this great show of merciless coercion and violence, this primitive elite was in every other regard—politically, morally, intellectually, culturally—unsure of itself and precariously positioned. Charles Francis Adams, himself a railroad executive, held this world in contempt: "A less interesting crowd I do not care to encounter. Not one that I have ever known would I care to meet again either in this world or the next; nor is one of them associated in my mind with the idea of humor, thought, or refinement."[32]

Ironically, it was thanks in part to its immersion in bloodshed that the first rudimentary forms of a more sophisticated class consciousness began to appear among this new elite. These would range from Pullman-like Potemkin villages to more practical-minded attempts to reach a modus vivendi with elements of the trade union movement readier to accept the wages system. But to begin with, this was a ruling elite that, Bartleby-like, preferred not to, until it had to.

Yet democratic protocols prevailed amid all the mayhem. The political arena, however much its main institutions bent to the will of the rich and mighty, remained ostensibly contested terrain. On the one hand, powerful interests relied on state institutions both to keep the "dangerous classes" in line and to facilitate the process of primitive accumulation. But an opposed instinct, native to capitalism in its purest form, wanted the state kept weak and poor so as not to intrude where it wasn't wanted. Due to this ambivalence, the American state was notoriously undernourished, its bureaucracy kept skimpy, amateurish, and machine-controlled, its executive and administrative reach stunted.

Moreover, the rhythms of uprising and repression encouraged a generalized great fear, which had as much to do with sexual, familial, and ethnic derangement as it did with the threat to conventional property relations. In this view of life, assaults on property were spiritualized and treated with a kind of malignant innocence as dangers to the moral health of society. Such a mentality was easily reduced to conspiratorial hysteria, racial insularity, and patriarchal bravado . . . as well as to feudal fantasizing. Every uprising, every confrontation, even daily doings in the mongrelized streets of the country's great metropolises, seemed nightmarish. They threatened a terrifying social perversion, a promiscuous mixing of the respectable and disreputable, and a kind of class miscegenation. Who or what was in control?

How hard to find a toehold on such shifting terrain. At one moment, pretending at aristocracy seemed appealing. But this purported aristocracy came of age in a culture saturated in the egalitarian individualism of its native land. Indeed it had presumably risen so high by disregarding the fixed hierarchies of a more deferential society. Yet that insouciance cut short attempts to produce and reproduce itself as an aristocracy. Inherently unstable, this amalgam tacked back and forth between a kind of imperial arrogance and democratic irreverence.

No society can live indefinitely in such a state, leaving the most vital matters unresolved. Even before the grand denouement of the Great Depression and New Deal arrived, an answer to the labor question was surfacing, one that would put an end to the long era of anticapitalism. Without intent to do so, it would become the antechamber to the Age of Acquiescence.

7

The End of Socialism

O ne can hear the footsteps of the Deliverer...Labor will rule and the World will be free." So wrote a young refugee from the Russian Revolution of 1905 to his infant daughter in 1918. Sidney Hillman grew up poor and pious in the Jewish Pale of Settlement in Lithuania, studying for the rabbinate. Then the labor question swept him away as it did so many millions of others throughout the West and even in the heart of the Russian autocracy.

Fleeing the czar's police, he ended up in America working in the garment industry. There he became one of the leaders of the great uprisings that paralyzed the rag trade in the years just before and after the tragic Triangle Shirtwaist Fire in 1911. By the time he penned these words to his daughter, he was the president of a fledgling new union, the Amalgamated Clothing Workers of America, run by Jewish and Italian socialists, that had managed to establish a robust presence in the men's garment industry. And the future seemed more promising still.

For Hillman and his comrades, for legions of others in and outside of the formal trade union movement, for many feminists and anti–imperialists, for those fighting against American apartheid or industrial autocracy, among ardent partisans of the Social Gospel scandalized by the established churches pandering to the rich, for people who hated the trusts and their threat to democracy and equality, labor's cause was a transcendent one. About unionizing to be sure, but also much more, it carried a messianic promise: if the proletariat could be liberated from the trials and tribulations of wage slavery, "the World will be free."[1]

Annus Mirabilis

Just a year after Hillman thought he could hear the Deliverer's footsteps, He/She arrived. Indeed, even before then, the Bolshevik Revolution had not only overthrown the czar but established a Soviet Republic in his place. This was an event of unimaginable inspiration in a capitalist world busy destroying itself. When the "war to end all wars" ended, insurgencies erupted most everywhere.

While the victors met in Versailles and tried to put back together again a world undone by war, two empires (the Austro-Hungarian and Ottoman) went out of existence. The Bolshevik Revolution threatened to overrun Europe. Factory seizures swept through Italy and France. Barcelona was paralyzed by a revolutionary strike. General strikes shut down Paris, Lyons, Brussels, and Glasgow. Uprisings spread to Norway, Holland, Sweden, and the newly hatched Czechoslovakia. The English government confronted a belligerent proletariat while at the same time fending off Irish Republicans preparing for civil war. Even the normally placid Canadians were in an uproar as general strikes shut down Winnipeg and Edmonton in the west and Toronto and Nova Scotia in the east. Early in 1919 a workers uprising in Berlin was crushed mercilessly and its leaders, Rosa Luxemburg and Karl Liebknecht, were assassinated (Liebknecht was shot in the back and Luxemburg's body was found floating in the Landwehr Canal weeks later). More successful if brief revolts happened in Bavaria and Bremen. Then Béla Kun, an inconspicuous radical Hungarian journalist, overthrew the Magyar land magnate and polo-playing Count Mihály Karolyi and created a soviet government in Budapest that lasted four months. A specter that had long haunted the Western world since at least the days of the Paris Commune had become flesh and blood.

The year 1919 marked the beginning of the end of the long nineteenth century. The leading capitalist economies of Europe were in shambles, physically devastated, mired in debt, demoralized. The chaotic rhythms of the street took over: the hot-blooded politics of resentment and revenge, of putsch and revolutionary insurrection. That once axiomatic faith in Progress, Reason, Private Property, and Liberal Democracy no longer seemed unassailable. On the contrary.

Fearsome and nightmarish for some, the risings seemed a harbinger of a world turned upside down, a pandemonium that would obliterate civilized life. After all, everything held sacred by bourgeois society stood condemned: the patriarchal family, private property, Christianity, the free market, parliamentary democracy, and, above all, individualism.

But for others the tumult was an augury of a new world. It promised to liberate humanity from poverty and industrial squalor, from self-destructive competition, racial and religious hatreds, war and imperial domination, and the exploitation of man by man. A new society of fraternal cooperation would nourish a new kind of human being, one no longer infected with the self-seeking possessiveness, envy, and will to dominate that seemed inherent in contemporary life.

America, in hindsight, might seem a placid place by comparison... but only in hindsight. Those alive in 1919 did not feel that way. Just as in Europe, deep-running social wounds bled onto the surface of public life. The seeds planted during the 1877 railroad strike and the armories built to intimidate future insurrectionists, the traumatic memories left behind by the bloodshed in numberless confrontations across the heartland of industrial America, the echoes of William Jennings Bryan's cri de coeur not to "crucify mankind on a cross of gold," the fiery call to arms of persecuted Wobblies, the exaltations and drear premonitions of the utopian and dystopian literature inflaming the American imagination—all of this converged in this fateful year, all year long.

In February a general strike erupted in Seattle. Even though Mayor Ole Hanson (elected with labor's support) denounced the strikers as

Bolsheviks and called out the Marines, the unions were actually a distinctly moderate collection of craft workers accustomed to coming to work in suits and ties. Decorum notwithstanding, the momentum of events soon led labor and its allies to set up a provisional government to assure carrying out municipal services. Although the strike was quashed five days later, people around the country were duly astonished that things could reach such a pitch of civil rancor.

Strikes large and small continued in an unending wave all through the year. They happened in coal mines (where there was talk of nationalizing the mines), on railroads, in lumber camps, on construction sites, among telephone operators, down in the subways, on the killing floors of the stockyards, even on Broadway. Each one seemed to harbor either the frightening prospect of social and political chaos, or an inspiring vision of general human emancipation. Taken alone, no one conflict warranted such reactions. And that is precisely the point. The times were out of joint.

After Seattle, two strikes in particular dominated this landscape of psychic derangement. In September, the police force of Boston walked off the job. Although these guardians of civil order—God-fearing Catholics—wanted merely to join the entirely respectable American Federation of Labor (AFL), every public official and every newspaper from Boston to San Francisco denounced them as "agents of Lenin." Commonwealth Avenue was compared to Nevsky Prospect in Petrograd. Lurid descriptions of a "Bolshevik nightmare" of terror in the streets became regular newspaper fare, even though the actual amount of looting and disorder remained remarkably limited. The otherwise timorous governor of Massachusetts, Calvin Coolidge, joined in the rhetorical overkill, refused to negotiate, and summoned the army and a volunteer militia of Harvard students. As the "savior" of Boston, he ignited an otherwise somnolent political career that eventually landed him in the White House.

Not long after the Boston police strike subsided, the nation's signature industry, steelmaking, became an inferno of vigilante terror as the steel companies and their political allies responded ferociously to a strike by their largely immigrant workforce. In obscure industrial hamlets across western Pennsylvania and Ohio, men, women, and children were beaten and jailed and cowed into submission. The strike began in September and raged through the balance of the year. By this time, an obligatory rhetoric of "red terror" poisoned the atmosphere.

Yet these allegedly Bolshevik steelworkers were made up largely of deeply provincial rural proletarians recruited from the steppes of eastern and southern Europe and the cotton fields of Alabama. There were radicals among their leaders—socialists, syndicalists, anarchists, Wobblies, and Communists; after all, at the turn of the century 46 percent of the delegates to the AFL convention voted for the Socialist Party platform, and in 1914 there were twelve thousand Socialist municipal officeholders across the United States. But most working the forges and foundries knew next to nothing about socialism or proletarian revolution. They were instead preoccupied with surviving this new purgatory of work life at the steel furnaces, so bestial and dangerous it is virtually unimaginable to Americans today.[2]

Hunting down radicals became a national obsession. Attorney General A. Mitchell Palmer (a onetime progressive-minded Democrat who favored women's suffrage and trade unionism) initiated a series of raids against radical organizations, begun deliberately on November 7, 1919, the second anniversary of the Bolshevik Revolution. His list of sixty-eight prominent persons allegedly holding "dangerous, destructive, and anarchist sentiments" included social workers Jane Addams and Lillian Wald and the historian Charles Beard. Thousands were arrested, headquarters were pillaged and wrecked, and posse-style justice prevailed. Hundreds of radical-minded immigrants were deported (including Emma Goldman, who, as she sailed out of New York on the U.S.A.T. *Buford*—dubbed by the press the "Soviet Ark"—with 250 fellow deportees, gazed shoreward and noted in melancholic irony: "It was my beloved city, the metropolis of the New World. It was America indeed, indeed America repeating the terrible scenes of tsarist Russia! I glanced up— the Statue of Liberty!"). When Palmer and his raiders were all done, they had discovered three pistols and no explosives.[3]

Vigilante terror ran alongside Palmer's official version. Wobbly organizer Wesley Everest, a lumberjack who had served in France, was cornered in the backwoods of Centralia, Washington, where he was castrated and hanged by an enraged mob of businessmen, American Legionnaires, and local thugs. Private corporate armed forces in collusion with local police and magistrates in steel country ran organizers out of town and herded intimidated strikers back to the mills or to jail.

Resistance, some of it violent, heightened the sense of final confrontation. Longshoremen in Seattle and San Francisco refused to load arms onto ships bound for Siberia and the White Russian counterrevolutionary army of Admiral Aleksandr Kolchak. In the bloodied coal mines and steel mills, Mother Jones (a fiery Irish-American labor organizer, a founder of the IWW, and considered by many mine owners as the most dangerous woman in America) rallied the strikers, declaring that "our Kaisers have stomachs of steel and hearts of steel and tears of steel for the 'poor Belgians.'" They were, according to Jones, "Czars" relying on the help of mercenary "Cossacks" to save their "slave" empire.[4]

Anarcho-terrorists mailed off thirty-eight bombs, hoping to incinerate the high and mighty, including John D. Rockefeller, Supreme Court Justice Oliver Wendell Holmes, and Secretary of Labor William Wilson. An Italian suicide bomber blew himself up outside Attorney General Palmer's Washington home. A house servant for Senator Thomas R. Hardwick lost his hand opening a package at the senator's home in Atlanta. Bomb scares continued through the year and into the next. The world's first "car bomb" exploded in July 1920 in front of the Morgan Bank at 23 Wall Street, where an Italian anarchist parked his mule-drawn wagon full of explosives. Thirty died, scores more were wounded.

Panic spread everywhere. There were hysterical calls for mass deportations. Plenty of rough-and-ready street "justice" was handed out to immigrants. A Connecticut clothing salesman went to jail for six months for saying Lenin was smart. In Indiana a jury took two minutes to acquit a man for killing an alien who had shouted "To hell with the United States." General Leonard Wood suggested deporting radicals in "ships of stone with sails of lead." A senator from Tennessee proposed shipping off native-born radicals to a special penal colony in Guam. Palmer denounced "the hysterical neurasthenic women who abound in communism." He worried about revolutionary heat "licking the altars of churches, leaping into the belfry of the school bell, crawling into the sacred corners of American homes to replace marriage vows with libertine laws." Evangelist Billy Sunday thought it might be a good idea to "stand radicals up before a firing squad and save space on our ships."[5]

No mishap was immune from this highly charged scapegoating, even the most improbable. A storage tank filled with 2.5 million gallons of molasses near Boston harbor exploded. Like a slow-motion tidal wave, forty-five feet high and seventy-five feet wide, the flood rolled irresistibly through the North End's streets, burying carriages, cars, horses, and warehouses and drowning people and animals. It took months for heavy-duty hydraulic pumps to get rid of the molasses. Horses stuck in the goo were put out of their misery. Naturally, anarchists were blamed. There was no proof.

Even New York City's Great White Way and Hollywood were infected. A strike of actors and stagehands in August shut down Broadway (and theaters in Chicago and elsewhere) for a month. Parades and street extravaganzas mobilized public support, including celebrity appearances by Eddie Cantor and others. There was a mass recitation of George M. Cohan's celebrated war song "Over There," which had been rewritten to highlight the unfairness of Broadway's businessmen. There was talk of replacing private theatrical producers with a national cooperative theater. In response Cohan—a major producer and patriot of the first order—challenged the loyalty of the striking thespians. Meanwhile, out on the West Coast, editorial writers, public officials, and religious figures warned away young women from a Hollywood they feared was becoming a kind of haven for bohemian Bolshevism, a place of loose morals and even looser attachment to the chastening regimen of family and hard work.

If the uproar had merely challenged the prevailing industrial and political order, 1919 would have been uniquely memorable. But the labor question interrogated all of American life.

Marked by a toxic chauvinism, the war years had aroused primitive fears about anything that seemed to threaten the distinctive Anglo-Saxon and Protestant character of the nation. Some mythic, organic "Americanism" might be lost. After all, the country was overflowing with aliens, immigrants from southern and eastern Europe of course—but, even more menacing, African American migrants from the South, headed north into unwelcoming cities and industrial workplaces. Bolshevism turned out to be a mortal threat not only to capitalism but to some more primal notion of what America was all about. It was a commonplace notion that "most of the hordes of immigrants who have been pouring into the United States from countries of Southern and Eastern Europe from lands inhabited by races impregnated with radicalism, Bolshevism, anarchy, belong for the most part to the lower strata of humanity."

Tragically, the labor question merged directly into the country's racial dilemma. The steel strike failed to humanize the industry in part because these impoverished and degraded workers didn't constitute a united proletarian army after all, the fears of their foes notwithstanding. They were instead "micks," "guineas," "Hunkies," "Polacks," and "niggers," whose mutual distrust and even hatred corroded their solidarity. The once despised Irish, now lodged at the top of the workplace hierarchy, thought of themselves as "white"; the Slavs and Italians couldn't be sure just what they were as they faced the contempt of their Irish foremen and gang leaders. But at least they knew they weren't "darkies." Even while the strikers were displaying extraordinary courage in facing off against United States Steel and the vast infrastructure of power it could bring to its defense, the strike became a theater of primordial tribalism, proving how impossible it was to separate the labor question from the race question. And African Americans could have no doubt they were the mudsills of the steelworker community, only allowed in at all to subvert the organizing efforts of their fellow workers as spies, as scabs, as people so intimidated and desperate they could be cynically manipulated.

On a summer's day that July in Chicago, a race riot erupted, larger than anything like it ever seen in America. Twenty-three black people died as did fifteen whites, while 291 were hurt. Twenty-six other towns and cities, including Washington, D.C., witnessed the same racial mayhem. Seventy-eight black men were lynched in 1919 and several burned at the stake, among them war veterans.[6]

Apocalypse then and there! The United States enjoyed no immunity. It too wrestled with a labor question that then had the power to call into question everything else. Nor was this belief merely the shared hallucination of extremists, of a marginal fringe of revolutionaries and counter-revolutionaries. If Sidney Hillman thought it imminent that "Labor will rule and the World will be free," so too did President Woodrow Wilson cable Congress from the peace negotiations at Versailles that "the question which stands at the front of all other questions amidst the present great awakening is the question of labor."

The Beginning of the End

Just a decade later everything had changed—yet on the surface nothing had. The country was suffering through the worst trauma in its history, bar the Civil War: factory occupations, street battles, general strikes, unemployment demonstrations, mine and public utility seizures by the freezing and desperate, blocked foreclosures and evictions, farmer rebellions, and anticapitalist political rumblings in response to the Great Depression made the 1930s seem much like 1919 or the most acrimonious outbursts from the Gilded Age. The language of public life was often just as overheated: "Tories of industry," "economic royalists," and "money-changers" faced off against "Bolsheviks," "nigger-lovers," and "Jews."

Moreover, resistance to the political and economic power of big business drew its energy from many of the same pools of hostility to capitalism that had boiled over periodically during the long nineteenth century. Small-town Middle America, clinging to what remained of its independence, still mustered up resistance to the predations of big-city banks and nationwide industrial corporations and retail goliaths. First- and even second-generation immigrants manning much of heavy industry still had at least one foot in Old World ways of working, marrying, raising a family, worshiping, and socializing. Their views of the world were not yet fully attuned to the imperatives of market society; it intimidated them just as it had their forebears. And it could also turn their intermittent rage into outrage, a moral leap capable of challenging the way the world worked.

Still something subtle but also profound *had* begun to happen. Joseph Schlossberg was a comrade of Sidney Hillman, raised in the same atmosphere of apocalyptic secular socialism. He would talk about the movement as the "fulfilling of a holy duty," and often invoked the "spirit of the sacred struggle." For years Schlossberg kept alive a kind of Old Testament socialist rhetoric—pristine, uncompromising, and martial in spirit, an eschatology of socialist deliverance. His keynote address at the Amalgamated Clothing Workers' founding convention was part jeremiad, part prophecy: "The ultimate aim of the Labor Movement is to bring the working class into its own, to transform the working class within a Capitalist Society into a free and democratic industrial republic.... Instinctively, the working class in this country obeying the dictates of their class interests hew their own path through the fossils of despotism, corruption, obsolete methods and ignorance...the Labor Movement, like a phoenix, rises from its own ashes." He went on to prophesy "universal working class solidarity and the end of the wages system."

Then, to an extent and in a way Schlossberg might never have anticipated, the wages system ended for millions. Moods grew more somber as the Great Depression leveled the economy. Bold visions of industrial democracy and millenarian futures gave way to a new emphasis on security and material well-being. Even before the cataclysm of 1929, a change in the atmosphere was detectable. J. B. S. Hardman was, like Schlossberg and Hillman, a founding father of the Amalgamated Clothing Workers and a tribune of labor's emancipation. But in 1928 he measured the vast time elapsed in a single decade: he noted that "the language that was used then no longer sounds familiar to our ears. The emotions that overwhelmed people in those momentous days fail to excite us today."

At the union's 1930 convention, Schlossberg proposed a more modest agenda than might have been anticipated just a half decade earlier: collective bargaining rights; a reduction in hours as a hedge against technological and cyclical unemployment; and unemployment insurance.

Hardman for one wanted to hold out. Although compelled to acknowledge that in the new age dawning, "many ideals of a former day appear to be devoid of meaning," he pleaded for their resurrection. Yet rhetoric far older than Marx, its moral injunctions, its illuminations, its psychological compensations, and its millenarian incantations sounded, to some at least, suddenly hollow. The metaphors seemed run-down, lacking sensual power; the idols were mortally stricken. If the cultural age of Marx and Bakunin, of the Jacobins and Chartists, of Debs and Sorel, of the Populists and IWW, and of the revolutionary general strike was passing away, unable to renew itself, a frightening indeterminacy loomed. What multifarious associations, symbols, heroes, villains, memorials, precepts, visions, oaths, and martyrs could ever provide the same social adhesion?[7]

Instead, a new culture—tutelary, contractual, possessive, mobile, and bureaucratic—had begun to flourish inside the union and would seed itself throughout the immigrant working class during the great social upheavals of the 1930s and '40s. It might be called bureaucratic modernism. Its accomplishments and its costs were historic.

What collapsed in 1929 was an ancien régime of industrial barbarism. At its base, millions of the rightless submitted with little recourse and less dignity to the autocracy ruling the workplace. Moral precepts and ideologies provided cultural ballast that helped make all this seem right and reasonable and even inevitable in a society which was on the contrary awash in democratic and egalitarian sentiments. A protracted era of primitive accumulation that depended on and embraced harsh social relations and gross inequities in the distribution of power and wealth encouraged this way of life...until it broke down completely.

A New "New World"

Civilized capitalism took its place. The New Deal Order has sometimes been taken to mean the set of reforms initiated by President Franklin Delano Roosevelt during his long reign. Many of these reforms had been incubated at the state level decades before his presidency: measures touching on child labor, hours and safety at work, minimum wages, tenement housing, and public health. Regulations of the food, drug, meatpacking, railroad, and other industries had highlighted the Progressive era in the decade before World War I. None of this would have come to pass without the chronic upheavals and impassioned anticapitalist yearnings characteristic of the long nineteenth century.

This was emphatically the case regarding the fiercely contested terrain of the workplace. Here too peace overtures predated the New Deal era. Pullman's experiment in town building and industrial paternalism had turned out to be a colossal blunder, but efforts to find a middle way never ceased. Around the turn of the century, the National Civil Federation, an organization of some of the nation's leading corporations, sought concord with the less militant and radically inclined trade unionists of the American Federation of Labor. A generation later, a business-sponsored version of industrial democracy known as "welfare capitalism" was initiated by such major corporations as AT&T, Sears, U.S. Steel, and General Electric. Corporate industrial democracy promoted "American plans" (so called to distinguish them from the tainted efforts at organizing workers by the era's suspect radicals), as an alternative to collective bargaining; these plans incorporated features ranging from profit sharing, bonus schemes, and retirement benefits to corporate medical clinics, cafeteria plans, lunchrooms, baseball fields, and water fountains and even simulacra of employee grievance machinery and company-created "unions." So long as the Roaring Twenties continued to roar, these undertakings fared well. Thus even before the old world came tumbling down, attempts to temper its harshness and ward off the worst were showing up at the country's signature businesses.

Still, the New Deal decisively turned the page on the long nineteenth century and its characteristic forms of industrial autocracy, laissez-faire permissiveness, social Darwinian amorality, and the mechanisms of primitive accumulation. It was either do that or follow the road map laid out by Andrew Mellon, the Jazz Age secretary of the treasury, who advised Herbert Hoover (the third president to serve under him, as one senator waspishly noted) that the way out of the Depression was: "Liqui-date labor, liquidate stocks, liquidate the farmers, liquidate real estate." That would "purge the rottenness out of the system. High costs of living and high living will come down. People will work harder, live a more moral life. Values will be adjusted, and enterprising people will pick up the wrecks from less competent people."[8]

Mellon's timing was off (today he might get more of a hearing). Back then, the New Deal shut the door on that "stark utopia." Its accomplishments distilled and nationalized impulses kept alive through two generations of resistance while stopping well short of the anticapitalism that had supplied their energy. Many reforms marked the new order, but the most "civilizing" included wage and hour laws, the outlawing of child labor, national recognition of workers' right to form unions and engage in collective bargaining, Social Security and unemployment insurance, and welfare for dependent mothers. Government regulation of banks and the financial markets as well as certain industries, regional economic planning and public works, forays into public low-income housing, and financial help for strapped home owners and farmers all helped put an end to the savageries of the long nineteenth century.

A new kind of capitalist economy offered a greater degree of equity between classes and an enlarged supervisory role for the state. It was underwritten by a Keynesian approach to monetary and fiscal policy designed to even out business cycles and especially to buoy up the purchasing power upon which a new economy relying on mass consumption depended. (John Maynard Keynes, a British economist long critical of laissez-faire economics and its moral indifference, had called for an activist government deliberately managing economic affairs). A phase of industrial capitalism seemingly on its last legs was given a whole new lease on life. Some would call it the American version of social democracy, some the welfare state, some the Keynesian commonwealth.

Bringing it into being was hard. Some in the inner circles of the Roosevelt regime — as well as veteran political reformers, social workers, urban policy makers, progressive congressmen and intellectuals, renegade economists, and sectors of mass-consumption-oriented and capital-intensive, advanced technology businesses — wanted the changeover to happen, but the old order was tenacious. As FDR confided to his treasury secretary, Henry Morgenthau, at the end of 1934, "the people I have called the 'money changers in the Temple'...are still in absolute control. It will take many years and possibly several revolutions to eliminate them."[9]

The Last Reveille

Creating this new world happened not only at the surface of public life — on the streets, in voting booths, on the factory floor, at picket lines and sit-ins, in legislative hearings, and at town meetings and assemblies of farmers. It was also made possible by small, more intimate transformations: in body language, in the grammar and vocabulary of everyday life, in eye contact where there had been none, by marrying outside the faith, by treating with skepticism the injunctions and prohibitions of elders, by insisting on the right to take a break to urinate even if the foreman insisted you wait, in the infusion of private concerns with public passions, in sensual feelings of self-empowerment, and in the dissolution of traditional identities and the fashioning of new ones.

None of what was accomplished could have happened without a welling up of popular outrage, organizational ingenuity, and courage. This ecumenical kind of bravery included the social and psychological courage to challenge weighty, coercive authority and generations of remembered intimidation, and the moral courage to defy ingrained racial and ethnic prejudices and social taboos, as well as geological deposits of self-deprecation.

What amounted to a secular great awakening left behind institutional, political, economic, and ideological legacies we are still familiar with. Indeed, many of them—Social Security, the welfare state, economic regulations, unions, deficit spending, labor laws, decent wages and hours, and unemployment insurance, as well as their filial descendants like Medicare and occupational health and safety and environmental protocols—we either take for granted or would like to see scrapped as a public nuisance. When they were born, however, they were ushered into the world by something less tangible but of enormous and rare tensile strength. They carried with them the aura of the extraordinary.

Exemplary above all of that spiritual upheaval was the labor movement. How odd. Unions, after all, are yet another set of tools useful in the trucking and bartering of ordinary commercial life. Today they carry the aura of narrow self-interest—or even of corrupted self-interest. During the era of industrial autocracy, however, forming them demanded individual and collective acts of sacrifice and fellowship, under the riskiest circumstances. Thousands not necessarily bound together by traditional ties of kinship, ethnicity, or religion nonetheless behaved as if they were fused by some new subatomic force just as compelling. The experience of embattled solidarity at auto plants, steel mills, department stores, and rubber factories; aboard ship, in warehouses, in locomotive and electrical assembly plants; in Southern textile mills and on the docks of San Francisco, driving long-haul trucks and reporting the news, making art and building dams, mining coal in West Virginia and packing meat in Chicago, was practical and exalted all at once.

Call it what you will, the labor movement of that earlier era was as much a freedom movement as the abolitionist movement had been or the civil rights movement would become. Had it not been so, millions would never have put life and livelihood, family and home, in such great peril. It's not that, given the Great Depression, they had nothing to lose; it's that they had everything to lose. That is why a kind of plain-spoken exaltation infused the experience and memories of those legions of the anonymous who marched, struck, and occupied the factories. A bedrock national credo had always held that freedom resided in the capacities of the lone individual. The uprising that gave birth to the Congress of Industrial Organizations (CIO) discovered instead that the empowerment of the individual depended on his or her "fraternal" intermingling with others in a common struggle for emancipation. After a historic sit-down strike in 1936 in Flint, Michigan, helped defeat General Motors, the most powerful corporation on earth, one worker recalled his own sense of liberation this way: "It was the CIO speaking in me."[10]

So it was for the invisibles all over the country. And that is why what they created was not foreordained, but instead was an opening up of possibilities. For a moment, the last moment in the country's history, alternatives to the prevailing order made their presence felt in public life—public ownership, radical redistribution of wealth, cooperative production for use, labor and government co-management of corporate affairs, democratic control of the shop floor, economic planning and public investment, rigorous trust-busting, independent political parties representing the dispossessed of field and factory. Generations later, their lasting collective creations—the organized labor movement and the New Deal regulatory and welfare state—seem by comparison paltry and withered, nearly lifeless.

But before we can reduce what happened then into today's quotidian concerns about decent wages and hours and fringe benefits, into those trade union institutions which seem weak and ossified, into those laws and agencies which for many constitute not much more than the alphabet of annoying government bureaucracy, it is important to reckon with the quite remarkable human material that gave birth to them. Moreover, it ill suits a society so given over to the pursuit of happiness as equivalent to the pursuit of material goods to hold in contempt institutions and laws that accomplish that goal at some level of decency for millions who without them would still live as their forefathers did.

Armed with the wisdom of hindsight, many argue there never were robust anticapitalist proletarian movements in America. They point to the divisive diversity of working-class composition along racial, ethnic, religious, gender, and occupational lines as fatally disabling. Never mind that the country experienced the most tumultuous and protracted upheavals against the capitalist way of things when those tensions were at their starkest and most abrasive.

What is undeniable is that the deposits left behind by that great freedom movement, whether initiated from above or below, no longer carry that same emancipatory charge. The frontier of anticapitalism, which had occupied a central site in the American political and cultural imagination for well over a century, closed down. Just as the U.S. Census of 1890 declared the western frontier closed and perhaps with it hopes of starting over, of "lighting out for the territories," so might a census of the country's spiritual makeup conducted sometime around 1950 have declared the frontier of alternatives to the way things were closed. Involuntary servitude was long dead. Wage slavery, at least as a tormented state of mind, was headed there. Peace was declared. Voluntary servitude beckoned. Whatever urges once existed to reach beyond a civilized capitalism, to replace the wages system of the long nineteenth century with something else, died away.

Death and Resurrection

Nor did those yearnings die a natural death. Their passing away was part tragedy and part by design, and this is the story of the convergence of the two.

Triumphant as it was, the labor movement of those years of uproar created—more than any other institution, public or private—a standard of living envied everywhere. In 1945, 40 percent of American families lived below the poverty line; only 44 percent owned homes; just 54 percent had cars. By 1970, 63 percent of Americans owned their own homes, only 10 percent lived in poverty, and there were as many cars as there were families. Not only did the economy grow at an annual average of 4 percent during the postwar era, but that growth favored the poor more than the wealthy. The bottom one-fifth of the population saw its income rise by 116 percent, compared with 85 percent for the top one-fifth. Spending on personal consumption rose from $195.6 billion in 1947 to $298 billion in 1960.[11]

The viability and longevity of mass consumption capitalism depended on that achievement. Sectors of the business and financial communities, oriented to and invested in mass consumption industries, not to mention the inner councils of the Roosevelt regime in and out of Congress, knew that as well as the labor movement. But it was the organized labor movement that compelled broad sectors of American industry still unwilling to engage in the new mechanisms of collective bargaining to nonetheless match the standards of living (wages, hours, vacations, holidays, pensions, health care, and more) that unions were winning for their members. These companies would rather do that than have to share other management prerogatives with the denizens of a once deferential shop floor.

An "American standard of living" and the forms of industrial democracy that made it possible and lent it a profound level of human dignity shattered the old order. But it also established a new one. From this time forward, all criticisms of capitalism from the left, no matter how militantly or defensively expressed, accepted the underlying framework of civilized capitalism installed by the New Deal. If that system failed to deliver the goods, so to speak, or violated the newly established elementary rights of working people, then it should be called to account. But not otherwise.

Moreover, the détente between classes enforced by the mechanisms of collective bargaining soon enough restored rights to govern how the corporation was run—especially how work was carried out on the shop floor—to management. This was after a brief interlude during which an insurgent labor movement had briefly but audaciously claimed that territory for itself. This new "social contract" was formally inscribed in postwar agreements in key industries, especially automaking ("the Treaty of Detroit"), which regularized cost-of-living wage increases and raises linked to productivity gains. Grander pretensions to actually share in high-level decisions about capital investment, product development, pricing, and other matters were abandoned even more quickly. In return, unions like the United Automobile Workers guaranteed labor peace for an extended period (such as five years) and with that a predictable cost and planning horizon for their management partners.

The historical logic embedded in the great victory of civilized over barbaric capitalism corroded away precisely those social and political instincts responsible for that triumph in the first place. Economic growth would become the solvent in which all those immemorial hard-edged social antagonisms of the long nineteenth century would dissolve. Progress had come to mean an ever-rising standard of living and a lawful respect for the rights of those who worked for wages.[12]

The material realities as well as the cultural beliefs and behaviors that once called such servitude, voluntary or not, into question were dead beyond resurrection. The good life now resided entirely within the near horizon of capitalism and its capacity to supply the goods. The pursuit of happiness, even if leveraged by social institutions like a union or government program, was ultimately something to be found in the private realm and through a simulacrum of freedom as material acquisition.[13]

Abstract historical logic, however, could never have carried such force all by itself. If the socially adventurous labor uprising became gradually less so, credit or blame must be spread around. Some, those most sympathetic to the larger crusade, tend to levy the heaviest blame on union bureaucrats abandoning the cause and becoming careerists or, worse, morally delinquent. But although true in some cases, that was probably the least significant factor in accounting for what happened.

Pressures mounted from all directions. The business community, its reputation rehabilitated by World War II insofar as it was credited with making the nation the "arsenal of democracy" and with running all the agencies of economic mobilization, was intent on restoring its political preeminence. While accepting for the time being the basic framework of the New Deal regulatory state and the essentials of the new "industrial democracy," it sought to curtail any further advance in that direction.

Unhorsing capitalism was never the New Deal's intent anyway. Especially since the outset of the war, the regime had largely come to agreeable terms with big business interests. It shed most programmatic overtures to universalize the welfare state and extend it into areas like health and housing. Structural reconfigurations of power relations in the economy, long-term economic planning, and state ownership or management of capital investments (commonplace during the war) were all offensive to the new centers of the postwar policy making, what soon enough would be widely referred to as the Establishment. Moreover, the "welfare state," for all the tears now shed over its near death, was in its origins in late-nineteenth-century Europe a creature of conservative elitists like Bismarck or David Lloyd George, and had been opposed by the left as a means of defusing working-class power and independence, a program installed without altering the basic configurations of wealth and political control.

As the center of gravity shifted away from the Keynesian commonwealth toward what one historian has called "commercial Keynesianism" and another "the corporate commonwealth," labor and its many allies among middle-class progressives and minorities found themselves fighting on less friendly terrain. If they could no longer hope to win in the political arena measures that would benefit all working people—like universal health insurance, for example—trade unions could pursue those objectives for their own members where they were most muscular, especially in core American industries like auto and steel.[14]

So the labor movement increasingly chose to create mini private welfare states. It achieved a great deal (and spent a lot of blood and sweat to do it): pensions and medical insurance, vacations, cost-of-living and productivity escalators, credit unions, and sick days—all that and more became the norm for a sizable segment of the American working class.

One consequence of that achievement was to blur the boundaries of class identity. "How American Buying Habits Change," a 1959 Department of Labor report, observed that it was harder and harder to distinguish working-class from middle-class consumption patterns, at least with respect to homes, furnishings, food, credit practices, vacations, education, and so on. This may have been the case for a rather restricted segment of the wage-earning, unionized population. Many remained deeply alienated from mainstream institutions and attached to more parochial, ethnic-based working-class identities. Nonetheless, blending of styles of consumption helped dissolve a consciousness of class into the amorphous universe of the middle class: the class that wasn't one.[15]

Erecting private welfare states through collective bargaining in core industry ended up aggravating the long-term isolation of the labor movement in ways it probably had not anticipated. Millions of working people were left out in the cold, especially those toiling in sectors of the economy like service and retail that would soon enough far outpace manufacturing employment. More often than not, these workplaces were occupied by women, minorities, and eventually immigrants. Labor laws championed by the insurgency of the New Deal had been written to exclude millions of them, not because the labor movement sought that result, but because business and agricultural interests were powerful enough to thwart the New Deal's labor-left. For these people working in what were then the economy's secondary sectors, industrial democracy and the American standard of living remained terra incognita.

Cold War Cultural Cleansing

A systematic ideological cleansing accelerated the tidal shift in the direction of the corporate commonwealth. A domestic "cold war," which began years before the international one got under way, was always directed against the New Deal and those circles most active trying to move it toward something resembling European-style social democracy. Even during World War II, but with immeasurably greater force right afterward, every element of that labor-liberal outlook—from racial equality to universal health insurance, from union power to public housing, from government regulation to economic planning, from welfare to women's rights, from academic freedom to free expression in the arts— was subjected to a withering assault. They were stigmatized as disguised forms of communism, indubitably "Un-American."

Many a struggle for equity and social justice went down to defeat as a result. Something even more fatal if less tangible happened: America engaged in a form of linguistic cleansing. The national vocabulary was effectively purged and with it that reservoir of social and political imagination dried up. Banning books, purging libraries of suspect literature, censoring movies, hectoring or firing radio and TV personalities, blacklisting writers, sacking teachers, defunding newspapers, all together created a climate of fear that chilled the atmosphere. Cold War anticommunism became a pathology infecting the homeland. Nominally waged on behalf of freedom, it emasculated it. Quickly it became too dangerous—verboten really—to think, act, and agitate across a broad range of issues, to use terms like "class," "class struggle," "plutocracy," "exploitation," or "ruling class," or even "racial equality," "public ownership," or "socialism." All of these and many more (with the exception of racial justice) had once been lexical commonplaces, part of the lingua franca of American life.

A culture so inhibited, engaged in a chronic self-censorship, loses its power to mount sustained resistance, to challenge vested authority— unless it became out of touch, as the Southern establishment soon came to be perceived. A state of permanent warfare (which as a state of mind is what the Cold War became) normalizes conformity, demands it in the public interest, is intolerant of deviation and dissent. Public debate grew increasingly claustrophobic, wrestling over distinctions without a difference. Were conservatives for business and liberals for government? Did that have much bite when the commercial commonwealth every day enacted their collaboration?[16]

The search for why the long nineteenth century boiled over with anticapitalist movements and ideas and sentiments, and the last half century has not, must measure the enduring impact of this long-ago moment of cultural repression. Language is, as a philosopher once put it, the "house of being." Many Americans—working hard, rewarded well, buying homes—were nonetheless left homeless.

Fortress or Prison?

For a labor movement compelled to circumscribe and censor its ambitions, there were other costs as well. To begin with, it split apart under the hammer blows of anticommunism. Its linguistic and programmatic purging was accompanied by a real purging of left-wing-led unions across a range of industries, including some of the movement's most dedicated cadres. The choice was to surrender to ideological intimidation or risk the wrath of a fear-induced political firestorm. The movement surrendered.

Its achievements in unionizing millions were historic. But to continue them was vital: either grow or lose ground. Cracking the "solid South," infamous for hostility to unions, and home (as the whole Sun Belt would eventually become) to firms running away from the threat of unionized labor, was strategically critical. The labor movement tried. But the attempt was doomed. The region's racial divisions were difficult enough to surmount. A one-party political system run by landlords, the labor lords of the textile industry, the mercantile elite, and captive Protestant churches also stood in the way. The anti-Communist persuasion that conflated unionizing and racial equality with communism stopped the CIO's Operation Dixie in its tracks.

Cut off from the South, the postwar labor movement inadvertently cut itself off from other pools of recruits as well. No doubt its own internal racial, ethnic, and gender prejudices must share the blame. They had always malfunctioned in just that way throughout the movement's history. Even though the CIO in particular was probably the most integrated and egalitarian-minded mass organization ever seen in America up to that time, the movement remained honeycombed with rules, protocols, and less formal dispositions that kept racial and gender hierarchies in place, blocking the arteries of its life-sustaining growth.

Erecting private welfare states and enlisting in the peaceable battalions of the middle class was not inevitable. Labor chose that path not because that was its first choice, and not because it was the corrupt one, but because it was losing its political weightiness and cultural puissance in the public arena. Here it was as much the victim of a pernicious state of mind, a deliberately perpetrated state of fear, as it was of the sheer political and economic throw-weight of big business.

Labor no longer appeared on the stage of public life battling for universal social welfare, championing the cause of all working people; it seemed increasingly concerned with its conspicuously better-off membership, which was also conspicuously white and male. The roots of today's scapegoating of unions by business, policy makers, and even ordinary but less protected working people go back to that. In our era, when most find themselves on the down escalator, it is easier and less risky to vent resentment at "privileged" workers, who in fact each day are themselves becoming weaker and weaker, instead of at those truly privileged circles who live well because so many others do not.

Tragedy lies beneath the triumph of the postwar era. In winning a fair deal at great self-sacrifice, dealing itself supplanted all those yearnings for emancipation, for something more than striking a good bargain in the marketplace. Yet without those liberationist desires there would have been no New Deal, only the old one. The end of what some have called the "proletarian metaphysic" disarmed the labor movement decades later, when rolling back the New Deal became the political fashion. The search for why the second Gilded Age went by without social upheaval and resistance, at least as compared with the original Gilded Age, must surely reckon with this, and much else besides.

It is time to explore the sources of submission.

PART II

DESIRE AND FEAR IN THE SECOND GILDED AGE

D on't tread on me!" is part of the genetic code of mythic America. So is it conceivable that over the course of a long generation, emerging during the last quarter of the twentieth century, the capacity and will to stand up against the presumptions of the powerful has atrophied? Has something gone missing, died away, or been reduced to some vestigial remnant that once upon a time invoked robust resistance to the usurpations of power elites?

This seems unlikely. Perhaps it's all an optical illusion, a case of political myopia. Just look around: the rise of the Tea Party all by itself strongly suggests that the "Don't tread on me" instinct is alive and well. Excoriating limousine liberals and know-it-all government bureaucrats stirs up hot political emotions. Establishments in both parties run from or curry favor with this right-wing populist belligerency.

Meanwhile, social movements from the left attacking entrenched privileges of gender, race, and ethnicity are now embedded in our political culture. Their victories, if not absolute, cause those reluctant to give up these old forms of domination to seek cover, apologize, or simply deny that their behavior means what common sense plainly tells us it means. Immigrants living in the shadows of semilegality, discrimination, and exploitation mobilize for their human and political rights. A passion for social justice animates NGOs and elements of the religious world. Grassroots community organizations blanket the country, and even a president is proud to have worked for one.

True, wars abroad drone on endlessly. Still, they do elicit fitful, episodic opposition. Corporations fouling the biosphere arouse chronic anxiety, doomsday prophecies, and occasional uproar. It is entirely possible to tour certain zones of the worldwide web and come away believing the country is boiling over with rage directed at war makers, bankers, and profiteers, that the status quo can't hold on much longer. All in all, the country remains a turbulent place. So why talk about acquiescence?

Furthermore, if today's bankers, corporate muck-a-mucks and their political enablers can perpetrate wrack and ruin and emerge pretty much unscathed, what else is new? We might like to imagine a heritage of popular combativeness in confronting the high and mighty, and memorialize heroic challenges by the "masses to the classes." In the soberer light of the country's real history, however, perhaps that is a fairy tale.

There are indeed serious objections to the idea that we have been living through an era of surrender.

Surrender to whom? While American culture has always been acutely allergic to any intimation that the country might be bedeviled by the Old World's class struggles, nonetheless something resembling a "ruling class" did rear its head now and then. There they were in plain sight: Loyalist aristocrats, the slaveocracy, robber barons, moneycrats, Tories of industry, the money trust, economic royalists, the Establishment, and other presumptive potentates did seem to exercise a hard-to-miss overlordship. You could usually distinguish them by their social breeding or education, or the way they talked and dressed, or by where they lived and whom they married and associated with, or by what they believed, and, most of all, by their wealth and their easy access to the instruments of political wherewithal, although these were not foolproof indicators. They might be admired and emulated, or loathed and their dominance challenged, but there they stood—faintly exotic, faintly alien American versions of a ruling class.

But then they vanished, dissolved into the polymorphous flux of postindustrial America. Can we any longer discern the profile of a ruling elite? After all, modern American consumer capitalism is irreverent to the core. It disrespects every established rank and order as "so yesterday," holds up to ironic mockery all vestiges of ascribed authority and tradition, scorns the old-fashioned unless it can repackage it ingeniously as nostalgia, as something newly and stylishly old. If our titans of industry and finance dress up like cowboys and construction workers, if they mimic the accents of good ole boys, if they are only one generation removed—if even that—from their roots in middle-class suburbia and no-name state colleges, is there any way of telling the difference between a "populist" ubermensch and the rest of us? Does it make sense to claim that we have been suffering from osteoporosis of the political backbone if the whole of society has become one gelatinous invertebrate mass? Under these circumstances, zeroing in on the powers that be is harder than pinning down the location and velocity of a subatomic particle, a quixotic crusade at best. Even if armies of resistance existed and mobilized for action, they might still have to ask "which way to the Winter Palace?"

If our times are to be singled out as "unnaturally" submissive, it is first of all essential to settle on exactly what's meant by acquiescence. There is the *1984* version and the *Brave New World* version. The first depends on brute mechanisms of intimidation, coercion, and studied deceit, physical and spiritual. The second relies on self-enslavement, where people come to embrace their own oppression, wallow in their own passivity, relish trivial distractions, and are pleasured into inertness, succumbing by choice. Is either of these scenarios apt today? Both perhaps?

Even if we acknowledge that the United States has in past times exhibited a penchant for notably violent social conflict, martial repression, and callous exploitation, certainly those overt forms of coercion have subsided substantially in more recent periods. The bloody triumph of the civil rights movement in the mid-twentieth century put an end to all that. America is now a democracy that behaves for the most part civilly, not as a bully (not here at home anyway). Yet might it be that, like a hide-and-seek ruling class, rumors about the dying away of fear as a mode of running things are greatly exaggerated? The politics of fear—the *1984* kind of acquiescence—may live a subterranean existence, under the radar but distorting the lives of multitudes. If millions of trees fall in the forest but no one notices, someone nevertheless may be wielding an ax.

What about that other way of giving in? This would include everything from self-administered anesthesia to the crafting of new forms of cultural legitimacy without which elites may find it too hard to get their way. Addiction to the multifarious delights of consumer culture, for example—from electronic gadgetry to crystal meth, from channel surfing to sugar-injected fast food, from buffo housoleums to logo-infested T-shirts—functions after all as a kind of deliverance, a part of daily life and an escape from it.

But it's a peculiar deliverance, an emancipation of the imaginary and the libidinal whose thrills and dreaminess are prefabricated in the factories and marketing ateliers of modern industry. Its pleasures seem compelled. So the emancipation it offers might be called oxymoronic, a liberation that happens strictly in private, that veers away from confronting the obsidian structures of social power and domination as they actually exist in the "outside" world. Maddeningly too, each "emancipator" comes and goes with frustrating frequency. Each liberating "high" has a short life expectancy and demands so much chronic refreshening it can feel enslaving. Yet and still, this is our realm of free will. We have a choice. We can always choose brand X. If this be acquiescence, why worry?

Or has some alchemical combination of *1984* and *Brave New World* ensured us a deeper domestic tranquility beneath the surface of our everyday political raucousness? The founders of the Republic wouldn't have had this particular psycho-political chemistry in mind, of course, but they were concerned with questions of authority, legitimacy, and "domestic tranquility." They pondered how to reconcile customary practices of social and political deference to disinterested elites, behavior to which in many ways they were still attached, with the breakthrough notion of popular sovereignty.

Since those formative days, modern capitalist societies, including the United States, have arguably remained libertarian and authoritarian at the same time. But the mechanisms of stability and coherence have changed. Of late, they invite the peculiar forms of self-expression made available through the "free" market while relying on internalized self-restraints and public ideologies—"family values" or "America is number one" revanchist chauvinism, for instance—to sedate the caffeinated energies of excessive individualism. Otherwise, that seductive world of the marketplace would unleash a torrent of centrifugal desires that, left unchecked, would end in anarchic nihilism.

In the end, to acquiesce might mean only that while the people may not actually rule, they grant, tacitly at least, that those who do are doing a creditable job and are running things more or less in the general interest. Over vast stretches of time, this is the normal state of affairs in many societies—how could they go on otherwise? Perhaps then, it is misleading to deploy the word "acquiescence." It conjures up images of the bended knee, when all we may have been witnessing here in America over the last generation is that mundane practice of going along to get along.

Business as usual in any society fissured by social cleavages, as most would admit ours is, means living day to day with submerged tensions. Various forms of surface compliance conceal instincts of the opposite sort. Public opinion polls, for example, regularly record sentiments in favor of higher levels of universal social insurance, redistributive taxation, workplace justice, and regulation of big business than the political system rarely comes close to acknowledging, much less doing anything about. This suggests that while the United States is formally democratic and egalitarian, people defer to the hegemony of wealth. Compliance is forthcoming (sometimes concealing a quiet resentment), either on pain of penalty (the corporation will outsource work abroad, flee to a tax-friendlier locale, fire troublemakers, and so on) or out of a genuine and indigenous belief in the efficacy and moral superiority of the business system itself. If what seems to be quiescence hides a muted discontent, perhaps we should not diagnose our current moment and recent past as particularly anemic.

All of these objections, caveats, qualifications, and ambiguities run counter to an allegation about an Age of Acquiescence. They carry weight, and they can be more definitely measured only against what used to pass for normal. Many would agree that there was a time, a whole epoch even, when the sinews of resistance were tougher and more resilient, and when the popular imagination audaciously leapt beyond the boundaries of business as usual. Great waves of social upheaval regularly rolled across the landscape of American life. Their reverberations lent public affairs a frisson we no longer sense. If there was such an era running through that long nineteenth century, it is dead. What killed it?

Fables of Freedom

Despots rely mainly on fear. They are masters of the means of coercion and intimidation, physical as well as psychological. Even the most brutal tyranny, however, seeks some measure of consent and for a time may win some. People may admire the tyrant for his frankness and audacity, his refusal to temporize—the way he embodies qualities they wish they could find in themselves and can thrill to vicariously. In the end, though, despots rule by blunt instrument.

Market democracies operate quite differently, and the element of consent is essential. This is not meant to imply that in these societies the politics of fear ceases to operate. On the contrary, it continues and may even flourish. But, as the economist Amartya Sen has noted, the "most blatant forms of inequality and exploitation survive in the world through making allies of the deprived and exploited.... Discontent is replaced by acceptance, hopeless rebellion by conformist quiet and...suffering by cheerful endurance."[1]

If the endurance is a "cheerful" one, that is because capitalist societies promise something a great deal more than the ability to endure. They begin as liberation movements offering deliverance from the material privations, as well as from the social and political constraints of premodern life that have frustrated the desires and ambitions of everyman, reserving them for privileged castes of blood and position. Freedom is the promissory note issued in return for willing assent. American democratic capitalism especially has made good on that promise again and again over generations. Free to move, free to till the land and keep its fruits, free to start a business, free to work (or not work), free to speak, worship, vote, and write, free to rise (or fall), free to enjoy the good life.

Material abundance in particular has for more than a century represented the most compelling form of freedom on offer. It is the boast of both political parties that they, uniquely, can provide it. Freedom from want, the prospect of economic security, was after all the watchword of New Deal liberalism; similarly, economic growth and middle-class material well-being constituted the core of the mid-1990s Republican Contract with America.

Social commentators and scholars have long credited the country's political and social stability to its remarkable capacity to provide a standard of living that until recently was unprecedented anywhere in the world. Around the turn of the twentieth century, Werner Sombart made his famous observation about socialism in America foundering on "shoals of roast beef." And at midcentury, the distinguished American historian David Potter argued that America as a "people of plenty" had eluded, thanks to the cornucopia produced by its marvelous economic machinery, what might otherwise have been bitter political and social acrimony arising out of the abrasiveness of class inequities.[2]

Miracles followed. Wage labor, once considered an incipient new form of slavery, became instead an avenue to freedom. The struggle for higher wages, and through them access to the American largesse by even the humblest worker, promised its own kind of emancipation, if not the anticapitalist one dreamed of during the long nineteenth century. This proved true enough for many if not everybody.[3]

Nor should this be looked down on as a form of "goulash capitalism" running parallel to the "goulash communism" of the Soviet Union, which was so mercilessly mocked by the Chinese a half century ago as an abandonment of communism's sacred trust to liberate mankind. Economic security and even material abundance carry their own forms of social, psychic, and spiritual liberation, first and foremost escape from the numbing intimidation of being without the wherewithal to get by, to raise a family, to preserve one's self-respect, and to not feel abjectly dependent.

Moreover, all the material artifacts of daily life come charged with social significance. What after all does formal equality amount to if only a select few possess enough by way of education, health, time, and technology (not to mention more mundane creature comforts) to ensure their own dignity and self-development? The struggle for "more" is no mean thing. In times past it has been an organic part of historic quests for a freer life.

Societies everywhere and at all times depend on tales of justification and purpose as much as they do on the means of tangible survival to hold themselves together. These might be thought of as fables, fictive approximations of the truth perhaps, but ones that both reflect and help constitute social reality. Ancestral visions of Progress, of the Invisible Hand, of socialism, of the cooperative commonwealth, or the Social Gospel's Christian commonwealth might be thought of as fables. Traditional tales of Christian redemption, as well as modern ones like the belief in a heroic revolutionary vanguard defying the philistines of the counting-house or even Nazism, also qualify. They carried with them mythic narratives, a sense of the immanent, shadows of the metaphysical. And despite their shortcomings and self-evident differences—their mutual enmity even—they shared a conception of emancipation as something essentially social.

But times have changed. Keynesian consumer capitalism and what is sometimes depicted as its mortal enemy, neoliberal, "free" market capitalism, have together turned earlier notions of freedom inside out...or what might be more aptly characterized as outside in. New fables of freedom spawned in the Age of Acquiescence are profoundly individual, no matter whether they are expressed as material desires or as exalted aspirations for self-empowerment. They are distinctly asocial, sometimes savagely antisocial. Cheerfully they celebrate Margaret Thatcher's drear axiom that "there is no such thing as society." Whatever else can be said about them, they do not constitute the raw material of social rebellion.[4]

Three fables of freedom in particular have marked the last half century: emancipation through consumption; freedom through the "free agency" of work; and freedom through the heroism of risk, a fable in which the businessman emerges as plebeian liberator. These tales were not invented when Ronald Reagan was elected president—their roots go far back into the American past—but they have substantially shaped the contours of our more recent remarkable quiescence.

Old wine in new bottles, these tales have mutated and matured in the new political economy of our times. The phase change from industrial capitalism to "flexible" finance-driven capitalism has lent these stories about the way things are and the way they need to be a compelling emotional coherence. Moreover, these are kindred fables; they bleed into and breed one another and together conduce to consent.

Mass consumption already constituted the foundation on which the New Deal's Keynesian commonwealth rested. The preeminence of finance in our new economy has not altered that. But it has vastly expanded the demographic and psychic reach of that economy. We may not have yet reached the terminal point predicted by Georg Simmel, the early-twentieth-century German sociologist and philosopher, in which "a life in boundless pursuit of pleasure makes one blasé. . . . It agitates the nerves to the strongest reactivity for such a long time that they finally cease to react at all." Still a certain enervation and even melancholy is sometimes detectable—or the opposite, a hysterical rushing about, a bug-eyed fascination with the next new thing, an infinite calisthenics of sensation. The desires and compulsions of consumer culture now drill down into the most impoverished social depths. And they permeate the most intimate regions of daily life, turning what was once thought to be untouchable by the calculus of the market—love, friendship, babyhood, wisdom, beauty, play, inner peace, redemption—into vendible commodities.[5]

Furthermore, because our new economic order has become an otherwise austere one—"lean-and-mean" especially when it comes to paychecks and the social wage—it has managed to sustain the consumer economy only by encouraging a universal indebtedness. That debt on the one hand functions as a source of primitive accumulation for finance. But on the other, it keeps the recyclable dream of freedom through acquisition alive while tethering it to an intimidating dependency on the creditor class. Consumerism has made play culture compulsive and obligatory.

Meanwhile, another and opposite cultural inversion would have us behave and believe that in our "brave new world," work has become a form of liberating play.

Flexible capitalism relies on—indeed, boasts about—its elasticity. That flexibility mainly refers to the way firms have managed to detach themselves from long-term relations with their workforce. Businesses enjoy the flexibility to respond to every perturbation in global demand most cheaply, recruiting workers when they need them without any ongoing obligations. Being flexible also means offloading functions once performed by the integrated corporation internally onto outside contractors and subcontractors, who may then be called into service or dismissed as the market dictates.

Together the casualization of labor and the shipping out of tasks has nourished a lively sense that in this new world work is undertaken at will by free agents. Men and women contract to undertake this or that project or job but, like their corporate partners, assume no continuing relationship, always remain alert to new possibilities, and retain their freedom as players in the marketplace—or so the story goes. In this way work, once to be escaped with as little pain as possible, a zone of dependency and constraint, seems to offer instead an unforeseen pathway to self-determination.

Involuntary servitude gave way to free labor; free labor turned into wage slavery; the affliction of wage slavery was eased by the American standard of living. Now we live, some of us anyway—an array of mid-level software designers, consultants, freelancers of a dozen varieties, even accountants and lawyers—in the era of voluntary servitude. It isn't "*arbeit mach frei*," but nonetheless the sense that work in the new economic order can be a form of self-emancipation thrives in certain quarters. Why accuse the inhabitants of acquiescing?

Of all the unlikely freedom fighters, denizens of Wall Street would have to rank as the most preposterous. The Street, after all, is the epicenter of that new global economic order. It was once known (and today is again known) as the "Street of Torments," a place to shy away from unless you were wealthy, connected, or perhaps preternaturally lucky. During the second Gilded Age, however, hoi polloi found its way to the Street in great numbers. Conservative pension and mutual funds became risk takers as the growth of the finance sector picked up steam. Moreover, information technology seemed to make the secrets of the Street transparent to everyone. Ordinary people came to harbor the dream of incalculable riches piled up overnight. More than that, they imagined the freedom to control their own fate just like those stock market champions idolized in the media, flexing their financial muscle and staring fearlessly into the unknown. Everyman could be a speculator if only he/she had the courage to seize the moment.

Heroes of our time had proved it could be done. Surfacing on the unlikely terrain of the marketplace, men from nowhere managed to challenge the corporate establishment. These warriors not only stalked the forbidding canyons of Wall Street but triumphed as well on the far frontier of advanced technology: the information superhighway. They waged war on the ancien régime of stuffed-shirt bankers and faceless corporate suits and they won. They became our culture's plebeian champions, our democratic plutocrats. What they had done was stunning and thrilling and reinvigorating the nation. More than that, the new economic and political order they midwived was open to all, or at least to a democracy of the audacious. Free at last.

Three fables of freedom have turned the more prosaic if systematic efforts to unwind the New Deal regulatory and administrative welfare state into an exhilarating series of stories full of moral purpose. However in touch they are with the most ingenious consumables, the most inventive new platforms for enterprising free agents, and the most exotic innovations in financial speculation, all three share a deeper coherence. They believe first of all in something quite old that has become youthful again: that the marketplace is the ideal matrix for fostering individual freedom, and that the dangers which may be part of that way of living are the price of liberation. This has always been a vital element of the national makeup, sometimes a more compelling one, sometimes less so. Freedom's demeanor in this incarnation is that of the steely isolate, the implacable loner, and a distinctly masculine grotesque but a seductive one.

Fables mutate. These three draw their persuasiveness from something newer as well: that the world as reconstituted by flexible capitalism has given birth to the free-floating individual, so unmoored from all those ties of kin, home, locale, race, ethnicity, church, craft, and fixed moral order that her only home is the austere one of the marketplace furnished in unforgiving arithmetic. Her selfhood is that of the abstract, depersonalized fungible commodity, a homunculus of rationalizing self-interest.

Every citizen is well aware of the triumph of free market ideology that began during the Reagan era. Indeed, in the realm of ideas there was no more evident or potent sign of acquiescence to the rule of capital than the hostility to all forms of government regulation and intervention into the economy. Some attribute this remarkable turnabout in thinking and public policy to the sheer persuasiveness of that bevy of think tanks, foundations, talk radio and TV "news" shows, and magazines launched with great fervor and dedication by the ascending right-wing political establishment.

Doubtless the doggedness and ingenuity of these policy intellectuals, together with the enveloping centralization and uniformity of the mass media (pace the social media), have mightily constrained and foreshortened what is thinkable, what is worthy of attention and what not, what rationales are credible and which ones are off the reservation. To get deeply rooted, however, required penetrating into the subsoil beneath the rational. After all, this constellation of free market thoughts and emotions, although always running in the American grain, nonetheless had to fight its way through a thicket of New Deal–inspired views and sentiments that ran in a different direction. After all, that New Deal persuasion was a worldview that had dominated the American political imagination for a half century.

Yet it succumbed. Something as earthbound as an overhauled economy—full of sunrise and sundown industries, ghost towns and edge cities, high-tech ateliers and sweatshops, international banks and transnational migrations of the uprooted, domestic deindustrialization and industrialization of the global South, planetary supply chains and big-box commercial megaliths, dying unions, emaciated or privatized public services, telecommunicating wonders and feral dogs roaming the wastelands of urban downtowns, new wealth, new poverty—has been kept aloft, in part, by the ephemera of the heart.

Fantasies can possess a tensile strength that belies their airy composition. These three do. They manage to efface reality's harshness. More than efface, they have allowed us to perform a kind of mental cosmetic surgery on the ugliness of dispossession and decline, inequality and exploitation, refiguring them as good or virtuous or fated. We can revel rather than revile, feel strong and empowered. William Butler Yeats put it well:

> We have fed the heart on fantasies
> The heart has grown brutal from the fare.

Fear: Reality Bites

Fantasy is powerful. But power is not all fantasy. What is truly remarkable about the grip these fables have exercised is that they managed it during an era when the most developed country on the planet was undergoing a protracted process of underdevelopment. If one clue to the mystery of acquiescence lies in the fables that enchant, we must also look to the way the starkness of flexible capitalism at ground level intimidates and demoralizes its latent opposition.

Fear wears many hats. There's the day-to-day, how-to-get-by variety: how to hang on to the home or pay this debt or that one or buy the medicine. Dare I complain if the CEO decides to disappear my pension? Will my union go under entirely if we put up too much of a fuss when the boss or the government tells us it is imperative we become lean-and-mean? There's the aspirational fear: how to pay for college and not get stuck in place; or negatively, the fear of falling, of failing, of that American nightmare of downward mobility. There's the fear that comes from abroad: What if my company and my job migrate overseas, or immigrants come here and take it? Or will I be deported if I mention to someone in authority that my employer is violating every labor law on the books? There's the fear of stepping out-of-bounds, of saying that which has become unsayable and "un-American."

Fear of the other has always bedeviled American society (and of course not only America). Racism was the cancerous phobia present at the creation. Those who argue the incapacity of resistance movements of the past to endure rightly point to this racial divide as exhibit A. More recently, just as the axis of social conflict moved away from the labor question to the race question, just as the institutional and legal edifice of American apartheid was being dismantled, a new racial consciousness and activism renewed the politics of racial fear. Racial rancor became the medium of a class consciousness that dared not speak its name.

Fear more universal and existential than the phobias about race accompanied the great transformation from industrial to global finance capitalism. This is the anxiety of loss, of cultural and moral disorientation, of being passed over. People of alien colors and beliefs and languages and customs threaten fixed moral standards, the way men and women relate, what should happen in school, what rights need protecting and why the need for so many new ones, where does patriotism reside, what authorities need to be respected. Evolving demographics threaten the primordial, the taken-for-granted way things were and would always be. And fear of decline and fall can breed a fierce, desperate resistance. Here, fear of loss and the fable of the free market conjoin to generate the most enduring form of resistance in our Age of Acquiescence: the rise of the populist right. Yet this turns out to be a resistance on behalf of restoration, one that doesn't pretend to confront the fundamentals as our ancestors once did.

And so there is a fear even more dreadful: namely, that we can no longer imagine a way of life and labor at odds with capitalism. The horizon is closing in. Everything in this inventory of acquiescence and fear also confronted our forebears living through the long nineteenth century, although in ways peculiar to that time — all, that is, except something so elemental it might pass unnoticed. Now but not then, capitalism seems the only answer to the riddle of history. We have become the slaves of a kind of fateful determinism, gussied up by supplications at the altar of technology and the marketplace.

Before exploring these fables of freedom and these politics of fear, it is important to see how this new species of flexible capitalism gave them life.

8

Back to the Future: The Political Economy of Auto-cannibalism

Hugh Carey was governor of New York in the middle 1970s. New York City was going bankrupt. Plenty of other cities and states across what was already by then known as the frost belt were in similar shape. However, in what was also then coming to be known as the Sun Belt, it was, relatively speaking, boom time. The population of the South and southwest would explode by 40 percent over the next two decades, twice the national rate. Meanwhile in Carey's words, Yankeedom was turning into "a great national museum" where tourists could visit "the great railroad stations where the trains used to run."[1]

Scenes from the Museum

Actually, tourists weren't interested. Abandoned railroad stations might be fetching in an eerie sort of way, but the rest of the museum was filled with the artifacts of recent ruination that were too depressing to be entertaining. It is true that a century earlier, during the first Gilded Age, the upper crust used to amuse itself by taking guided tours through the urban demimonde, thrilling to sites of exotic depravity or ethnic strangeness, traipsing around rag-pickers alley or the opium dens of Chinatown, or ghoulishly watching poor children salivate over store window displays of toys they could never touch.

Times have changed. Better out of sight and out of mind. Nonetheless, the national museum of industrial ecocide, a mobile collection moving from city to city, grew more grotesque from year to year, decade to decade.

For instance, Camden, New Jersey, had been for generations a robust, diversified small industrial city. But by the early 1970s, its reformist mayor, Angelo Errichetti, said it "looked like the Vietcong had bombed us to get even. The pride of Camden...was now a rat-infested skeleton of yesterday, a visible obscenity of urban decay. The years of neglect, slumlord exploitation, tenant abuse, government bungling, indecisive and short-sighted policy had transformed the city's housing, business, and industrial stock into a ravaged, rat-infested cancer on a sick, old industrial city." If we keep in mind that the mayor could describe things this way over forty years ago, and that we can still read stories today about Camden's further decline into some bottomless abyss, it can help us reckon with how long it takes to shut down a whole way of life.[2]

Once upon a time Youngstown, Ohio, was a typical smokestack city, part of the steel belt running from Pennsylvania through Ohio and on into the heavy-industry core of the upper Midwest. As in Camden, things started turning south in the 1970s. Over a ten-year period beginning in 1977, the city lost fifty thousand jobs in steel and related industries. By the late 1980s, when it was "morning again in America," it was midnight in Youngstown: foreclosures all over town, epidemic business bankruptcies and criminal and domestic violence, collapsing community institutions including churches and unions and families and municipal government, physical and emotional maladies left untreated. Burglaries, robberies, and assaults doubled after the plant closings. Child abuse rose by 21 percent, suicides by 70 percent in two years. There were an average of two thousand personal bankruptcies annually during the mid-1980s. One-eighth of Mahoning County went on welfare. The city filled up with the detritus of abandoned homes: work clothing, unpaid bills, scrap metal and wood shingles, shattered glass, stripped-away home siding, canning jars, swing sets, dead storefronts. Fifteen hundred people a week visited the Salvation Army's soup line. *The Wall Street Journal* called Youngstown "a necropolis," noting miles of "silent, empty steel mills" throughout the Mahoning valley and a pervasive sense of fear and loss. Bruce Springsteen would memorialize that loss in "The Ghost of Tom Joad."[3]

The steel mills of Gary, Indiana, were built on a thousand acres of swampland and sand dunes by Elbert Gary, chairman of United States Steel during the first decade of the last century. His idea was to flee the growing labor pressures and municipal regulations of Chicago and Pittsburgh by putting up a "disposable city." Just to be sure, the company rerouted the Calumet River so it might serve as a barrier between the mill and the town. *Harper's Weekly* commented that "the strategic position" of the mill "indicates a premonition of trouble. The Gary steelmills will be an open shop and the swarming hordes of Huns and Pollacks will think twice...before crossing the medieval mote [*sic*] to gain the industrial stronghold beyond."

The best-laid plans go awry. In 1919 Gary exploded during that year's steel strike. Martial law was declared and a thousand troops of the Fourth Division of the U.S. Army quashed the uprising. One reporter observed that "the magic city has become a weird nightmare." Another nightmare, just as bleak in its own way, was a half century down the road. By 1985, the deindustrialization of the steel belt had left one-third of Gary's population living below the poverty line. Dispossessed steelworkers in the "magic city," who had once made $15 to $20 an hour, were lining up at Wendy's hoping to work for $3.35.[4]

If you were unfortunate enough to live in Mansfield, Ohio, for the last forty years, you would have witnessed in microcosm the dystopia of destruction that was unfolding in similar places. For a century, workshops there made stoves, tires, steel, machinery, refrigerators, and cars. Then Mansfield's rust belt got wider and wider as one plant after another went belly-up: Dominion Electric in 1971; Mansfield Tire and Rubber in 1978; Hoover Plastics in 1980; National Seating in 1985; Tappan Stoves in 1986; a Westinghouse plant in 1990; Ohio Brass in 1990; Wickes Lumber in 1997; Crane Plumbing in 2003; Neer Manufacturing in 2007; Smurfit-Stone Container in 2009; and in 2010, GM closed its most modern and largest stamping factory in the United States and, thanks to the Great Recession, Con-way Freight, Value City, and Card Camera also shut down.

Midway through this industrial calamity, a journalist echoed Hugh Carey's words as he watched the Campbell Works of Youngstown Sheet and Tube go dark, musing that "the dead steel mills stand as pathetic mausoleums to the decline of American industrial might that was once the envy of the world." What's particularly impressive about this dismal record is that it encompassed the alleged boom times of Reagan and Clinton. Through "good times" and bad, Mansfield shrank, becoming skin and bones. Its poverty rate now is 28 percent and its median income is $11,000 less than the national average. What manufacturing remains is nonunion, and $10 an hour is considered a good wage. Mansfield's fate was repeated elsewhere in Ohio—in Akron, for example, once the rubber capital of the world, whose dismal decline was captured by the Pretenders in "My City Was Gone."[5]

In the iciest part of the frost belt, a *Wall Street Journal* reporter noted in 1988 that "there are two Americas now, and they grow further apart each day." She was referring to Eastport, Maine. There the bars filled up with unemployed and underemployed. Although the town was the deepest port on the East Coast, few ships docked there anymore and abandoned sardine factories lined the shore. The journalist had seen similar scenes of a collapsing rural economy from "coast to coast, border to border": museums displaying boarded-up sawmills and mines and storefronts, closed schools, rutted roads, and ghost airports.[6]

Closing up, shutting down, going out of business—last one to leave, please turn out the lights! So it was in towns and cities around the country. Public services—garbage collection, policing, fire protection, street maintenance, health care—atrophied along with the economic musculature. So too did the physical and psychic makeup of people, their body chemistry and moods and relations with others—things we don't customarily think of as economic "assets," but without which society grows weak and morbid. High blood pressure, cardiac and digestive problems, and mortality rates tended to rise. So too did doubt, self-blame, guilt, anxiety, and depression. The drying up of social supports among friends and workmates haunted inhabitants of these places just as much as the industrial skeletons around them.[7]

When Jack Welch, soon to be known as "Neutron" Jack Welch for his ruthlessness (and anointed by *Business Week* as "the gold standard against which other CEO's are measured"), took over the running of General Electric in the 1980s, he set out to raise the stock price by gutting the workforce. Welch was frank: "Ideally you'd have every plant you own on a barge ready to move with currencies and changes in the economy." Either that or shut them down (or at the very least keep amputating). During his first two years at the helm of GE, Welch laid off more than 70,000 people (20 percent of the workforce), three years later another 60,000 were gone. But imagine what it was like in places like Schenectady, which lost 22,000 jobs; in Louisville, where 13,000 fewer people were making appliances; in Evendale, Ohio, where 12,000 who used to make lighting didn't anymore; in Pittsfield, Massachusetts, where 8000 plastics makers got laid off; and in Erie, Pennsylvania, where 6000 locomotive workers got pink slips.[8]

Life as it had been lived stopped in GE and other one-company towns. Nor did it always happen at the hands of an asset stripper like Neutron Jack. Take Solvay, a town near Syracuse. Solvay Process, a maker of soda ash, went belly-up in the mid-1980s, thanks to the inexorable economic mechanics of deindustrialization. When it did, the bars closed, the luncheonettes closed, the local trucking companies did too, and marriages ended and cars got repossessed, houses got foreclosed, and the local government all but closed as tax revenues shrank by half.[9]

Two traveling observers making their way through this American wasteland in 1984 depicted such places as "medieval cities of rusting iron." It was a largely invisible landscape filling up with an army of transients, moving from place to place at any hint of work, camped out under bridges, riding freight cars, locked out of overstuffed mission houses, living in makeshift tents in fetid swamps, often armed, trusting no one, selling their blood, eating out of Dumpsters.[10]

Nor were the South, the rest of the Sun Belt, and the mountain west immune to this wasting disease. At first, the region grew robust at the expense of the aging industrial heartland. Local political and business elites actively recruited up north. They had a lot to offer: low taxes, municipal and state subsidies, loans, and land grants, plus no unions to speak of. The old Confederacy together with western newcomers like Phoenix or Orange County executed a historical about-face, making deindustrialization a form of regional revenge; the former "colonies" were now the headquarters for banks, mass retailers, and low- and high-tech manufacturers.

But the financial imperatives driving deindustrialization were eventually felt everywhere. Empty textile mills, themselves often runaway migrants from the north, dotted the Carolinas, Georgia, and elsewhere. Half the jobs lost due to plant closings or relocations in the 1970s happened in the Sun Belt. High-tech manufacturers also shut down. When Kenmet, a maker of capacitors and other sophisticated electronics, closed in 1998 in Shelby, North Carolina, the town and plant were likened to a "morgue," "a morbid place" of resignation, and its people were sometimes accused of "rural malingering." One such "malingerer" had this to say: "We're up a creek [if] anybody gets sick or dies. There's just that little feeling in the pit of your stomach like please don't let disaster come."[11]

Ten years later in Colorado Springs, one-third of the city's streetlights were extinguished, the police helicopters were sold, the budget for watering and fertilizer in the parks was eliminated, and surrounding suburbs closed down the public bus system. In Prichard, Alabama, monthly pension checks to the town's 150 retired workers stopped. During our Great Recession, one-industry towns like Elkhart, Indiana ("the RV capital of the world"), Dalton, Georgia ("the carpet capital of the world"), Blakely, Georgia ("the peanut capital of the world"), or Lehigh Acres, Florida (the housing boom), were closing libraries, firing the police chief, and taking other desperate survival measures. Tax revenues that used to pay for these elementary services were no longer available, thanks to the imploding of local economies and public policies that sought to appease big business by reducing or wiping out their tax liabilities.[12]

After the financial system tanked and budgets shriveled, Wilmington, North Carolina, could no longer provide fire protection because it couldn't pay to replace worn-out motors for pumping water. Streets had become nearly unnavigable as they crumbled from disrepair; garbage got picked up less often; upkeep of public gardens, parks, and community centers stopped. Sidewalks rotted; recycling ended. Cops and firemen shared in the general demoralization.

Even exemplars of the Sun Belt industrial miracle were at pains to sustain it. Phoenix, for example, had with great success invited in a broad range of industries, many of them at the technological cutting edge. By the turn of the new century, however, the city was well along the roadway to a postindustrial future. That prospective future had already become the present in such once unlikely places as San Jose, the capital of Silicon Valley, and in this case the future wasn't working. Verging on bankruptcy, California's third largest city was closing libraries, letting go city workers in droves, shutting down community centers, and asking residents to put up with gutted roads: "We're Silicon Valley, we're not Detroit. It shouldn't be happening here. We're not the Rust Belt," lamented one shocked city councilman.[13]

MIT released a study in 2010 about America's 150 forgotten cities, all doomed by deindustrialization. Not forgotten but down and out were such hallmarks of the country's industrial rise and triumph as Buffalo, Cleveland, Albany, and Allentown, topping their list of the country's "Ten Dying Cities."[14]

Running on Empty

Detroit—no metropolis has been more emblematic of tragic decline from the outset of our era of disaccumulation right up to the present day.

Once a world-class city that was full of architectural gems, with a population in the 1950s that had the highest median income and rate of home ownership of any major American city, the Motor City now haunts the national imagination as a ghost town, like all ghosts dead, yet alive. Once the nation's fourth larger city, with 2 million residents, its decrepit hulk is home to 900,000. In one decade alone, from 2000 through 2010, the population hemorrhaged by 25 percent—that's nearly a quarter of a million people, or about the size of post-Katrina New Orleans.

Vast acreage—one-third of the metropolitan land area, the size of San Francisco—is now little more than empty houses and empty factories and fields gone feral. A whole industry of demolition, cordage, waste disposal, and scrap metal companies has sprung up to tear down what once was; *Plant Closing News,* which began in 2003, is just one new enterprise that chronicles the Motor City's decline (teardowns average one hundred each month). With a jobless rate of 29 percent, some of Detroit's citizens are so poor they can't pay for funerals, so bodies pile up at mortuaries. Bus routes have been eliminated, as have streetlights. Plans are afoot to let the grasslands and forests take over, to shrink-wrap the city, or to give it to private enterprise—or maybe all three.

Take the story of the Detroit Zoo. Once a fully populated public-owned home for wildlife of all sorts, it was nearly privatized in 2006. While an outcry stopped that from happening then, new management reduced it to the barest minimum of zookeepers and animals for them to care for. An associate curator once in charge of elephants and rhinos went in search of other work as his wages were disappearing along with the animals. He found a job with the city chasing down feral dogs, whose population had skyrocketed as more and more of the cityscape went back to wilderness.[15]

Thanks to information technology there are now websites offering "our delightful selection of de-industrial t-shirts, art, photography, and drawings," including posters and postcards for those tourists susceptible to schadenfreude first dreamed of by Hugh Carey. Anything can be aestheticized in our postindustrial age, including dereliction and decay. In

Detroit, according to the writer Paul Clemens, who spent a year "punching out" in a closing auto plant, this hypersophistication, part high-mindedness, part environmentalist chic, has become a cottage industry in its own right, converting industrial wastelands into artistically designed parks.[16]

In the Motor City (and in other core industrial centers like Baltimore) "death zones" have emerged, where neighborhoods verge on medical collapse.

Looking Backward

Perhaps these stories of decline and decay merely constitute local instances and symptoms of a familiar story about capitalism's penchant for "creative destruction." Old ways die off, sometimes painfully, but that's part of the story of Progress. New wonders appear where old ruins stood and people get healthier and wealthier, if not necessarily wiser.

But what if Edward Bellamy's time traveler from 1888 woke up in Boston in the year 2000 and found to his dismay that society seemed headed back to where he'd come from? Cities were decaying, people were growing poorer and sicker, bridges and roads were crumbling, sweatshops were growing more common, more people were incarcerated than anyplace on the planet, workers were afraid to stand up to their bosses, unions were barely managing to stay alive, the air, water, and land were filling up with poisons, schools were failing, daily life was growing riskier, debts were more onerous than most could have imagined, inequalities were starker than ever.

A recent grim statistic suggests this dystopian view may be not quite as far-fetched as it might otherwise seem. For the first time in American history the life expectancy of white men and women has dropped. Researchers have reported that the life spans of the least educated have actually fallen by about four years since 1990. The steepest declines were among white women lacking a high school diploma, who lost five years of life, while for men the drop was three years. These numbers not only are unprecedented for the United States, but come very close to the catastrophic decline for Russian men in the years following the collapse of the Soviet Union.

Because these life and death statistics are linked to where one ranks in the economic/educational hierarchy, they are also evidence of a country's ever-growing inequality—in this case, a fatal inequality. The life expectancy of African Americans has always and still does trail far behind that of the white population (although now because of this recent decline, black women and less educated white women are in the same boat).

But the more global import for assessing what's been happening over the last generation or so is captured by another number: as of 2010, American women had fallen to forty-first place in the United Nations ranking of international life expectancy, from fourteenth in 1985. Among developed countries, American women now rank *last*. Younger Americans die earlier and live in poorer health than their counterparts in other developed countries. Indeed, death before the age of fifty accounts for about two-thirds of the difference between males in the United States and one-third for females as compared with their counterparts in sixteen other developed countries.[17]

Why? This demographic crash landing is so unanticipated it is mystifying. The obesity epidemic, rising rates of smoking among women, wider and wider abuse of prescription drugs, guns, spreading psychosocial dysfunction, millions and millions lacking health insurance, overwork, "death zones"—singularly and together—are getting looked at. Whatever the final explanation, this social statistic is the rawest measure of a society in retrogression, of a country in the throes of economic anorexia. At the most elementary level, it is stark repudiation of one of the nation's most coveted conceits: that the New World is the land of Progress ne plus ultra.

And there is one other marker of this eerie, counterintuitive story of a developed nation undergoing underdevelopment. It too is a reproach to an equally cherished national tenet. For the first time since the Great Depression, the social mobility of Americans is moving in reverse. Every decade since the 1970s, fewer people have been able to move up the income ladder than in the previous ten years. Now Americans in their thirties on average earn 12 percent less than their parents did at the same age. Danes, Norwegians, Finns, Canadians, Swedes, Germans, and the French all enjoy higher rates of upward mobility than Americans. Remarkably, 42 percent of American men raised in the bottom one-fifth income cohort remain there for life, compared with 25 percent in Denmark and 30 percent in the notoriously class-stratified land of Great Britain.[18]

We have become familiar with this lament of what is loosely called "the vanishing middle class." Except for the top 10 percent, everyone else is on the down escalator. The United States now has the highest percentage of low-wage workers (earning less than two-thirds of the median wage) of any developed nation. The standard of living for most Americans has fallen over the last quarter century, so that the typical household income in 2012 was just what it was twenty-four years earlier. The comedian George Carlin once mordantly quipped about what can be described only as a lost illusion, "It's called the American Dream because you have to be asleep to believe it."[19]

The Political Economy of Decline

During the long nineteenth century, wealth and poverty lived side by side. So they do again today. In the first instance, when industrial capitalism was being born, it came of age by ingesting the valuables (land and inorganic resources, animals and vegetables and human muscle power, tools and talents and know-how, and the ways of organizing and distributing what got produced) embedded in precapitalist forms of life and labor. Because of this economic metabolism, wealth accumulated in the new economy by extinguishing wealth in these precapitalist older ones.

Whatever the human and ecological costs, and they were immense, the hallmarks of Progress, at least in a strictly material sense, were also highly visible. America's capacity to sustain a larger and larger population at rising levels of material well-being, education, and health was its global boast for a century and a half.

These statistics about life expectancy and social mobility suggest those days are over with. Wealth, great piles of it, is still being generated, some of it displayed so ostentatiously it is impossible to overlook. Technological marvels still amaze. Prosperity exists, although those living within its charmed circle constitute a less and less numerous caste. But a new economic metabolism is at work.

Primitive accumulation at the expense of noncapitalist ways of life accounted for that earlier epoch of Progress. For the last forty years, however, prosperity, wealth, and progress have rested in part on the grotesque mechanisms of auto-cannibalism, or what has been called disaccumulation, a process of devouring our own.[20]

Traditional forms of primitive accumulation continue elsewhere— across the vastnesses of rural China and Southeast Asia, in the villages and mountains of Latin America, in the forests and plains of Africa. In these places, peasants, peddlers, ranchers, petty traders, scavengers, handicraftsmen, and fishermen get engorged by great capitalist enterprises that are often headquartered abroad. These hundreds of millions provide the labor power and cheap manufactures that buoy up the bottom line of global manufacturing and retailing corporations, banks, and agribusinesses.

Here in the homeland, however, the profitability and prosperity of privileged sectors of the economy—first of all, in the arena of finance— have depended instead on stripping away the meat and bone from what was built up over generations.

Once again a new world had been born. This time it depended on liquidating the assets of the old one. This liberated capital might be shipped abroad to reward speculation in "fictitious capital" (currency and commodities markets, securitized debt, and so on). Or it might be invested to restart the engines of primitive accumulation in the vast global outback. The rate of domestic investment in new plants, technology, and research and development began declining in the United States during the 1970s, and the falloff actually accelerated in the gilded '80s. Dismantling took many forms: deliberately allowing plant and equipment to deteriorate until useless, using it as a cash cow via resale, milking profits and sending them elsewhere rather than reinvesting to update facilities, shutting down part of a plant and running it at low levels, or selling off parts to a jobber.

During the 1970s alone, between 32 and 38 million jobs were lost due to this kind of disinvestment, which was common practice in old (New England textile factories) and new industries alike (New England aircraft manufacturers). Manufacturing, which after the Second World War accounted for nearly 30 percent of the economy, by 2011 had dropped to a bit more than 10 percent. Since the turn of the millennium alone, 3.5 million manufacturing jobs have vanished and 42,000 manufacturing plants closed. On average between the years 2000 and 2011, seventeen American manufacturers closed each day.[21]

Nor are we witnessing the passing away of relics of the nineteenth century. Of the 1.2 billion cell phones sold in 2009, none were made in the United States. In 2007, a mere 8 percent of all new semiconductor plants under construction globally were located here. The share of semiconductors, steel, cars, and machine tools made in America has declined precipitously just in the last ten years or so. Even the money sunk into high-tech telecommunications has been largely speculative, so that only 1 to 2 percent of the fiber-optic cable buried under Europe and North America was ever turned on, even at the height of the dot-com boom. Today, only one American company is among the top ten in the solar power industry (photovoltaic cells), and the United States accounts for a mere 5.6 percent of world production. Only GE is among the top ten in wind energy. Much high-end engineering design and R&D work has been expatriated as well. By 2004 America trailed China in exports of high technology. The portion of printed circuit boards, which are at the heart of advanced industry, produced here at home has steadily declined and now accounts for 8 percent of global output compared with 26 percent in 2000. The cherished belief that stuff made in America is inherently of superior quality is encouraged by companies like Apple. The company cultivates that idea in its iPhone ads, noting that the product is "designed in California." But it's not built there. Today there are more people dealing cards in casinos than running lathes and almost three times as many security guards as machinists.[22]

Meanwhile, the fastest growing part of the economy has been the finance, insurance, and real estate (FIRE) sector. Between 1980 and 2005, profits in the financial sector increased by 800 percent, more than three times the growth in nonfinancial sectors. During the ten years from 1978 to 1987, profits in the financial sector averaged 13 percent. From 1998 through 2007, they came in at a stunning 30 percent.[23]

Creatures of finance, rare or never seen before, bred like rabbits. In the early 1990s, for example, there were a couple of hundred hedge funds; by 2007, there were ten thousand. A "shadow banking" system consisting of hedge funds, private equity firms, security brokers dealing in credit instruments, and an array of mortgage entities grew up alongside the conventional one to account for half of the whole financial industry before the crash of 2008. A whole new species of mortgage broker now roamed the land, supplanting old-style savings and loan institutions and regional banks. Fifty thousand mortgage brokerages employed four hundred thousand brokers, more than the whole U.S. textile industry. A hedge fund manager put it bluntly: "The money that's made from manufacturing stuff is a pittance in comparison to the amount of money made from shuffling money around." Forty-four percent of all corporate profits in the U.S. come from the financial sector compared with only 10 percent from the manufacturing sector. Lawrence Summers, Bill Clinton's last secretary of the treasury, succinctly summarized where matters stood: "Financial markets don't just oil the wheels of economic growth; they are the wheels."[24]

Resting on the Ruins

Too often these two phenomena—the evisceration of industry and the supersizing of high finance—have been appreciated as parallel to but not organically tied to each other. Yet another fable, adorned with the hieroglyphics of differential calculus, tells a reassuring story. Sad it might be that, for some people, towns, cities, and regions, the end of industry meant the end. But that is (as it always has been), so the myth goes, only the unfortunate yet necessary prelude to a happier future pioneered in this latest case by "financial engineers" equipped with a new technical know-how to turn money into more money while bypassing the intermediary messiness of producing anything. And lo and behold: prosperity! This tale, however, contains a categorical flaw.

Actually, the ascendancy of high finance was premised on gutting the industrial heartland. That is to say, the FIRE sector not only supplanted industry but grew at its expense—and at the expense as well of high wages and the capital that used to flow into those arenas of productive investment.

Think back only to the days of the junk bonds, leveraged buyouts, megamergers and acquisitions, and asset stripping in the 1980s and '90s. What was getting bought, stripped, and closed up—all in order to support windfall profits in high-interest-paying junk bonds and the stupendous fees and commissions paid to "engineer" these transactions— was the flesh and bone of a century and a half of American manufacturing. Wall Street's renewed preeminence, its own "morning again in America," was in every way bound up with this midnight vanishing of a distinct species of American economic and social life. For some long time now, our political economy has been driven by "I" banks, hedge funds, private equity firms, and the downward mobility and exploitation of a casualized laboring population cut adrift from its more secure industrial havens.

"Deindustrialization" is antiseptic terminology for social devastation. In fact, it marked a fundamental overturning of a whole way of life, transforming the country's economic geography and political demo-graphics, bearing with it enormous social and cultural ramifications. Whole towns, regions, unions, churches, schools, local businesses, and community hangouts, political alliances, venerable traditions, and his-toric identities went down with the smokestacks. Feelings of despair, loss, and resentment filled the emptiness.

In their landmark 1982 book *The Deindustrialization of America*, Barry Bluestone and Bennett Harrison plotted this fateful interconnection. Deindustrialization, as they saw it, entailed the diversion of capital "from productive investment in our basic national industries into unproductive speculation, mergers and acquisitions, and foreign investment." This did not occur by happenstance; it was because the rate of profit in American industry began a long-term decline in the 1970s in the face of height-ened competition from the reconstructed, postwar economies of former enemies and allies alike.[25]

For the first time in nearly a century the country bought more than it sold on the international marketplace. Trade deficits became a perma-nent fixture of the U.S. economy. Signs of decline mounted. The U.S. share of global GDP fell from 34.3 percent in 1950 to 24.6 percent in 1976; American oil production declined from 50 percent after the war to 15 percent; steel from 50 percent to 20 percent. Japan captured the home electronics market (TV, video, numerically controlled machine tools) as well as big chunks of the car, textile, and shoe businesses. Germany did the same in metalworking. The American share of the world market in manufactured goods shrank by 23 percent. Productivity growth slowed and even shrank by the end of the 1970s. During the next decade, the Bureau of Labor Statistics estimated that between 1.5 and 2 million jobs evaporated each year as factories and ancillary businesses shut down.

National alarms went off. In 1974, *Business Week* published a special issue on "The Re-industrialization of America" (how naïve that sounds now, when talk about how to re-create American industry is mainly dis-missed by "experts" in the age of finance as Luddite babble). *The New York Times* ran a five-part series on the same subject and Congress held hearings. Remedies of various kinds were applied. Some, like compelling international rivals to raise the value of their currencies relative to the dollar, helped save or enlarge American export markets temporarily. Corporate profits could also be sustained artificially by cutting taxes, by loosening the constraints of government regulation, by floating ever-larger budget deficits in part to finance a vast expansion of the arms industry. Forcing down costs, especially labor costs and the social costs of the welfare state, would lessen the pain by increasing it. This made union busting and cuts in social programs and infrastructure maintenance and replacement a fixture of public life. Slicing away at the accumulated fat of corporate middle-level management and the rusting productive facilities they managed became part of the tactical repertoire.[26]

None of this could in the long term solve the underlying, intractable problem of depressed profit rates, overcapacity of production, and the paucity of enough lucrative outlets for new investment. Only depressions performed that kind of radical surgery, with great thoroughness and ruthlessness. By denuding the economic landscape of less remunerative enterprises, those that survived such deep downturns could start afresh, buying up cheaply bankrupted assets, and paying needier workers a fraction of what they once earned. Draconian credit tightening of the sort attempted by Federal Reserve Board chairman Paul Volcker at the end of the 1970s came too scarily close to simulating that kind of across-the-board triage. Indeed, it was too unsettling a reminder of that solution infamously suggested fifty years earlier by Secretary of the Treasury Andrew Mellon when he recommended curing the Great Depression by allowing it to run its course and "liquidate labor, liquidate stocks, the farmers, liquidate real estate." Volcker didn't venture quite that far, but did manage to produce the Reagan recession of the early 1980s. More dying branches of American industry were pruned away; however, the cure threatened to be worse than the disease. The recession was the severest since the 1930s.[27]

Short of this sort of heroic purging of the economy, however, currency manipulations, military spending, government-financed trade deficits, rejiggering the tax structure in favor of business and the wealthy, social austerity, deregulation, and an armored assault on the ossified structures of corporate America would have to do. These measures produced good-enough results during the Reagan era, creating a chimera of prosperity—an illusion, that is, unless you were attached to one of the charmed circles surrounding the petrochemical, finance, real estate, and telecommunications industries.

It was all too easy to be seduced by the flourishing of various forms of "paper entrepreneurialism," by the escalation of corporate profits, by the magical mushrooming of venture capital (up 544 percent during the decade), by the frantic race among universities to set up "entrepreneur" course offerings, and by the atmosphere of luxe that made its debut at the Reagan inaugural ball. A thriving rentier class—those relying on various forms of investment income (interest, capital gains, rent, dividends)—made it harder to see that the percentage of national income paid out in wages and salaries fell by one-tenth. Few noticed that during the same decade the income of the bottom 10 percent of the population (25 million people) also fell by one-tenth—this was the first time since the 1930s that such a sizable number of citizens had suffered a serious decline in their standard of living.[28]

A rentier society is not necessarily a prosperous one. Actually, the growth in GNP was much less than it had been during the 1950s or '60s, and even less than the lamentable '70s. Net business investment fell and there was a great shrinkage in new capital formation, notwithstanding the tax cuts that were designed to encourage it. The fifty corporations receiving the largest tax breaks from the Reagan cuts of 1981 actually reduced their investment over the next two years.[29]

Asset stripping and financial deregulation in particular thus worked in tandem. Amending, paring down, and repealing a slew of financial prohibitions and supervisory agencies did not cause capital resources to move away from production into various forms of financial speculation.

Instead, these measures expedited an outflow of capital already under way, thanks to the dilemma of profitability in American industry.

For example, we think of usury laws as medieval legislation. But as a matter of fact, usurious rates of interest were illegal in the United States as late as the 1970s. Then they were modified or abolished. So too, Federal Reserve regulations once required minimum down payments and maximum periods of repayment for housing loans, and another set of regulations required the same for credit card loans for cars, appliances, and durable goods of all sorts. Beginning during the Carter administration and accelerating during the Reagan and Clinton regimes, all of this was dismantled. Commercial banks were once restricted on the interest rates they could pay on deposits. By 1982 they weren't. Later in the decade, they were allowed to underwrite commercial short-term paper, municipal bonds, and mortgage-backed securities. And, by the end of the Reagan years, they could even underwrite equities (that whole class of investments which, unlike bonds or most other loans, entailed ownership rights but also were much riskier), making it up to 25 percent of their business.

Inflation and opening up the sluice gates of financial speculation made it difficult for savings and loan institutions to compete because they were still limited by law in what they could pay depositors and what they could invest in. So those rules were jettisoned, and S&Ls even started putting people's savings into high-risk junk bonds, securities that would soon enough plummet in value but only after sucking dry the material wherewithal of the companies they were used to purchase. All this ended in the savings and loan debacle at the end of the Reagan administration, when 1000 of the 3400 S&Ls went bankrupt or lived on only as "zombie banks." (Zombie banks are financial institutions with a net worth less than zero that continue operating thanks to government support.)

Between 1985 and 1992, more than 2000 banks failed; only 79 had gone under in the whole of the otherwise dolorous 1970s. In the Clinton administration more prohibitions were relaxed; most notably, the

Glass-Steagall Act, the New Deal law that separated commercial from investment banking, was repealed. These actions, including the freeing of the derivatives market from any government oversight, produced the asset bubbles that blew up in the stock market, dot-com, and, later, sub-prime mortgage debacles. New laws opened the door to the creation of financial holding companies that could do anything they pleased— including loaning, investing, and speculating—regardless of the barriers which had once separated these quite different, sometimes counter-posed, activities.[30]

Boom times under Reagan, Clinton, and George W. Bush were pre-mised on the securitization of everything in sight, from mortgages and student loans to credit card debt. A voluminous thesaurus of financial engineering inventions appeared: first exotic arcana like OIDS (original issue discount securities) and PIKS (payment in kind securities), then the deeply mystifying CDOs, credit default swaps, and off–balance sheet vehicles. There were bonds that paid interest in the form of other bonds. Wall Street became adept at converting even the homeliest forms of debt like car loans, boat loans, credit card bills, RV loans, and student debt into "asset-based securities." Banks became megabanks as they com-peted for the riskiest, most lucrative paper. The bigger they got, the risk-ier they became. The whole system was so highly leveraged and precarious it was acutely vulnerable to the slightest disturbance.[31]

Deregulation outside the financial sector had the same withering impact. Carter initiated the deregulation of airlines, trucking, and rail-roads. Reagan was even more zealous, eliminating restraints on oil prices and electric and gas utilities. Telecommunications followed. Low-ering costs was the rationale and sometimes that happened, sometimes not. For example, in the electrical power industry those states that deregulated in ways promoted by the energy company Enron saw their rates rise by $48 billion more than the average costs in states that retained traditional regulations.[32]

Long gone were the days when Wall Street did what it was purported to do: namely, raise capital to finance industry and other long-term enterprises. As one observer noted, collateralized debt obligations raised "nothing for nobody. In essence they were simply a side bet—like those in a casino—that allowed speculators to increase society's mortgage wager without financing a single house."[33]

Worse than that, however, the freeing of finance unleashed it to leech away the values accumulated over generations in American industry. Arguably the strategic goal of neoliberal policy was to liberate the powers of finance (while suppressing the social wage). The idea was to expand the mechanisms and techniques for originating, mobilizing, and marketing debt through the ingenuity of financial engineering at the expense of tangible resources while calling on the government (that is, the rest of us, free market ideology notwithstanding) to assume the moral hazard and social risk when default beckoned. Marx observed long ago that "all this paper actually represents nothing more than accumulated claims, or legal title, to future production."[34]

Tithing the underlying economy in this way left it anemic and vulnerable. Under the regime of lean-and-mean, which remains with us to this day, hurdle rates for profits remained so high that the only way to meet them was to reroute capital out of long-term commitments (to research and development as well as to plant and equipment) and into portfolio investments in commercial and residential real estate, buying up companies (often for resale), or in stock trading or currency hedging that generated short-term earnings.

All of this facilitated the merger and acquisition and leveraged buyout mania on the Street. At the same time it led to a relentless lowering of labor standards and unionization because industries could no longer easily pass along some labor costs to consumers now that they were unregulated. As a result, workers in all these sectors—pilots, machinists, truck drivers—found their wages squeezed, their unions thrown on the defensive and surrendering to two-tier wage structures. New hires— that is to say, the future working class—would be compelled to move backward in time. Moreover, they would be accompanied on their journey by small-town and rural America. Deregulation of the whole transportation network penalized small towns, smaller cities, and low-income areas generally, as they lost airline and railroad connections, paid jacked-up local phone rates, and receded into invisibility.[35]

Not greed but rather the rigors of a survivalist competition to stay ahead of the profit curve produced a kind of economic brinksmanship. As the time horizon for realizing earnings grew shorter, capital was mis-allocated into financial manipulations, unproven technologies, and real estate, all of it heavily leveraged, its risks camouflaged. Little was added to the net stock of productive resources (except in the telecommunications industry, where too much was added and for the same speculative purposes.) But as a consequence, a lot was added to the bank accounts of traders, brokers, bankers, and top managements who psyched out the market correctly.[36]

Fire in the Hole

Corporations in trouble, no longer able or willing to finance themselves with retained earnings, needed to please Wall Street to keep afloat. And they did so for two decades and more by the kind of ferocious cost-cutting "Chainsaw" Al Dunlap made famous at Scott Paper and Sunbeam. Dunlap had a bulldozer voice and a personality to go with it. He was apt to crow about his working-class parentage—his father was a union shop steward at a shipyard, his mother worked at a five-and-ten—to show his sympathies as he slashed and burned. Best-selling author of *Mean Business*, he earned his spurs by immediately laying off one-third of the blue-collar workforce (11,000 people) and shrinking the white-collar battalions from 1600 to 300 at Scott Paper.

Harley-Davidson, long practiced in this same art, was still at it during the Great Recession. The motorcycle maker stopped hiring in America and projected cutting loose more than one-fifth of its workforce, making up the lost capacity by ratcheting up the hours of those who remained. Practices of this kind were also common at corporations like Ford, General Electric, Alcoa, and Hasbro. Stock prices invariably soared as the mayhem descended. This strategy of deliberately wasting away was especially attractive to companies during the crisis periods of the dot-com collapse and the Great Recession.

Alternatively, a firm might look for new revenue not in manufacturing but by creating its own financial auxiliaries to speculate in everything from Eurobonds to currencies, credit cards and home mortgages, leases and insurance. Companies like General Electric and General Motors did this with a vengeance. GE Capital was responsible for 40 percent of GE's revenue by 2008 and half its profits, dollops of which came from betting on collateralized debt obligations until they soured. Meanwhile, GE's outlays for research and development dropped by 20 percent in the 1990s. Enron, before it became infamous, derived a similar share of its revenue not from power generation, but from lending, trading, and other financial activities, including fraud. It practiced a kind of commercial savagery. When a brush fire broke out in California, exacerbating that state's summertime electrical energy crisis, an Enron trader, overjoyed that rates would rise, exclaimed, "The magical word of the day is 'Burn Baby Burn.'" Another talked about the money they "stole from those poor grandmothers in California."[37]

Investing in mergers and acquisitions was an appealing alternative only because the underlying assets of the companies being commingled or bought could then be pared down or liquidated, and pensions and health insurance obligations could be defaulted on, with the costs passed on to the public treasury. Devalued assets could in turn be picked up at bargain-basement prices and resold. Indeed, the point of most transactions was to buy in order to sell, which tended to leave long-term investment out in the cold.

It is only a slight exaggeration to say that the new corporations emerging out of this bazaar of buying and selling were in a new business: the fabrication of companies to trade back and forth. During the 1980s, nearly a third of the largest manufacturing firms were acquired or merged. It would be more apt to call all this churning rather than investing. In 1960, institutional investors held stock for an average of seven years; that was down to two years by the 1980s.[38]

The Afterlife

Disaccumulation thus waged war against capitalism on behalf of capitalism. Absorbing or discarding the plant, equipment, and human resources locked up in manufacturing and other enterprises enriched the financial sector by eviscerating these other forms of capitalism. This should not be confused with what happened during the long nineteenth century. Big corporations and trusts then did drive smaller competitors into bankruptcy or take them over. But the net effect, looking at the situation strictly from the standpoint of production, was to enlarge the productive wherewithal of the nation's capitalist economy.

Nor was the merger and acquisition mania of recent days like the conglomerate rage of the 1960s, where companies diversified their portfolios and eluded antitrust law by acquiring, usually with their own funds, a grab bag of unrelated businesses. In that instance, the corporation as a social institution remained in place. True, the conglomerate era left behind behemoths of inefficiency and managerial ineptitude and the lean-and-mean era would admittedly administer a purgative. But that corrective was a harsh one with immense collateral damage.

Moreover, many of the companies gobbled up, their allegedly incompetent managements evacuated, turned out to be better superintended by their old guard than by the buy-and-sell artists who momentarily replaced them. So, for example, high-octane rhetoric-propelled deals like the merger of Chrysler and Daimler-Benz in 1998, which predicted costs would be saved, economies realized, and markets expanded. Two years later—once income had plummeted, market capitalization had grown anemic, share prices were halved, workers had been downsized, six plants had closed, and assets auctioned off—the deal was called a nightmare. Many others ended likewise, but their failures paid large dividends on Wall Street.

As one analyst has described it, the modern corporation has now diffused into a nexus of contracts in which shareholder value is served first of all and last of all by managements acutely sensitive to that constituency alone. American industry was melted down to provide a vast pool of liquid capital that could be rechanneled into purely speculative trading in paper assets—stocks, bonds, IPOs, mortgages, derivatives, credit default swaps, structured investment vehicles, collateralized debt. And that covers only the relatively humdrum. What about trading bundles of insurance contracts for the terminally ill? Securitization was the alchemist's stone of dispossession. Tangible assets got liquefied and turned into bundles of tradable intangibles.

Most of this had negligible job-creating impact. But it offered rates of return no longer available elsewhere in the economy. It did, that is, until it didn't. What was conceived of as ways of dampening risk (what else after all is a "hedge" fund supposed to do?) ended up aggravating it past the breaking point. After the dot-com crash of 2000, nearly all the thousands of IPOs of the late 1990s fell below their initial offering price. Half of those not already out of business were selling for $1 a share or less. The values incinerated in that implosion matched the value of all the homes in the United States. Their financial engineers had long since moved on.[39]

Just a few years later, during the global financial meltdown, the homes themselves would go extinct, washed away in an unnatural disaster. Between 2008 and 2011 three million people lost their homes. Eleven million homeowners found themselves "underwater" by 2011. Thirteen trillion dollars in houses and stock went up in smoke. By 2010, family income, long on a treadmill sloping down, was lower than it had been in the late 1990s. Investment in plant, equipment, and technology as a portion of GDP was less than in any decade since World War II. One in every seven Americans was being chased by a creditor. Some, in desperation, became reckless gamblers, loading up on even more precarious forms of debt in a futile race to stay one step ahead of the sheriff, engaged in a kind of self-sabotage.[40]

Yet for a generation financial engineers—and their ideological apologists—imagined themselves as crusaders. They were out to save the "exploited class" of shareholders being gulled by complacent and sometimes corrupt management. One business school professor noted that "maximizing shareholder value" was "embraced as the politically correct stance by corporate board members and top management." It was a "mission-driven cause" that "overcame the wrongful allocation of capital and embodied the sacred identity of profit and private property."[41]

Wrongful allocation indeed! What were often depicted as rescue missions turned out to be sophisticated forms of looting. Capitalism in whatever form has always encouraged such behavior, especially with regard to alien societies—and particularly those inhabited by people with the "wrong" complexions, physiognomies, and customs. Alongside the plundering, however, law-abiding enterprise grew up. But in our era of finance-driven speculation, the line between criminal looting and conventional "investment" grew hazier.

A preponderance of evidence accumulated suggesting that investment banking had become increasingly and even inherently corrupt. An avalanche of insider trading, market manipulation, misrepresentation, favoritism, kickbacks, conflicts of interest, and frauds of the most exotic variety has led one observer to describe the last twenty years as the "age of deception." It's unlikely that all of a sudden a whole subculture had descended into the criminal underworld (although the temptations to do so had arguably never been higher, and some obviously succumbed). More plausible and more worrying is that deception had become the new normal. Every player—"I" banks, regulators, IPO promoters, mutual fund operators, hedge funds, auditors, rating services—had been reared in a system whose whole purpose was to game the system. This was not a secret but a boast.[42]

The Poverty of Progress

America remains the world's second manufacturing center, behind China. This is true even though the U.S. economy has lost its technological lead in many sectors, despite the wholesale hemorrhaging of manufacturing jobs during the Great Recession, and notwithstanding data-rich predictions that millions more jobs will be exported abroad over the next decade or so. What remains at home, however, will survive mainly because of the austere circumstances working people have been compelled to accept if they want to work at all. The Great Recession accelerated an onslaught of wage cutting, furloughs, two-tier wage hierarchies, and doubled job assignments already under way for two decades. Moreover, deindustrialization, as devastating as it has been, hardly captures all that has been devoured by the new order of finance-driven flexible capitalism.[43]

Wounds appeared everywhere. Infrastructure rotted, becoming inefficient and downright dangerous. The United States now ranks twenty-fifth in the quality of its infrastructure, trailing Brazil, India, and China in its transportation network, for example. One-quarter of highway bridges were recently deemed "structurally deficient" and another third poor or mediocre by the American Society of Civil Engineers, who also gave the nation's roadways a grade of D minus. Other elements of the infrastructure fared better, getting a grade of D plus in 2013, up from the D of four years earlier. Public transportation also improved from four years earlier—it got a D. While Europe spends 5 percent of its GDP and China 9 percent on infrastructure, the United States manages only 2.4 percent. According to investment banker Felix Rohatyn, "Three quarters of the country's public school buildings are outdated and inadequate. It will take $11 billion annually to replace aging drinking water facilities; what was budgeted for that, before sequestering, was less than 10% of that. Unsafe dams have risen by a third and number 3500. Half the locks on more than 12,000 miles of inland waterways are functionally obsolete."[44]

Neglect, however, is only half the story. Certainly letting public facilities decay helps suppress the social wage supported by tax revenues, some of which actually comes from corporate America. One way to further reduce the corporate tax bill is to allow public services to deteriorate. While it may affect the daily lives of ordinary people, making them more unsafe, unhealthy, or inconvenient, in a land where the well-off insulate themselves from the public arena through access to private goods and services, this wasting away of public hardware is not so hard to bear. And not borrowing to replace worn-out bridges, tunnels, power plants, and waterworks cheapens credit for leveraging more lucrative if speculative endeavors in the world's marketplaces: fewer demands for capital makes it less costly.

Something even more retrograde has been going on at the same time. Our neoliberal infatuation with the free market and the irresistible political influence of big business has led to the rediscovery and updating of the Enclosure Acts of eighteenth-century England. What had then been "the commons"—land, water, forest, and wildlife, available to all—was by legislative fiat converted into the private domains of Britain's landed elite. Here in the United States over the last generation, public facilities, resources, and services—waterworks, transportation, public lands, telecommunication networks, airwaves, herbs, forests, minerals, rivers, prisons, public housing, schools, health care institutions, in sum everything from zoos to war-fighting—got privatized, turning the commonweal into profit centers for the incorporated. One writer has called this the "gutting edge of accumulation by dispossession." It also goes on abroad, inscribed in trade agreements, where, for example, all the costs of environmental regulation and protection, if they are allowed at all, are borne by the host countries.[45]

Over the course of the last quarter century, poverty grew, crippled lives, and wore new faces. Some reappeared as the urban wretchedness the turn-of-the-century reformer Jacob Riis would have recognized. More showed up in the countryside and even in derelict suburbs; indeed the numbers of the suburban poor are now the fastest growing. Rural poverty reached 17 percent by the 1980s, its growth fed by the decline and death of extractive and smaller industry. During the new millennium's first decade, the numbers of people categorized as living in "extreme poverty," especially in the suburbs and in Midwestern cities, grew by one-third. And the biggest leap in people living below the poverty line happened in the Sun Belt, in places like Coral Gables and Fresno.

Between 2004 and 2007 (that is, before the Great Recession struck), more than 30 percent of Americans were poor at least once for two months or more; by 2007 one-third of all children lived in households that had been poor for at least a year. And just as the economy capsized in 2008, 40 percent of the 40 million officially poor people were "very poor," meaning their incomes were less than half of what the government defined as poverty level. Close to 40 million people depended on soup kitchens or food pantries.[46]

Many of the impoverished were and are the marginalized unemployed. Back in 1978, Senator Edward Kennedy warned of the rise of "a permanent underclass"; and the 1980 Census recorded astonishing levels of poverty—over 20 percent—in cities like Newark, Atlanta, Miami, Baltimore, and Cleveland. Viewed by the overclass as "unreachable," victims of their own cultural derelictions, excesses, and addictions, these people were disproportionately African American. This ascription implicitly functioned for many as the cause of what needed to be explained. That the deterioration of the economy, the shift in its center of gravity toward finance, the anemia and isolation of the labor movement, and cowardly public policy might better explain their exclusion grew less and less palatable in a culture infatuated with the market.[47]

But millions more work. And even during the Clinton boom years a white underclass emerged along with a rainbow underclass of new immigrants. By 2010, more than 15 percent of the population (46 million people) was living in poverty, the highest proportion since 1993. As of this writing, more people rely on food stamps—44 million—than ever before. Even before the Great Recession, the Agriculture Department estimated that 35 million people were "food insecure." Some resort to food auctions, where items are cheap because they're often past their sell-by dates. And as it had during the first Gilded Age, poverty descended into a shadow land of the criminal: local laws proliferated outlawing panhandling; harassing the homeless became commonplace; begging, loitering, camping, or sleeping in parks could land you in jail; there were even laws to warn off vagrants and outlaw squeegee guys.

When poverty captured headlines during the first Gilded Age, it was inextricably bound up with exploitation at the workplace. When poverty got rediscovered in the early 1960s, it was, on the contrary, more often associated with exclusion from the workplace in urban ghettos, in exhausted rural regions in Appalachia, and elsewhere. Now we've come full circle and poverty, more often than not, is associated once again with the sweatshop labor that Jacob Riis and others made infamous. When McDonald's held its first-ever national hiring day in 2011, it signed up 62,000 people, more than the net job creation of the whole national economy in 2009. Those 62,000 were lucky to be plucked out of a pool of 938,000 applicants, a rate of acceptance lower than the entering freshman classes at Princeton, Stanford, and Yale. What awaited these fortunate ones was the lowest average wage then on offer in the American economy, less than half of the prevailing wage.

McJobs are the signature accomplishment of a faux recovery. A new category of the "near poor" was created to account for this swelling population of those who toil yet can barely manage to get by. About 50 million people now live in such near poor families. The largest increase in private-sector jobs during the "recovery" has been the low-wage food services and retail sectors. While 23 percent of the jobs lost during the Great Recession were low-wage ones, 49 percent of new jobs are low wage. Many are temporary in the retail, waste management, food services, and health care fields.

If you're old and lucky (which usually means you belong to a union still capable of defending its members), you might hang on to where you got. But if you're young you might well be headed down even before you get a chance to start rising. Entry-level wages for male high school graduates have dropped 19 percent since 1979; for females by 9 percent. The median income for men in their thirties is 12 percent less than it was for their fathers' generation. As of 2005, two-thirds of young working people with a high school degree had no health insurance, compared with one-third in 1979. Households of people from twenty-five to thirty-four years old are carrying debt loads that exceed their annual income. They can't afford housing, college, or cars.[48]

And once again immigrants, legal and illegal, make up a large proportion of the sweated labor force: 27 percent of drywall workers; 24 percent of dishwashers; 22 percent of maids and housekeepers; 22 percent of meat and poultry workers; 21 percent of roofers. Through the subcontracting arrangement now preferred by lean-and-mean flexible corporations, millions of these people work for major companies.[49]

Convict labor, in the nineteenth century a staple of industrial and agricultural enterprise, is making a comeback. The largest incarcerated population on earth (next is Rwanda) has become a pool of forced labor for a range of private and public enterprises, including many of the Fortune 500. The Corrections Corporation of America and G4S (formerly Wackenhut) sell inmate labor at subminimum wages to Chevron, Bank of America, AT&T, and IBM, among others. Corporations can, in most states, lease factories in prisons or lease prisoners to work on the outside making office furniture, taking hotel reservations, fabricating body armor, butchering meat, and sewing pants.[50]

Fear of falling, always the nightmare underside of the American dream, became a reality for millions cut adrift from once secure anchors in the economy. Even castoffs from white-collar jobs at banks and insurance companies found themselves lining up in pinstriped suits at Family Dollar stores for jobs paying $11 an hour. The country's economic geography shifted accordingly. Thus the portion of Americans living in middle-income neighborhoods shrank; in 1970 about 65 percent of families lived in such communities, but by 2011 only 44 percent did.[51]

A cycle of creeping economic superfluity emerged decades ago. First furloughs, followed by brute pay cuts and the silent intimidation to work harder for less or else. Whether in unions or not, workers enjoying the modest pleasures of middle-class life were compelled to shed them. Like those at the Sub-Zero company in Wisconsin, which made freezers and ovens, where it was either a 20 percent pay cut or the company was off to Kentucky or Arizona or south of the border. Thousands of identical dilemmas presented themselves over the last generation. The outcome was invariably the same, so that anecdotal misfortunes became the open sores of a social disease. Now millions consider themselves fortunate if they can find any kind of job, often at the lowest ends of the hierarchy as home health aides or waitresses, willing to accept painful wage cuts. On average a worker losing a stable, decent-paying job was likely to see his or her earnings fall by 20 percent over the past quarter century.[52]

What once was the conventional forty-hour work week became for many a fifty- or sixty-hour week, in part because people held down two jobs and in part because the wonders of advanced electronics tethered employees to their jobs 24/7. One out of six middle managers worked more than sixty hours. Down at the lower end of the workplace hierarchy, security guards at G4S, for example, averaged the same. At other venues if hours didn't go up, workloads did. If family income managed to just tread water, it was because 70 percent of women with children under the age of seventeen work now (59 percent of them with children under six) compared with 13 percent in 1950. Making matters worse, the United States is one of only four countries—Liberia, Swaziland, and Papua New Guinea being the others—that does not mandate paid maternity leave.[53]

The Temporary Forever

Many of the afflicted—young, middle-aged, and even older—slid down into a provisional world of informal or temporary employment. The president of a temp agency in Toledo observed, "What I'm seeing is a large number of very talented people who are trying to land anything. Everyone is moving down." What is sometimes called "contingent labor" has grown at an accelerating rate for decades. During the 1980s, it grew far faster than the U.S. labor force as a whole: ten million (or 25 percent) of the jobs created during the Reagan years were temporary ones. That pace picked up in the 1990s, by which time contingent workers accounted for one-fifth of the total workforce. It showed up in virtually all sectors of the economy, in fields and factories, at construction sites and warehouses, at offices and retail outlets. "Permatemps" made up more than a third of Microsoft's workforce in the late '90s. Temp agency revenues from placing professional workers doubled.[54]

"Flexible labor"—that is to say, disposable workers—met the imperatives of a declining, deregulated, and finance-driven economy. Mergers and acquisitions obeying lean-and-mean protocols, along with the flight of capital abroad, created a vast pool of idling, available labor. It sped up the process of deskilling and the disassembling of complex work into simpler tasks. Competition following deregulation generated intense pressures to lay off permanent employees. The premium placed on short-term financial results further ratcheted up those demands to compress labor costs as a way of funding leveraged buyouts. Temporary labor became the twentieth century's fin de siècle version of Marx's "reserve army of the unemployed," now folded into huge, bureaucratic temp agencies and mobilized on permanent standby. All have become free agents—free, that is, of the security of tenure, retirement income, health care, vacation days, sick days, holidays, and any possibility of effectively voicing their displeasure in the workplace. Employers large and small are thereby also freed of legal obligation to pay into Social Security, Medicare, or unemployment insurance accounts, to respect wage and hour laws, or to pay workmen's compensation.

This flotilla of free-floating working people—some call it the "precariat"—now make the hotel beds and clean the toilets, grow the food, harvest the food, serve the food, man the call centers, care for the sick and the young, dig the ditches, build the buildings, stock the warehouses, drive the trucks, landscape the villas, clear the wreckage, sell the merchandise, design the website, enter the data, and flood the temp agencies, all without any way of knowing where and how they'll manage day to day, month to month, year to year. Even nurses, scientists, accountants, lawyers, and teachers work on "contingency." The ingenuity of "human relations" professionals has been tapped to create a breviary of contingent work: day laborers, independent contractors, on-call workers, freelancers, temps, and part-timers. By far the most exotic subspecies is the oxymoronic permatemp, someone who works at the same place for years but always confined inside the gulag of temporary employment with all of its indignities, lower wages, lack of benefits, and all-around exclusion from company perks. Microsoft is not the only notorious user of the permatemp as high-tech menial; Hewlett-Packard, Verizon, and Intel also employ them.[55]

FedEx, for example, is a major user of the "independent contractor" category of labor. Nominally, its drivers "own" their own trucks but are in every conceivable way controlled by FedEx. However, because they are nominally "owners" they are ineligible for protection by the nation's labor law and don't qualify for benefits, workmen's compensation, or unemployment insurance.[56]

Worse yet is the lot of the migrant agricultural laborer. Our country is in a literal sense fed by degradation. Workers live and toil amid filth, crammed into barrackslike shelters not fit for animals, smuggled across borders by "coyotes" into twenty-first-century forms of indentured servitude. Like their nineteenth-century rural antecedents, they seem utterly isolated in the American outback; but they actually labor, through a "flexible" network of contractors and subcontractors, for the largest retailers in the world.[57]

So vulnerable, ignored, unable to exercise elementary rights, living outside the law's protections, often foreign, sometimes "illegal," this world bears some of the features of a caste. Profits depend on its exploitation. Perhaps even more telling, so too do whole ways of life. That bazaar of high-end consumption, all its pleasures and conveniences, rests on this underworld, willed into invisibility. Our system of financial capitalism or "credit capitalism" relies to some considerable degree on the geometric multiplication of the working poor not only in the global South, where we are accustomed to finding it (and largely ignoring it), but now here at home.[58]

Another Day Older and Deeper in Debt

Debt, the original mechanism of primitive accumulation (both when capitalism was getting started in the West, and later when it was bringing the global South under its imperial sway), has likewise been eating away at the innards of everyday living for a long time now. It is an affliction of the old and young, low- and middle-income earners, the unskilled and overcredentialed.

Debt sometimes acts as the Dr. Jekyll and Mr. Hyde of commercial society. For some it has been a blessing, for others a curse. For some, the moral burden of carrying debt is a heavy one. And no one lets them forget it. For others, debt bears no moral baggage at all, presenting itself rather as an opportunity to advance, and if proved insupportable, is dumped without a qualm.

It turns out that those who view debt with a smiley face, who approach it as an amoral pathway to wealth accumulation, and who tend to get forgiven the larger their defaults, come from the higher echelons of the economic hierarchy. Then there are the rest, who get scolded, foreclosed, and dispossessed, leaving scars that never go away, wounds that disable the future. This upstairs-downstairs differential class calculus might be called the politics of debt. In our modern era of disaccumulation, this social arithmetic has taken on a poignant irony when it comes to hearth and home.

Securitizing mortgages (subprime and other kinds) and turning them into collateralized debt obligations traded around the world epitomized the "paper entrepreneurialism" turn-of-the-century capitalism had become. Rewards were unimaginably lush on all the Wall Streets of the planet. Mutating homes into securities, and treating them as ATMs, as millions did, fatally undermined an older cultural order which our financial age capitalism could treat only as an impediment.

Facing the social upheavals of the Great Depression in the 1930s, including the anger generated by mass foreclosures, the New Deal had rushed through various housing and farm finance reforms. They expressed the deep conviction articulated by President Roosevelt that "a nation of homeowners, people who own a real share in their own land, is unconquerable." This was a bipartisan persuasion. Republican president Coolidge, a Vermont puritan, believed "no greater contribution could be made to the stability of the Nation and the advancement of its ideals than to make it a Nation of home-owning families." Presidents before and after Silent Cal, including FDR, felt likewise that the savings and loan industry was premised on the notion that "a man who has earned, saved, and paid for a home will be a better man, a better artisan or clerk, a better husband and father, and a better citizen of the republic." Their reasoning once seemed straightforward enough: "Thrift is a disciplinarian of self-denial, temperance, abstemiousness, and simple living."

How alien that now sounds to a world in which the home reemerged as a cash cow—until it could no longer be milked. Cautiously constructed mortgages once functioned as the lubricant of social stability and appealed to empowered circles like the Roosevelt administration for just that reason. The unchaining of debt turned that world upside down. It unsettled, intimidated, and in the end ravaged the "homeland," and not only at home.[59]

Household debt in 1952 amounted to 36 percent of total personal income; by 2006 it accounted for 127 percent. Between the late 1970s and the late '90s the average monthly charge on credit cards climbed from 3.4 percent of income to 20 percent. In 1980, fewer than 1 percent of all financial institutions offered home equity loans, but by the end of that decade, 80 percent of all banks and 65 percent of savings and loans did. If you were under the age of thirty-five after the turn of the millennium, you belonged to the "debt generation," relying on credit for education, housing, and health care as debt levels grew at twice the rate of income.

You could borrow to get a boat, a degree, a place to live, or just to stay alive. Financing poverty proved lucrative, for example. Taking advantage of the low credit rating of poorer people and their need for cash just to pay monthly bills or to eat, some check-cashing outlets, payday lend-ers, tax preparers, and others levied interest in the mid three figures. And many of these poverty creditors were tied to the largest financiers, including Citibank, Bank of America, and American Express.

Poor or not so poor, pressure to fall deeper and deeper into debt had less to do with uninhibited appetite than it did with the pervasiveness of insecure employment, the decline in state supports, and slowing economic growth, especially among the elderly, young adults, and low-income households. Credit promised to function as a surrogate "plastic safety net." A sizable majority of low-income households resorted to credit not to live the high life, but to meet emergency bills and basic living expenses. But as income levels shrank, the net sagged...and then ripped.

Poor or not so poor, shouldering freight loads of debt became increasingly impossible. The portion of disposable income spent on servicing debt rose from 10 percent in 1983 to 14.5 percent in 2006. For older and younger people and low-wage earners, over half their pretax income went to servicing their debt. Nor were there any savings left to cover the deficit: the amount of personal income saved in 1979 averaged 8.9 percent; it was nearly negative, at 0.6 percent, in 2007. Personal bankruptcies quintupled since the late 1970s; between 1980 and 2005, they leapt from about 300,000 annually to 2 million.[60]

Meantime, when FIRE caught fire, it got bailed out, which is a kind of double-indemnity form of auto-cannibalism. After all, the sector first grew mighty by ingesting the surrounding economy; when the markets did a free fall, the commonwealth was again tithed to keep them from crashing. Champions of the risk society off-loaded risk, when it became too risky, onto the shoulders of everyone else—leaving the whole social fabric at risk.

Tunneling Down

Retrogression has a stark arithmetic. During the past thirty years, hours of labor have gone up (nine weeks per year longer than the work-ethic-obsessed Germans; the average middle-class American couple works 540 hours—that is, three months—more each year than the same couple did a generation ago); the number of years people work during a lifetime has gone up; the number of family members working has gone up; and the proportion of family income needed to reproduce the next generation (child care, health, education) has gone up.

Nose-to-the-grindstone calisthenics, however, have left the social organism not stronger but dehydrated. One-quarter of the workforce earns less than the poverty level for a family of four; 50 million live in poverty or near poverty, and that number increased by about 30,000 people each year during the post-dot-com boom; the number of families with children under six living in poverty has gone up; the number of impoverished children rose too, ten times faster than the increase in the total number of children; one-third of those kids live in households that can't consistently afford to eat; and the United States has the highest infant mortality rate of any of the twenty developed countries that belong to the Organization of Economic Cooperation and Development (OECD), as well as the highest incidence of obesity, mental illness, and consumption of antidepressants.[61]

Alternative markers of social well-being have also tracked steadily downward. *Fortune* magazine predicted in 1967 that wages would rise by 150 percent between then and the year 2000. As it turned out, real income in 1990 was exactly where it had been when those prophecies of good times ahead were first enunciated. "Morning again in America" dawned only for a favored sliver. Wages have at best stagnated while productivity rose markedly. The gross disparity in the distribution of income and wealth, more skewed than ever before, has by now become a commonplace of public notice, inscribed memorably in the Occupy Wall Street rubric "We are the 99%."[62]

Public health care declined and the need for private insurance rose; housing prices and interest rates became more volatile. Once productivity and wages had risen in tandem, doubling between 1947 and 1973. Since then, productivity has increased by 84 percent while the average hourly wage has stayed flat. The value of the minimum wage declined precipitously during the whole era, by a third just in the ten years between 1979 and 1989, way below the poverty threshold. Even after the latest full increase in the federal minimum wage took effect in 2009, its real value is less than it had been a half century ago.[63]

A generation ago, one-third of workers in the private sector had traditional defined-benefit pensions (including 84 percent of those working in companies employing more than 100 people); now 16 percent do, as corporations shifted into 401(k) plans or froze pensions, or just got rid of them. No matter, as according to the Pollyannas of the new order, people will "e-tire" (meaning they had better join the ranks of the precariat or suffer the consequences) instead of retire. They were invited, by proponents of the new order, to practice the arts of "self-actualization" in their sunset years. Three-quarters of low-wage workers had no employer-paid health insurance, and three-quarters no sick days.[64]

Fifty years ago, half of those who just lost a job received unemployment insurance. Before the Great Recession, that proportion had declined to a third (and less than one-fifth for low-wage workers). That was itself a symptom of the precarious downward trajectory set in motion by capitalism's vaunted new flexibility. Millions now compelled to work part-time or irregularly, on board when needed, overboard when not, could no longer meet the minimum monthly earning requirements to qualify for unemployment benefits.

Alongside those lucky enough to have regained some means of livelihood, a demoralized band of the long-term unemployed, numbering at least 1.5 million people, has gathered, having all their insurance exhausted after 99 weeks. The "99ers" come from all walks of life, including the college-educated, middle-management castoff who found himself not only out of work but evicted, down to his last couple of hundred dollars, and about to move into his car. Shape-ups forming outside home-improvement stores and plant nurseries in Las Vegas included jobless immigrants alongside Anglos. On average, people now stay unemployed for six months, a figure never seen since such statistics were first recorded in 1948. During the Great Recession, an astounding 19.4 percent of all men in their prime earning years (twenty-five through fifty-four) were jobless—this was also a record. The "99ers" are making up a minisociety of the superannuated.[65]

All sorts of public provisioning and protection, not just unemployment insurance, grew similarly more scarce. "Welfare as we have known it" was abolished by the Clinton administration. Federal training programs for the technologically unemployed shrank drastically. Federal housing subsidies have dropped by two-thirds since the 1970s. During the Reagan years, spending on food stamps declined by 17 percent, school lunch programs by a third. Today, preschool enrollments are among the lowest in the developed world. The value of Pell grants for low-income college students, which once constituted 84 percent of tuition, by the first decade of the new century covered only 32 percent.

Auto-cannibalism acquired its own special vocabulary. What we once called firing has been euphemized as "business process engineering," as "slimming," "right-sizing," "rationalizing," "focused reduction," "reinvesting," "outsourcing," "release of resources," "redundancies," or more cheerfully, "career change opportunities." Only rarely did someone speak more plainly, as did Labor Secretary Robert Reich when he acknowledged in 1996 that "the job security many workers experienced in the three decades after World War II is probably gone forever." On the other side of a widening class chasm, the language of predatory triumph trumpeted the new order—for example, best sellers bore such chest-thumping titles as *Barbarians at the Gate*, and *The Disposable American*. Intel CEO Andy Grove chose *Only the Paranoid Survive* as his book's title to capture the pathology that had become the new normal.

Conservative pundit George Will noticed which way the wind was blowing when it first began in the early 1980s and was amazed: "This represents a transfer of wealth from labor to capital unprecedented in American history. Tax revenues are being collected from average Americans...and given to the buyers of U.S. government bonds—buyers in Beverly Hills, Lake Forest, Shaker Heights, and Grosse Point and Tokyo and Riyadh. If a Democrat can't make something of that, what are the Democrats for?"[66]

Indeed! It was reasonable to suppose, as many did over the decades to follow, that this drift of events would run aground on the shoals of resistance to such gross inequality, injustice, and decline. That did not happen, not among Democrats certainly, but also more portentously perhaps, not among those on the front lines whose lives were being reengineered and sometimes dismembered by the new capitalism. Embedded deep within the political and cultural life of the new order were the mechanisms of acquiescence, the means of persuasion and coercion, the promise and fear, that kept it aloft.

9

Fables of Acquiescence: The Businessman as Populist Hero

Cornelius Vanderbilt has been called America's first tycoon. Yet during his lifetime and afterward, he was often enough depicted (sometimes by himself) as the people's champion, challenging the prerogatives of an established elite. There was some truth to this. In the decades leading up to the Civil War especially, he and other upstart businessmen demanded open access to state-authorized franchises for ferry services, steamboat routes, railroads, and other vital public conveyances. Up to then, these enterprises had been granted exclusively to the politically well-connected families of older mercantile and landed interests. During the antebellum years, especially during the presidency of Andrew Jackson, these circles were regularly denounced as monopolists and aristocrats. All sorts of aspiring entrepreneurs in town and country called for universal incorporation laws to open up the marketplace. Future tycoons like Vanderbilt associated themselves with this democratic struggle against capitalism on behalf of capitalism.[1]

Napoleon-like legends have periodically burnished the reputations of American tycoons ever since. One half of that myth—the better-known half—celebrates in the ascendant businessman those qualities of the warrior, commander, and conqueror commonly associated with the

French emperor (Vanderbilt's nickname was the Commodore). The other half, however, is more taken with the contrary plebeian story of Napoleon's rise from social obscurity; the man from nowhere, the lowly officer in the Grand Army of the Republic who by virtue of his sheer audacity and native shrewdness came to lead that army as it overthrew the monarchies and potentates that had ruled Europe for centuries. Napoleon: the Emperor of Democracy.

America has been particularly infatuated with the version of this story that features the businessman as popular hero, a figure combining imperial mastery with everyman beginnings. The country's vast terrain, rich resources, egalitarian credo, and common market have made that remarkable rise out of the inconsequential to Olympian heights reality enough for enough people to lend that legend enduring appeal. And as the Vanderbilt version of this Napoleonic tale reminds us, this is more than a simple story of rags to riches. It is also in its own way a stirring account of class warfare. Together they comprise the singular romance of our native bourgeoisie.

Under normal circumstances, the quotidian concerns of the counting-house, the prudential caution, and the preference for peaceable trucking and bartering do not make the bourgeoisie a likely candidate for heroic exploits and valorous adventure. True, in the Old World, an aura of idealism and heroic bravery accompanied the protracted combat of the rising middle classes against an entrenched feudal order. Blood was spilled on behalf of a new conception of human freedom. Here in the New World, however, once the Revolution accomplished its work, the confrontation with a formal hierarchy of privileged castes (excepting the slave power) was an attenuated one. What remnants hung on from the colonial era, bound together by family ties, breeding, education, and inherited wealth, and deferred to by ordinary folk—Boston's Brahmins, New York's Knickerbockers, Philadelphia's Gentlemen—were more or less quickly overwhelmed by the furious pace of economic transformation, territorial expansion, and the democratization of everyday social life, not to mention the opening up of the political arena to the vox populi.

Yet in what was hypothetically a uniquely classless society, upper classes kept coming into and going out of existence. The most powerful were anchored in various forms of landed, commercial, financial, and, soon enough, industrial property. Their longevity, however, was not assured. This is first of all testimony to the economic fluidity of the expanding marketplace, which kept opening up new commercial opportunities. Nonetheless, to effectively seize the moment often required contesting against those who already had a grip on the levers of economic and political wherewithal.

So began a version of class warfare that pitted striving men from nowhere against those who probably just yesterday had arrived at the heights. At times those challenging the prevailing hierarchs, however much they might have desired to join them, cast their cause in the language of republican individualism, equality, and freedom. Periodically this peculiar crusade renewed that otherwise incongruous experience of a rising nouveau riche mounting the barricades. When this happened, the businessman could emerge as the paladin of emancipation and win an extraordinary degree of public esteem and moral authority.

No stranger interlude in the saga of the businessman as emancipator has cropped up than the one we have lived through during the second Gilded Age. This fable of the financier especially (as well as the techno-entrepreneur) as freedom fighter has made its unique contribution to that mood of acquiescence which so starkly distinguishes our own Gilded Age from the original.

The Aging of the Establishment

Beginning in the 1980s, a cadre of financial outliers, men lacking the credentials of the Wall Street insider, launched an assault on the white-shoe establishment. America's leading corporations and banks found themselves in the crosshairs. How odd! A century before, Wall Street and the Fortune 500 stood as the impregnable redoubts of what many identified as the country's ruling class. Now hot-tempered agitators dressed in neckties and armed with briefcases determined to overthrow the old guard and in the process save the American economy—indeed, not just the economy but the nation.

Save it from what and from whom? By the 1980s, the economy had floundered for a decade, afflicted simultaneously with hyperinflation and levels of unemployment not seen since before the Second World War. Core industries seemed increasingly unable to match the performance of their counterparts in Europe and Japan. Trade deficits, which in the nineteenth century marked America's status as a developing nation, reappeared as if time was headed in the wrong direction. The postwar global monetary system invented and presided over by the United States collapsed.

Alongside this depressing experience of economic retrogression and aggravating it at every point was a more general sense of national decline. Defeat in Vietnam, OPEC's defiance of the West, and the humiliation of American captives in Tehran were all mounting evidence that the "American Century" was ending prematurely. Mores and beliefs that had long governed family life, relations between men and women and children and their parents, sexuality, and traditional sources of legitimate authority had lost their grip. Watergate punctuated the disorientation.

Who to blame? Many candidates were naturally offered up. What since the 1950s had been frequently identified as the Establishment was one favorite. Defined and described in various ways, it was pictured by most people who believed in its existence as an interlocking directorate whose components included top management from the Fortune 500, Wall Street, and key regional financial centers; executive branch appointees to leading posts within the national security state and military, often with first careers on Wall Street; intellectuals at think tanks engaged in long-term strategic planning about both foreign and domestic affairs; shapers of public opinion running the nation's principal metropolitan print media and broadcast television; and those occupying the inner councils of the two major political parties.[2]

The social profile of this milieu tended to reflect its members' shared background as upper-class Protestants who had often attended the same or similar private preparatory schools and Ivy League colleges. They had grown up in an archipelago of luxuriant enclaves and secluded mansions running along both coastlines or nestled near their prime holdings in the industrial heartland. After college they socialized in a set of exclusive men's clubs. That provincialism was counterbalanced by travels and associations around the world, making them self-consciously cosmopolitan. They helped steer nonprofit foundations, moved easily between the private sector and public positions, and usually cut their teeth by running major corporations and banks, if they weren't lifetime military men.

Ideologically they were at peace with the main institutions and political arrangements of the New Deal administrative and regulatory state, some of which they had helped to create. Bipartisan or nonpartisan by preference (although often genetically Republican), they accepted the postwar concord that allowed a substantial if constricted role for the labor movement in the nation's political affairs and acknowledged the wisdom of some if limited government oversight of the economy. They were as well the architects and inheritors of the postwar American imperium, including the Marshall Plan, NATO, the World Bank, the International Monetary Fund, and the Bretton Woods system of fixed exchange rates.

Most of all, they were confident that judicious applications of Keynesian fiscal and monetary policy could ensure growth and immunize the economy and society against the cyclical social and political chaos of the past. This was the regnant illusion of the postwar order: that in this way an inherently amoral capitalism could be wedded to some gentlemanly code of conduct. The free market, left to its own devices, might in fact be a moral imbecile. But its longings to be wild and free of all constraints could be domesticated by those wise enough to do the taming.

Common background, breeding, experience, and beliefs prepared the Establishment for one mission above all: to ensure postwar stability. In the words of one historian, they were "American democracy's only natural aristocracy." And they were world-class managers.[3]

Managerial capitalism was born along with the modern, publicly traded, multifunctional, multidivisional corporation around the turn of the twentieth century. It was meant to replace the dynastic version of family capitalism. Those owner-operated enterprises had built up the great industries and fortunes of the nineteenth century. But they had done so at the cost of chronic economic uncertainty and intermittent disaster as well as severe social antagonisms that kept threatening to burn the house down. A handful of corporations establishing oligopolistic positions across a range of industrial and commercial sectors, overseen by an even more select group of investment bankers, were designed to end that era of internecine competition and turmoil.

During the earlier period, the property owner and manager was the same person or family (the great trunk-line railroads, thanks to their enormous capital requirements, expanse, and intricacy, were the first exception to this). Under the new dispensation of the publicly traded corporation, a cadre of professional managers and directors presided over these highly complex organizations. They were to ensure each such corporation's efficiency, longevity, and of course its profitability.

Severing ownership from management had many consequences. For one, the corporation emerged as an impersonal entity (even though in law it was and still is treated as a "person"). Its leading management team need not reflect any longer the personal interests, prejudices, obligations, or local loyalties of a dominant patriarch. As professionals—expert in finance, sales, technology, or production—managers were compelled to take actions that might not immediately show up in higher stock prices or dividends. Taking root at first in complex business enterprises, the management outlook quickly exfoliated across a wide terrain, defining life beyond the sphere of production. Its emphasis on efficiency and predictability and its intense desire for rationalized means of control to normalize conflict and ensure stability became maxims applicable to all great bureaucracies, public and private.

Little room was left within the interior of these featureless machines for the romance of the adventuring entrepreneur. On the contrary, the manager assumed the role of the invisible functionary. Dynastic capitalism was a relic. Long live the corporation.[4]

For some this would prove frustrating; not so, however, for the ostensible owners of the corporation. In fact, the widening class of shareholders were not prepared for or interested in taking on the responsibilities of running the enterprise that normally attached to ownership. Rather they focused on the present or future value of its stock. Moreover, the diffusion of stockholders made it hard to check managerial autonomy. While well rewarded, often with equity stakes in the company as well as handsome salaries, the new management class possessed a fungible set of skills and experience that allowed them to move from one corporation to another. Building up a patrimony was no longer organically linked to the capital accumulation of a singular enterprise.

So too, the modern corporation was not as instinctively averse to government meddling as its dynastic predecessor had been. To be sure, it resisted all far-reaching proposals for public ownership, government planning, price fixing, central banking, vigorous antitrust action, oversight of the stock market, and government-sanctioned collective bargaining. But it recognized the tactical usefulness of laws to ensure fair competition, rate setting on the arteries of transportation and power generation, state mediation of labor conflicts, and government help on other matters that would enhance the stability and predictability of corporate affairs (and, not so coincidentally, do away with the nuisance of smaller, upstart competitors who couldn't afford to live by those rules).

Attitudes about dealing with the workforce also altered along with the phase change from family (or dynastic) capitalism to corporate capitalism. On the one hand, virtually no modern corporation was prepared to accept independent unions on the shop floor until the New Deal era. However, company-initiated and -controlled forms of welfare capitalism allowed for company-created unions, profit sharing, stock ownership, recreational and health facilities, and even pensions. These were pragmatic overtures taken up in order to reduce the enormous expenses of high labor turnover, and incidentally encourage bonds of loyalty where once only estrangement and animosity prevailed. Dynastic capitalism had dealt with this problem more mercilessly.

Other constituencies were also treated with greater forbearance. By the very nature of its size, capital commitments, production cycles, marketing efforts, customer base, and ties to government, educational, and research institutions, the new corporation was compelled to engage in long-term planning and multiple-party negotiations. Maintaining good relations (including public relations, as brand names and corporate logos became strategic marketing devices) with communities, suppliers, customers, and others who inhabited the enterprise's wider universe became a variable within management's calculus.

A mystique grew up around the practice of managerial capitalism. Obedient only to the dictates of efficiency, the corporation was allegedly cleansed of the unseemly greed and cruelty that typified robber baron days. In this idealization managerial capitalism presented itself and often enough was accepted by the outside world as a mechanism of public service: a minicommonwealth of workers, consumers, shareholders, and local communities. Those who ran these enterprises deployed power benignly, having expropriated the primary functions of the old expropriators. They held the public interest in trust, as such firms would not hesitate to claim.

Halfway between truth and a tall tale, this account eluded some discomfiting realities. There was little effective check on how these managers used their power; nor was their social conscience strengthened by regular exercise. Politically they were first among equals when it came to getting their way. Their loyalty above all was to their own self-advancement, tracking through the treacherous terrain of the corporate hierarchy. In its pursuit, these dispassionate professionals could become downright nasty and unscrupulous. So too, this milieu's sense of noblesse oblige is easy to exaggerate, committed as they were to moneymaking, guided by principles no loftier than "work and win/strive and succeed." While they were well educated, their approach to knowledge was strictly instrumental: shrewd rather than wise. Profitability was always the leading priority.

Nonetheless, measuring profit, when and how often to take that measure, and what to do with accumulated surpluses, did not always or necessarily coincide with the interests of shareholders. Today that would be considered heretical.[5]

"Shareholder value" as the only value that ought to govern decision making in the boardroom is the orthodoxy of our time. To lend ballast to that claim, its advocates intimate its pedigree goes all the way back to the beginning of capitalist time. But that was not so in Adam Smith's day or during the long nineteenth century that followed. Stock exchanges, once they became significant, were infrequently used to raise capital for long-term investment; rather they were a vehicle for cashing in and cashing out by individuals or were used in more or less ingenious ways by financial institutions trading for the short term. Reinvested earnings, commercial loans, and bond issues instead constituted the lion's share of capital resources for the modern corporation. This practice continued well into the twentieth century. Between 1950 and 1973 nonfinancial corporations funded 93 percent of capital expenditures out of internal resources. During this period, 70 percent of corporate profits on average were reinvested in the company as opposed to 30 percent in 1929.[6]

Shareholder value as an ideology and faith, no matter its claim to axiomatic truth and longevity, was actually invented a mere generation ago to overthrow the ancien régime, itself increasingly dysfunctional. The faith's underlying premise that shareholder value would be protected and enhanced by a studied ruthlessness again and again proved faulty. In so many leveraged buyouts, takeovers, mergers, and acquisitions, shareholder value declined over the long term, corporate performance fell, and the "discipline" of debt, which was supposed to make these firms pit-dog fit, ended up sinking otherwise entirely viable concerns. Nonetheless, we now pay obeisance to the belief that those who have essentially nothing to do with the running of these businesses—and in most instances have little or no intrinsic interest in what they make or do, and whose collective identity as a mass of individual owners changes almost daily—by right and tradition ought to control them.[7]

How Do You Spell Disestablishmentarianism?

Managerial capitalism together with the New Deal political order defined the contours of stability for two generations. The Establishment took the credit and then suffered the consequences of its excessive self-confidence. When everything began unraveling in the 1970s, the liberal elite that had run the country since the Great Depression apparently ran out of answers. David Rockefeller complained that "people are blaming business and the enterprise system for all the problems of our society."[8]

More than economic ineptitude and corporate obesity were at stake. The political and cultural landscape became harder to navigate. The Establishment seemed to have allied itself with the ghetto. Its commitment to civil rights and affirmative action (to which it assented only under pressure) suggested it was jettisoning its political marriage of convenience with the white working and middle classes. And its will to defend the empire had fissured and grown too timid, its credibility and legitimacy eroding on the left and right. What one writer has called "the end of victory culture," culminating in the horrific calamity of Vietnam, fatally undermined the puissance and credibility of the Establishment. Plus it seemed far too sympathetic to the counterculture's mockery of the conventional moral and social order.[9]

So profound was its loss of authority that the Establishment began failing to reproduce itself. Its offspring no longer felt attached to its traditions, manners, and religious rituals, stopped going to law school or disdained joining the family business, married outside its exclusive social circle if they married at all. Children sometimes ended up on the other side of the barricades, assaulting the family compounds and corporate boardroom. (Indeed some members of the SDS's Weather Underground faction hailed from Social Register families.)[10]

The Establishment was losing its footing everywhere. In its heyday, it seemed to share core values with its subjects, at least with regard to work, patriotism, piety, modesty, moral discipline, reserve, and racial privilege. Now this liberal elite seemed to have repudiated all that, which ate away at the sentimental ties binding it to ordinary working people. The stigmata of race, drugs, unorthodox sex, irreligion, and suspect patriotism seemed to mark an ancien régime gone to seed. They became the telltale markers of a potent new fable: that of the limousine liberal, a group soon to become the bête noire of right-wing populism.

Liberators in Pinstripes

Economic calamity and elite paralysis nourished another oddly related fable: the Wall Streeter as heroic revolutionary. In this tale, the corporate old guard had become ossified and sclerotic, complacent, bureaucratic, and risk averse. On their watch the economy was withering away, losing its combative muscle, its indigenous American taste for the audacious. What native entrepreneurial urges still lived on were disabled by a bewildering labyrinth of government regulations, restrictions, and inhibitions. Together business and public bureaucracies were responsible for the arteriosclerosis afflicting the national economy. They needed dismantling. Fortunately, there were men ready to face the Goliath.

A capitalist version of liberationist theology, at one time the eccentric faith of outlying circles of revanchist businessmen and marginalized conservative intellectuals, gathered momentum all through the dolorous 1970s. An aged ideological alloy combined reverence for the free market with a seething resentment of state interference and the servile demoralization it allegedly encouraged.

Such ancient ideas were now defended by the latest applications of differential calculus and probability theory. But what gave this old-time religion added force, first of all among a rising generation on Wall Street and soon among a milieu of nerdy techno-entrepreneurs, were the unprepossessing social origins of these young men.

Precisely because many of them, like Ivan Boesky and Carl Icahn (or for that matter Bill Gates or Steve Jobs), were not to the manor born, but were instead strivers from the middling classes, they genuinely believed and were able to convince legions of followers and admirers that they had come to storm the fortresses of the ancien régime. Richard Fuld, who eventually ran Lehman Brothers and ran it into the ground, attended the University of Colorado and hawked bonds for a living. AIG was founded by the son of a woman who ran a boardinghouse; he later turned it over to Maurice "Hank" Greenberg, whose father owned a candy store on the Lower East Side. Greenberg in turn appointed Joseph Cassano, the son of a Brooklyn cop, to manage the London-based credit default swap operation. Stan O'Neal, who mismanaged Merrill Lynch into near bankruptcy, was the son of a farmer turned GM worker. Carl Icahn, the son of a cantor, was a lower-middle-class kid from Queens whose smarts got him to Princeton and then to Wall Street. Once there, he exercised a raging temper and a petulant contempt for the old-boy network from whom he regularly extracted tribute in the form of "greenmail" that temporarily at least allowed top management to hold on to its executive suites.[11]

Self-proclaimed champions of the disenfranchised shareholder and saviors of a business underclass denied access to life-sustaining bank credit, men like Icahn turned Wall Street into a combat zone where the forces of market freedom faced off against the overlords of yesteryear. The inventors of this ideological drama were capable of the most cynical and self-interested deceptions while remaining true believers in its underlying moral allegory and economic axioms: the shareholder as the oppressed victim, management as the great usurper.

It was this sense of mission that transformed these corporate raiders, merciless practitioners of the lean-and-mean approach to corporate reorganization, into cultural heroes during the Reagan era and beyond. They promised to open up the marketplace for capital to that discriminated-against mass of American businessmen who lacked the size and connections to command the attention of the big banks. They fearlessly attacked the entrenched managements of the very largest corporations whose timidity, addiction to routine, and limited vision kept stock prices artificially depressed, depriving their shareholders of their rightful gains. In this brave new world, the formal legalities of property rights trumped all other social claims. This was the "right" ne plus ultra that the New Deal had momentarily abridged.

Ironically, as time passed, each new hosanna to the shareholder invoked a more and more migratory, shadowy presence, a kind of mass-less mass, whose purpose in life seemed less and less to do with owner-ship and management and more and more to do with speculation. The idea of being tied down to a particular piece of property in the age of financialization seemed like a fool's game—until everything went smash.

Every act of this Wall Street insurgency had its disinterested or even nonmaterial justification. If their outsized mergers and acquisitions made them stunningly rich, they produced handsome returns for holders of mutual funds, college endowments, savings and loan institutions, and pension funds that bought the high-risk/high-return junk bonds which financed these transactions. If men like Saul Steinberg, Carl Icahn, and Ron Perelman and the immaculately coiffed circle of anonymous suits serving them seemed almost indecently awash in money, at least they worked liked demons to get it, putting in inhuman hours, beginning their days at four in the morning, ending them at midnight. For them, hard work, an American sacrament, was an aphrodisiac; they were a liv-ing reproach to the stereotypical Wall Street banker whose day began at ten and ended at three, with an intermission for a three-martini lunch.

Taking on the stuffed shirts like Felix Rohatyn of Lazard Freres or the urbane, French-accented Michel Bergerac, head of Revlon (as Ron Perelman, an uncouth upstart out of Philadelphia, did in his hostile take-over of the company in 1985), was depicted as class warfare, American-style. The have-not-enoughs were confronting the have-too-muches (even though Perelman himself craved nothing more than to climb to the summit of social notoriety). Somehow, the fate of the American dream seemed to be at stake. And if in the immediate aftermath of root-and-branch corporate reconfigurations, landmark industrial plants shut their doors; if whole communities became ghost towns; if middle management lived in terror of its own extinction—in the long term, this was a kind of tough-love patriotism; it would strengthen America against its rivals in a global economic jungle where only the fittest survived.

When they lobbied ferociously for a defanging of the government's regulatory apparatus or for the repeal of keystone pieces of New Deal legislation like the Glass-Steagall Act, these young lions did so to extend the realm of freedom, to remove the dead hand of the government bureaucrat, and to unleash the creative energies of the enterprising individual. The willingness to be savage, and to wear that savagery like a medal of honor, was the whole point; this was a revenge fantasy against America's white-shoe crowd, who had forfeited their right to rule.

A choir of youthful publicists provided intellectual cover for the new knighthood. In his best-selling *Wealth and Poverty* (its title an ironic and perverse echo of the Henry George classic), George Gilder explained that "to help the poor and middle classes one must cut the taxes of the rich." Fatuities like this soon became commonplaces of our political life and remain so to this day.[12]

No mere public policy scrap, this was a crusade with a metaphysical bottom line. Richard Dorman, Reagan's deputy secretary of the treasury, lambasted the business establishment as "bloated, risk averse, inefficient, and unimaginative." Freedom morphed into a synonym for free enterprise. An anti-elitist revolution from above, it exuded a messianic aura. Corporate America was to be saved from itself, from its fat cat complacency. Stripped of poorly earning assets, malingering workers and their featherbedding unions, and doddering and absentee managers, American business would rise again. Only men who had risen from social obscurity could appreciate and meet the challenge. They came armed with the necessary irreverence, fearlessness, and appetite for the new. They could reinvent the world in their garages or sweep away those cobwebbed gray flannel suits. Only they had the foresight to spot, and the derring-do confidence to resurrect, companies languishing in commercial oblivion, financially distressed but latent with untapped potential. They could be freed, but it would take the valor of a new financial knighthood.[13]

Michael Milken's Aladdin-like junk bond leveraged buyouts, mega-mergers and acquisitions made him the chief knight of the realm. Raised in California, nerdy, married to his high school sweetheart, residing in the same suburb he grew up in, supremely arrogant, yet notably modest in what he drove, dressed in, and lived in, he was perhaps an unlikely candidate for the role. He nonetheless exerted a mesmerizing influence, a charisma that had limos lining up on Rodeo Drive in Beverly Hills at four in the morning to do deals, convinced, as one of his more perfervid admirers gushed, that "Michael is the most important individual who has lived in this century." Why not? Contemporary observers thought they spied a social revolution in the making. Milken was its Lenin.

Household names in American business—TWA, U.S. Steel, Gulf Oil, Walt Disney—were all of a sudden in play and threatened with absorption into some alien acronym of financial abstraction. One-third of the companies on the Fortune 500 list in 1980 no longer existed as independent entities a decade later. Employment rosters at the Fortune 500 fell from 16 million in 1979 to just over 11 million in 1993. Three thousand mergers worth $200 billion took place in 1985 alone. By the end of the century, *Fortune*, anointing America "a Trader Nation," announced that there was "a revolution underway, and it's changing the way we invest and work and live."

Milken's social revolution overturned Wall Street's historic hierarchy. The firm he worked for, Drexel Burnham Lambert, had been distinctly minor league; now it and a handful of other new arrivals, like Kohlberg, Kravis, Roberts & Company, were cock of the walk. "Relationship banking"—that genteel world lined with mahogany walls hung with Old Masters, resting on time-tested traditional dealings between partic-ular banks and their corporate mates, a relationship premised as much on family and social ties as it was on mere moneymaking—gave way to (indeed, was run over by) "transactional banking." Here every new deal was open to negotiation, each a new test for some Wall Street financial house to prove its commercial bona fides all over again, and all deals were subject to the singular criterion of the highest return produced in the shortest time.

Nasty microbattles for control took place inside venerable firms like Lehman Brothers, where languorous Ivy League patricians turned out in rimless spectacles and the omnipresent breast-pocket hankie were challenged by shirtsleeved, uncouth, cigar-chomping geeks from the trading floor staring out at the world through stylishly obtuse, thick-framed black glasses. As one magazine profile noted, Mesa Petroleum's T. Boone Pickens, a corporate raider of the first rank, although a WASP, "never loses a chance to dramatize his persona as a plain-talking country boy engaged in a populist battle against an effete elite." Frank Lorenzo, who wrestled to the ground the old-line management of Eastern Airlines, was the son of a Spanish immigrant who went out of his way to emphasize his ethnic origins by listing his given name in *Who's Who* as "Francesco." It was all symbolic of fresh blood getting pumped through the aerated arteries of an aging financial organism.[14]

An All-American Infatuation

No arena of cultural endeavor remained immune to the charisma of these young Turks. Preachers and newspaper editors, magazine entrepreneurs and board game creators, novelists, playwrights, moviemakers, and television soap opera producers, historians, book publishers, gossip columnists, and even choreographers were all infected with a kind of bug-eyed fascination. Treating the financier as a messiah was already afoot when the economy first turned down in the seventies. In *The Financier*, Michael Jensen invoked the "I" banker as a kind of holy magician: "His art is arcane. But just as the rainmaker promised to draw from the sky that drop that nourished the farmer's crops, so these latter day rainmakers draw from the people and institutions around them the dollars that one needed to build the nation's factories." In an atmosphere like this, those who covered the news or searched it for sources of entertainment couldn't take their eyes off what Michael Thomas, a columnist for *Manhattan Inc.* (perhaps the magazine most single-mindedly zeroed in on doings on the Street), waspishly dubbed the "new tycoonery."[15]

Catholic theologians like Michael Novak joined televangelists in scouring the Bible for injunctive commandments to multiply and accumulate. Televangelist Jerry Falwell found "the free enterprise system... clearly outlined in the Book of Proverbs." Great wealth, Falwell professed, was "God's way of blessing people who put him first." He and his fellow evangelicals certainly practiced what they preached, transforming their ministries into multipurposed businesses that included theme parks, cable TV stations, colleges, and hotels. Nor were they shy about flaunting their personal opulence. Jim and Tammy Faye Bakker had six houses, one of which came equipped with an air-conditioned doghouse.

New magazines like *Success*, *Manhattan Inc.*, *Venture*, and *Millionaire*, and the relaunched *Vanity Fair* (as well as established ones like *Esquire* and *The New Yorker*) sprang to life as awestruck documentarians of the era's power-suit costuming, its manly horseplay, its philanthropic social climbing, its O.K. Corral financial stare-'em-downs and shoot-'em-ups. Power portraits of the biggest deal makers marveled at their all-around fitness, their regimen of physical workouts that prepared them for all-nighters. A high-end athletic club offered the "Fitness Program Fast Enough for Wall Street." These were financial athletes at the peak of their game, in it not for the money alone but for the je ne sais quoi that always seems present at the mystic heart of all true sportsmen, men like the financier Asher Edelman, known as "the Liquidator," who confided his "Nietzschean desire for control." Bond traders made out like professional hit men and boasted of "ripping the faces off" opponents (who sometimes turned out to be their clients). More cerebral samurai of the financial wars carried around copies of *The Art of War* by Sun-tzu, the Chinese Clausewitz. *Forbes* rhapsodized about Michael Milken's "one-man revolution"; *Business Week's* cover story compared the junk-bond master with Morgan; *Institutional Investor* anointed him "Michael the Magnificent."

A whole subgenre relived familiar tales of transfiguration. For instance, there was the story of Bruce Wasserstein (playwright Wendy's brother), who grew up in the middle-class neighborhood of Midwood in Brook-lyn, spent time as a poverty worker and Nader raider, only then, like some character out of *The Big Chill*, to go on to negotiate the four largest corporate mergers in American history. He was compared with a blood-ied general perpetually embattled. Wasserstein enjoyed homelier com-parisons: "I'm a craftsman, no different than a carpenter or a painter."

Moreover, Wasserstein's incongruous beginnings turned out to be not so odd after all, as a small cohort of young men living on the fringes of the counterculture and the "new left" brought its feistiness and irrever-ence, if not its politics, to this bizarre version of the class struggle on Wall Street and to the information superhighway. A face-off at an unsexy institution like Lehman Brothers between two otherwise colorless figures—one, Lewis Glucksman, a jowly merchant; the other, a onetime political functionary, Pete Peterson—got dramatized in the media as a facsimile of mortal combat, a tale of "greed and glory." Arbitrageur Ivan Boesky's book *Merger Mania* modestly attributed his triumphs to hard work and common sense. But this was mere rhetorical gesture since everyone knew his real allure was that of the riverboat gambler. Nick-named "Piggy," he was a charmer with a long history of skirting the law.[16]

Slang from the Street insinuated itself into the language of everyday life. And whole thesauruses migrated in the opposite direction—from civilian life back to the front lines—to capture the atmosphere of blood-thirsty romance. Metaphors for corporate mergers leaned heavily on the language of sex and violence, ranging all the way from chivalrous mar-riage to rape. There was talk of "white knights," of "shotgun" corporate marriages, of "financial angels" and "sweethearts," not to mention "sleeping beauties" targeted by a rogue's gallery of "black knights," "killer bees," and "hired guns." This was a refreshed vocabulary stripped of the politesse of the Establishment, earthier and closer to the *Volk.* Here was the metaphoric vocabulary of a Wall Street state of mind spo-ken from coast to coast.

Wall Street R Us

However improbable it might have seemed to our ancestors, this fable of Wall Street heroism on behalf of democracy managed to enchant. By the turn of the millennium, a cultural democratization of the Street was widely visible. It had grass roots. First of all, by then roughly half the population participated in the stock market, if only passively through their pension funds and other forms of institutional investment. Moreover, the Street's reputation had undergone a miraculous makeover. Those hoary suspicions of old had faded away. More than that, the Street had become for many a zone of liberation, visionary exultation, national pride, and entertainment. A great many people had come to think of the stock market as a place that welcomed outsiders; not merely welcomed them, but empowered them; and not only empowered them but put them in touch with the zeitgeist of the new millennium. Ordinary folk could become homesteaders on Wall Street's virtual landscape, where they might stake out their claim to freedom: freedom from workday tedium, from the press of material want, from the demeaning deference to employers and haughty elitists in business and government. A chemical engineer in New York credited his involvement in the stock market with a miraculous change in his thinking: "It gave me the feeling of control over my life I never had before." Susie Vasillov, owner of a housewares store and a stock market player, spoke for many: "And whether you're a mommy or the owner of a tony housewares shop, we're all businesspeople. I think it's a great thing that's happened to the country." Shareholder Nation had arrived.[17]

Toy manufacturers simulated the excitement about piratical cutthroatery with aptly titled board and video games like Greed, The Bottom Line, and Arbitrage. Book publishers discovered an insatiable demand for titles purporting to illuminate the mysteries of business gamesmanship: *The Money Game*, *The Takeover Game*, and dozens of others featured the stories of financial "geniuses" and takeover Michelangelos.

Newspapers and magazines were full of glad tidings about Wall Street as the latest form of the vox populi. CNBC, CNN-FN, Bloomberg, and others responded and encouraged the insatiable appetite for investment news and advice. Financial news plus sports accounted for half the editorial content of many newspapers. By the 1990s, the sheer overwhelming presence of stock market news on TV and radio, the proliferation of talk shows and whole new cable channels where market analysts became video celebrities, the inundation of the airwaves by commercials for brokerages, online trading websites, and other avenues of mass enthrallment were all evidence that someone was listening.[18]

They were doing more than listening. Average folk were predicating their spending plans on the leverage their assets in the stock market presumably provided. Home building and buying, car purchases, vacation getaways, big-ticket consumer electronics, air travel, and consumer durables in general stayed afloat, in part, atop the bubble. People wore wristwatches that beeped when IBM stock hit its owner's price threshold. A Florida dentist confessed to tracking his investments in between patients, sometimes between X-rays and fillings.

Day-trading, which became wildly popular by the mid-1990s, particularly invited hoi polloi, all sorts of people who might not otherwise have ventured anywhere near the Street, to indulge and overindulge. They seemed consumed by normal consumer anxieties about being left out and left behind, but also by the sort of thrills, titillation, and lightninglike action that popular culture in general thrived on. *Newsweek* called it a "blood sport." A Connecticut billboard touting offtrack betting captured the sneaky thrill: "Like the Stock Market. Only Faster."

Investment clubs for schoolkids and octogenarian ladies and everyone in between sprouted up everywhere. They were as much pastimes as they were financial undertakings. By 1990 there were about seven thousand officially registered clubs, with probably three times that number organized on a more informal basis. More than a third were all female. The most famous was organized by a group of women in Beardstown, Illinois. They published *The Beardstown Ladies' Common Sense Investment*

Guide, which flew off bookshelves since the ladies had done quite nicely, thank you, on the stock market. (Later it turned out the club's books had been cooked, although innocently.)

High schools introduced investment into the curriculum; by the late 1980s, 350,000 students were playing the Stock Market Game in class and competing in tournaments that went on for weeks. In Arlington, Massachusetts, seventh graders formed teams called the Wizards of Wall Street, the Money Machine, and Stocks R Us. Summer camps added playing the market to their menu of daily activities. Mothers who thought teaching their children about Wall Street would be empowering could buy *Wow the Dow,* a kiddie's guide published by Simon and Schuster. When the Four Seasons Hotel in Boston set up a "dollar and sense investment camp," a local magazine editorialized: "If kids get hooked on saving and investing, America's future could be free of dependence on foreign capital . . . and the nation closer to a balanced budget."[19]

Fever dreams like this were in one sense nothing new when it came to depicting the Street as the pathway to riches. Yet what was different was the way visions of El Dorado were interwoven with the merry informality of consumer culture and the expectations of social emancipation. Wall Street, once a popular symbol of aristocracy, inequity, and oppression, now promised to overthrow itself and have a lot of fun doing it. The Bull is dead. Long live the Bull.

The Narcissism of Victory

Back-shelving the Protestant catechism about hard work and frugal living, the staple wisdom of an earlier era, the element of risk now got top billing in an economy increasingly dominated by financial high-wire acts. It was a more precarious world, but a fairer one, or so declared scholars like Milton Friedman or Peter Berger. The latter's *Capitalist Revolution* likened the system to a great wheel of fortune that spun in a way that best assured material progress and social mobility.[20]

This kind of liberatingly brutal frankness reached its comic-opera apotheosis when Ivan Boesky addressed the graduating class at Berkeley's business school in 1986. There he proudly recalled his working-class, Jewish immigrant origins and famously assured the graduates that "greed is healthy," a revelation they greeted with a healthy round of applause. Boesky's bon mot had become an axiom of the new age. Immortalized by Oliver Stone's Gordon Gekko in the film *Wall Street*—although Gekko managed to lend it an added moral wallop through a critical emendation of the original: "Greed is good"—it hung on even when the party seemed over.

And why not? By the time Boesky made his remark, whole flotillas of students from the nation's top colleges were disembarking at Wall Street. Recruits in unprecedented numbers streamed into an army of investment bankers, money managers, venture capitalists, and corporate lawyers, financial re-engineers armed with higher mathematics and determined to make over America. They constituted a new praetorian guard of "the best and the brightest," a group who wore their SAT scores and Ivy League diplomas like escutcheons of their right to rule. Meritocracy, narrowly defined as "smartness," served as social camouflage, an egalitarian façade concealing a single-minded fealty to the inexorable laws of the market. Conveniently, it buried out of sight the less flattering reality of socially privileged backgrounds that accounted for what was otherwise depicted as an act of self-creation. It was a parody of democracy. An insidious ideal, it degraded the egalitarian credo of earlier times, replacing it with devil-take-the-hindmost apologia for gross and growing inequality.

Such remarkable self-assurance amid the wreckage is breathtaking. Speaking at St. Paul's Cathedral in London in 2009, Brian Griffith of Goldman Sachs invoked the Son of God: "The injunction of Jesus to love others as ourselves is recognition of self-interest.... We have to tolerate the inequality as a way to achieving greater prosperity and opportunity for all." His boss, Lloyd Blankfein, was pithier, claiming, amid the ruins, that he was "doing God's work" supplying money for companies to hire people to make things. For his part, just when the economy hit rock bottom at the end of 2009, President Obama praised Blankfein and Jamie Dimon (the head of JPMorgan Chase) as "very savvy businessmen," noting that he did not "begrudge people success or wealth."

The transfiguration of moneymaking into a fearless quest for self-discovery and self-invention was married to a grander and older idealism about America as a "redeemer nation," holding a perpetual tutorial for the rest of the planet. It was a chiliastic creed that combined eschatology and chauvinism enlisted on behalf of imperial bullying abroad, balm after years of decline and defeat.

Even the shattering of the world financial system couldn't shake this article of faith. An executive at an international hedge fund put it this way in 2011: "We demand a higher paycheck than the rest of the world. So if you are going to demand ten times the paycheck, you need to deliver ten times the value. It sounds harsh, but maybe people in the middle class need to decide to take a pay cut."

All of this fueled a contagious triumphalism not confined to the Street or corporate boardroom. The aroma of renewal and power smelled all the sweeter as the Japanese and Germans, onetime pretenders to economic supremacy, were compelled to swallow enormous mouthfuls of U.S. debt, to suffer the loss of their trade advantages with the up-valuation of the yen and the deutschmark, and to bring their "economic miracles" to a screeching halt, from which the Japanese struggled to recover for decades to come. In his 1985 State of the Union address, President Reagan boasted that the United States would become "the investment capital of the world."[21]

Invasion of the Body Snatchers

To the victor belong the spoils. It took no time at all for these rebels against the old order to morph into plutocrats, revolutionary plutocrats perhaps, but decidedly gilded ones. Reagan's first inaugural ball started it all. A *New York Times* article headlined "A New Opulence Triumphs in the Capital" captured the moment and went on to describe "an upwardly mobile suburban sensibility founded on buying power and unabashed appreciation for luxury." One grande dame feeling her oats huffed, "It's getting a little tiresome to always have to apologize for ourselves." She needn't have worried. The ball was called "a bacchanalia of the haves," a marriage of the "New Right and the New Rich." Diana Vreeland, style guru and confidante of the Reagans, sized up the future: "Everything is power and money and how to use them both.... We musn't [*sic*] be afraid of snobbism and luxury."[22]

The afterhours social life of these young moguls had a narcotic effect on journalists. They filled page upon page with who wore what and who sat next to whom and what edible artwork was served at the latest fete for the Metropolitan Museum of Art. Saul Steinberg, the period's most notorious greenmailer and an original corporate raider from the late 1950s, was ushered into society at a gala affair covered like a coronation. The Brooklyn-born son of a plastic manufacturer, Steinberg, his former corpulence trimmed away, was welcomed aboard thanks to a newly mastered social poise and his generous disbursement of funds to the favorite cultural institutions of the city's elect. These nouveau robber barons competed with rock stars for off-the-business-page coverage in style-conscious publications like *New York* magazine, which meticulously traced their footsteps across the art market, the city's nightlife, and the white sands of the Hamptons. Journalists mapped the social geography of their residential splendor, often enough teardowns in newly fashionable faubourgs replaced by kitsch palaces equipped with tanning parlors, motorized chandeliers, petting zoos, and heliports. Still, even Robin Leach, the voyeuristic host of *Lifestyles of the Rich and Famous*, who made a career of televising the geography of excess, found an all-gold house—walls, floors, ceilings, crockery, a gold-dusted Rolls-Royce—"obscene."[23]

Male sartorial display became an item of editorial comment as well as commercial advertisement. Wall Street in particular modeled a return to a kind of rococo extravagance: red suspenders, assertive midriffs encased in vests that simulated the look of nineteenth-century clubmen, custom-tailored suits from the Old World that gave off a lambent shimmer. *Manhattan Inc.* invented a column called "Power Tools," offering advice on power fashions, including a $135 silk scarf embellished with a Napoleonic

bee design and a late-nineteenth-century ebony, ivory, and gold walking stick available at $485. Aston Martin slyly promised prospective cus-
tomers that the car would "demoralize thy neighbor." Yachts were
selling at such a clip that by the mid-1980s the Atlantic and Pacific
Oceans were assigned their own area codes—871 and 872. There was a
run on fur coats for Cabbage Patch dolls, prompted by ads informing
customers "it comes in 23 colors, including envy green." Tiffany and
Company mounted a window display for a $50,000 diamond necklace
that included a bag lady sitting in a cardboard box reading *House and
Garden*.

Yearnings of this sort echo the quest for "pecuniary decency" identified a century earlier by Thorstein Veblen as proof you belonged to the
elect. That urge to be sure, plus a pernicious version of an indigenous
American egalitarianism: "The more equal people become the more
relentless their desire for inequality."[24]

Enthusiasts of their own celebrity, the new tycoons loved to posture
and pose as *philosophes*, gurus, and style setters. The media ate this up,
"the luxe, calme, and volupte that business success or inherited wealth
can bring." Gossip columnist Suzy Knickerbocker summed it up: "Perhaps it's dreadful that money is God, but that's the story." More
gimlet-eyed reporters, however, noticed that these business Olympians
could pull all-nighters only because they employed a bevy of servants to
clean up after them: personal shoppers, hairdressers, gift buyers, mani-
curists, and half a dozen other "experts" to keep the rest of their mundane existence on track. Even magazines like *Manhattan Inc.* ran features
in which the reader got to learn about the uglier personal as well as professional attributes of the newly risen, including their peculations, frauds,
and gargantuan overreachings. Newspapers occasionally found some
spare ink to measure the gulf opening up between the nation's have-nots
and the Mount Everest of wealth piling up on Wall Street.[25]

All but the most zealous and unabashed registered a certain queasiness
about the sudden appearance of a new plutocracy. But this unease failed
to seriously disturb the surface of public life. Michael Thomas and Lewis

Lapham performed exquisitely comical dissections of the mores of the new moneyed elite, but these left little imprint behind. Instead, the cultural climate sustained an air of ironic knowingness, arch, yet at the end of the day fascinated and awestruck. Even books like *The Bonfire of the Vanities* and *Liar's Poker*, meant to puncture the infatuation, failed to undercut the mythos of the plutocrat as rebel. Nor did they intend to: the comic cynicism of *Bonfire* was, after all is said and done, the standpoint of a world-weary acknowledgment of the way things are and have always been.

Nothing, no jokes and no moralizing, could disrupt the new normal. Staying power like that was all the more remarkable since it survived in one form or another the bubbles and busts of the next twenty years—the 1987 stock market crash, the savings and loan debacle and bailout, the collapse of the "Asian tiger" economies, the Russian implosion, the mathematical fiasco of the hedge fund Long-Term Capital Management, Latin American meltdowns, and the dot-com implosion at the turn of the millennium. The Bull kept charging, though even before this cascade of crises, mounting evidence suggested that this tale of the financier as revolutionary and national savior was indeed a fable.

Undressing Napoleon

Once the crises did hit with alarming frequency, the fable's credibility should have been further undermined. Shareholder value, always an evanescent phenomenon attaching to a floating population of transient traders, proved vulnerable to precisely those measures taken to buoy it up. Often enough, the allegedly senile managements that had run these acquired properties turned out to be much more adept and knowledgeable about how to manage them than the financial outliers who leveraged their purchase on a sea of debt. Nor was this supposedly lifesaving debt used to fund reinvestment in new plant and equipment or in longer-range research and development. Several years after they were issued, most junk bonds turned out to be precisely that: "junk" securities whose rate of return declined if they didn't default.

Beginning with the S&L bailout, the notion that new paladins of capitalism relied on themselves and their mastery of the free market, taking their punishment like men when they faltered, seemed like so much disposable cant. Preaching about getting the government off the businessmen's back couldn't stand up against the desperate pleas for that same government to save them. As one observer noted, the bailout state proved beyond any doubt "the non-ideological character of the American faith in money. No economic theory, no political coronation, no wall of rhetoric or line of thought can survive a loss of 500 points on the Dow."

Moreover, the conspicuous consumption of the nouveau plutocracy inevitably earned the era a reputation as the country's second Gilded Age. The parallels were obvious. There was the same insatiable lust for excess, the vulgarity of what one wag described as "robber baron aesthetics." Inequality in the distribution of wealth and income increased at a speed never before seen in American history, even in the Gay Nineties.[26]

While ten million lost their jobs to plant closings and layoffs during the Reagan "recovery," compensation packages for the ten leading corporate CEOs ballooned 500 to 700 percent since 1980, and average CEO pay, twenty-five times that of the average hourly production worker in 1968, was nearly one hundred times that amount by the 1990s. Nor was there any consistent correlation between the increase in CEO compensation and corporate performance or shareholder gains.[27]

Shades of Jay Cooke's Ogonzt castle and Jacob Riis's rag-pickers alley now and then caught public attention. Amid industrial ghost towns, soaring rates of child poverty, central city rot, shuttered mines and factories, and small-town atrophy, *Business Week* observed, "The great divide between rich and poor in America had widened in perhaps the most troubling legacy of the 1980s." Social commentator Kevin Phillips, invoking a relevant historical parallel, described this national drama as a "tale of two cities." And like the original Gilded Age, the new one was quickly sunk in a miasma of corruption. Suspect dealings honeycombed the federal bureaucracy—HUD, EPA, FAA, the Agriculture Department, the VA, FEMA, the Federal Home Loan Bank Board, the Health and Human Services Department, the Transportation Department, the Consumer Product Safety Commission, the Bureau of Land Management, OSHA, and the Pentagon all had scandals during the Reagan years. Favors for lobbyists, polluter violations buried, corporate functionaries consulting for government agencies, bribes, kickbacks, fraud—a whole shadow economy carried on incestuous relations with the public treasury. The Charles Keating–Lincoln Savings and Loan debacle implicating five senators as the eighties ended, or the Jack Abramoff–style crony capitalism at the turn of the twenty-first century, matched anything on offer from a century earlier, including the Credit Mobilier, Whiskey Ring, and other notorious scandals that had provided Mark Twain with raw material for his first best seller, *The Gilded Age.*

By the turn of the millennium, K Street (ground zero of crony capitalism, named after the Washington street where lobbyists gathered) had become so powerful that it didn't so much lobby for particular legislation as it wrote the laws itself or chose who would regulate its constituents. Enron got to vet the new head of the Federal Energy Regulatory Commission, for example. This was a form of merger and acquisition of business and government on the grandest scale. Government, it turned out, was neither the problem nor the solution; it was merely expedient or it wasn't.[28]

Meanwhile the hippest pioneers of entrepreneurial self-reliance trailblazing on the Silicon Valley techno-frontier seemed to be champions of an irresistible future, seers, fabricators of Progress like those path breakers in the days of the iron horse and electric light. People like Bill Gates, Steve Jobs, Andy Grove, and Mark Cuban were as much a part of the plebeian business mystique as their Wall Street counterparts—men from nowhere, self-confident, impatient with business as usual, and audacious when it came to challenging the old corporate and technological order. Moreover, unlike their Wall Street analogs, because they worked on the frontiers of science, they added something special to the fable of the businessman as revolutionary. Here was entrepreneur as the bearer of the inevitable, in touch with underlying mechanisms of the cosmos, a traveler to a place no man had been before. Defy that if you dared!

Yet so much of what these men achieved relied on decades of government-sponsored research and technological development, encouraged by the Defense Department and the rest of the national security state. So much for the reigning faith that government needed to go extinct—though acknowledging that debt was predictably rare.[29]

Finally, as ideology, shareholder value as the only value bore a striking resemblance to the social Darwinism of that earlier time, both functioning as rationales for the callousness—one might call it the self-conscious social unconsciousness—of the 1%. Yet few felt ashamed. Only when the system went belly-up did the whole mythos of the businessman as the people's hero temporarily deflate, as onetime "masters of the universe" became wards of the state.[30]

Robber Barons vs. Gilded Plebeians

Mimicking each other in so many ways, these two gilded elites separated by a century nonetheless elicited quite different reactions: fear and loathing back then, enduring populist romance in our time. Why?

When the captains of industry and finance lorded it over the country in the late nineteenth century, no one would have dreamed of calling them rebels against either some overweening government bureaucracy or some entrenched set of "interests." There was virtually no government bureaucracy to rebel against, and these men were themselves "the interests," Wall Street chief among them. People like J. P. Morgan, E. H. Harriman, and Jay Gould worried about being overthrown, not about overthrowing someone else. How different this is from the faux-radical rhetoric of the more recent past, with its pointed barbs directed at busybody, obstructionist regulators, sclerotic corporate managements, and timorous financiers. A Gilded Age peopled by irreverent, leonine youngsters out to shake up the old order has a distinctly different feel from one run by lugubrious, bearded patriarchs whose very physical heft cried out their sense of overlordship and reverence for good order.

And then there is the Gordon Gekko factor, a parodic invention worth remembering. His icy bloodthirstiness and candor, on the one hand, make him loathsome in ways that would have been familiar to generations of Americans who'd never run across a corporate raider and wouldn't have known the difference between an LBO and a PhD. He's pure parasite. He leeches off the hardworking, productive enterprise of others, embodying a moral antinomy going as far back as one cares to look. "I create nothing, I own," he boasts to his young protégé. Merciless when it comes to dealing with his opponents, he orders his chief aide, "the Terminator," to "rip their fucking throats out. Stuff them in your garbage compactor." He's a moral sleaze as repugnant as Jay Gould, the original "Mephistopheles of Wall Street."

Yet Gekko is also a new creature. There is something irresistible about him. It is not merely the devastating combination of single-minded decisiveness, animalism, and sexual allure. Even more tempting is his breathtaking self-confidence and showmanship. And even more than that is his astonishing power to persuade. Gekko is unscrupulous beyond compare, but he succeeds first of all not through skulduggery. He triumphs in the same way that the Wall Street upstarts of this new gilded era first did, by a mesmerizing invocation of shareholder value as a form of liberationist theology. He's not a destroyer but a savior, not only of companies, but of "that other malfunctioning corporation called the United States of America." There is a purgative cleanliness to his rhapsodic exaltation of greed. It offers a metaphysical thrill: "Greed is good. Greed is right. Greed works. Greed clarifies and cuts through and captures the essence of the evolutionary spirit. Greed...has marked the upward surge of mankind." Gekko is a charismatic grotesque who has mastered the art of mass communication, appealing to the darker side of the popular imagination. He doesn't talk down, he doesn't patronize. Instead, he fraternizes with the people, abandoning the socially irritating presumptions of the Establishment and those earlier incarnations of what in the nineteenth century was sometimes referred to as "the shoddy aristocracy."

That whole ragtag assortment of warrior metaphors drawn helter-skelter from disparate civilizations—from antiquity to medieval Europe, from the Wild West to futuristic, high-tech, sci-fi heroes: a Grand Guignol of titans, black knights and white knights, gunslingers, conquistadores, predators, and barbarians at the gates—lay anchored in an amoral savagery, an unbridled individualism nesting deep within the vengeful psyche of a disarmed and demobilized society. The power to resist its call diminished inversely with each new addition to the Forbes rich list. But this surrender did not entail any bending of the knee. After all, the aristocracy of the first Gilded Age had gone away.

Minus the oddball exception or two, the new tycoonery of the Age of Acquiescence, as Gordon Gekko reminds us, did not fancy itself an aristocracy. It did not dress up like one or marry off its daughters to fortune-hunting European dukes and earls. On the contrary, many of its leading figures regularly dress down in blue jeans, construction worker regalia, and cowboy hats, affecting a kind of down-home populism or nerdy dishevelment. However addicted to the paraphernalia of flashy display they may be, the new capitalist elite does not pretend these are the insignia of ruling-class entitlement.

Feigning simplicity and the art of the ordinary, they are apt to enter into informal friendships with the help that would have scandalized the paternal habits of yesterday's elect. Once upon a time, the lower orders aped the fashions and manners of their putative betters; now it's the other way around. The new breed of plutocrat shed the quasi-aristocratic demeanor that for generations had defined the haute bourgeoisie: studied indolence, complacency, cool ennui, ironic distancing.[31]

Even the fears of our newly risen are categorically different, living in dread not of class conflict but of the IRS, criminals, con men, terrorists, and, as Tom Wolfe memorialized in *The Bonfire of the Vanities*, the urban underclass. A plutocracy that embraced the populace nonetheless retreated behind locked gates, spiked hedges, floodlights, electronic surveillance gadgetry, and personal bodyguards.

Like any nouveau climbers, they also lived in dread of falling back into the obscurity they came from. But they didn't stage tableaux vivant, hold masked balls, and cook up fake genealogical credentials to prove blue-blooded lineage. They did hunker down, however, in walled-off worlds, nurserylike Edens that encouraged not only a sense of entitlement but a delusional social ignorance and escapism, one lacking in discipline. In this universe far, far away you could travel in a limo with a hot tub; patronize a Madison Avenue butcher who stocked antelope, elk, bear, mountain sheep, eland, lion, cape buffalo, hippopotamus, llama, yak, and opossum, in case you had grown bored with ordinary red meat; and send your children to a "mini couture" run by Giorgio Armani.[32]

All of this stood as a kind of libidinal counterweight to the hyper-rationalism inspired by the rigors of the market, its protocols of risk management, and the celibacy of numbers. Tangible evidence of triumph like this enhanced the illusions of omnipotence. The faux-revolutionary plutocrat was perhaps convinced, and certainly convinced others, that he needed to be left alone so that he could fulfill his mission. Only he and his kind could create jobs, as if that were his principal purpose, as if there were still—as there once was in traditional societies—real sanctions, obligations, and customs that commanded the social use of privately held means of production. In real life, however, there are today little or no such obligations, only the comical fancy of the businessman as missionary job creator.

Neither sybarite nor statesman, the plutocratic rebel is an odd duck and an elusive target. Indeed, it is no longer even apt to talk of a leisure class (at least in the way Thorstein Veblen conceived of a milieu in hasty flight from anything tainted by work). After all, our moguls of the moment are workaholics. When it comes to doing deals, they convey a commanding presence. Yet in the larger arenas of public life, they don't seem to come naturally armed with the "habit of command," having been raised on the narcissism of popular culture and its cult of self-absorption. This withering away and erasure of the very notion of ruling classes carries profound political consequences. Having an aristocracy to kick around, even an ersatz one like the American version, was politically empowering; lacking one is disorienting. It may generate anxieties. Confronting the realities of power and wealth threatens the understructure of private property in a way that challenging the undemocratic, elitist practices and pretensions of an alien nobility did not. To question the inherent rationality and rightness of the prevailing way wealth is made, distributed, and controlled is a taboo not easily violated. To acquiesce may be less disquieting and at the same time cater to the evergreen hope that the road to self-enrichment remains open.[33]

The Politics of the Vanishing Ruling Class

Our populist plutocrats are more adept than their Gilded Age predecessors were at mastering democratic politics. The old leisure class was distinctly allergic to the seamier aspects of courting the populace. Some tycoons like Mark Hanna put in long hours running party affairs from the top. Others got involved if they needed a tax break or tariff by calling upon their kept senator. By and large, however, this world relied on the federal judiciary, business-friendly presidents, constitutional lawyers, and public and private militias to protect their interests.

Savvy corporations became more engaged at the dawn of the twentieth century, lobbying, helping conceive and write legislation, and fending off invasions (not always successfully) of party fiefdoms by irate farmers, angry ethnics, urban machines, and middle-class reformers. They even sought avenues into proletarian precincts, encouraging the more compliant elements of the trade union movement to work out the terms of a social peace they could live with. Beginning in the 1970s, however, business elites became acutely more political-minded, penetrating deeply all the pores of party and electoral democracy. This meant going so far as to craft alliances with elements of what their predecessors—who might have blanched at the prospect—would have termed the dangerous classes.

Conservative elites first turned to populism as a political strategy thanks to Richard Nixon. His festering resentment of the Establishment's clubby exclusivity prepared him emotionally to reach out to the "silent majority," with whom he shared that hostility. Nixon excoriated "our leadership class, the ministers, the college professors, and other teachers...the business leadership class...they have all really let down and become soft." He looked forward to a new party of independent conservatism resting on a defense of traditional cultural and social norms governing race and religion and the family. It would include elements of blue-collar America estranged from their customary home in the Democratic Party.[34]

Proceeding in fits and starts, this strategic experiment proved its viability during the Reagan era, just when the businessman as populist hero was first flexing his spiritual muscles. Claiming common ground with the folkways of the "good ole boy" working class fell within the comfort zone of a rising milieu of movers and shakers and their political enablers. It was a "politics of recognition"—a rediscovery of the "forgotten man"—or what might be termed identity politics from above.[35]

Soon enough, Bill Clinton perfected the art of the faux Bubba. By that time we were living in the age of the Bubba wannabe—Ross Perot as the "simple country billionaire." The most improbable members of the "new tycoonery" by then had mastered the art of pandering to populist sentiment. Citibank's chairman Walter Wriston, who did yeoman work to eviscerate public oversight of the financial sector, proclaimed, "Markets are voting machines; they function by taking referenda" and gave "power to the people." His bank plastered New York City with clever broadsides linking finance to every material craving, while simultaneously implying that such seductions were unworthy of the people and that the bank knew it. Its $1 billion "Live Richly" ad campaign included folksy homilies: what was then the world's largest bank invited us to "open a craving account" and pointed out that "money can't buy you happiness. But it can buy you marshmallows, which are kinda the same thing." Cuter still and brimming with down-home family values, Citibank's ads also reminded everybody, "He who dies with the most toys is still dead," and that "the best table in the city is still the one with your family around it." Yale preppie George W. Bush, in real life a man with distinctly subpar instincts for the life of the daredevil businessman, was "eating pork rinds and playing horseshoes." His friends, maverick capitalists all, drove Range Rovers and pickup trucks, donning bib overalls as a kind of political camouflage.

"Live free or die" might have been their adopted motto. Calls to dismantle the federal bureaucracy carried a certain populist panache. Huffing and puffing about family values proved a cheap date for the new gilded elite that otherwise couldn't care less. A graphic novelist drove the point home by depicting them as "sunshine rednecks" and "weekend good ol' boys."[36]

A generation's worth of this kind of political theater has made it second nature. When, for example, rival candidates for the governorship of Connecticut faced off in 2010, they were in fact both men of stupendous wealth, possessed of all the educational, residential, and other material insignia of privilege—prep and Ivy League schooling, private planes, oceangoing yachts, hotel-sized homes. But the Republican made sure to be seen eating egg salad at a diner wearing blue jeans. His Democratic rival dressed up in a "barn jacket" and rolled-up sleeves, garb suited to telling tall tales in aw-shucks lingo about his early struggles to start his own business. Jeff Greene, otherwise known in Florida as "the Meltdown Mogul," had the chutzpah (hardly alone in that, however) to campaign in the Democratic primary for a Florida Senate seat in a Miami neighborhood ravaged by the subprime debacle—precisely the arena in which Greene had grown fabulously rich. There he rallied the people against Washington insiders and regaled them with stories about his life as busboy at the Breakers hotel in Palm Beach. Protected from the Florida sun by his Prada sunglasses, he alluded to his wealth as evidence that he, a maestro of collateralized-debt-obligation speculations, knew best how to run the economy he had helped pulverize, punctuating that point by flying away in his private jet securely strapped in by his gold-plated seat buckles.[37]

Mitt Romney provided the near apotheosis of this fable. Denounced even by his Republican rivals as a "vulture capitalist," he nonetheless put himself forward as a credible candidate for president based mainly on his record as a salvationist hero of business in distress. The ex-governor of Massachusetts kept shooting himself in the foot by reminding voters of his gilded life and gilded friends. But he rested his quest for the presidency on his experience running Bain Capital, a private equity firm he claimed was the workingman's best friend.

Business lobbyists quickly mastered the art of masquerade. Journalist Jonathan Chait notes one striking case. A rally was convened to support George W. Bush's tax cuts for the wealthy. It was planned, according to a campaign memo, so that "visually this will involve a sea of hard hats. The Speaker's office was very clear to say they do not need people in suits....AND WE DO NEED BODIES—they must be DRESSED DOWN, appear to be REAL WORKER types, etc." Lobbyists who attended the rally were indeed provided hard hats. In another instance, the political director of the National Association of Manufacturers dressed in a rugby shirt and a faded blue "Farm Credit" hat. When *The Wall Street Journal* attacked renegade rich people who actually favored the estate tax as "the fat cat cavalry," it confirmed that virtually anyone could play this game.[38]

True enough, there is a long history of political patronizing of this kind, going at least all the way back to Andrew Jackson's time. Arguably, the essential genius of the American political tradition consists of this complex choreography: accommodating the passions and interests opened up by the protocols of democracy without disturbing the underlying equanimity of capital accumulation and rule by propertied elites. It is a balancing act made even more complicated by the heightened fluidity of the American experience of class hierarchy, perhaps best captured by that old but still cogent observation about "shirtsleeves to shirtsleeves in three generations."

Nonetheless, rarely if ever in the past has the plutocrat so rooted himself in plebeian culture, erasing all that remained of the habits of deference once expected to inform relations between rulers and the ruled. Nor did he before now build bridges to the lower orders by pointing out precisely what separates them—namely, his unapproachable wealth—using it as a credential of his all-Americanism. Nor have such alliances, when they existed, lasted nearly as long. Nor have so many businessmen assumed second careers as elected officials without any prior experience; on the contrary, many have pointed to their lack of personal political experience as their chief virtue. That, plus offering their long years spent running companies as proving their unique aptitude to govern. Michael Bloomberg, whose billions plus managerial genius won him three terms as mayor of New York City, is perhaps the most illustrious example. There are many others, including: Meg Whitman, the onetime CEO of eBay who lost a race for governor in California; Carly Fiorina, who ran Hewlett-Packard and then tried, unsuccessfully, to become a senator from California; the victorious governor of Michigan, Rick Snyder, once chairman of Gateway; Rick Scott, another winner as governor of Florida after a career as a health care entrepreneur; the serial loser Linda McMahon, whose decades running, along with her husband, World Wrestling Entertainment wasn't enough to launch her into a new career as senator from Connecticut; and then of course, for comic relief, there is always "the Donald." In pointing out their business savvy and experience as their singular qualification for holding office, it is as if these people, and numerous others running for less visible local and state offices around the country, were trying to get elected to the board of directors of America, Inc.

Populist plutocracy reconfigured the age-old problem of legitimacy, of the underlying sources of consent on the part of subordinate classes to the rule of tiny, wealthy elites. The new plutocrat makes a convincing case that he is of the people, expresses their deepest desires and aspirations, and governs in their name. So, for example, the *Herrenvolk* democracy over which the George W. Bush administration presided epitomized this marriage of corporate elitism to blue-collar, white-skinned cowboy populism. Without an establishment to overthrow, resisting the rule of the déclassé feels like pushing on a string.

Moreover, this new plutocratic milieu is far less defined by a shared ethnic genome; cultural beliefs, social clubs, school ties, even geography are far more diverse, as is its basic demographic profile. These traits, or rather the lack of a common set of shared traits, comes with the territory; it's a world in constant motion, rootless, as mobile as the capital flows streaming here and there that define it. Consequently, the profile of the plutocracy becomes ever more indistinct. Its disappearance becomes part of the general leveling down of cultural distinctions that constitute the age.[39]

What a wondrous transformation—a vanishing act really—so disarming, so essential to the Age of Acquiescence. The rise of a populist plutocracy that comes to power with counterfeit credentials of its own manufacture, thereby contributing to its self-erasure as a ruling class: the final nonconfrontation.

10

Fables of Freedom: Brand X

People stocked backyard bomb shelters with survivalist essentials and their favorite comestibles, planning on a life underground. The nose cones of intercontinental ballistic missiles pointed at great cities all over the Northern Hemisphere. Lethal submarines patrolled the depths with enough fire power to incinerate the planet. End-game theorists plotted scenarios for "mutual assured destruction." Diplomats walked on the brink of a global precipice, playing a grotesque, adolescent game of chicken.

Amid all this Armageddon-like fist waving, an odd kind of domestic squabble broke out in a kitchen in, of all places, Moscow. At a world's fair in that city in 1959, Vice President Richard Nixon and Soviet premier Nikita Khrushchev faced off in an argument about just who would bury whom and how. That "kitchen debate" would become one of the more memorable chapters in the history of the Cold War. For the American side, it distilled the essence of how capitalism and wage slavery might be reconciled and freedom preserved.

Instead of pointing to their muscle-bound arsenals, the two world leaders challenged each other about which society was likely to produce the best stoves, washing machines, televisions, electrical appliances, and other consumer delights. Said Nixon, "To us, diversity, the right to choose...is the most important thing. We don't have one decision made

at the top by one government official.... We have many different manufacturers and many different kinds of washing machines so that the
housewives have a choice.... Would it not be better to compete in the
relative merits of washing machines than in the strength of rockets?"

The vice president's boasting about the six-room "model ranch
style house" (the epitome of the country's consumer ideal), which was
the central attraction at the American exhibition, had dual intent. Maybe
a ranch house would (and maybe it wouldn't) bury communism abroad.
But what it would more definitely do was bury communism and class
conflict at home; of that the American leader was confident. The labor
question that had disturbed the domestic tranquility for a century at last
had an answer: free choice.[1]

The All-Consuming

Consumer culture, in its own everyday way, channels desire into forms
of expressive self-liberation. It feeds an atmosphere of invidious distinction and cravings for immediate gratification. It is hardly a recipe for
communal fellow feeling. This is not news: Tocqueville observed this
phenomenon long ago, in its infancy. Since then, historians have discovered the first signs of "consumerism" further and further back in the
past.

Since Nixon's famous debate with Khrushchev, it has been almost
unnatural to question the organic connection between freedom and the
American standard of living. In the free-world West, one was free to
choose from a wonderland of brands X, Y, Z, ad infinitum. Choice was
the summa of freedom—free, that is, as George W. Bush would remind
us decades later, to shop.

Nixon's boast can't be taken lightly. The embodiment and exfoliation
of human creative powers in kitchenware and jet planes, in lifesaving
pharmaceuticals and central heating and air-conditioning, in telecommunications and food enough to keep billions alive is, whatever else one
might say about it and the way it was accomplished, stunning. This is
Progress with a capital P as perhaps the gods meant it to be.

The vice president, however, was speaking politics not teleology. America had discovered the antidote to class warfare. If the material gratifications on sale were made widely accessible and alluring enough, it would temper the social resentments of the past. It would deliver a rough approximation of the country's egalitarian credo. And it would cultivate a sense of individual autonomy and self-reinvention that would neuter earlier quests for freedom aimed at dismantling the prevailing hierarchies of power and wealth.

Ironically, this was the New Deal talking. The New Deal came into being as the culmination of generations of struggle against precisely those hierarchies. Sit-down strikes, rent strikes, citywide general strikes, tenant farmer strikes, home and farm occupations, seizures of shuttered coal mines and public utilities by the desperate, bloody demonstrations of the unemployed, anticapitalist political parties, and populist movements to "share the wealth" had all challenged the institutions of constituted authority. They were rare acts of courage. They were as much about human dignity and democracy and social justice as they were about feeding and clothing and housing the destitute. The same can be said about the New Deal as a political order insofar as it confronted entrenched power and opened up the political arena to the voiceless.

In its finished form, however, the New Deal order resolved those fulminating antipathies by installing mass consumption capitalism. This was as much a political solution to the heated confrontations set off by the Great Depression as it was an economic cure for that national trauma. Working classes once kept orderly by the rhythms of machine labor and managerial discipline would instead defuse their discontents in the individualized pursuit of invidious distinctions and material comforts. After a long decade of severe privation and terrifying insecurity, yearning for a safe haven took precedence. Memories of that trauma remained fresh for half a century.

New Deal reform—ranging far afield from the Wagner Act and the Fair Labor Standards Act to the National Industrial Recovery Act, the Tennessee Valley Authority Act, the Rural Electrification

Administration, and the Wealth Tax Act—was in part conceived as a way of rebuilding the economy by redistributing income and extending the market for mass-consumption-based industry. And this was the way allegiance to a system that had virtually collapsed, causing millions of casualties, could be restored. That was what President Roosevelt meant when he pointed out to those economic royalists and Tories of industry who bitterly opposed the New Deal that he was saving capitalism, not setting out to destroy it. The wages system of old was to be civilized. Either that or else . . .

The all-consuming selves we take for granted today are "merely empty receptacles of desire." Infinitely plastic and decentered, the modern citizen of the republic of consumption lives on slippery terrain, journeying to nowhere in particular. So too, nothing could be more corrosive of the kinds of social sympathy and connectedness that constitute the emotional substructure of collective resistance and rebellion.

Instead, consumer culture cultivates a politics of style and identity focused on the rights and inner psychic freedom of the individual, one not comfortable with an older ethos of social rather than individual liberation. On the contrary, it tends to infantilize, encouraging insatiable cravings for more and more novel forms of a faux self-expression. The individuality it promises is a kind of perpetual tease, nowadays generating, for example, an ever-expanding galaxy of internet apps leaving in their wake a residue of chronic anticipation. Hibernating inside this "material girl" quest for more stuff and self-improvement is a sacramental quest for transcendence, reveries of what might be, a "transubstantiation of goods, using products and gear to create a magical realm in which all is harmony, happiness, and contentment . . . in which their best and most admirable self will emerge at last." The privatization of utopia! Still, what else is there?[2]

The Sounds of Silence

Neither the architects of the New Deal nor Richard Nixon could have foreseen where the logic of consumer culture would lead or how deeply it would saturate the social order. Some public intellectuals of distinction did. Together these men turned the immediate postwar decades into an intellectual tour de force, but they left few footprints on the social order.

John Kenneth Galbraith, a loyal New Dealer, was also an audacious proponent of Keynesian mass consumption economics as an antidote to the derangements of the business cycle. Yet a decade after the end of the war he was issuing jeremiads about the "affluent society," about how it crowded out public goods and corroded social consciousness. *The Affluent Society* (1958) and a string of books by Galbraith that followed were best sellers, widely talked about, debated, denounced, and defended. Just as popular were books like *The Hidden Persuaders* (1957) by Vance Packard, which vividly described the black arts of the advertising industry and its remarkable ability to manipulate desire. His examination of how motivational research and other subliminal psychological tactics choreograph expectations and desires was especially chilling as Packard demonstrated their deployment in the political arena as well.

High-spirited as the era seemed to be, there were lamentations about the stupefying spread of mass culture, about the machinelike conformity characteristic of not so much the assembly-line worker as the "man in the gray flannel suit" manning the managerial bureaucracies of the corporate world. Consumer culture enticed everybody, but perhaps it found its most perfect vessels among the millions who made up what David Riesman and his co-authors (1950) called "the lonely crowd." Here was a reconfiguration of the social psyche so hollowed out and vulnerable that it needed to be regularly confirmed in its existence by outside authority. But that authority had become so amorphous, ambiguous, and diffused it left its subjects in a chronic state of anxiety. While this "new man" was by necessity open to the world, no longer a slave to tradition, he was infinitely pliable, paying obeisance to taste or opinion makers in the realm of material goods as well as in moral and intellectual matters. Here were the seedlings of a new middle-class acquiescence, although Riesman himself did not explicitly make that judgment.

Onetime left-wing intellectual Daniel Bell announced the "end of

ideology" (1960). While this turned out be a grossly premature predic-
tion, what Bell put his finger on was the passing away of the "proletarian
metaphysic" and all that it had portended about the social transformation
of capitalist society. Indeed he argued that all the grand humanistic ideologies born out of the Enlightenment were exhausted. Proletarian revolution was the last such grand historical romance. Bell's was not a
lament, but nonetheless detected the dolorous world that would fill the
vacuum. These dreams of transcendence had been replaced by a narrow-
gauged system of technical adjustments to social dysfunction, bearing no
larger social promise.

Bell's book was fiercely debated. But the ranks of those still believing
in the proletarian mission were dwindling. A new generation of 1960s
radicals would undertake a fresh exploration for some new "agency of
social change" to play the liberating role that History had once assigned
the working class. Herbert Marcuse seemed to speak to that vacuum, but
his *One-Dimensional Man* (1964) was more a piercing look at the new
culture of acquiescence than an agenda for the future. It somberly
observed the decline of revolutionary potential in the West as a pacified
population became captives of "false needs" nurtured in the emporiums
of consumer society. The very aptitude for critical opposition had withered, especially on the part of a working class enmeshed in the prevailing capitalist order. Marcuse—for all that he was championed by a
young generation of spirited "new leftists"—sounded a deep pessimism,
closing his remarkably successful book with these drear words from the
Marxist social critic Walter Benjamin: "It is only for the sake of those
without hope that hope is given to us."

Here then was a culture of opposition, or so it seemed. It hardly was
compelled to live underground. Magazines, books, even movies probing
this new world enjoyed big audiences. The subtle machinations of corporate advertisers, the neglect of public space and the "public household," the alienated loneliness of the "other-directed" man in the gray
flannel suit, the numbing atmosphere of suburbia, the simmering tension
between the moral imperatives of the work ethic, and the libidinal

yearnings for immediate gratification were no secret. That they might together mute the cacophonous social uproar of the long nineteenth century was cause for worry by those who detected these social undercurrents. Indeed, some said so. Each in its own way announced the end of the long nineteenth century.

So what is remarkable is not that some noticed this shift in the historical center of gravity, but the inexorable way in which these forebodings didn't in the end matter. Their cultural deposits were shallow. True they fueled, especially, the countercultural currents of the sixties. But those were soon swallowed up by the tidal waves of consumer culture, reabsorbed, and then tossed ashore onto the marketplace. Indeed, for just that reason they failed to get a grip down below because the undertow was running in the other direction.[3]

A core paradox was only then surfacing: namely, that if self-expression and self-development could become vendible commodities, that experience could also become disempowering, mocking the quest for individual authenticity. Implicit in a consumer economy floating on a great reservoir of debt is that if you're having some trouble gratifying your desires, or just getting by, neither the problem nor the solution is social, but simpler and more personal than that: borrow. Life is about now. Between 1979 and 1997 the rate of personal bankruptcy rose by 400 percent. Moreover, shifting the search for meaning and release inward would devalue the political experience, which after all inherently happens in public. Our recent financial calamities are illustrative.[4]

Today, many corporations producing for the mass market have fled the United States for cheaper manufacturing platforms abroad. However, precisely those financial imperatives that led industry to abandon the homeland have actually strengthened the consumer culture syndrome and, by the way, undermine the wherewithal to engage in collective resistance. Perhaps the more profound tragedy ushered in by our highly leveraged economy, an economy resting on debt, is not the precarious condition of our financial institutions. Rather, it is the degree to which ordinary people are inveigled in and dependent on what these masters of the universe have invented. It would be hard to exaggerate the extent to which the average American has become addicted to debt. The numbers even before the financial debacle were astonishing. Between the late 1970s and the late 1990s the average monthly charge on credit cards nearly quadrupled. In 1980 only 1 percent of financial institutions offered home equity lines of credit; by the end of the decade 80 percent did. The market grew from $1 billion to $132 billion. Indeed, thanks to the diligence and ingenuity of the FIRE sector, the whole mass consumption economy, not just the housing market, recently found itself underwater.

Years before the global financial meltdown, Americans had become negative savers. What else were they to do when wages stagnated, jobs vanished, and the safety net frayed, but the yearnings invoked by Nixon had become ever more irresistible? The moral of that story is not that they had become naughty by some Victorian measure of frugality, but that living on a credit card is to exist in the perpetual present, a vantage point antipathetic to the future orientation embedded in the political movements of yesteryear.

Just as inimical is the acute sense of personal responsibility and guilt indebtedness carries with it. That moral torment overwhelms political instincts to indict the systematic causes of this very intimate dilemma. Instead, each and every one of us is separately to blame for our own self-indulgence. This persuasion holds even though the most deeply indebted—our peak financial institutions—walk away from their debts, passing them on to the public treasury, without a qualm.[5]

Today consumer culture penetrates the lowest depths of proletarian life. Its seductions envelop even the working poor. Living day to day, one medical emergency, car breakdown, or child care crisis away from bankruptcy and eviction, preyed upon by a vast industry of poverty profiteers (slumlords, check cashers, loan sharks, credit card companies, and the like), the working poor nonetheless devote a sizable percentage of their meager income to the fabricated fancies of consumer culture. And why not? In a world overrun with the search for psychic balm, this is the arena that matters most, the one that promises so much by way of personal liberation and reinvention. Leveraged by debt, consumer culture has helped make the state of permanent wage labor—even a declining, downwardly mobile one—tolerable.

When the ghettos of black America erupted in one insurgency after another through the mid- and late 1960s, this profound insult and provocation was already detected. A witness before the Kerner Commission convened in 1967 to investigate the causes of these urban explosions, a conservatively inclined representative of the National Business League, noted, "It is to be more than naïve—indeed it is a little short of madness—for anyone to expect the very poorest of the American poor to remain docile and content in their poverty when TV consistently and eternally dangles the opulence of our affluent society before their hungry eyes." Looting was another form of shopping![6]

Freedom to Shop and Shopping for Freedom

Arguably, there was always something otherworldly about shopping and the installment plan. Unnerving at first, it took decades for people schooled in the habits of frugality and thrift to feel at ease morally about going into debt. Taboos about debt dating far back were still part of the country's cultural DNA. People might not know that "God helps those who help themselves," "If you would know the value of money, go try to borrow some," and "For he that goes a borrowing goes a sorrowing" came from Ben Franklin's *Poor Richard's Almanac;* still these adages aroused misgivings.[7]

More disorienting yet was the promise (made so compelling by the graphic and verbal art of the advertising industry) that through an otherwise simple transaction—for a car, TV set, living room couch, soap, deodorant, a pack of cigarettes, or items far more exotic—you could become a different person or multiple persons. At a stroke you could shape-shift, try on one identity then discard it for another, become alluring, aloof, wise, mysterious, powerful, respected, heroic, or loved by ingesting those qualities along with the package they came in. This kind of freedom was vertiginous, but also thrilling.

Thrill seeking of this peculiar sort channeled the desires of wider and wider segments of the upper middle classes in cities and suburbs in the late nineteenth century. During the Jazz Age of the 1920s, it seeped down into the middling classes, made inroads among the better-off working classes, and traveled out into rural and small-town America. Buying on the installment plan became routine. The Great Depression aborted the installment plan for the time being—there was no credit to be had. But it was sorely missed. Much of the social and political energy of that remarkable decade was directed toward ways of restarting the engine of mass consumption and the ideological convictions that made it hum.

Once World War II was over with, it hummed. The "kitchen debate" captured what had become an all-consuming way of life. The *Journal of Retailing* (a trade magazine) reached for the injunctive: "Our enormously productive economy demands that we make consumption our way of life, that we convert the buying and use of goods into rituals, that we seek our spiritual satisfaction, our ego satisfaction in consumption." A down-and-dirty version of this view of life had already topped the hit parade in Louis Jordan's 1946 song, "Let the Good Times Roll":

> Hey everybody, let's have some fun
> You only live but once
> And when you're dead you're done, so. . .
> If you want to have a ball
> You got to go out and spend some cash.[8]

A decade later, *Fortune* magazine summed up the sensory experience of the new American everyman: "Nearly everything he sees, hears, touches, tastes, and smells is an attempt to sell him something. To break through his protective shell the advertisers must continuously shock, tease, tickle or irritate him, or wear him down by the drip-drip-drip Chinese water torture method of endless repetition. Advertising is the handwriting on the wall, sign in the sky, the bush that burns regularly every night."[9]

Long before that issue of *Fortune* was available on the newsstand, Marx referred to the "artillery of commodities"; a century later, that artillery constituted the main arsenal of liberal democracy. It could and sometimes did shoot to kill. Recent studies show that "big food" corporations, for example, target children as a ripe market for unhealthy eating; some kids actually show signs of loyalty to brand X even before they can speak. Toddlers recognize the golden arches of McDonald's before they know the letter m. For many youngsters this is a skill worth unlearning, since they are likely to choose foods with familiar logos and a lot of that food is high in sugars, fat, and sodium. Neuroscientists have discovered that seeing a familiar food logo trips the pleasure and reward regions in children's brains. Such are some of the pathologies of liberal democracy.[10]

Liberal democracy, however, almost didn't make it. When the Great Crash of 1929 opened up the abyss, calling everything into question, the old regime did not discreetly abdicate. It took a great act of political rebellion to revivify the consumer economy, extend its reach to embrace all social classes—except the "invisible" poor—and erect the political institutions designed to stabilize and sustain this peculiarly American version of consumer capitalism and social welfare. That is why we continue to think of the New Deal (along with the Civil War) as a singularly transformative moment in the country's history, one in which the country's president felt compelled to acknowledge that the rich and powerful hated him and that "I welcome their hatred."

But one person's revolution can be the next person's ancien régime. It took another rebellion, this time apparently directed against the consumerism of the new liberal order, to bring consumer culture to places where no man had gone before. History obeys its own logic, if it has one at all.

The Death and Rebirth of Consumerism

War, segregation, nuclear terror, patriarchy, and poverty turned the 1960s into a decade of resistance, the last one to remind us of what once was. Iniquities of that magnitude were by themselves enough to fire up people. There was something else at stake as well, however.

Conspicuous among those mounting the barricades were suburban, middle class, college-bound offspring of Depression-era parents. They rebelled as well against precisely the consumer-based life that the New Deal order had made possible. They hated its conformity, its obeisance to conventions of dress, sex, and deportment, its preoccupation with material possessions, its keeping-up-with-the-Joneses social climbing, its social unconsciousness and circumscribed imagination, and the hypocrisy and inauthenticity of its "other-directed" rituals of self-presentation—the banality of a culture absorbed in creature comforts and how to acquire them. This counterculture flamboyantly rejected all that and reveled in its own outrageousness. However, what began as a grand act of *épater les bourgeois*, a defiant laboratory of collective self-estrangement, soon enough evolved into a narrower existential search for personal authenticity.

Many were enthralled by the counterculture's "do your own thing" cry for release from social convention even though they themselves never participated in its more exotic effusions. And as the years went by, they discovered that this intensely individual experience was available for purchase on the mass market, or rather by a market that had been finely segmented to accommodate a broad range of tastes, identities, and styles. The evolution of the standardized mass market into a profusion of niche markets tailored to meet the particular desires of more and more finely delineated subcultures was both a commercial triumph and a political one. Commercial diffusion accelerated the atomizing of social life. No longer did the market help define an everyman. Instead it paid to cater to dozens of real and imagined lifestyles anchored in social status, age, ethnicity, occupation, race, and the idiosyncrasies of taste.

Ever since General Motors differentiated itself from Ford back in the 1920s by offering a range of car models aimed at different segments of the buying public (Ford, on the contrary, was famous for selling you any color Model T as long as it was black), companies have recognized the value in targeting subsectors of the mass market. This was certainly the case during the postwar decades. By the 1970s, the extent to which markets could be subdivided into precisely defined social-psychological niches had expanded exponentially. *Business Week* claimed that the "breakout of consumers by age group ('the Pepsi generation'), income, education, geography, ethnic background and use patterns" by "selective selling or market segmentation" was so pervasive "that the terms 'mass market' and 'mass media' have almost become misnomers."[11]

Tom Wolfe dubbed the 1970s the "Me Decade," a fitting moniker as its insatiable cravings for self-fulfillment and spiritual awakening were quickly catered to by corporate America. Products once sold as standardized items for everyone were rebranded as carriers of defiance, as ways to thumb your nose at inhibitions and traditional authority, and as outward manifestation—in what you wore or ate or drove or played with—of your inner psychic emancipation, your capacity for self-expression.

Every highway, byway, and alleyway of desire was tracked down, mapped, and furnished with "customized" goods, from watches and perfume to fashion, music, regional foods and wines, from ancient, sacred practices of physical fitness to high-tech specialized sporting equipment. By the 1980s, cable TV was developing channels catering to every desire: cooking and modeling, pornography and sports, and, eeriest of all, in the next decade the desire for "reality." Eventually, after the turn of the century, cable channels even offered relief from the afflictions of overindulgence, providing therapeutic entertainment for those so swamped by stuff they couldn't make it out of their own homes: *Hoarders* and *Storage Wars* had some answers. Dressing up (or down), trying things on (or taking them off), breaking taboos, eroticizing the inanimate, romanticizing the pedestrian, and thawing out iced-over wells of imagination could be exhilarating, opening up new zones of freedom. Illusory idiosyncrasy could be mass-produced. Big business had few qualms even about making fun of itself and its robotic suit-and-tie image if that improved the bottom line. Fox TV was entirely at ease with the occasional mockery of capitalism on its longtime hit series *The Simpsons*.

However, an economy and way of life invested in the hunt for endless novelty corroded moral faculties that already rested on less evanescent foundations. Aesthetics supplanted ethics, appearances and images took the place of narrative meaning. In this brave new world—without the anchorage of tradition, without the imagined and vivid intricacies of kinship, without the past living on in the detail of everyday life—meaning became a scarce social commodity. Living in what one commentator called "the windowless room of the current event" erased historical memory (or replaced it with kitsch nostalgia), without which a society has a hard time figuring out not only where it came from but where it might be or should be heading.[12]

Down the Rabbit Hole: Politics in Private

A political economy rooted in capital accumulation depends on the moral psychology of delayed gratification and naturally looks to the future. But a political economy based on mass consumption, especially one ruled over by finance and trading and undergoing disaccumulation, is oriented toward instant gratification and the perpetual present. It may be prey to a psychology of arrested adolescence and moral indifference.

Citizen consumer came to adopt the vantage point of the passive spectator in his relationship to the public world and to accept politics as another arena of stylized marketing. Minute inspections of the character traits of candidates made politics into a form of reality TV entertainment. Politics became a hybrid form of shopping and gossip.

For all of American history, the political universe was occupied by work-related groups: laborers, farmers, businessmen, and so on. After World War II, these "identities," while still operative, tended to diffuse—particularly workers and farmers—and carried less social weight. Consumer culture created new identities based on lifestyles so that, for example, the working class became a group first of all concerned, like all others, in levels of material possessions and social status. After all, they shared in the same media of popular culture as everyone else and tended to identity anyway as "middle class" based on their levels of consumption and the ubiquity of middle-class values. "Quality of life" supplanted concerns about power, and the political coherence of a working-class interest subsided accordingly.[13]

Lifestyle politics encouraged alliances based on tastes, appearances, and identities that could be tried on and discarded. Punk and goth, for example, became faddish experiments in a kind of noir urban romanticism for East Village bohemians. These were then taken up by white suburban teenagers as the costumes of antic cultural rebellion. Working-class young people of color did the same with hip-hop. The mimicking gangsta swagger against "the Man" that ensued among white middle-class kids was all act without action. Moreover, it carried with it a patronizing consolation: that they too could aspire to a soulful suffering and raise an irreverent middle finger, as if that summed up the story of black America. It was angry theater, a triumph of surface over substance, and politically meaningless, except in private.

Flexible capitalism encouraged this political dissolution. At every turn, that economy undermines trust and stability and lives in the moment. Like consumer culture, it is inherently hostile or at best indifferent to the sphere of social welfare, which is premised after all on recognizing our mutual dependence and obligations. Neoliberalism could be embraced as a kindred emancipation, one in which the unencumbered free market released the individual from social constraints. Emancipation could converge on digestion. It might be found in the streets but could also be found in the kitchen or in all the erogenous zones of the stimulated psyche. Embracing this new world's egoism and its distracted, pleasured passivity left the organs of civic mobilization anemic from disuse.[14]

Hipster Capitalism

Ronald Reagan ascended to the presidency on waves of nostalgia for an older, mythic America, one of traditional family values, god-fearing and full of love for what we now call the homeland. Sure enough, the politics of restoring and protecting the homeland grew ever more vigorous as a result.

Yet the irony of the Great Communicator's reign was that it also unleashed torrents of mercenary greed, inaugurating what many would soon enough describe as a second Gilded Age. Alongside reveries about *Leave It to Beaver* and Tom Sawyer's America grew up something quite alien. Under the aegis of the new "flexible" finance capitalism and even before Reagan assumed office, capitalism and the counterculture had fallen in love and gotten married. Old antagonisms from the 1960s melted away.

The yuppie, that infamous embodiment of self-regard of the post-apocalyptic 1970s, was one version of this new union. A workaholic, toiling away at tasks usually lacking in meaning beyond the superficial, he and she became at the same time maestros of hip consumption. Fiercely ambitious, determined to rise in conventional ways, yuppies eschewed the more outré forms of the counterculture. But they avidly ingested whole lifestyles, some borrowed liberally from hippie insouciance, but now without the patina of rebellion: all style, no substance, but allowing for every manner of theatrical self-invention. That, together with cold cash, made for a composite personality with an empathic sense of entitlement, empowerment, and off-the-rack (designer) individualism. This was a privatized universe of gated communities, malls (rather than town squares), health clubs (not parks), private schools and private security (not public schools and police), private rather than public sanitation, fire, water, and hospital services. Republicans or Democrats, they were enthusiasts for Ronald Reagan's core conviction that "what I want to see above all is that this remains a country where someone can always get rich."

Still, as cosmopolitan, hip explorers on a journey of self-discovery they were not a ready audience for the cultural restorations that Reaganism also seemed to entail. Insofar as this milieu adopted a view of the outside world, more often than not its sympathies lay with gender and racial equality, sexual liberation, multiculturalism, and the whole manifest of social liberalism: whatever seemed to open the doors to the free flowering of the individual. In this regard, a much broader population — the "new middle class" of techies, professionals, and white-collar people staffing public and NGO offices—that otherwise did not cultivate the yuppies' pretentiousness or avidity for money shared in this distinctive quest for individual liberation, often in ways too iconoclastic for the yuppie social climber.[15]

Even the most bohemian ecologies became fodder for the market's infinite ingenuity. Hipsters, artists, and hipster artists along with a broader "creative class" became the objects of a real estate strategy. Decrepit working-class barrios were reclaimed and upscaled, though cheaply and with enough of the decrepitude cunningly preserved to add antibourgeois allure. Trendy neighborhoods were nicknamed and branded as commercial ventures underwritten by an unspoken politics of acting out, a pantomime of symbolic disaffection with no discernible social impact except on the bottom line. Shops, museums, and art itself could function as what developers called "urban activators." In fact, the atmosphere of hipster knowingness chilled whatever social action, commitment, vision, or moral seriousness this kind of fashionable disaffection might imply. A *David Letterman Show* promo made the point this way: "An hour of celebrities talking about themselves constantly interrupted by commercials. Hey America, the pride is back." This was indifference in its aggressive mode.

"Capital has no home," George Bernard Shaw observed. It is always a transgressor, a disputer of tradition and champion of equality in the abstract while reproducing material inequality in real life: the yuppie was homeless in just this new way. Many others would join their spiritual ranks, but without their more outsized material accoutrements, as the economy came to rest increasingly on the fabricating and manipulation of mass desire and fantasy. No hidebound prejudices, customs, and authorities from the past could be allowed to stand in its way . . . unless of course they could be rebranded and packaged nostalgically—Marlboro men, faux rednecks, family and family dog behind white picket fences, peasant coffee gatherers, yeomen-farmer wheat growers, and smithies and handicraftsmen in leather smocks—and sold into their own special niche markets.[16]

Shopping for Jesus

Yuppiedom in particular seems a practically foreordained outcome of consumer culture unchained. The same is not self-evident about people undergoing religious reawakening. Yet the persuasion that the marketplace is a carrier of freedom has taken root even among the pious. If wealth once made them uneasy, arousing anxieties about the way it might corrupt the soul—enslave it to the devil, one might say— adherents of today's "Prosperity Gospel" are no longer troubled in that way.[17]

Indeed, freedom from sin through discovering or rediscovering Christ comports well with success in the market in this latest revision of the Gospels. Reverend Terry Cole-Whittaker, a preacher from the early days of televangelism, kept her audience upbeat about finding Jesus with the help of a "prosperity campaign kit." It worked to bring you closer to the Lord, plus made you wealthy while you were getting closer. A Georgia-based minister with the wondrous name of Creflo Dollar runs a Pentecostal church where he preaches this hosanna to prosperity in sermons called "Thinking for Success" and "Overcoming the Fear of Lack." A huge megachurch in Houston with 47,000 parishioners is presided over by Joel Osteen, whose best-selling book *Become a Better You* advises that God "created you to live abundantly" and provides counsel on how to succeed.

One minister in Mississippi delivered this piece of economic theology, which might go down well among many academic economists: "The poor will follow the rich, the rich will follow the rich, but the rich will never follow the poor." A five-million-copy best seller called *The Prayer of Jabez* by the preacher Bruce Wilkinson talked about God rewarding Wall Street portfolios. Founder of the Faith Exchange Fellowship, Dan Stratton wrote a book aptly entitled *Divine Provision: Positioning God's Kings for Financial Conquest.*[18]

Love of luxury and wealth has permeated the daily doings and the theology of televangelists for decades now. Missionaries rely on the principal medium of consumer culture, television, to deliver their message. Their tax-exempt multimedia empires are, after all, big business, and they have hardly been shy about exhibiting its showiest desserts, including multiple mansions and private jets. Such luxuries were to be piled up in God's counting room as evidence of capitalism's moral benevolence and its promise of individual freedom: a kind of eschatology of material success, signs of God's grace, free enterprise as a biblical injunction.

Evangelical right-wingers have unequivocally endorsed supply-side economics (the notion that cutting taxes on business and the wealthy will not only generate more investment but in so doing actually increase tax revenues), applauding the gathering in of wealth by the wealthy in the interests of general prosperity and seeing that money as a divine gift, a blessing. Pat Robertson called the theory, which most economists have dismissed as bogus and which runs in the face of all previous Christian theology, "the last truly divine theory of money creation." Robertson, Jimmy Swaggart, Jerry Falwell, and others less luminous have crafted a ministry that marries the irreconcilable: nineteenth-century morality and twentieth-century consumerism. In this metaphysics, Jesus is sometimes depicted as rather well-to-do and the market as God's workshop.[19]

Echoes from the past can be heard in these modern-day sermons. The most frequently delivered public lecture of the late nineteenth century was called "Acres of Diamonds." The Reverend Russell Conwell (founder of Temple University for boys from the lower classes) traveled the country and the world to spread the word that there was no incompatibility between the teachings of Jesus and the amassing of wealth. Briefs on behalf of laissez-faire economics were regularly delivered from the pulpits of affluent Protestant denominations. A kinship with the Prosperity Gospel there surely is.

Yet what the Reverend Conwell wanted to emphasize in his more than two thousand appearances was the holy connection between the virtuous life and ascetic accumulation. Nowadays the weight falls instead on feeling justified about living the good life. The atmosphere of public life is permeated by piety. To some considerable degree, however, this now functions as a way to avoid recognizing that capitalism has become a moral idiot, wildly longing to break free of all inhibition. What would the Prosperity Gospel make of Cotton Mather's warning that "the cursed hunger for riches will make man break through the laws of God"?[20]

Yuppies and the reborn live at the polar regions of our society. That they both can be infatuated with consumer culture is one mark of how pervasive it is and how disarming, morally and politically. No biological process, no psychic recess, no sacred ritual is beyond its reach.

Inner Peace

Demands and desires that might once upon a time have been addressed through the organs of social life—kin networks, neighbors, village norms—can now be resolved (or so it would seem) through the so-called commodification of intimate life. Especially among mobile classes of professionals, managers, lawyers, consultants, and the like, farming out tasks and decisions about the most personal matters is common, abetted immeasurably by the internet. Experts on love, matchmaking, marriage planning, conception, child raising, shopping, mental dilemmas, household organization, friendship, aging, and death are there in great numbers to take over on these matters.

What Arlie Russell Hochschild calls "emotional capitalism" in her book *The Outsourced Self* amounts to a willful outsourcing of these most idiosyncratic aspects of the self to the marketplace, where they are reconceived as business problems. And sometimes this works well, especially among the overworked who can afford it and have no time left to worry about matters that by their nature require a lot of time. "Domestic outsourcing" can include corporate concierges, "dial a wife" carpooling services, or getting aging parents into the old-age home. Corporations provide similar onsite services, including breast-feeding, wedding preparations, and teenage counseling. Virtually anything then can be turned into a saleable commodity, assuming there's enough of what economists call "effective demand," meaning cold cash.

What it also implies, however, is that the market is essential in arenas where it once seemed to have no place. Conversely, it would imply an eroding lack of self-confidence, of ineptness at living at some basic level. And by default it erases any lingering connection between these vital concerns and the tissues of social life that are not first channeled through the market. This is acquiescence at its most willing.[21]

Millions seeking material comfort and through it some experience, no matter how fleeting, of liberation, but who neither qualified as yuppies nor felt comfortable among the ranks of the pious, nonetheless found release in neighboring regions of the psyche. A new expressive self, incubated in the shopping mall, is so differently put together than that old utilitarian, work-oriented and often guilt-ridden self of bygone days. This new man discovered pathways to empowerment in a universe of therapeutic media: self-help best sellers, Oprah and Phil Donahue, and a tidal wave of psychological counselors, clinical psychologists, and social workers. By the mid-1980s there were more therapists in the United States than librarians, firefighters, or mailmen.

What might once have been diagnosed as social dilemmas or as matters of sin and salvation were reconceived as forms of personal or moral failings, medical problems treatable by chemistry, or as dysfunctional behavior that experts in social adjustment could remedy. It is a telling commentary on our times that "co-dependency" is widely considered an illness, although it is not listed in the DSM.

Here consumer culture merges economics and psychopathology. Chronically restless, unsatisfied, and anxiety-ridden, people cycle through endless rounds of consumption because it seems to offer a way out. This is not salvation in any religious sense. Nor does it offer the secular redemption once associated with the Enlightenment, democracy, or socialism. Rather, it is salvation through repeated momentary sensations of personal well-being, the promise of the "propaganda of commodities." But what it delivers is inherently fleeting; otherwise it wouldn't work commercially. While satiating one discontent it seeds another. It is as well inherently antisocial because its insatiable cravings arise from a deep-seated sense of being cut adrift in a world of all against all. And what seems an escape into the private realm becomes instead the invasion by the public worlds of the market, the corporation, and the state into territory once considered out-of-bounds.[22]

Yet this fable of freedom endures. As a prophylaxis against social unrest it has worked well. And if it presumes a war of all against all, then that brave new world of the lone combatant has offered up charms of its own. To that fable of the free agent we now turn.

11
Wages of Freedom:
The Fable of the Free Agent

Steve Roberts, a freelance journalist, recounted his adventures traveling across the country on a bike equipped with the latest electronic gadgetry. His recumbent bicycle, dubbed the "Winnebike," was, according to one observer, "a machine that eloquently symbolized the daring notion that people could indeed be free, follow their dreams, and break the chains that had always bound them to their desks."[1]

"Workers of the world unite! You have nothing to lose but your chains" is not what Roberts had in mind. On the contrary! Roberts was not suggesting some collective takeover of the means of production by fellow bikers. He was not in flight from the wages system or wage slavery; if anything they were in flight from him. That is to say, Roberts was voicing a faith that in the new world of flexible capitalism, which was finding less and less use for permanent employees, a new category of emancipated labor—the free agent—was being born. Facilitated in his case by information technology, the work life of the free agent could become a dream life. Still paid a wage or a fee by some property owner, this new species of worker was nonetheless liberated to do his own thing, even if his own thing belonged in the end to someone else. Wage slavery was going extinct; hail the new regime of voluntary servitude.

A Dream Deferred

How strange! A specter haunted the American social imagination for generations. Falling into the ranks of wage labor opened up an abyss. At the bottom awaited deprivation and dependency, an insult to human dignity. Life there was reduced to machinelike movements of the closely monitored "hand." This was a zone of social oblivion and political inconsequence. Getting by, getting noticed, getting respect—all waited on someone else's sufferance. You might have to reside in that gray world temporarily. That was tolerable. But to spend a whole life that way was not; it was the antithesis of the American dream, at least in the way it was first formulated.

No matter what precautions might be taken, the wages system guaranteed a precarious fate, full of perils. Descending into it proved far, far easier than climbing out of it. The gratifications, dignity, and independence that derived from building up some piece of propertied legacy of your own became more a taunt and a provocation than a promise, out of reach for most. This passion for self-possession, to be obliged to no man, was in the American grain and would never go away, no matter how often rebuffed. It would be goaded on by those infrequent instances when obscure men of rare good fortune or monomaniacal will, not overly burdened by scruple and hungering beyond the ordinary appetite, mutated modest ambition into imperial self-aggrandizement. Titans were objects of envy and resentment, but also of emulation. But of course that was the sheerest fantasy for most, hard to sustain in the teeth of wage slavery.

Now, wondrously, flexible capitalism has alchemized the torments of waged work, turning them into the pathway to freedom. At least Roberts and multitudes of others are convinced. Can this be so? Is acquiescence just another word for emancipation?

During the middle decades of the last century, so long as that armature of civilization surrounded the labor market—the right to organize, unions, unemployment and disability insurance, minimum wages, maximum hours, retirement income, safety regulations, grievance procedures, health insurance, job security, progressive tax rates, and public services—the wages system carried with it an aura of fairness and social justice, if not exactly freedom. Fair or not, it struck most as a great improvement over the lot faced by their ancestors. The insecurity, poverty, and hyperexploitation of those days seemed if not entirely wiped out, then confined to the margins (especially if you were white and male), remnants sooner or later to be done away with.

When that fortress began to weaken in the 1970s, and when the walls began to fall in the decades that followed, some were naturally alarmed. Trade unions, community organizations, spokespeople for inner cities, surviving New Deal Democrats, and others cried out—but not too loudly, and they soon adopted deeply defensive postures.

One response, however, was shockingly unanticipated. It welcomed the return to a free market in labor as, indeed, liberation. Some fancied themselves free agents set loose to make it on their own.

Mudsills and Middle Classes

How odd this fancy seems. Our new system of flexible global capitalism, including the American branch, is increasingly a sweatshop economy. There is no denying that brute fact in Thailand, China, Bangladesh, Vietnam, Guatemala, Honduras, and dozens of other countries and regions that serve as platforms for primitive accumulation. Hundreds of millions of peasants have become proletarians virtually overnight.

Here at home something analogous has been happening but with an ironic difference. On the one hand, millions of impoverished peasants, peddlers, urban scavengers, fishermen, and casual laborers from the planet's southlands have migrated into the sweated industries of new low-grade sectors of the American economy. For some, this journey nonetheless represents a substantial material improvement over their former condition and is undertaken with enthusiasm. Most had no choice as their old ways of life and making a living were being gutted by inexorable mechanisms of global agriculture, trade, and finance. In days gone by, they would have been seen (if seen at all) simply as a division within the army of wage labor. Nowadays, however, major corporations connive to treat them as free agents; as "associates," "temps," or "contractors." Any subterfuge will do if it can plausibly suggest they are "free" enough of any legal obligations on the part of their putative employers to pay or otherwise treat them with decency. Free agency of this kind is hard to tell apart from earlier forms of involuntary servitude. Nonetheless, it may buttress the consoling delusion that the zone of freedom is expanding, so why get unduly exercised about exploitation at work?

At the same time, flexible capitalism has set in motion what might be called the unhorsing of the indigenous American middle class. All those supports for respectable middle-class existence are corroding away. Here too a psychological safety net of free agency offers to cushion the fall.

People in sombreros and people wearing white collars have entered a vast new zone of precarious labor. Some have no choice but to recognize their proletarian fate. Others reimagine it as a way to recuperate what is slipping away and, better than that, as a new freedom.

"Middle class" is a slippery category, one that has always had vaguely defined boundaries. Once it seemed intended to encompass small property-holders and assorted professionals. Then it came to embrace people doing white-collar work at the midlevels of corporate and government bureaucracies with a certain amount of education and skilled manual or technical knowledge. With the advent of mass consumption capitalism, "middle class" came to mean mainly, although not only, a certain material standard of living—that is, a category of consumption rather than work.

Moreover, in the past and still today, it functions as a national ideal, the original version—the American version—of the classless society to which we all do or ought to or will someday belong. In that capacity it has worked as a prophylactic against the contagion of "class warfare." And its effectiveness in that regard has improved precisely to the degree that "middle class" has come to signify a basket of consumables without any reference to the hierarchies of production.

If that middle class is shrinking or vanishing, as so many observe, it is because our new order of flexible capitalism is turning it into a proletariat. Those millions of wage earners whose middle-class standard of living shielded them from that less enviable social status are finding it increasingly difficult to believe anymore in their immunity. Instructed to reeducate themselves for work life in postindustrial America, they end up training for jobs that don't exist, a fact of life even before the Great Recession. Instead they line up for low-wage jobs wearing suits, the secondhand castoffs from earlier lives in banks and insurance companies.[2]

But this downwardly mobile middle class still lives a world apart from the mudsills of society, where immigrant and native workers slave in ways thought extinct. During the first Gilded Age the sweatshop seemed a noxious aberration. It lawlessly offered irregular employment at substandard wages for interminable hours. It was ordinarily housed helter-skelter in a makeshift workshop that would be here today, gone tomorrow. It was an underground enterprise that regularly absconded with its workers' paychecks and made chiseling them out of their due into an art form.

Today, what seemed abnormal no longer does. At the turn of the twentieth century, the sweatshop ran against the grain of economic consolidation, the integration of functions characteristic of the multidivisional complex corporation. But under the regime of flexible capitalism, downloading of those operations once performed internally reproduces facsimiles of the sweatshop as the new norm. True enough, it has also encouraged the proliferation of petty enterprises—subcontractors, consulting firms, domestic work companies, temp agencies—fertilizing the soil in which our age of democratic capitalism is rooted. But the tidal drift is in the other direction: the recruitment of huge armies of casual labor.

The planet's peak corporations such as FedEx and Microsoft depend on this system. Indeed, they have thrived on it. Redefining workers as independent contractors is a free pass for major companies to circumvent both labor laws and obligations to provide all kinds of fringe benefits, from health care and retirement to vacations and overtime.[3]

Wage theft, especially in the less visible world of smaller businesses, has become a national scandal. A study of labor markets in Chicago, Los Angeles, and New York in 2008 revealed the severe extent of wage theft among low-wage workers, especially women and the foreign-born. No labor law was left inviolate: overtime, minimum wage, illegal deductions, misclassifications to elude coverage under the Fair Labor Standards Act or to escape unemployment and disability insurance legal commitments. Manufacturing, repair services, and domestic work were the sectors where the most pervasive transgressions occurred, but no arena was immune.[4]

Newly flexible proletarians—a permanent population of the impermanent, a reserve army of the marginally employed—work for Walmart, for auto parts or construction company subcontractors, on the phones at direct-mail call centers, behind the counters at mass market retailers, in plastics and toy workshops, doing light electrical assembly work, entering data and filing forms in office warrens, sweeping up for custodial firms, on the line at food-processing centers, digging and pruning and planting for landscapers. They include not only immigrants but a swelling population of the downwardly mobile native-born, now making a dwindling percentage of what they used to. They account for about 20 million people, perhaps an eighth of the total workforce, their number multiplied alongside the downsizing of the old economy. And no labor statute, usury law, or health and safety inspection—not to mention a union—comes close to mitigating their circumstances. This is becoming the reality at many industrial sites, service centers, and retail outlets as well as across the whole logistical supply chain of our mass consumption economy. So too, the relative job security such employees once enjoyed is gone, leaving them vulnerable to the lean-and-mean dictates of the new capitalism: double or triple workloads; or even worse, part-time work always shadowed by humiliation and fear; or even worse yet, no work at all. For these people, whether newly arrived immigrants or the dispossessed of industrial America, talk about the emancipation offered up by the unfettered free market in labor has been a cruel joke.[5]

Free at Last: White-Collar Nomads

Not so, however—not at first anyway—in the white-collar Tomorrow-land of free agent techies, software engineers, videographers, graphic designers, marketing "consultants," and freelancers of every conceivable description, from lawyers and engineers to statisticians and medical practitioners. Not so either—at least not at first—for that whole endangered species of middle managers trying to reinvent themselves as useable pieceworkers.

How could that be? On the one hand, they now were living a precarious existence, under intense stress, chronically anticipating the next round of layoffs if they happen to still be regularly employed. Once members in good standing of the middle class, they found themselves on the down escalator relocating to a place no one could mistake as middle class. And their future looked bleaker still: according to Princeton economist Alan Blinder, another 40 million jobs are likely to be off-shored in the next two decades and will include many white-collar positions like tax preparers, radiologists, programmers, securities analysts, mortgage originators, and other favored occupations of the new economy. Finally, as if to add insult to injury, many of these positions, envied and sought after for their high skill, inventiveness, and creativity, end up being not only insecure, but boring, subject to intense surveillance, and without those ladders of upward promotion the old paternalist giant corporation took for granted.[6]

Yet for a long time and even now, many celebrated their new status, a fact that registers how deeply the notion of the free individual as a lone player in the marketplace had triumphed. It proved a purgative persuasion that could leave one feeling cleansed of moral and social entanglements, dressed in spare existential armor, and fortified with a frontiersman's sense of adventure, as if that old territorial frontier out west had migrated into cyberspace and to the extraterritorial world of commercial interchange. One academic observer extolled the new way of life associated with the creative class of symbolic analysts who purportedly carried around the means of production in their heads, freeing them of old dependencies in this new world of flexible production: "People have come to accept that they're on their own—that the traditional sources of security and entitlement no longer exist or even matter." Today, unlike the sturm und drang of the industrial era, layoffs, downsizing, and other rigors of the free market provoke "no picket signs, no demonstrations, not a peep from the politicians.... We simply accept that there is no corporation or institution that will take care of us—that we are truly on our own." Uncertainty is the new normal, one worthy of a nation of pioneers.[7]

Management texts echoed that free-spirited techno-mad biker Steve Roberts: "The portable office offers freedom to work when and where we please, to realize our aspirations to set up and run our own business, to pursue business and leisure interests and to create more time." A Department of Labor report observed that employees valued telecommuting—even though they were staff workers, not free agents—because they felt more "independent" and "self-sufficient" or, for more down-to-earth reasons like taking care of family obligations.

Yet since the 1990s, workers in the United States have been working longer hours anytime, anywhere. Americans work 350 hours more every year than Europeans, even more than the Japanese, famous for their diligence. "Anytime, anywhere" means in most cases when and wherever an employer needs them.[8]

If the old regimes of explicit bureaucratic rules and routines seemed to vanish, they were replaced with new forms of power and surveillance. Some operated through wired-up apparatuses (one was attached to Steve Roberts's bike) or the ubiquitous cell phone tethering free agents to their taskmasters round the clock. Better were the invisible internal police patrolling the psyche of the precariously positioned "self-activator." Free as the agent might imagine himself to be, with only fleeting loyalty to any particular organization, nonetheless he remained the creature of the system of flexible capitalism. After all, the outlook of neoliberal flexible capitalism sees the self as the ultimate resource, self-exploitation another name for self-expression, and the more pliable and more malleable the freer. The free agent's behavior ideally acted out all those traits upon which the new economy rested: mastery of personal relations, manipulator and charmer, user of others, deft reader of power dynamics, trawling for the main chance.[9]

According to the free agent persuasion, this flexibility represented enhanced mobility. Proponents "declare their independence" and think of themselves as "micropreneurs." In a book called *Free Agent Nation*, published around the turn of the millennium, Daniel Pink defined these new citizens as "free from the bonds of large institutions." He and she had become "agents of their own future" and new "archetypes of work in America." They lived by their wits, these "self-employed knowledge workers," and "fashion their work lives to suit their own needs and desires."

The advent of a more flexible economy had teleported us from the age of the organization man to the age of the free agent. Once to be expropriated was a threat, the ultimate declension to proletarian status. Now to be without property, except the portable type carried around in your neurons, could feel like you were shaking free of the corporate oppressor, escaping the "iron cage" of the bureaucracy. The free agent was managerial material—itself a form of self-flattery—in the sense that he or she was managing the self and practicing a kind of emotional engineering, especially in settings where outside supervision is less feasible.[10]

People were free to "create their own gig on their own terms." They could remodel their work lives as craftsmen: customized and creative, leaving behind those dehumanizing mechanisms of dependency and command, the mind-numbing routines and repetitions of the old division of labor. It was a kind of postindustrial version of "up from slavery."[11]

Hosannas like this became a kind of ethical persuasion, cunningly in line with the lean-and-mean precepts of flexible capitalism. Dutiful physical exertion was no longer enough. Especially in the exfoliating service industries, what was required was communication skills, social talents, and emotional commitment—people had to like you, not just be served by you. Smiley faces were to be worn at all times, no matter how arduous it might be to keep one going. In an atmosphere of chronic insecurity, Apple could tell its employees, "Money shouldn't be an issue when you're employed at Apple. Working at Apple should be viewed as an experience." Indeed! Now mechanisms of efficiency and cost-cutting entailed colonizing the emotions.

A free agent with his or her sense of self-management is more apt to be adaptable, to make that self-investment, and to muster up the enthusiasm rather than merely that old-time obedience. As one observer noted, the point in this interactive environment was to "master the art of seeming to love the job, become part of the job."[12]

"Professionalization" of wage work has become a new form of self-presentation. As the sociologist Andrew Ross points out, it even penetrates styles of consumption, especially dress. Techo-creative workers in science and information technology adopt a "no collar" nonconformist mentality. It is explicitly counterposed to the standardized uniform of older forms of white-collar work. "No collar" is supposed to suggest the creativity and individuality of this free agent world. A more theatrical and idiosyncratic costuming is meant to express this whole mythos of the free agent life—risky, creative, iconoclastic.[13]

Free agents are hardly stand-ins for everyman. But nonetheless they constitute a remarkably heterogeneous group: home-based proprietors, temps, permatemps, freelancers, "e-lancers," independent contractors, independent professionals, "infopreneurs," part-time consultants, "interim executives," "troubleshooters," and even nominally full-time telecommuters hopping from company to company. Pink estimated (probably overestimated) 33 million people or one-quarter of all working Americans fell into this category.[14]

It is improbable at best that a sizable segment of the precariat ever found the notion of free agency seductive. For these millions set free in the precarious world of flexible capitalism, their newfound freedom as casual labor amounted to freedom from economic security, freedom from health care and the wherewithal to retire, freedom from all those protections standing between decency and destitution. Many are forced to become debt serfs, tithing a quarter of their income to service their credit cards and banks. Even when Pink's book was published in 2001, temporary workers between the ages of twenty and thirty-four earned 16 percent less than traditional employees, 55 percent had no health insurance, and most had no pensions. Numbers since then have steadily worsened. Flex-time often ended up substituting one form of face-to-face submission to factory or office floor authority for a new means of electronic surveillance.

Employee surveillance has become increasingly ubiquitous. The American Management Association estimates that more than half of U.S. companies deploy some form of electronic monitoring. Mobile phone tracking catches up those free agents who don't work in a static location. It has made its presence felt among the ranks of professionals, ranging from computer programmers and loan officers to stockbrokers (as at Charles Schwab) and veterinarians.[15]

However, for a subspecies of this precariat—articulate, wired, ambitious, hip, and ingenuous all at once—the seduction was a powerful one. To begin with, that old social contract which swapped corporate loyalty for security was in tatters anyway. One independent web designer working in New York City's Silicon Alley had been laid off twice since graduating college in 2005 and run out of unemployment checks. Now he operates out of his studio apartment, where just nine paces separates his desk from the kitchen. He sums up his ambivalence about how he's managing, the emotional seesaw of life in free agent Tomorrowland: "It's great, it's scary, it's worrisome, it's stressful; it's exciting."[16]

Then there is the constitutive illusion of IT, that the means of production could be somehow downloaded from complex organizations to anyone owning a computer. So too, the aura of professionalism still clings to occupations like that of the videographer even while working conditions leave them at the mercy of their "flexible" employers; however, they are excluded from the traditional production guilds that still offer real protection. Professionalism serves as a psychological wage, presumably compensating for economic deterioration. And it didn't hurt that, especially in the United States of Amnesia, a great majority of Americans living at the turn of the millennium were not around during the Great Depression. They didn't carry with them its searing lessons about what it can mean to be a free agent with no way home in a capitalist economy flat on its back.[17]

More than a livelihood was at stake. This was a full-blown romance about a way of life. Swap lifetime employment at a single organization for a chancier but exhilarating run at trading on talent; small is good, big is not better; forget balancing family life and work, blend them instead; retirement is so twentieth century now that we're free to double-down and reinvest in our old age, call it "e-tirement" for "self-actualizing older Americans"; power to the people, not the corporate "man"; free agents make the best villagers, re-creating its yesteryear hominess through interest groups and information-swapping support groups, and in other useful forms.

Here too was an ideology and a sensibility that converged on that of the counterculture, which had long since been mainstreamed. This new vantage point on work stressed "being authentic," measuring success by your own calculus, and setting your own priorities. So pervasive became the love affair with risk as the genetic marker of the American genius that not to take a chance, to stay put, became itself a sign of failure. Now however, a generation removed from "turn on, tune in, drop out," the momentum had shifted. This end-of-century profound individualism found release through joining the market, not, as it once had, by storming it or thumbing its nose at it. The golden rule was revised for the lean-and-mean twenty-first-century free agent nation and goes like this: "I'll help you because in the future I know you'll help me." The great French sociologist Emile Durkheim had a century earlier identified this behavior as the "social pathology of egoism." Use others as they would use you.[18]

Precepts of financialization seeped into the pores of everyday life, making this way of thinking seem completely natural. "Today, just as they do in their financial lives, individuals are achieving security through diversification. Security means investing their human capital in several clients or projects rather than in tying it up in a single one. . . . The free agent provides talent (products, services, advice) in exchange for opportunity (money, learning, and connections)." Not exactly. What's being traded is not only muscle or intelligence but the slippery, mutable self. How disempowering is that, breeding as it must an intense self-policing?[19]

At its most utopian or dystopian (depending on how you see things), this body and soul identification with the marketplace and the arts and crafts of self-exploitation produced an idea for a new financial instrument: the "individual public offering," an offering up for speculative trading of all those kinetic and potential energies and talents encased in the flesh and bone of the actual person, something already on the market for boxers. Prizefighter Nation! These "free agent IPOs" have been imagined as "micro offerings," say for publicly held authors, who might sell shares in themselves and divvy up royalties with shareholders. The writer proposing this argues that "savvy investors might be better off investing in a promising individual than an existing company. That person will likely be around for decades earning income and paying dividends." Naturally to keep shares liquid, he notes, an exchange will be required. He suggests calling it FASDAQ. Eventually, there will be mutual funds and maybe even an index fund weighted to include "the 500 best publicly held free agents in a dozen representative fields." Wackier still, enthusiasts observing the stock market tech boom at its height in the late 1990s predicted that by 2003 "not only will every person in America hold stock in an Internet company, each person will be an Internet IPO." David Bowie's venturing into this IPO new world was cited as the first prominent example of what was in store for the future. You could see the handwriting on the wall: "The blinding pace of Internet IPO's" was a "defining event"; eventually it would accomplish the "merging of shares and bids with skin and bones."[20]

Or take reality TV. The biggest media corporations in the world now flexibly reposition themselves by hiring nonunion contingent workers, in what is otherwise a highly unionized sector of the economy, to produce low-budget, low-cost entertainment. Writers are effectively demoted to "story editors" and actors are reclassified as "contestants." They are fished out of a vast reservoir of TV wannabes for what is after all another form of temp work, paying about $700 a week if that; sometimes they get nothing, functioning as interns, part of what one writer has labeled Intern Nation.

Jobs in the culture business are especially envied. They promise not only transit to middle-class status but lives of creativity and autonomy. The allure is so strong "real" lives may be made sacrificial offerings to get there. Reality TV, for its "stars," becomes a form of pure self-exploitation. These "actors" require an infinite adaptability, ready to respond to the constant flux of the market's demands; the search for work turns into a form of enforced entrepreneurialism. The pace is often a killing one. Competition is so fierce any thought of organizing in collective self-defense is seen as futile. Since these shows frequently adopt the format of a game, getting fired is just one rule of the game. No one is at fault. So too, the promise of self-expression turns out to be delusional. You do your job as "scripted," and identify with it. Indeed, to do well means to be constantly at work.[21]

The Invisible Chains of the Meritocracy

Delusions of self-reliance have induced deeper hallucinations of self-empowerment among this new high-tech/creative middle class. Information technology purports to turn work into play, to invite mass participation and communication, to break down hierarchies, and to open up unexplored territories of social power. Yet none of this happens. Nowhere else than in this world of creative labor is the outsourcing of piecework more common; nowhere is the pace of work more demanding, the hours longer; nowhere is job insecurity more the norm; nowhere is old-fashioned employer-funded health insurance more a fading memory; nowhere is planning for the longer-term future more pointless.

A Microsoft senior vice president did the remorseless arithmetic determining the fate of even the most skilled in the globalized economy. "Going global," he said, "extends the effective work day to about sixteen to eighteen hours." The labor market in India, he noted, produces "quality work at 50 to 60% off the cost...two heads for the price of one." Free agents might not have steady salaries they could count on anymore in this brave new world of pay for performance. But along with that injunction to perform or else came the promise of sharing in the future spoils through bonuses, stock options, commissions, and so on—should they happen to materialize.[22]

Still, this same milieu, its portfolios full of advanced degrees and technical know-how, believes deeply in the ideology of meritocracy. It is the form of thought and belief most natural to market culture generally but especially suited to its new population of technomads and other free agents who are convinced sheer smartness must win out. The precepts of meritocracy will thus inscribe a kind of natural inequality—that is, the only true equality is that of devil take the hindmost: the less meritorious, the less deserving.

The meritocracy imagines it has overturned the old systems of class hierarchy. But merit, as Fredric Jameson points out, "is at least partly class-based. Parents with money, education and connections cultivate in their children habits the meritocracy rewards." And the new meritocracy ends up displaying many of the vices of the old aristocracy—snobbery, social unconsciousness, self-regard, insularity—and far fewer of its virtues. But why dwell?[23]

Flexible capitalism has bred two kinds of homelessness. The old-fashioned variety originates in poverty and foreclosures. A brave new kind is, on the contrary, the heroic homelessness of the free agent. Capitalism generally, and mass consumption/flexible capitalism emphatically, leaves no stone where it found it. Everything from a home to a child to an education to a friend can be reduced to a fungible form of speculative investment, inherently temporary, of the moment, ready for the discard pile. Everything runs on the surface: no depth, only appearance. Mastering the confusion is seen by some as a form of freedom. The fable of the free agent revels in that liquid state of being and in the challenge of that mastery. It is the utopia that never apologizes for the mess it leaves behind. Many people, not only inhabitants of the symbolic workplace, came to relish an image of themselves as purveyors of change, restless, infinitely versatile, a rolling stone but without the angst.

There is pathos in this urge to break free of bureaucratic confinement. Like the original counterculture, initially it drew on anticorporate energies, resenting the hierarchies and uniformities, the sterility and impersonal deployment of power by the corporate bureaucracy. But when the mythos of the free agent rose to prominence a generation later, leaving the corporate world wasn't a choice but a brute fact of life.[24]

At the end of the day, free agents were speculating on themselves like any other investment. An ideology of professionalism (what one scholar has called "white collar nationalism") suppressed any instinct to identify as working class. There was no real room in this hermetic universe for anything that even faintly gestured toward home and community, much less a sense that this paradise was bifurcated by a grossly skewed distribution of power.[25]

On the contrary, what the fable promised was a muscling up, a power trip all your own. The sensibility nurtured by this salient of the new amoral economy combined an affirmative sense of "you're worth it" with an implicitly sadistic injunction to "earn it." One writer has called this "the financialization of the self." This may have amounted to a coarsening of the individual. But it is a coarsening that tragically disguised an underlying vulnerability to life under hypercapitalism. There is no denying its appeal, its alluring promise of liberation. By making the individual amenable to the purposes of the newly flexible, decentered corporation, free agency kept him or her as its loyal functionary. It may have elided the social origins of that passionate yearning to be free. Yet at the same time it contributed its own psychological gratifications to the Age of Acquiescence.[26]

Flexible capitalism, however, is more than a novel form of cultural seduction and psychotherapy. It is after all a lean-and-mean way of doing business. To keep going, even in the face of the hardships and degradations it breeds, the new capitalism resorts to other, less salubrious alternatives. Fears of many varieties also work in favor of acquiescence.

12

Journey to Nowhere: The Eclipse of the Labor Movement

As an economic organism the labor movement barely registers a pulse. Politically its heartbeat is more detectable but just how or whether those compressions oxygenate its other vital organs is hard to tell. A historic low point was reached in 2012, when the percentage of unionized workers in the private sector declined to a level not seen in a century—an anemic 6.6 percent. This was the woeful anticlimax of a long generation of decline.

How unlikely that seemed as the tumultuous decade of the 1960s ended. Trade unions represented more than a third of the workforce; teachers and other public sector workers all over the country had achieved the right to organize and bargain collectively; nonunion companies felt the pressure to meet union standards of wages and benefits; Great Society programs enlarging the welfare state, especially Medicare and Medicaid, were law thanks in large measure to the labor movement's political clout; key industrial unions like the United Automobile Workers could claim genuine credit for helping bring down Jim Crow; and while the leadership of the AFL–CIO saluted the Cold War and the hot one in Vietnam, some national unions and their affiliates joined the antiwar resistance that helped effectively depose a sitting president.

Depending on which end of the looking glass we peer through, this might be judged a Panglossian view of the way things really were. After all, the head of the AFL–CIO, George Meany, refused to attend the 1963 March on Washington (or allow his group to endorse it) because he along with J. Edgar Hoover believed Martin Luther King to be a closet Communist or fellow traveler. The federation's foreign operations did yeoman work undermining labor and political movements abroad that didn't subscribe to the dogmas of the free world. Compared with earlier times, little dissent was tolerated within most major unions when it came to major issues of foreign or domestic policy, not to mention on matters of union economic strategy. Construction unions (and not only them) fiercely resisted efforts to dismantle the racial protocols in place for generations that kept jobs there lily-white. (Indeed thirty years earlier, the AFL had lobbied hard to exclude a nondiscrimination clause from the Wagner Act so as to protect its segregated locals.) Concrete efforts to organize the open-shop South were scarce and, except when bound up with the civil rights movement, avoided. And the rest of the unorganized parts of the labor force were left that way.[1]

Many people today look back at the entire midcentury period with great fondness, wishing for its revival. So it is useful to note that what was once called labor-liberalism included in its makeup much of what now seems deplorable. Yet it is at the same time striking how robust the institutional and political capacity of working people to stand up to the "interests" was, as compared to the sorry state of the union now.

Last Reveille

At no time was that muscularity more on display than during the early 1970s, when an avalanche of strikes marked the end of the long 1960s. The first years of the new decade witnessed the largest strike wave since the great postwar shutdowns of 1945–46, when the labor movement last took to the streets to determine not only its own fate but the future of the country.

Nearly every province of the economy was shaken: mailmen and teachers, coal miners and steelworkers, farmhands and auto assemblers, garment makers and long-haul truckers, meatpackers, longshoremen, construction and subway employees, telephone operators, and railroad and social workers all walked out, some more than once and some, as in the case of the postal and subway workers, defying the law. Two hundred thousand postal employees ignored a Taft-Hartley injunction and their own frightened leaders, making theirs the largest wildcat strike in American history. In New York City, drawbridge workers took home fuses, electrical components, and keys so the bridges remained upright. Long-haul truckers stopped trucks moving goods into cities like Cleveland. The governor of Ohio ordered 4100 National Guardsmen into the streets.[2]

If there was a proletarian moment during the insurgent sixties, this was it, even if it crossed time zones into the seventies. It was the nature of these uprisings as much as their timing that made them so. Many were initiated by rank-and-file workers (often these were wildcat strikes, undertaken against or without the approval of the union bureaucracy). In steel, coal, and elsewhere, they meant to overthrow an entrenched and often corrupt leadership. These shop-floor militants were just as frequently young men and women, some Vietnam veterans, deeply influenced by the counterculture, the civil rights and black power movements, feminism, and the antiwar movement. Their beards, beads, long hair, and Afros, as well as their insouciant disregard of established institutions on the shop floor and union hall, marked them as kindred spirits to the sixties' antic antiauthoritarianism. The president of the UAW Local in Lordstown, Ohio, called the strike at the General Motors factory there "the Woodstock of the working man."[3]

So too did their demands break the mold of conventional collective bargaining and echo a broader impulse to throw a wrench into the machinery of postwar liberal society. Most famously, at the newly opened GM plant in Lordstown (running the fastest assembly line in the world), strikers were worked up about the intense speed of the assembly line, the overbearing discipline imposed by management, the numbing

343

routinizing of their jobs, the demeaning hierarchies of race and gender that permeated the workplace, and the dangers to their health and their souls. More pay, once the universal solvent of these antagonisms, was no longer a foolproof lubricant.

For a brief few years, "your money or your life" became a trickier question to answer. Even the government felt compelled to pay attention. A 1973 report, "Work in America," described an epidemic of what it called "blue collar blues" sweeping through the best-rewarded precincts of industrial America.[4]

Yet the tide was turning. One reason for ratcheting up the pace of work at Lordstown and elsewhere was to fend off the competition from European and Japanese industries flooding the market with lower-cost goods produced with more modern technologies. Huge chunks of the world market in household electrical appliances and metalworking were lost to Japan and Germany respectively. So too in steel and in America's signature industry, cars, where 22 percent of the domestic market belonged to Japan by 1980. This was the beginning of what became the long decline of American industry still under way today.

More immediately, the rest of the 1970s was marked by economic stagnation in the West, particularly in the United States. Here inflationary and speculative pressures on the dollar and the abandonment of the Bretton Woods fixed exchange rates exacerbated the impulse to drive down labor costs. Trying to maintain forward momentum when the economy was headed in reverse was a task even a more unified movement would have found difficult.[5]

But however spirited, the upsurge remained a splintered one. Despite its breadth and energy, and notwithstanding its occasional victories over major corporations, the government, and its own union hierarchs, the strike wave of these years did not actually measure up to the one after the war or the ones that made the thirties so memorable. It is not only that the triumphs were few and often not lasting. Unlike their predecessors, these were often provincial affairs, local to one union or one company or town. They rarely cross-fertilized and never established an organizational presence as a coherent movement. While activists expressed cultural and ideological affinities with the era's zeitgeist of resistance and liberation, these remained largely implicit, matters of life-style and attitude, not the elements of a programmatic alternative to the crisis of confronting Cold War labor-liberalism.

To be sure, there were exceptions to all these "defects." The postal employees, communications workers, and coal miners confronted whole industries and even the federal government. Especially in the auto indus-try but elsewhere as well, efforts to conjoin the struggles for racial and class liberation took root. Running against the prevailing winds in the private sector, the decade witnessed great union gains among public employees, especially among women and African Americans. The gen-eral restiveness breathed new life—if only momentarily—into what remained of the more reform-minded circles of the New Deal inside the Democratic Party. Nonetheless, the last proletarian rising did indeed turn out to be the last and least of them. At the outset of the 1970s, 2.5 million people participated in strikes involving at least 1000 workers; come 1980 that number had shrunk to 300,000. Industrial unions began a massive hemorrhaging. The consequences were grave not only for the life expectancy of the labor movement but for all those outside its ranks.[6]

Stormy Weather

In the gravest offense to the amour propre of the American credo, the arrow of history pointed backward. Once industrial unions were firmly entrenched after the war, the gap between this primary labor force (those unionized or by economic osmosis enjoying the unions' benefits without belonging) and secondary workers living outside that charmed circle, usu-ally in nonindustrial sectors, had lamentably widened for a generation. Now it began to narrow. But that wasn't good news. What it signaled instead was that the deindustrialization and de-unionization of primary workers brought them ever closer to the working and living conditions of the swelling ranks of the secondary labor force. In meatpacking, steel, air-craft, flat glass, clothing, petroleum refining, or wherever one looked, earnings fell precipitously, on average by 43 percent. Between 1979 and 2012, the productivity of the average American worker, after inflation, rose by 85 percent but the average, inflation-adjusted wage increased by only 6 percent and wages in manufacturing declined by 21 percent.

You might be picking crops, answering the telephone, packing fish, stocking warehouses, emptying bedpans, entering data, serving up food, cleaning hotels, or minding the megastores of America's domestic third-world economy. Or you might still be toiling on the shrinking reservations of core heavy industry, surviving the latest round of lean-and-mean downsizing, clinging to your unions, skills, and middle-class aspirations. No matter, as all increasingly felt the sting of hyper efficiency drives and social stagnation.[7]

Invisibles working in the shadow lands of the secondary sectors had always lacked the security, dignity, material compensation, and rights that had defined civilized capitalism. Now their once envied brothers and sisters felt these afflictions as well. "Brothers and sisters"? Even that language felt archaic.

On the Road to Surrender

One reason for the decline was that a sclerotic union bureaucracy— lacking in imagination and political courage, cognizant perhaps that the world they'd known was turning against them but hoping the old formulas would still compute, anxious to hang on to what they had (access, influence, treasuries)—stood in the way. The hierarchs of the AFL-CIO were by this time light-years removed from the more audacious imaginings of their predecessors. A century earlier, even the AFL, its allergy to anticapitalist radicalism notwithstanding, talked about "the class struggle" and held the state in suspicion. Now management prerogatives had become sacrosanct as George Meany explained in 1976: "Who are you if you are a labor man on a board of directors? Who do you represent? Labor does not want to run the shop. In the United States participation is absolutely and completely out."[8]

It was hard enough to face up to the assaults of powerful and determined steel, coal, and auto companies, and to neutralize the racial demagoguery that had stifled organizing in the South for generations or the psychological and cultural phobias that left women workers out in the cold. How much harder to attempt all that when, in as many cases as not, the bureaucracy left behind as the institutional legacy of an older era's democratic rebellion now disowned its own inheritance.

Betrayal, however, no matter how often it may have happened, is too thin an explanation for the historic undoing of a movement that had changed the face of twentieth-century America. Plenty of fresh blood was in any event pulsing through the arteries of the workplace, ready to revitalize its fighting capacity. The rebellions were evidence of precisely that. But they faced more formidable enemies than an encrusted labor bureaucracy.

The Wages of Disaccumulation

Economic slowdowns, not to mention actual retrogression, are hard to weather under any circumstances. There was nearly a decade of such regress, beginning in the mid-1970s and continuing through the early Reagan years. In the heartlands of American industry, the homelands of the labor movement, this slide never ended, even while other segments of the economy picked up. Even before the financial meltdown of 2008, machine tools, consumer electronics, auto parts, appliances, furniture manufacturing, and telecommunications equipment had become anemic imitations of what they once were. We still haven't touched bottom.

High levels of unemployment—over 10 percent during the Reagan recession of 1981–1983—alongside unprecedented inflation in the high teens made collective bargaining into at best a series of defensive maneuvers. This was in part the point of a deliberately induced severe contraction, otherwise known as the "Volcker recession," perpetrated by the Federal Reserve chairman to squeeze the last drop of cost-driven inflation out of the economy. Unemployment and bank failures reached levels not seen since 1940 and records were set for bankruptcies and farm foreclosures. It had become an axiom of mainstream economics that there existed a "natural rate of unemployment"; a rate lower than that would produce inflationary pressures on labor costs. As Reagan adviser David Stockman explained, unemployment "was part of the cure, not the problem." Paul Volcker would later candidly observe that "the most important single action of the Administration helping the anti-inflation fight was defeating the air traffic controllers' strike." He was driving home the point that labor unions were responsible for American industry's lack of competitiveness. Destroying the air traffic controllers' union was a high-visibility way of demonstrating the government's determination to break the power of unions more generally.

As one company after another shifted its operations either into the right-to-work (i.e., nonunion) South and Sun Belt or abroad, the labor movement's leverage further diminished. What new manufacturing jobs got created here were mainly sited in these "growth" regions. By 1972, over a quarter of the U.S. manufacturing workforce lived in the South. Outsourcing abroad was an irresistible strategy. The large-scale export of jobs first emerged as the economy entered the downward spiral of the seventies. Even at that early juncture, one-quarter of all new capital investment by U.S. companies in electrical and nonelectrical machinery, transportation equipment, chemicals, and rubber manufacturing was happening abroad, mainly in Europe. By the 1980s, investment in the third world (notably Brazil, Taiwan, Mexico, and South Korea) accelerated, as did the flow of finished goods back into the American market.

Saving money was not the only reason to relocate work offshore. "Off-shoring strategies are more about shifting relations of power than gaining efficiency," observed one management scholar. Well before the new system was branded "flexible," management had recognized the wisdom of reversing old practices by decentralizing production, thus weakening the leverage of unions. After the Flint sit-down strike of 1936–37, for example, GM never again wanted to be held hostage by worker actions in a single facility so vital it could shut down its whole far-flung enterprise. The company soon enough began breaking apart and relocating plants around the country, especially in the South, to weaken the sinews of solidarity.

As a global phenomenon, flexible accumulation made the obstacles to union growth that much more formidable. It allowed for quick changes in location and the divvying up of production units into smaller and smaller sites, which tended to discourage joint action. Differences in labor law from one country to the next, not to mention the sometimes sharply opposed outlooks of workers in less developed regions hungry for work at any price, made joint union action all the more difficult.[9]

Workplaces are mini-political as well as economic organisms and what may seem to obey a strictly economic logic usually carries a hidden agenda about who's in charge. Under the new regime of flexible production, companies off-loaded functions once performed internally to outside contractors and subcontractors. Many of these operated as nonunion facilities. In part that was precisely the point, its effects showing up right away on the bottom line. Disaggregating the production process in this way also eroded the social ties that often underlay union sentiment in more centralized work environments.[10]

In some cases, like trucking, what flexibility turned out to mean was transforming employees into independent contractors—independent therefore of most labor protections and union representation, and free to absorb the costs of equipment and fuel that were once the burden of the trucking companies.

Flexibility on the shop floor sometimes meant installing "quality circles" and other forms of faux worker participation in planning and executing work routines. This studied overture to making work life more democratic and creative turned out to be a kind of participatory-management discipline. To some very considerable degree, work discipline in a capitalist economy must always be internalized if its system of free wage labor is to function smoothly. Under flexible arrangements this became even more emphatically so.

Moreover, in a society saturated in the democratic atmosphere given off by the civil rights and women's liberation movements, it was inevitable that zeitgeist show up eventually on the shop floor. Management initiatives that purported to invite greater degrees of shop-floor democracy, abetted often by compliant unions, were the ghostly remains of the liberationist impulses set loose by the earlier rebellion against work, now translated into the sterilized if fashionable argot of labor-relations experts. And quality circles and other managerial experiments inviting worker input did indeed sometimes improve efficiency and productivity. They were a bottom-line pick-me-up, but not much else.[11]

Tread water if you can. That became the unspoken rule of thumb within the shrinking ranks of organized labor. Businesses drove the point home, insisting on and, in most cases, winning major concessions. Wage increases went from meager to none to less than none as one round of concessionary bargaining followed another, decade after decade. In a finance-driven economy infatuated with sophisticated mathematics, differential calculus, and Gaussian copulas, simpler arithmetic told the good news and the bad: layoffs = high stock price. For example, at Sears when 56,000 people lost their jobs, the company's share price rose 4 percent; Xerox shares increased by 7 percent when 10,000 workers were handed pink slips. And this was happening in the boom years of the 1990s. During the Great Recession, what began as furloughs in both the private and public sectors quickly devolved into layoffs and, for those who went hats-in-hand begging to remain on the payroll, brutal wage cuts of 20 percent and more.[12]

More than wage givebacks were demanded by employers who threatened — even though it was illegal to do so — to pack up and move unless they got what they wanted. Fringe benefits — vacation days, medical insurance, pensions, holidays, job security, and more — were sacrificed in an atmosphere of fear and intimidation. Cowering, even if there was no other practical alternative, did little good: de-unionization or fatally weakened unions spread plaguelike throughout the industrial heartland, including at major corporations like Phelps Dodge, Eastern Airlines, Greyhound, Boise Cascade, and International Paper. In 1983, more than half of telecommunications workers were union members, but fewer than 30 percent would be by the turn of the millennium. Teamster union members accounted for 60 percent of the drivers in 1975 but only 25 percent by 2000. Wages during that stretch fell by 30 percent, by 17 percent in steel, by 40 percent in meatpacking.[13]

Soon enough, even the future was offered up in appeasement. Beginning in the 1980s and accelerating rapidly after that, unions began agreeing to two-tier wage arrangements in which new hires—young men and women in the main—would come on board at wages (and benefits if they kept any) half or even less than half of what existing employees were making—and with no real hope of ever catching up (new contracts now contain a lifetime cap on pay). A newly hired auto-worker today brings home about what his grandfather did in 1948. In an economy of diminishing expectations, all of this was met with barely more than a whimper of discontent.

Once rare, two-tier arrangements now cover 20 percent of all union contracts, and not just in heavy industry but also in retail, nursing, supermarkets, and among public workers. And these tiers (a caste system of veterans and "B-scalers") define health and pension benefits as well. That this further corrodes the basis of an already fragile solidarity is a painful reality, one likely to grow harsher.[14]

Down and Out in the Brave New World

Alongside the carcass of the old economy a new one was being born. Not the glamorous one in the Silicon Valley and Alley on the two coasts, but the grittier, shabbier, under-the-radar one found in mass retail outlets, fast-food franchises, Inland Empire warehouses, assembly-line laundries, hotel kitchens and bathrooms, day-care centers and hospital wards, landscapes of the elect, garment sweatshops, casinos, fly-by-night construction camps, data-processing and call centers, tomato fields and almond groves, packing plants, fish factories, and taxicabs.

Here is where the work goes on that makes high-end lifestyles possible, the underbelly of "new class" prosperity and its global city. Here, given its distinctive darker complexion, is the new caste serving the new class. Here the mechanisms of the free labor market operate inexorably not only to depress standards of living but to discourage and demoralize the will to resist. Here in this vast twilight zone firings are instantaneous, severance unheard of. Here malnourishment, bad housing, homelessness, drugs, and bad health have everyone living on the precipice, with no margin for error.

In 2007 a quarter of those classified as poor were employed full-time, all year. Most lived in an isolating, fearful climate, subject to chronic police surveillance, new vagrancy laws, and stop-and-frisk profiling; if they were unfortunate enough to have to turn to welfare, they had to first pass a battery of drug tests, paternity tests, criminal background checks, and school attendance tests: a recipe for docility if ever there was one. Too much fear, too much desperation, too much was at stake, especially for those birds of passage from abroad, whether here legally or not, or for those refugees from deindustrialization just hanging on.[15]

Technological marvels, heralded as signposts of a new and liberated economic era, carried with them a nightmarish underside. Electronics of all sorts and the microprocessor in particular allowed for a level of constant surveillance of the workforce and measurement of its output. These systems may count every keystroke made by data-entry and data-processing clerks. "Telephone tapping" at call centers allows for real time oversight. Active or magic badges track an employee's movements and locations. Video surveillance techniques, once envisioned by Frederick Taylor (the godfather of scientific management), now help in performance evaluations. While initially electronic surveillance focused on clerical workers in finance, insurance, and telecommunications, it is now common among waiters, nurses, hotel maids, and others. All sorts of workplaces, from Verizon phone centers (where the pay is good) to Walmart store aisles (where the pay is lousy) subject their employees to a minute and threatening scrutiny and a dense rain forest of penalties for every infraction, everything from unlicensed bathroom breaks to unauthorized schmoozing. Airlines, for example, run a performance evaluation system for flight reservation and sales agents. At one airline, agents are expected to handle 275 incoming calls a day with a 90 percent booking ratio. If they fall below that standard, they get disciplined; so too if a call lasts more than 215 seconds or if an agent should take more than twelve minutes away from the computer to use the bathroom. American Airlines installed remote-controlled surveillance software to supplement its listening devices at its Dallas–Fort Worth operation.

All of this seeps into the psyche of workers, so that soon enough they become their own disciplinary police. And that is exactly how the originators of prison surveillance schemes like Jeremy Bentham's "panopticon" expected them to work. Titles used by temp workers for their online zines capture the ire of many: "McJob," "Working for the Man," "Contingency Crier," "Guinea Pig Zero," and others constitute a literature of anger, resentment, and on occasion revenge and sabotage. Speeded-up work and spiraling levels of stress became the norm for nurses in assembly-line surgeries in Boston, Guatemalan fish packers in New Bedford, and every subspecies of labor in between.

Lean-and-mean meant doubling up on work assignments without complaint and keeping your head down to avoid the next round of employee triage; after all, someone enlisted in the army of temporary workers could fill your spot on a moment's notice.[16]

To be caught in this web of flexible accumulation (or what might more aptly be called "flexible dispossession"), pressured from all sides and in precarious circumstances wherever you turn, breeds a distinctive emotional chemistry: part anxiety, part depression, part stupefaction, hopelessness, dread, an immobilized passivity. And all the while the tormented worker is supposed to be wearing a smiley face, adding emotional effort to an experience that conspires against such feigned happiness.

Fear inside the black box of the workplace is arguably the common state of life in all capitalist economies. Power is vested in the holder of the property title, whose writ is law. People work there at will—that is to say, at the will and on the terms dictated by property, however that property may be embodied. There are only two exceptions that restrain that prerogative. Unions may. Or the government may. Unions in these newer sectors of the economy are largely unheard of. But what about the government?[17]

Down by Law

Government too has seemed blind to and sometimes complicit in what was going on. Lately "wage theft" has become a public scandal. Employers all over the country think nothing of violating labor laws covering minimum wages, overtime pay, hours of work, and safety regulations—all the basics of civilized capitalism. Beating the system is the system. They know no one is watching. Heading back to the future in this way has become the norm for millions of working people. It started decades ago.

Official indifference or open political hostility to the rights and material necessities of labor picked up steam soon after the rebellions of the early 1970s died away. Just moments after he assumed office, Ronald Reagan fired all the striking aircraft controllers (their union had actually supported his election) and permanently replaced them (at first with the army). This was widely perceived by the business community as a signal that times had changed. Unions could be confronted more aggressively, their rights challenged or abrogated and their striking members replaced permanently with others who once upon a time had been but no longer were called scabs.[18]

Even before the Reagan years, the Supreme Court had ruled that workers could not strike for the duration of the union contract, no matter how routinely the contract was circumvented or violated. So began a backward march into the nineteenth century, when the injunctive power of the government was regularly deployed to break unions and their strikes. (Indeed, by far the most common use of the Sherman Anti-Trust Act from its passage in 1890 until the New Deal was not, as one might suppose, to break up monopolies, but as the legal justification for issuing injunctions against union strikes, considered illegal combinations in restraint of trade.) This proved a notably effective weapon against some of the wildcat uprisings of the seventies as well. The exception was the miners' strike of 1977–78, which lasted 110 days. That walkout occurred in defiance of President Jimmy Carter, union president Arthur Miller, and a Taft-Hartley injunction ordering the men back to work. Victory or not, the government was making it plain which side it was on. While organizing drives had once culminated in union victories two-thirds of the time, by the end of the seventies the labor movement was losing in a majority of cases, and matters only grew worse after that. The Wagner Act, once called labor's emancipation proclamation, became itself a bureaucratic maze ingeniously deployed by management legal teams to delay the resolution of grievances and organizing drives until the stamina and resources of their labor adversaries were exhausted. Much of this happened under Democratic as well as Republican administrations.

Funds and personnel to enforce labor laws were whittled away over the decades to follow. A serial violator of health and safety laws was picked by President Reagan to run OSHA. It took a court decision to force the agency to enforce its own mandates. The National Labor Relations Board was increasingly staffed by people friendly to business; Reagan even appointed Donald Dotson, who had devised anti-union strategies for Wheeling-Pittsburgh Steel, to run it.

Rulings made organizing increasingly difficult. Management practices once considered "unfair" under the Wagner Act of 1935 became commonplace. For example, captive meetings, in which employees were compelled to listen to management's antiunion propaganda, were normalized. Threats to move or shut down a plant if its workers organized, also a legally "unfair" way to cow the workforce, were largely ignored. Reprisals for organizing, including firings, all of which were presumably outlawed, became instead customary. Elections to decertify unions, once rare, no longer were.[19]

Class Consciousness from Above

Political mobilization by the business community and by legislative satellites like the American Legislative Exchange Council (an organization founded in the 1970s of conservative politicians and policy wonks, heavily funded by major corporations like Exxon Mobil and Koch Industries, which formulates prospective legislation across a broad range of issues) further eroded government labor protections in states around the country. Class consciousness in these quarters rose markedly beginning as the Keynesian synthesis disintegrated. In 1971, Lewis Powell, later a Nixon appointee to the Supreme Court, wrote a memo to the United States Chamber of Commerce. It did not mince words: "The American economy is under broad attack.... The overriding first need is for businessmen to recognize that the ultimate issue may be survival—survival of what we call the free enterprise system, and all this means for the strength and prosperity of America and the freedom of our people."[20]

Among the first to answer that call to arms was the Business Roundtable. An organization run by two hundred top CEOs—representing the core of American capital-intensive manufacturing, including Ford, GM, DuPont, Alcoa, GE, and AT&T—it was created in 1973 to counter hostility to the corporation then still percolating in public life. It originated specifically in an effort to defang the labor movement and its campaign to repeal crippling clauses to the Taft-Hartley Act that outlawed the union shop and helped make the South impregnable for union organizers.

Peak corporations mobilized to repress the rise in construction costs in particular, but in manufacturing more broadly. The National Right to Work Committee, founded decades earlier by former Congressman Fred Hartley, achieved a great victory when President Gerald Ford vetoed a law that would have legalized "common site" picketing—meaning the right of different construction crafts to support one another at the same site. Another business confection, the Public Service Research Council (colloquially known as Americans Against Union Control of Government), helped force President Carter to back away from labor reform. Business sponsored PACs grew at the rate of one per day in the 1970s.[21]

When, in 2011, Scott Walker, the newly elected governor of Wisconsin, moved to deprive the state's public workers of their rights to engage in collective bargaining, mass demonstrations and even an occupation of the Capitol in Madison ended in defeat as did the subsequent effort to recall the governor. Indeed, public employees, especially teachers and their unions, became the scapegoats of choice all over the country. By 2012, the momentum established decades earlier climaxed. In Michigan, where the heart and soul of industrial unionism was born, the legislature passed a right to work bill that was unthinkable just months before, and actually followed the Democratic Party's national victory. And Michigan wasn't the only state in the union heartland to do that and more. Child labor laws were chipped away at in states like Utah, Minnesota, Maine, Ohio, and Missouri, allowing young people (as young as fourteen) to work in formerly prohibited industries or eliminating the need for work permits or relaxing rules that prevented youth from working until ten at night on school days. Newt Gingrich suggested putting poor children to work in "the cafeteria, in the school library, in the front office," so they could have the same chance as middle-class kids "to pursue happiness." Meantime, a federal study found that young workers (between ages fifteen and seventeen) suffer from higher rates of work-related injuries compared with those twenty-five and older.[22]

To the Right of Bismarck

Assaults on the social welfare state further undermined the wherewithal to stand up to the new order. Unemployment insurance covered a declining segment of the workforce and a declining percentage of income. On the eve of the financial meltdown in 2007 one-third of the unemployed received payments compared with one-half in the 1950s; less than one-fifth of low-wage workers were eligible, blocked by new barriers requiring minimum monthly earnings to qualify. Those still clinging to benefits could bring home on average only 35 percent of their weekly wage. Federal training programs for the technologically displaced shrank from $17 billion in 1980 to $5 billion in 2005. The federal minimum wage, already at the poverty level in 1980, fell another 30 percent below that in the next decade. After it was finally raised in 2007, its real value in 2009 would still be less than it had been a half century earlier.

Federal housing subsidies diminished by two-thirds since the seventies, even as rents and prices rose. Family provisions essential to the modern work experience—day care, paid maternity leave, health care, living wages, and paid sick leave—were provided in niggardly amounts, cut, or never even got a serious legislative chance. Federal government metrics kept the poverty line out-of-date and way below the level needed to maintain a decent way of life: a nifty way of keeping down the numbers of those eligible for aid. Privatization of what everybody once took for granted were public goods—water, education, public housing, transportation—further depressed the social wage.

Abolishing "welfare as we have known it," as the Clinton administration managed to do, was a way of enlarging the pool of vulnerable, low-wage workers with no other option but to become, if they were able, employees at will, no matter the terms and conditions of their work. What had been maligned as "welfare dependency" was traded in for a new dependency on businesses rooting in soil fertilized by need. And so the business community vigorously supported welfare "reform," especially its provisions allowing for flexible wage scales as an end run around the minimum wage and its tax subsidies and training grants. It made for an attractive package indeed, in particular in a tightening labor market. All in all, welfare reform added a million low-wage workers to the labor pool by 2002.

Defunding college education at an accelerating rate, at a time when it was seen as the only pathway to upward mobility, reproduced a demoralized population of working-class and eventually middle-class youth, adding still more pressure to the households they came from. In 1980 state governments contributed nearly 80 percent of the cost of undergraduate education; now students bear more than one-half. Pell grants, which once accounted for over 80 percent of tuition, were paying

32 percent by 2005. Student debt now runs about $1 trillion; more than 40 percent of twenty-five-year-olds in 2013 carried student debt, and 60 percent of them owed more than $10,000.[23]

O Brother Where Art Thou?

Where, one might reasonably ask, was the Democratic Party while its core social constituencies were suffering? The party of the New Deal last acted like it was one in the late 1970s. Back then it mustered support for labor reforms to overcome some of the crippling aftereffects of the Taft-Hartley Act and other obstacles to union organizing. Onetime vice president Hubert Humphrey, along with prominent elements of the business community (Ford, Harriman Brothers, the Bendix corporation, and other major manufacturers hoping to recoup their position in an increasingly competitive global marketplace through government subsidies for research and development and new technologies), tried as well to address the initial phase of deindustrialization by resurrecting old New Deal proposals for a national development bank. Humphrey and his allies called for capital controls to stop the outflow of manufacturing investment to Mexico, Brazil, and East Asia. And they tried resuscitating the full-employment legislation that had been defanged just after World War II. However, these propositions died in Congress and had no real friend in the White House, signaling that the party of "labor's emancipation" was already on its way elsewhere.[24]

It went in search of new followings in the emerging middle classes among socially liberal professionals, technocrats, and other white-collar commuters from the suburbs. African Americans remained loyal Democrats thanks to the civil rights legislation of the 1960s. But in part for that same reason other blue-collar constituents began migrating away to various forms of racial populism championed by third-party demagogues like George Wallace or even into the arms of the Republican Party. The GOP embraced the silent majority's resentment of limousine liberals and their countercultural and multicultural allies. Demography, racial politics, and cultural emancipation converged to shift the Democratic center of gravity in the direction of the new class.

George McGovern's 1972 presidential campaign first signaled which way the wind had started blowing. The McGovern coalition excluded the labor movement as a conservative element. In turn, the labor movement excluded the McGovern campaign, which it found obnoxious to its cultural and patriotic instincts. (Labor abstention no doubt contributed to McGovern's crushing defeat.) The embryonic New Democrats found a fresh comfort zone in the liberated individualism of identity politics, its moral concerns trumping the economic ones of the old party.

That political migration from economic to cultural politics caused no discomfort in corporate boardrooms, which were ready to view these new identities as so many lucrative niche markets. By 1990 one-half of the Fortune 500 companies employed a full-time staff to manage diversity. But the social liberalism of identity politics also set in motion a logic of fragmentation that could chisel away at the fragile solidarity of an earlier era, especially as that solidarity had itself always carried within it latent fissures and inequities of race and gender and work hierarchies. And after all, the immersion in identity politics was by definition a recognition and a celebration of difference, a huddling together of the same in contradistinction to the not-same, a solidarity premised on division.[25]

President Jimmy Carter was an alien inside the contracting political universe of New Deal labor-liberalism. Carter the technocrat was aptly described by Stuart Eizenstat, his chief domestic adviser, as "the first neo-liberal Democratic president, fiscally moderate, socially progressive, and liberal on foreign policy issues." Despite Carter's subsequent reputation as a global humanitarian, the techno-liberalism he articulated was ethically challenged. It was the culmination of a century of cultural evolution that sought to reduce politics to a matter of expertise and the manipulation of public sentiment to support ends already agreed upon in circles of the knowing. The idea was to dampen down social abrasions and political confrontations and to resolve them by means of political psychotherapy and social engineering.

This was a worldview compatible with the automatic mechanisms of the self-regulating market. It appealed to the new class of suburban professionals and technocrats captivated by the mirage of cost-benefit analysis as an end run around the bloody-mindedness of politics. Its ardor for government economic activism cooled while it warmed up for the corporation. What links still existed between the social liberalism of the new class and the economic liberalism of the working class were wearing out. More than growing apart, these became armed camps with middle-class social liberals facing off against conservative populist "hard hats." A new political chemistry, allying the neoliberalism of the business class and the social liberalism of the new class, became electorally feasible.

After Ronald Reagan's election, what remnants there were of New Deal populism and class consciousness were shuttered away in some attic of the Democratic Party. Legions of working people, whether unionized or like the thirty million or so unorganized working poor, could expect little help anymore from that quarter. They had been abandoned not only by government but by the political machinery their forebears had created to help them cope.[26]

Carter was in effect a precursor of the Democratic Leadership Council's neoliberal champion, Bill Clinton. The council formally made its debut after Ronald Reagan's overwhelming re-election. It recognized the supremacy of the business model for running the country. This included reducing taxes on corporations and the wealthy. And it applauded deregulation, already well under way during the Carter years, in trucking, the airline industry, natural gas, electrical power, and, most tellingly, in finance — a fatal deregulation in the case of the savings and loan business. It was even endorsed by liberal heroes like Edward Kennedy and Ralph Nader and by figures from the other shore like Milton Friedman.

The marriage of Bill Clinton to Robert Rubin, who came from Goldman Sachs to run the Treasury Department, would consummate this union of Democrats and Wall Street. As the Clinton era ended, a journalist summed up this historic makeover: "The precinct of money, traditionally rock-ribbed Republican, has become one in which Democrats are more comfortable. In many ways, the democratization of money has led to the Democratization of money. As the 1990s wore on, the Clinton Administration grew not only to tolerate and appreciate the markets but even to love and embrace them."

A long parenthesis in the history of American political culture had closed. It amounted to a belated recognition that the whole medicine chest of countercyclical remedies on offer from Keynesian economics and the political chemistry that had made them possible had failed to cure the structural crisis of American capitalism—or at least that the political party where they had been incubated was no longer prepared to defend them.[27]

Fear and Self-Loathing

Poverty can crush the will and amputate the future; everything becomes a matter of getting from one day to the next. Resignation sets in or, worse, depression. As the twentieth century drew to a close, one-quarter of the workforce—that is, 36 million people—earned less than the official poverty level for a family of four, three-quarters of them had no company health insurance, eight of nine no pension, three-fourths no paid sick days. Matters only grew tougher when governments pared away at what programs there were left to alleviate the hardship. What was to be done? And who was to do it?[28]

Mass incarceration was one "solution" pursued with a vengeance for decades. It freed up the streets and put a lid on unemployment, and while doing that exported the ominous shadow of the prison into the barrios. Rise up against that if you dare!

Or, if you were one of the millions of illegal immigrants keeping whole sectors of the economy afloat, you might call out your sweatshop employer. But this rated as the highest-risk behavior. The feds might be lurking nearby; ICE (Immigration and Customs Enforcement) is well-known to be raiding and deporting people like you, sometimes thanks to tips from employers who want to shed recalcitrant workers. Keeping your mouth shut and your hideouts hidden might seem far wiser.[29]

Betrayed and abandoned, cut adrift or superannuated, coerced or manipulated, speeded up, cheated, living in the shadows—this is a recipe for acquiescence. Yet conditions of life and labor as bad as or even far worse than these once were instigators to social upheaval. Alongside the massing of enemies on the outside—employers, insulated and self-protective union leaders, government policy makers, the globalized sweatshop, and the globalized megabank—something in the tissue of working-class life had proved profoundly disempowering and also accounted for the silence.

Work itself had lost its cultural gravitas. What in part qualified the American Revolution as a legitimate overturning of an ancien régime was its political emancipation of labor. Until that time, work was considered a disqualifying disability for participating in public life. It entailed a degree of deference to patrons and a narrow-minded preoccupation with day-to-day affairs that undermined the possibility of disinterested public service. By opening up the possibility of democracy, the Revolution removed, in theory, that crippling impairment and erased an immemorial chasm between those who worked and those who didn't need to. And by inference this bestowed honor on laboring mankind, a recognition that was to infuse American political culture for generations.

But in our new era, the nature of work, the abuse of work, exploitation at work, and all the prophecies and jeremiads, the condemnations and glorifications embedded in laboring humanity no longer occupied center stage in the theater of public life. The eclipse of the work ethic as a spiritual justification for labor may be liberating. But the spiritless work regimen left behind carries with it no higher justification. This disenchantment is also a disempowerment. The modern work ethic becomes, to cite one trenchant observation, "an ideology propagated by the middle class for the working classes with enough plausibility and truth to make it credible."[30]

Moreover, the marketplace is not the workplace. A society preoccupied with exchange, with the world of the market, loses sight of the place where real value is created, wealth distributed, and power deployed. The democracy of consumption, while having a lot to recommend it, is not the incubator of inspiring self-sacrifice which social movements live on. The nineteenth-century critic John Ruskin observed, "It is not that men are ill fed but that they have no pleasure in the work by which they make their bread and therefore look to wealth as the only means of pleasure." However, if that workaday world is remembered at all today, it is naturalized, turned into an inevitability, and made into an ontological category so as to be beyond interrogation.[31]

Poverty did sometimes manage to occupy center stage. But this was not poverty arising out of exploitation at work. It was first of all the "invisible poverty" detected in the early 1960s, which on the contrary originated in the exclusion from work. Alternatively, there was the specter of poverty, again racially inflected and highly visible, but as a cultural not economic phenomenon, as a failure of the will—the will to work. Significantly, there were no more "Work in America" reports, at least none commanding nationwide attention like the one issued in 1973. Why worry about the "blue collar blues" in an economy where many are so cowed and anxious that any job will do? And something even deeper was tunneling away at the self-respect and public stature of the workingman.[32]

The shift from industrial to finance-driven capitalism was accompanied by a cultural phase change whose impact on the self-esteem of working people and on their public regard was disarming and devastating. Escape from proletarian life and social status has long been an American promissory note. Yet a contrary impulse to make a place in the sun for the working classes has coexisted for generations alongside those feelings of shame, failure, or denial.

No longer is this the case. Even the labor movement wants to depict itself as middle class, in a studied aversion to using a social category— the working class—that fits it well but is now so stigmatized that it is better left buried. As one writer notes, even those pop culture figures who, by virtue of everything they do at work should be seen as working class, are rather portrayed as middle class, be it the Simpsons or the characters on *Friends* or *Gilmore Girls*. Should it crop up, this invisible class is treated as an exotic species at best or at worst as a failure, as throwaway trash. Manual labor is disrespected in favor of what is depicted as "real" creative work, often abstract, done in an office, numerical, image-laden, and paper-bound. A world once highly visible, wretched, and inspirational all at the same time has dropped beneath the horizon of our common consciousness.

In this postindustrial world not only is the labor question no longer asked, not only is proletarian revolution passé, but the proletariat itself seems passé. And the invisibles who nonetheless do indeed live there have internalized their nonexistence, grown demoralized, resentful, and hopeless; if they are noticed at all, it is as objects of public disdain. What were once called "blue-collar aristocrats"—skilled workers in the construction trades, for example—have long felt the contempt of the whole white-collar world. For these people, already skeptical about who runs things and to what end, and who are now undergoing their own eviction from the middle class, skepticism sours into a passive cynicism. Or it rears up in a kind of vengeful chauvinism directed at alien others at home and abroad, emotional compensation for the wounds that come with social decline.[33]

At lower levels of the working-class hierarchy, it is stunning how many still living in poverty blame themselves for their predicament, for making "bad choices." Then again, it's really not so surprising in a society that has largely erased their presence except to judge them delinquent. Who can't sense the collective frown that derides working-class dress codes, eating habits, what they drive and what they smoke, their feckless social and moral attitude about work, childbearing and child-rearing practices, early marriages, leisure pursuits—in sum, their whole unstylish lifestyle. And the connection to race is organic, a way of erasing and replacing class with race. All these improprieties are associated in the public mind with blacks and Latinos even while felt to be characteristic of a whole class.

Once upon a time the exposure of urban misery and squalor aroused middle-class sympathy, even outrage. Now the reaction is more likely one of fatalistic resignation. Thus when Jacob Riis put together a book of words and pictures about life in the slums of late-nineteenth-century Gilded Age New York, it shocked and nauseated middle-class readers. It helped ignite a national crusade to do something about what was considered a social scandal. A century later the television drama *The Wire* might have been our own era's version of Riis's *How the Other Half Lives*, detonating a similar explosion of outrage. It was after all a scorching indictment of the way our modern breed of pitiless capitalism simply writes off vast tracts of humanity, in this case both the black and white working and impoverished classes of Baltimore.

Yet "indictment" does not quite capture the mood and vantage point of the TV serial. It was rather a kind of visual requiem pervaded by a mournful hopelessness about the scene it paints, about the abyssal cynicism and corruption of the city's political class, its police hierarchs, its business leaders, its school bureaucrats, its media lords, its ghetto spokesmen, and even those remnants of the labor and civil rights movements mounting a last-gasp, enfeebled resistance. The last man with heart left in terminal Baltimore turns out to be a drug-dealing killer.

Tragic fatalism of the kind conveyed by *The Wire* is a version of our general condition that accepts as natural and inevitable what might have alarmed and agitated past generations. What comes to seem normal is assumed to be not only real but right, or is not noticed at all, or is so frequently noticed its impact becomes negligible.

Vanishing is disempowering in the extreme, especially if you're still right there. In a society infatuated with business titans and Olympian managers, commanding presences because they are in positions of command, the managed shrink in self-estimation. Deprecating and denigrating this underworld is a reflex, one that becomes part of the collective unconscious. As Senator Phil Gramm observed, "No poor man ever gave me a job." Dissing these "losers" became a nasty commonplace, not beneath even President George H. W. Bush's press secretary Tony Snow, who remarked: "Upper classes have always pulled societies forward economically—and their conspicuous prosperity has always aroused the jealousies of the lower classes. The envious set out to strip the rich of their lucre believing mistakenly that by redistributing income they could make everybody affluent." Snow's was a kind of social cowardice that runs away from confronting the structure of power and wealth actually responsible.

This may have always been true, but more emphatically so once wage slavery is accepted as destiny, as history's end point, when all that has come before it is gone. Or as Margaret Thatcher put it: "There is no alternative."[34]

O Brother Who Art Thou?

Naturally, the brutal process leading up to this monumental disappearance caused internal bleeding. In a society that was giving itself over to the uninhibited pursuit of self-interest, unions were increasingly treated as the most piggish institutions out there, strictly out for themselves—especially their bureaucrats, who were likened to gangsters of the first order. While corruption is chronic in all sorts of institutions, especially in government, politicians never tire of raking unions over the coals for behavior they turn a blind eye to when it crops up among more powerful transgressors.

Where unions managed to achieve and hang on to some semblance of power, security, and dignity, they were greeted by a sour turn in the public mood. That mood swing was caused by a general decline in all those precious things that make life supportable for those not lucky enough to be in unions. Resentment instead became the emotion *du jour* and unions got chastised for not having to suffer quite as much as everybody else—everybody, that is, except those privileged circles who didn't have to suffer at all.

Inflation was blamed on the unions. Stagflation was blamed on the unions. Union members were coddled, too immune to the discipline of the market, too well paid. If in the distant past low wages were once the problem, now they were the solution. Why not pick on teachers' unions for the sorry state of public education and the even sorrier prospects of the kids in attendance? Teachers and their unions after all don't carry the heft of hedge funds looking to privatize schools and willing to make insupportable claims about the wonders of a charter school regimen.[35]

Racial resentment has always cut a broad swath through working-class life, making enemies where there might have been brothers. The rights revolution of the 1960s, while supported by many trade unions, was opposed by others—most conspicuously, in the construction trades. Then, as pressures of economic decline began to set in, resentment about affirmative action, school busing, tax-supported poverty programs (however meagerly funded), and other needs-based, tax-supported social welfare initiatives boiled over.

Actually, this resentment was less evident among union workers than among white working-class men and women outside the ranks of organized labor. Wherever it cropped up, it wedged apart groups that might have been and in some large measure had been living approximations of "solidarity forever," of that subversive social emotion, sympathy, which the Taft-Hartley Act went out of its way to criminalize. An irony of tragic proportions happened. People once standing shoulder to shoulder in the struggle for economic justice were now divided into hostile camps by the same conundrum.[36]

Nor was this debilitating only in a practical sense. What lent the labor movement of the 1930s and the various anticapitalist currents before then such a large presence was the instinct, expressed only episodically, to identify its cause and objectives with the lowliest. Now, jealousy about the gains, however limited, of those beneath them, those still living on the mudsills of modern America, corroded precisely that socially more embracing instinct.

A better-off white working class bought into a notion originally concocted by the haute bourgeoisie of the first Gilded Age: there were *two* working classes, one respectable, hardworking, manly, orderly, cleanly turned out, and a second one that was dirty, dangerous, debauched, and unmanly. This demobilizing fantasy was already the price paid in the immediate postwar years for losing the battle in the public sphere to extend social welfare and resorting instead to the far more restricted private realm of collective bargaining.

More crippling even than that, this growing parochialism, embedded in the politics of identity no matter what victimized population was hoisting its flag, changed the way people viewed the world. Making sense of what's out there is never a matter of individuals apprehending it directly. Rather knowledge, especially social knowledge, is mediated by all those relations and connections in which everybody is entwined— from the intimate immediacy of the family to the remote nation-state. Breaking down the Berlin walls that balkanize social life into sovereign territories—family, kin, neighborhood, ethnic and religious tribes, primordial hierarchies of race and gender, manual and mental labor—is rare. When it does occur, however imperfectly and briefly, people caught up in this overturning, in this act of organizational artistry, may reconceive the world and their own place in it. The mutuality, the underlying interdependence, that accounts for the existence and the identity of every modern individual becomes palpable. You might call that the epistemology of revolutionary change. In plainer language it is what animated the mass strikes of the Gilded Age or what the Flint sit-down striker recalled after that victory when he said, "It was the CIO speaking in me."

What is therefore most pernicious about the recent ascendancy of free market thinking is perhaps not so much the triumph of its public policies. Rather, it is how its spirit of self-seeking has exiled forms of communal consciousness, rendered them foolish, naïve, woolly-headed, or, on the contrary, sinful and seditious. A cultural atmosphere so saturated with these suspicions is a hard one in which to maintain or create movements or institutions built on oppositional foundations.

The postwar "grand bargain" which traded in anticapitalist aspirations for the American standard of living and the welfare state was already a first step headed that way. The siege mentality of the Reagan era further entrenched this behavior. Worse, that atmosphere became the polluted air breathed by everyone. Even those still tied to the remnants of what once were assemblies of resistance, zones where the world might be reimagined, were weighed down by the torpor of a regnant self-interest. Hunkered down in their bunkers, unions began to behave as they had been caricatured by their foes: wheelers and dealers, wise to the ways of the world, bailing out as the boats flooded. To envision an escape from that fate seemed like proposing to abolish the law of gravity.

Manning Up

Weakness and defeat, the exhaustion of old remedies, living as cultural and social ex-communicants, all this could not help but demoralize. And it made inviting as well other forms of consolation and reassertion. Political seductions aimed at hard hats, at silent majorities of ordinary, hard-working people, at the upholders of family values, and at those who still got dirty when they worked with their hands while those in suits and ties shuffled papers were persuasive to many. The counterreaction to the racial politics of the 1960s fertilized the soil in which hostility to government could root.

Richard Nixon's approach to shoring up his social support rested on this démarche in cultural politics aimed at the white working class, something he borrowed from George Wallace's assault on the liberal establishment. Meanwhile, his vice president, Spiro Agnew, trafficked in alliterative homilies designed to arouse anxieties about manly men and their despoilment by the "effete" and the "effeminate" establishment.

While this seduction merchandized a warehouse full of issues, from crime and drugs to abortion and subversion, at its most primitive it indicted the liberal elite for taking money from the people who worked to give it to those who wouldn't.

For example, Louise Day Hicks, a leader of the fiery protest movement in Boston against busing and affirmative action, saw the contest as one between "rich people in the suburbs, and the working man and woman, the rent payer, the home-owner, the law-abiding, tax-paying, decent-living, hard-working, forgotten American." Looking through the other end of the telescope, Charles Murray saw in his best seller *Losing Ground* a state-created caste of nomadic outsiders, poverty program addicts, immoralists, poverty-stricken pariahs, and parasites.[37]

Nixon sought to capture the sense of resentment and alienation that had been vividly depicted in "The Revolt of the White Lower Middle Class," an article by Pete Hamill. The president loved that article, which was mined in turn by his Labor Department secretary, George Shultz, for a report called "The Problem of the Blue Collar Worker," which sympathized with the worker's sense of being forgotten and passed over. Nixon's team went to great lengths to woo the AFL hierarchy, including heads of the construction, longshoremen, and teamsters unions, as well as police and firefighters. And so too, the Nixon administration seized on the latent identity politics of the white working class, appealing to thirty-three separate ethnic groups from Bulgarians to Syrians, transmuting indigestible class issues into the comfort food of cultural genuflection.[38]

What Nixon inaugurated became Republican orthodoxy for a generation. And since it worked, why not? Many working-class Americans saw little relief and less respect headed their way from the desiccated ranks of the New Deal. The Democratic Party had become the captive of a milieu that repudiated much of what they cherished: marriage, the paterfamilias, and patriotism; sexual orthodoxy and social conventions; and also class consciousness. The trick that produced Reagan Democrats from blue-collar precincts in some numbers was not to erase a sense of class identity but to neuter it politically, to make it turn inward—to privatize it, so to speak.

As the distinguished literary critic Terry Eagleton points out, for a long time issues of gender, race, ethnicity, identity, and culture were inseparable from "state power, material inequality, the exploitation of labor, imperial plunder, mass politics, and resistance and revolutionary transformation." Then the links got severed. We have grown accustomed to speaking about the "Southernization" of American politics. Alongside it emerged the Southernization of the American working class, its retreat into make-believe. Perversely, a form of cultural flattery invited white male workers especially to take pride in their own degradation as rednecks, in the stereotype of them as stupefied marginalia. One ingredient of this cultural curative buoyed up a deflated masculinity. A world less and less respectful of the working-class male breadwinner, one chipping away at his material wherewithal, one where women in the workplace seemed trespassers and transgressors outside their proper place, could be seen by a man as a threat to a primordial status as well an implicit indictment of his own failure to provide. It incited a kind of angry, vengeful, homophobic muscle flexing and altered the chemistry of working-class life. Together with racial fears and resentments, this was a cocktail of class consciousness mixed by political and business elites whose every motivation and policy initiative meant to subvert the class consciousness that still survived from earlier days and that stood in their way.[39]

Popular entertainment and the graphic fantasies of commercial art made this cultural persuasion the spiritual sustenance of everyday life, as Jefferson Cowie has described in his book *Stayin' Alive*. Even while legions rose against the prevailing industrial order in the early 1970s, Archie Bunker, with his amusing dumbness and bigotry, showed up as the media's favorite image of the white working-class male. In other depictions this simulacrum of the genuine blue-collar article might be less benighted, or simply pathological, as in *Easy Rider*. He might be hapless and marginal—"history's loser," say, like John Travolta in *Satur-*

day Night Fever—or, on the contrary, patronized as the bearer of authenticity, hence the suddenly fashionable fascination with country-western music and mores, epitomized by Merle Haggard's "Okie from Muskogee."

Heroes like Rambo, Dirty Harry, or Charles Bronson in *Death Wish*, and antiheroes like Al Pacino in *Dog Day Afternoon* or Robert De Niro in *Taxi Driver*, and men in commercials wearing shirtsleeves and bandannas and driving pickup trucks through rough country all became icons of a stylish new working class. What distinguished it was its hypermasculinity, its warriorlike penchant for revenge, its contempt for conventional institutions of authority, and its fealty to the family. Here was a mythic figure, full of latent (or not so latent) fury, a narcissistic, infantile rage, often mirroring the enemy's. It was a masquerade of control, needing no one but concealing a social hopelessness. This working-class hero might rush in to protect the underdog, but only to lapse into the age's all-enveloping cynicism.

Debasement masquerading as empowerment or just plain debasement without psychic compensation became de rigueur. This recombinant bouillabaisse of bluegrass, gospel, hillbilly, and cowboy music turned the epithet "redneck" into a boast. One fundamentalist preacher/singer captured the inversion in a song:

> No, we don't fit in with the white collar crowd
> We're a little too cowboy and a little too loud.
> But there is no place I'd rather be than right here,
> With my red neck, white socks, and Blue Ribbon Beer.

The literary critic Roger Shattuck itemized the elements of this "savage ideal," which "combines shiftlessness and energy, yeoman stock and degeneracy, hedonism and paternalism." When it was still capable of shouting out, the cri de coeur came in ways that aroused personal not social protest: Johnny Paycheck's song "Take This Job and Shove It," for example. The roar echoing from the punk rock scene was just as inward, cramped in civic ambition, minimalist in its vision, reinforcing as a *point d'honneur* its own marginality.

If public life can suffer a metaphysical blow, the death of the labor question was that blow. For millions of working people, it amputated the will to resist.[40]

13

Improbable Rebels: The Folklore of Limousine Liberalism

W hat do Glenn Beck, Henry Ford, Father Coughlin, Joseph McCarthy, Barry Goldwater, George Wallace, and Spiro Agnew have in common? They are or were all warriors in a peculiarly American version of the class struggle. A motley crew otherwise—a TV and radio shock jock, a Midwestern carmaker and folk hero, a Detroit priest, an alcoholic senator from Wisconsin, a "maverick" politician from Arizona, a Southern demagogue, a dishonored and deposed vice president— each in his own way took up arms against the ruling class. For the last half century or so, the representative figure of that ruling class has been widely recognized under a memorable alias: the limousine liberal.

Strange warriors engaged in a strange war. For generations the proletarian specter did, just as Marx had prophesied it would, haunt the capitalist imagination and the citadels of power. No more, not in the West, where it is more supplicant than fire-breathing dragon. Instead, during our own generation of acquiescence, the most enduring and hot-tempered resistance to the established order of things has arisen in the more temperate climes of the heartland's middling classes. It is a recurring itch that never seems to go away. It is a cri de coeur full of a sense of injustice and resentment: something is being lost, something vital has been kidnapped by limousine liberal elites and can be redeemed only by their overthrow. Newly born middle classes have combined with older ethnic white working classes in a sustained assault on the Establishment.

Should we call them the "irreconcilables"? Are they rebels? Are they restorationists? Are they merely pawns in someone else's game? Their stamina suggests at least one conclusion: they are the resilient offspring of our reconfigured capitalism. And their ancestral roots go well back into the last century.

Revolutionary Elitists

When the New Deal order first began to fall apart at the seams, back in the 1960s, a New York City political apparatchik from the Bronx named Mario Procaccino won the Democratic Party's nomination for mayor. His foe, John Lindsay, running for reelection on the Liberal Party line, had been congressman representing the "silk stocking district" on Manhattan's wealthy east side. Procaccino is the one who coined the term limousine liberal during the 1969 nasty primary campaign, to characterize what he and his largely white ethnic following from the city's outer boroughs considered the repellent hypocrisy of elitists like Lindsay: well-heeled types who championed the cause of the poor, especially the black poor, but had no intention of bearing the costs of doing anything about it.

After all, they were insulated from any real contact with poverty, crime, and the everyday struggle to get by, living in their exclusive neighborhoods, sending their kids to private schools, sheltering their capital gains and dividends from the tax man, and getting around town in limousines, not subway cars. While not about to change the way they lived, they wanted everybody else to change, to have their kids bussed to school, to shoulder the tax burden of an expanding welfare system, to watch the racial and social makeup of their neighborhoods turned upside down. These holier-than-thou rich folk couldn't care less, Procaccino declaimed, about the "small shopkeeper, the homeowner.... They preach the politics of confrontation and condone violent upheaval."

Limousine liberals have been with us ever since. As a matter of fact, they were part of the political landscape decades before Procaccino came up with his bon mot.

Today, people like Glenn Beck, Sarah Palin, and Michele Bachmann echo similar complaints. Beck excoriates progressive elitists who detest and work to undermine the protections invented by the founding fathers to safeguard "individual natural rights (like property) as the unchangeable purpose of government." Fancying himself an amateur historian, Beck has taken us back to the prehistory of the limousine liberal during the turn of the century Progressive era. Although quick to distance himself from conspiracy mongers, in describing this original iteration of the limousine liberal Beck feels compelled to acknowledge that "there's a point when conspiracy is not a conspiracy; it's just true." Beck and Tea Party partisans everywhere have pledged a war to the finish against this strange species of elitism.

Strange indeed! Here in the homeland we don't easily resort to the language of class struggle. Normally it offends "true" Americans like Beck, who think of class warfare, if they think of it at all, as alien, something they have in Europe or had in Russia—but not here certainly, not in the New World where classes were providentially banned from the beginning. Still, Beck (as did his forebears) does talk this talk, gets his hackles up over an upper-crust claque that's been running the country off the rails for nearly a century. He pillories the ruling class, warning of "the inevitable rise of tyranny from the greed and gluttony of a ruling class." In St. Louis, a Tea Party leader boasts that "the Tea Party scares the hell out of the ruling class."[1]

Glenn Beck is more a fabulist than a historian; he makes up stories, omits what's inconvenient, tells half-truths, and specializes in a kind of lachrymose vitriol. Nevertheless, he's onto something, as was Procaccino.

First, limousine liberals constitute something new in the long sweep of time. Elites, ruling castes and classes, aristocracies, and the like normally defend the existing order of things. The limousine liberal, on the contrary, is an agent of change. Moreover, the "limousine liberal" epithet has evolved as a peculiarly slippery, elastic category. Over time it has come to embrace a great deal more than wealthy, cosmopolitan elitists like Lindsay. The stigma has attached itself with ever greater force to a heterogeneous milieu of government bureaucrats, social engineering policy wonks, politically connected Ivy League academics, and mainstream media savants: a whole new class of the comfortably situated and socially liberal whose contempt for working- and lower-middle-class folkways and conventional morality is exceeded only by their own self-regard and appetite for the next new thing. One might call this version of limousine liberalism a "ruling class plus." However warped this picture, it resonates.

Second, this species of elitism arrived on the scene just about when Beck says it did, as the nineteenth century turned into the twentieth. That's when corporate capitalism supplanted family capitalism and the peculiar form of class struggle Beck alludes to began.

Anonymous, impersonal, and amoral, corporate capitalism is radical. In the end, nothing—no matter how ancient or revered—can stand in its way in its irresistible quest to accumulate. It may profit from racial segregation or gender discrimination, for example, but it does not depend on those arrangements to exist and may at any particular historical moment find they get in the way. Its commitment to the family and to religious and traditional moral values is contingent, subject always to the higher mathematics of the bottom line. It is a perverse irony that those who champion capital's insatiable appetite come to seem the vanguard of Progress and simultaneously purveyors of an amoral, uncivilized brutishness. As John Maynard Keynes, otherwise a high priest of limousine liberalism, once put it: "Modern capitalism is absolutely irreligious, without internal union, without much public spirit...a mere congeries of possessors and pursuers."[2]

Family capitalism, however, in which property and marriage are bound together to make up what we know as the bourgeoisie, is conflicted; it's eager to grow but only within the circumscribed confines of the propertied, morally disciplined individual and the dynastic household. At every concrete historical moment the entrepreneur, or that vast population of wannabe businesspeople, attach their pecuniary behavior, accomplishments, and desires to distinct local communities, regional attachments, family aspirations, ideals of manhood, specific products and forms of workmanship, concrete historical traditions, religious values, and sheltering racial or ethnic enclaves—a whole social universe.

Around the turn of the twentieth century—Beck's primordial moment—the antitrust movement waged war against the new corporate order. This was one member of an extended family of anticapitalist insurgencies, of which populism was the most celebrated, directed against finance and corporate capitalism. It indicted high finance and the trusts for destroying livelihoods and ways of life. It attacked big business as well for undermining democracy. It condemned the amorality and decadence of Wall Street, the way the new corporate order corroded the moral and religious armature protecting the family. And it reverberated with a sense of violation: "Don't tread on me!"

Antitrust activists, along with populists and others suffering dispossession, rose up to defend a society of independent producers, a familiar society of Christian virtues, hard work, self-reliance, and family continuity. Much of that is far removed from what Glenn Beck is alluding to. Still, there is a kinship, a real genealogy that joins the animosities, cultural forebodings, and economic anxieties of the Tea Party to this older universe of family capitalism under siege.

Capitalism Against Capitalism

Mutations, occurring periodically over the course of the twentieth century, evolved into the latest iteration of this peculiar discontent, the Tea Party. The social and emotional makeup and political objectives of neither the Tea Party nor its predecessors are summed up by a single-minded devotion to family capitalism. They were as likely to capture the enthusiasm of the small shopkeeper as well as the patriarchal pride of the dynast, to flatter the dignity of the skilled mechanic while slandering his union, and to denounce big government while depending on it. Still the faith, the ambition, and the anxieties of family capitalism touched them all.

Henry Ford, an American folk hero, was the first if improbable avatar. By World War I he had identified the enemy: limousine liberalism *avant la lettre*. The automobile magnate was the country's iconic family capitalist. That may seem odd—after all, he employed tens of thousands in dozens of sophisticated factories, some the size of several football fields. But the Ford Motor Company was a privately held family firm, whose founder meant to keep it that way. Like so many anonymous entrepreneurs before him in midsized cities and towns across Middle America, the independent family-owned enterprise was a cherished achievement as much as it was a source of patrilineal continuity. Amid a society increasingly overtaken by gigantic, impersonal corporations run by faceless men in suits—managers, not owners—Ford stood there as an outsized emblem and champion of an imperiled way of life. He was family capitalism's superhero, as close to a romantic figure as the inherent workaday countinghouse spirit of the bourgeoisie is likely to produce, as good as it got.

Ford hailed from, loved, and in people's minds personified all the cherished virtues of small-town America. He was a lover all right, but also a hater. Especially he hated Jews, bankers, and Bolsheviks. This was not a case of serial hatreds. Rather it was a composite animosity in which that trio of Jews, bankers, and Bolsheviks in collaboration loomed up, in Ford's eyes, as a singular threat to the continued existence of the American *Volk*, to that whole integrated universe of private property, the patriarchal family, and God—the bedrocks of bourgeois society.

Starting in 1920, Ford caused to be published a series of articles in the *Dearborn Independent* (a newspaper he controlled) under the general rubric of "The International Jew." The series ran for more than a year, was reissued as a book, and became a best seller.

Anti-Semitism had always been part of American life; Ford wasn't breaking new ground there. What particularly exercised him was the power of finance capitalism. After all, elite circles of investment bankers had midwived the birth of the publicly traded giant corporation around the turn of the century, and those great combines were now managed and directed by emissaries from the banks. Their power and influence was obnoxious to Ford. "It is the function of business to produce for consumption and not for money and speculation," he declared. He was so committed to this producerist variant of anticapitalism that when he set up his giant tractor plant at River Rouge (and made the whole company an entirely privately held concern), he noted, "In the new tractor plant there will be no stockholders, no directors, no absentee owners, no parasites." Nor was the overwhelming influence of these "parasites" limited to the continental United States. International finance, which Ford thought to be dominated by if not exclusively limited to Jewish investment banking houses, plotted to overturn all of Western civilization.

Anti-Semitism and suspicion about banking parasites had been common currency long before the carmaker came along. And citizens of Middle America had been experiencing night sweats about communists since the Paris Commune. What lent Ford's ravings such grit was the way he managed to connect such disparate anxieties about the changing nature of American life to the nefarious doings of this cabal. His great discovery was to unearth how these fiendishly clever banking conspirators had enlisted the help of their inveterate class enemies. Ford's "The International Jew" might be thought of as the folk Marxism of the middling classes.

Ford's epiphany was the moment when limousine liberalism was first conceived: the ruling class pronounced as subversive. Ford was the epitome of family capitalism, champion of the work ethic, defender of what we could call today "family values," abstemious, frugal, modest, methodical, diligent, independent, and a benevolent patriarch. What he feared, what he wanted to alert his countrymen about, was a profound existential threat. Wall Street in league with a godless Kremlin was the fount of a pervasive hedonism that mocked all that the heartland held dear while driving it out of existence.

Ford's articles ranged widely across the terrain of modern life in a painstaking effort to unearth the hidden pathways linking this satanic conspiracy to every Sodom and Gomorrah of postwar America. Here they were peddling pornography through their control of the movie business. Tentacles extending into the criminal underworld, they ran vast stock frauds to loot the innocent. Determined to undermine what was left of the nation's self-discipline, they saturated the country in boot-leg gin. Because they were the masterminds of the publishing industry, they arranged for an endless flow of sex and sensationalism in newspa-pers, magazines, and pulp novels. They fed the nation the same titillat-ing diet of cheap thrills and sexual innuendo in one scandalous Broadway production after another, thanks to their backstage domination of the Great White Way. "Jewish jazz," bankrolled by the same circles, was on its way to becoming the national music, its mood and rhythms an open invitation to the lewd and lascivious. Encouraging every form of vanity and self-indulgence, pandering and promoting an ethos of immediate gratification, the conspiracy was the incubator of a modernist debauch.

That specter of a sinister league of bankers and Bolsheviks would remain an undercurrent of popular political unease from that time for-ward. Profiles of the leading protagonists changed over time; Jews, bankers, and Bolsheviks slowly receded from view or morphed into pointy-headed corporate and government bureaucrats, effete intellectu-als, silk-stocking politicians, social engineers, cultural nihilists, one-worlders, and latte-sipping yuppies—in other words, a menagerie of the well-born and well-bred who had gone to seed, become acolytes of a way of life in which "all that's solid melts into air," and were running (and ruining) the country.[3]

The Limousine Liberal Family Tree

Ford's conspiratorial sense of history—an active element of populist cosmology long before the automaker arrived on the scene—has remained a live idea ever since. But during the 1930s, there began a portentous shift in Conspiracy Central from Wall Street and the City of London to Moscow—and even New Deal Washington. Anticommunism, already a vital element of Ford's politics of fear and paranoia, lent an especially toxic ingredient to the populist politics of family capitalism.

Demagogues such as Father Charles Coughlin, the "radio priest" from the Shrine of the Little Flower outside Detroit, invoked Ford-like images of fat cat parasites, gold-obsessed eastern bankers, usurious Wall Street Jews, and their red revolutionary allies. Coughlin won legions of impassioned followers among small-town businessmen and farmers, the working and "lace curtain" Irish-Catholic lower middle classes, aspiring white-collar entrepreneurs, and others who resented "Rockefeller, Morgan, and their crowd." What these middling sorts feared and resented was the disruption of local economies and traditional social mores by intrusive outsiders: giant-sized corporations and a self-aggrandizing big government, poking its nose into matters like education, race, and family relations, which were none of its business. Theatrical and bombastic, Coughlin likened the New Deal to "a broken down Colossus straddling the harbor of Rhodes, its left leg standing on ancient Capitalism and its right mired in the red mud of communism." Moreover, his growing sympathy for Nazism was not so shocking. Fascism after all had its roots, partly, in a European version of populism, nurtured by a post–World War I disgust with the selfishness, incompetence, and decadence of cosmopolitan elites, as well as a bellicose racial nationalism.

Coughlin's followers loathed big business and big government, even though at the time big government was taking on big business. But "Don't tread on me" meant a defense of local economies, traditional moral codes, religious authority, and established ways of life that seemed endangered by national corporations as well as the state bureaucracies that began to proliferate under the New Deal. Coughlin's radio addresses (forty million people listened spellbound over thirty stations) and his newspaper, *Social Justice*, filled up with references to the "forgotten man," an image first invoked by FDR on behalf of the working poor.[4]

From its inception, "forgotten man" populism positioned the middling classes against the organized power blocs of modern industrial society: big business, big labor, and big government. Kindred images would resurface in the years ahead, especially during the tumultuous 1960s (in Nixon's appeals to the silent majority) and in the Tea Party's wounded sense of exclusion. But in the era following World War II, the movement's center of gravity shifted away from the world of business and finance, away from matters of economic justice, and instead directed its ire at the cultural pretensions and moral perfidy of the nation's new elite.

The Lost Cause Reborn

This distinctive form of populism became ever more restorationist and ever less transformative, ever more anticollectivist and ever less anticapitalist. "Parasitism" remains a key word in the populist dictionary but was now deployed to skewer the poor when once it excommunicated the rich. What were subordinate themes in the old-style populism—religious rectitude, racial and ethnic homogeneity, national chauvinism, and the politics of paranoia—now sounded the dominant note.

Joseph McCarthy, who found his following among the same social groupings attracted to Coughlin, came within a whisker of actually baptizing this peculiar elite with the epithet invented twenty years later by Mario Procaccino. McCarthyism and the Cold War marked a decisive turning point in the transmigration of economic to cultural populism. In the global war against communism, after all, hostile talk about capitalism was virtually verboten. McCarthy emphasized instead the mortal dangers of the New Deal state, infected at its root with Communist-inflected collectivism. The archetypical enemy looked the same: Anglo-Saxon, Ivy League financiers, bankers with "grouse-hunting estates in Scotland," and New Deal government commissars, an aristocracy of destruction. It was the grouse hunting, however, not the economic overlordship, that aroused McCarthyite resentment. The domestic cold war, whose real enemy for many was the New Deal much more than it was the Soviet Union, left behind many casualties. It committed a kind of cultural genocide, purging and proscribing whole families of languages—

not only populism—whose deep grammar had once interrogated capitalist injustice, exploitation, and amorality.

McCarthy went right for the heart of the WASP establishment. How galling that these traitors who hailed from the most privileged precincts of American society, beneficiaries of the country's great wealth, its best education, its highest social honors, and the most eminent public offices, worked to undermine the homeland! Those centers of privilege, which more than any others had for generations inflamed the anticapitalist and populist emotions of millions, those bastions of good order and reaction—Wall Street, Harvard, the corporate boardroom, and the white-shoe law firm—now stuck in the craw of people in a feverish panic over the threat of revolutionary upheaval, of communism abroad and subversion at home.

McCarthyism was no marginal persuasion. One of McCarthy's fellow senators, Robert Taft of Ohio, leader of the Republican Party's Midwest conservative wing, vented his general resentment against those eastern Wall Street internationalists in control of the party, claiming, "Every Republican candidate for president since 1936 has been nominated by Chase Bank." Numerous Republicans denounced the Marshall Plan as a "bold socialist blueprint." McCarthy referred to Secretary of State Dean Acheson as "this pompous diplomat in striped pants" with his "phony British accent," parading about with his "cane, spats, and tea-sipping little finger." Warnings went out that men like John McCloy, U.S. High Commissioner for Germany "with a top hat and silk handkerchief" (who would indeed later go on to run Chase), were ill equipped to deal with the worldwide Communist conspiracy because they belonged to it.[5]

Long before Mario Procaccino penned his one claim to fame, the transmutation of America's ruling class was thus well under way. And increasingly its most inflammatory features were defined by its social and cultural attributes. Its economic privileges and superordinate positions atop the country's peak corporations and government departments were now taken for granted, perhaps now and then resented but little more than that.

Barry Goldwater's insurgency inside the Republican Party mainstreamed what up to the 1960s had remained a marginal if influential politics. Was the Arizona senator a rebel? Yes, if you keep in mind his condemnation of the too liberal elite running the Republican Party. In his eyes they represented a clubby world of Ivy League bankers, media lords, and "one-worlders." Phyllis Schlafly, who a decade later would lead an antifeminist backlash, crusaded for Goldwater. Her campaign tract, *A Choice Not an Echo*, skewered a power elite of financiers, publishers, and government officials revolving around people like Averell Harriman, the Rockefellers, and Secretary of the Treasury Douglas Dillon: a Wall Street cabal disloyal to America, a dangerous band of domestic subversives.[6]

Above all, Goldwater was an avatar of today's politics of limited government. He was an inveterate foe of all forms of collectivism, including unions and the welfare state. (And this is not to mention his opposition to civil rights legislation.) He might even be called the original "tenther"—that is, a serial quoter of the Tenth Amendment to the Constitution, which reserves for the states all powers not expressly granted to the federal government; for Goldwater and others after him, such federal intrusions simultaneously upset the racial order and transgressed the rights of private property.

As the Goldwater opposition sunk its grass roots into the lush soil of the Sun Belt and the South, its desire to restore an older order of things was palpable. The senator's followers were quintessentially middle-class congregants of the church of family capitalism. Yet they were oddly positioned rebels. Unlike the declining middling sorts attracted to Coughlin and others in the 1930s, they came mainly from a newly rising middle class, nourished by the mushrooming military-industrial complex: technicians and engineers, real estate developers, upscale retailers, military subcontractors, owners of construction companies, middle managers, and midlevel entrepreneurs who resented the heavy hand of big government while in fact being remarkably dependent on it. On this new frontier their way of life relied on an ingenious and bipartisan array of tax breaks, government loan guarantees and subsidies, public works (like roads, bridges, waterworks, and irrigation systems), zoning protocols, federal housing, and urban development agencies and grants. But they were not about to pay any attention to that element of their ascendancy, which would have spoiled their amour propre about the free market and self-reliance.

These Sun Belt conservatives could be described as reactionary modernists for whom liberalism had become the new communism. How shocking—or not—when Goldwater won the 1964 Republican presidential nomination in a knockdown brawl with the party's presidium, led by New York governor Nelson Rockefeller.[7]

George Wallace, Alabama's segregationist governor, accelerated this transformation of the economic populism of yesteryear into the cultural populism of the late twentieth century. Wallace inveighed against gilded know-it-alls using their levers of power over the government, the media, the judicial system, the universities, and the philanthropic foundations to upset the prevailing order of things: "Do we have an elitist government?... They've decreed it's good for the people to do certain things. And even though the people don't like to do it, they must do it because this super-elite group is so determined." The governor was addressing, as he put it, "the man in the textile mill," the "barber and beautician," and "the little businessman."

Style sometimes is substance. Both Vice President Spiro Agnew, with his invective directed against what he labeled the "nattering nabobs of negativism," the "pusillanimous pussyfooters," and the "effete corps of impudent snobs," and Governor Wallace weren't afraid to taunt the bourgeoisie, to talk outside the box, and to violate Anglo-Saxon taboos against the unsayable. The irony is that once this kind of rhetorical impiety was part of the arsenal of working-class defiance of capitalist good order; now it was retrofitted on behalf of law and order. No matter! Any movement worth its salt needs this emotional energy. On high school football fields and parking lots, at shopping malls and stock car tracks, in Elks halls, fairgrounds, and drugstores, speaking to blue-collar and first-generation white-collar workers and second-generation Okies, Wallace roused feelings of nostalgia for a culture headed for extinction. He mixed it with rage against all those—hippies, atheists, and "pseudo intellectuals"—who might be considered the camp followers of limousine liberals.[8]

Patricians like William F. Buckley, editor of the *National Review*, denounced this kind of politics as "Country and Western Marxism," creeping in from the hinterland. He had a point: Wallace was all at once an anti-elitist, a populist, a racist, a chauvinist, and a tribune of the politics of revenge and resentment. His appeal was to an expanded universe of family capitalism that embraced the upper reaches of the white working class. He defended the hard-hat American heartland mainly by hailing its ethos of hard work and family values, not by proposing concrete measures to assure its economic well-being. Wallace railed against the arrogance of Washington bureaucrats, the indolence of "welfare queens," and the impiety, moral nihilism, and disloyalty of privileged long-haired, pot-smoking, antiwar college students. He hated the "Yankee establishment," conflating the "filthy rich on Wall Street" and the "socialist beatnik crowd running the government."

Still, Goldwater and Buckley dismissed Wallace as a New Deal populist because the governor endorsed federal funding of education, job training, unemployment insurance, public works, and increases in Medicare and Social Security payments. The separate streams of working-class racial populism and the populism of family capitalism would one day converge, but not yet. Still, men like right-wing strategist Richard Viguerie early on sensed the party worth taking over was Wallace's American Independent Party, not the Republicans.[9]

Precariously positioned blue-collar workers, beleaguered by taxes, inflation, and the collapse of the racial, sexual, and moral old order of things, hunkered down to defend the value of their mortgaged homes, the autonomy of their local schools and their ethnically and racially familiar neighborhoods. This was a kind of proletarian version of family capitalism—claiming territorial space as its communal property—that enlisted race as another medium of class struggle.

Wallace's racial antistatism became a worksite for conservatives and segregationists fashioning a common political identity and logic. Soon enough, it would no longer be taken for granted that conservatives were natural-born elitists. On the contrary! Wallace, a new kind of populist conservative, was an outlier, an outlaw for law and order—defiant, non-acquiescent, and ecumenical. And he aspired to be something more than an unreconstructed redneck son of the South: "It is basically an ungodly government," he said. "You native sons and daughters of old New England's rock-ribbed patriotism . . . you sturdy natives of the great Midwest, and you descendants of the far West flaming spirit of pioneer freedom, we invite you to come and be with us for you are of Southern mind and Southern spirit and Southern philosophy, you are Southern too and brothers in our fight."[10]

When Wallace ran in the Democratic presidential primaries in 1964, he'd polled big numbers not only in the South, but in industrial states like Michigan, Indiana, and Wisconsin. His supporters included working-class folk but also people from lower-middle-class suburbs and farms who had loved Joe McCarthy. His earthy, hillbilly wit and his scorching denunciation of Judas-like parasitic elites were aimed at everyman. In Michigan a large UAW local endorsed Wallace during the 1968 primaries. A survey found one in three union members in the state preferred the governor, as did 44 percent of all white workers in Flint. A crowd of twenty thousand attended a Wallace rally in 1968 at a sold-out Madison Square Garden in New York City. Before he was shot during the 1972 primary campaign season (he had won 42 percent of the Florida vote, finished second in Pennsylvania and Indiana, and won in Michigan and Maryland), his campaign registered the early signs of the nation's economic bad news. Wallace championed the tax-burdened middle class and its anxieties about inflation, deploring "welfare loafers" living off "liberal giveaway programs." He declaimed, "Middle America is caught in a tax squeeze between those who throw bombs in the streets...while refusing to work...and the silk stocking crowd with their privately controlled, tax-free foundations." A hard hat, a home owner, a cop, a steelworker, a taxpayer, a barber: the borders of the aggrieved and angry spilled across class lines. "We're sick and tired of the average citizen being taxed to death while those billionaires like the Rockefellers and the Fords and the Mellons go without paying taxes."[11]

Popular Front on the Right

"Blue-collar aristocrats," proud of their work, mingled with modestly salaried white-collar people. These latter included sales and accounting clerks, banking and insurance functionaries—who were often as routinized and subordinate as manual workers but cherished illusions about the nature of their work, their security, and their mobility that set them at a remove, and who considered it a great social accomplishment to have escaped manual labor. Together they fitted into a social space also populated by small retailers, building contractors, and service operators. Sometimes compliant and even admiring of the upper orders, at other moments they simmered with resentment over the privileges and immunities of those protected circles, worried about their own less secure status.[12]

As this protean movement enlarged its social reach, it also muted its overt racism; the civil rights movement, including its limousine liberal supporters, had made such attitudes verboten. So, as the movement penetrated widening circles of the "respectables," it relied instead on a color-blind opposition to limousine liberal initiatives like affirmative action, court-ordered school busing, and poverty programs. Racism that dared not speak its name voiced instead an inverted set of class animosities that long ago had also been declared impolitic and unpatriotic.[13]

Thus, "Country and Western Marxism," Buckley's snide innuendo notwithstanding, showed up elsewhere in the ranks of conservative populism. Procaccino's paisan from Brooklyn's Italian American Civil Rights League believed that "oil, steel, insurance, and the banks run this country." Around the same time, Louise Day Hicks, the leader of the antibusing movement in Boston, explained that the war there was a contest between "rich people in the suburbs, and the working man and woman, the rent payer, the home-owner, the law-abiding, tax-paying, decent-living, hard-working, forgotten American." Race and class tensions intermingled in Boston and other metropolitan centers and encouraged a thirst for revenge against the central committee of limousine liberalism.[14]

Class conflict may have been proscribed by the Cold War. But its pulse was easily detectable even in unlikely precincts of the "new right." William Rusher, a key Buckley collaborator at the *National Review* and the most populist inclined of its inner circle, described the new configuration of petty producers, "which includes businessmen, manufacturers, hard-hat blue-collar workers and farmers," against nonproducers. For Rusher those layabouts could be found in the knowledge industry, the media, the educational establishment, among federal bureaucrats, foundation functionaries, and on the welfare rolls. He called them the "verbalists."

Paul Weyrich, a godfather of the populist right and cofounder of the Heritage Foundation, observed, "Big corporations are as bad as Big Government.... They are in bed together." Indicting big business for its gutlessness had become a conceit of the new right. The corporate world, in this view, had caved in to the unions and curried favor with government bureaucrats. Nor was the indictment limited to the outliers of American society. Senators Paul Laxalt of Nevada and Orrin Hatch of Utah excoriated business leaders as "gutless wonders," "inheritors who have never known what it's like to put everything on the line, to meet a payroll."

Weyrich was right of course. But by this late date no rebel of conservatism was seriously proposing an assault on Wall Street and the Fortune 500. On the contrary, the language and style of these latter-day middling insurgents were infused with managerial locutions. They were prone to defer to and to emulate business leaders for their savvy and braggadocio. Older preoccupations with the money trust and monopoly faded.[15]

The Lost Soul of American Politics

Now the most intimate matters were at stake: the raising of children, the relations between men and women, neighborhood turf, God, and the racial status quo. When a cabinet-level Department of Education was created in 1979, fear and anger about government obtrusiveness crested. An alarmed correspondent in *The Right Woman* (a now defunct journal of the antifeminist new right) wrote, "There is an underlying assumption . . . that the correct education of children is the primary responsibility of the state. . . . This view is contrary to Judeo-Christian tradition which always maintained that the education and care of children is the primary responsibility of parents. . . . To interfere or to attempt to interfere with parents' rights is a violation of the First Amendment rights."

Pat Robertson, the Machiavelli of evangelical politics as the creator of the Christian Coalition (who, by the way, was a Yale Law School graduate with a senator for a father), condemned "the humanistical/atheistic/hedonist influence on American government" that comes from its control by the Trilateral Commission (founded by David Rockefeller) and the Council on Foreign Relations. Phyllis Schlafly's Eagle Forum, Beverly LaHaye's Concerned Women for America, and her husband Tim's American Coalition for Traditional Values mobilized to take over a government diseased by "secular humanism" and to restore the moral order, "the traditional values of Western civilization."[16]

Highfalutin bloviating of this kind, however, conceals something more poignant. A society in which the ground is always shifting under everybody naturally gives rise to a contrary yearning to slow down, to find a resting place, especially to restore some moral sure-footedness. Many, whether religious or not, can sympathize with the resolve of one evangelical woman: "I have moral absolutes. The majority of the population doesn't even think they exist."[17]

Radical shifts in religious sensibility help measure the distance traveled from the age of resistance to the Age of Acquiescence. During the first Gilded Age, religious denunciations of the established order often originated outside the mainstream, even in renegade denominations. Now, instead, analogous religious circles censure what their ancestors applauded and applaud the free market orthodoxy their forebears censured. What has stayed the same, however, is the thoroughgoing integration of economic and moral perspectives.

A telling instance of this organic worldview surfaces now and then on the Christian right; for example, take the crusade against homosexuality. Conservative populist circles are apt to not only portray gay behavior as unnatural, socially destructive, and evil but also to identify homosexuals as belonging to a wealthy and privileged elite using the influence of money to impose their morality. (As a matter of fact, however, the homosexual population earns on average 10 to 26 percent less than heterosexuals.)

Indeed, sexuality has for a generation become a political lightning rod of choice (as well as a cultural obsession). What began in the late 1960s as a broadening of radical politics ended up displacing them. Instead sexual politics became a stalking horse for the Christian right.[18]

Analytically, it is possible to separate out the economic and the moral desires and anxieties of family capitalism. But in the everyday life of this resistance movement, they were and are vital organs of the same body politic. So it was that the Equal Rights Amendment was essentially defeated in the Sun Belt states, where family capitalism was flourishing. Here, too, the work ethic, which had always carried with it a distinctly masculine inflection, could recover from the emasculation that threatened it in the dolorous precincts of the corporate bureaucracy. Starting up a family business could be lucrative and therapeutically soulful. Moreover, the growth of the Christian right was not concentrated among the poor or blue collar or less educated. Instead, it flourished in the fairly prosperous suburbs of the South, southwest, and Midwest. A profile of a typical gathering would be apt to include teenagers from private Christian schools, businessmen in suits, matrons sporting diamond earrings, and people wearing L.L.Bean wool skirts and wool sweaters. By the early 1990s, one-half of all college graduates were awaiting the return of Jesus. When they congregated, the appeal was as much about social tradition as religious devotion to all those habits of hard work, self-sufficiency, and social mobility that were the outward signs of a pious life.

For the evangelical world more generally, the state plays the role once performed by the diabolic financial arachnid of nineteenth-century Populist dramaturgy: it is a demonic beast, ravenous for power, working in league with global finance including the International Monetary Fund, the World Bank, and Beck's favorite, the Federal Reserve. It manipulates and extirpates the remnants of democratic individualism. And it must be said that minus the satanic imagery, they have a point.[19]

For decades now, the Trilateral Commission has taken a leading role in this morality play: "the western world's most powerful bankers, media leaders, scholars, and government officials bent on radically changing the way in which we live." Big Brother, as George Orwell certainly knew, can also wear a capitalist fright mask. Fundamentalists look around the modern world and see Babylon, where, the Book of Revelation tells us, "the merchants of the earth weep and moan over her ruination."[20]

Chronic cultural warfare over matters of sexual identity, school curricula, and family values were related fronts in a common assault. Jerry Falwell's Moral Majority spilled over naturally into the antitax rebellion of the late 1970s (comprising the infamous Proposition 13 in California, to limit property taxes, and like-minded movements in states around the country). It drew much of its strength from home owners and small businesspeople suffering what was then decried as "bracket creep." *The New York Times* called the tax revolt a "modern Boston Tea Party." The *Times*, which in the eyes of the new right was the chief outlet for the limousine liberal viewpoint, was poking fun at the movement and its leader, Howard Jarvis. Progressives called him a corporate shill. But, at least to begin with, he wasn't, as he waged an independent struggle against a prevailing tax structure that was devouring middle-class people as inflation vaulted them into higher tax brackets.[21]

What was once a marginally suspect language of opposition, surfacing and then resubmerging, has remained a vital part of our political grammar and vocabulary ever since.

Some Call It Treason

A potent emotional logic is offered up to explain this penchant for subversion on the part of the privileged classes. Their pampered lives sap their wills and cut them off from the grass-rooted patriotism of more common folk. Their cosmopolitan lifestyle exposes them to an armada of cultural viruses that eat away at that bedrock individualism which made the country what it was, or what their critics imagine it was. Their urbanity implies a kind of impiety, a social and psychological dissipation, and a loss of frontier vigor. Concealed behind the impersonal exterior of the bureaucratic welfare state, these mandarins of upheaval cultivate a primal urge to subordinate the free but self-disciplined individual—celebrated by the family capitalism of yore—to the lockstep rhythms of the leviathan state.

Oddly enough, actually existing specimens of the limousine liberal have become scarcer and scarcer. Precious few captains of industry or titans of finance show up on the barricades of social and cultural upheaval. At one time not long ago they did. For example, the war on poverty was widely supported not only by the new class of liberal social engineers but also by broad ranks of the managerial and professional classes and by businessmen like Henry Ford II and Sol Linowitz (a lawyer, diplomat, onetime chairman of Xerox, and close associate of David Rockefeller). Urban rehabilitation and redevelopment, a highly visible element of the limousine liberal portfolio in the 1950s and '60s, functioned as a kind of state capitalism. Subsidized and monitored at the federal level, it was executed amid much interest-group wrangling by municipal governments across the country. The meshing of the corporation and the civil service and political bureaucracies produced what one observer called "finpols"—financial politicians whose economic function entailed deep penetration of government labyrinths. The Economic Opportunity Act of 1964 owed a great deal to pressure from below from the rediscovered poor, but also much to elite circles active in formulating the whole démarche in domestic policy. A political sore point to be sure, these elite reformers in the end conceived of the remedy as an administrative matter. (Apply just the right mix of social and psychological expertise, and moral and political questions tend to drop out of the equation; call it the domestic version of "crackpot realism.")[22]

For a long generation, however, the core of American big business and finance has tended to line up on the side of conservative fiscal and monetary policy and deregulation, which has become a bipartisan persuasion. But neoliberal capitalism also has no objection to the social and cultural reforms of that same era (racial and gender equality, for example). The modern American corporation, as a matter of sound business policy, is among the more politically correct institutions in the country. The capitalism of the *Volk*, on the other hand, holds no intrinsic appeal for the avowedly multicultural corporation (except perhaps as a marketing strategy). Capital's logic is strictly commercial, a matter of the arithmetic of cold cash, not morals. Its purified indifference may upset the tradition-minded, but resonates well with the highly charged self-righteousness and social liberalism of the new class of deracinated, upwardly mobile professionals, technocrats, midlevel financial engineers, new-media makers, liberal academics, and so on. They don't drive around town in limousines and don't make strategic decisions for corporate America. They may not even be shareholders. But there is a shared meritocratic worldview and a disdain for all those inhibitions and vestigial institutions standing in the way of individual self-empowerment and self-gratification and self-realization; the politics of authenticity as flight from all those customs and traditions is, after all, the siren call of capitalism.

New in function and style, just like all elites, this newest one naturally adopts the condescending position. It looks down at the lower middle class as mediocre, provincial, conformist, rigid, and prudish. Partisans of political correctness, this new class doesn't think of challenging the foundations of the political economy, but rather themselves become the target of the morally appalled populism of family capitalism. Caricatures of this elite world deployed by their aggrieved putative victims are abundant and overripe, captured by an article in *The Atlantic* as "pierce-nosed Volvo-driving France-loving…latte-sucking tofu-chomping holistic Waco neurotic vegan weenie perverts."

These vanguards of the modern elevate the authority and presumed "expertise" of state and corporate bureaucracies and staff their managerial hierarchies. They take the view attributed to them by their foes, a tutelary presumption that they know best. Dismissing the distress and anger this produces as so much antediluvian maladjustment is near-sighted at best. Instead, the calisthenics keeping the state healthy lead inexorably to the fundamental disruption and evisceration of older institutions and ways of arranging life—families, neighborhoods, school systems, churches, parks, streets, stores—that anchor and lend tactile meaning to abstract worlds of space and time. From the standpoint of the limousine liberal power elite, this is all salutary, progressive, and rational. But at ground level, this is perceived as the work of a malignant establishment, a privileged ruling class heedless of the human costs involved in its diktat.[23]

The Past Is Not Even Past

Limousine liberalism has lived a long time in the American imagination—from Ford to Beck. Why? It has risen and subsided without any inherent connection to the ups and downs of the economy, although it may be inflamed by either. Many once assumed that after the great antitrust movement was defeated in the earlier part of the twentieth century, family capitalism had breathed its last. Not so!

While there was a sharp decline in small-sized manufacturers at the turn of the twentieth century, that had slowed by midcentury, when such firms accounted for 25 percent of total manufacturing employment. During World War II, the war economy incubated new industries and new companies in newly industrializing regions of the country like Texas, California, and the southwest—Arizona and its capital, Phoenix, particularly. The southland's countryside and burgeoning suburb/cities ardently wooed business to resettle there. The region was an entrepreneurial paradise of no unions, low wages, free land, tax abatement, and subsidies. Half of all foreign investment in the United States after 1970 went to the South. The federal government fertilized the region's industrial landscape with oil depletion allowances, agricultural subsidies, pipelines, and a network of defense/aerospace installations. All of this served the needs of big business but also as a hothouse for ancillary businesses. William Faulkner summed it up: "Our economy is no longer agrarian. It is the Federal Government."[24]

And if manufacturing proved less hospitable, the service sector beckoned. Flood tides of immigrants formed pools of ethnically based entrepreneurs, some in the backwaters of the informal economy. If big box retailers dominated the standardized mass market, the infinity of new niche subcultures and their inexhaustible desires could be supplied by boutique lifestyle enterprises. By the end of the 1970s, 40 percent of service workers were employed by small firms with fewer than twenty employees; it was even more so in retail.

Impressive as these numbers are, they can't capture the social and psychological implications. Petty business relies first of all on personal capital and on personal, familial labor. Its economic tolerance for the needs and desires of wage labor can often be low. The smallholder artisan populism of the nineteenth century drew local petty producers and their working-class neighbors and customers close together. That is far less so today. In the age of lean-and-mean, keeping labor unions restrained and labor costs repressed means survival. Keeping government agencies out of business affairs is something big corporations can handle with their flotillas of lawyers. But the small businessman has to live with it.

So too, in the survivalist world of start-up enterprises, it is common practice to raise seed capital by mortgaging the family house. When house and home were then vaporized by the big banks during the recent financial firestorm, fury over the bailout of Wall Street helped ignite the Tea Party everywhere.[25]

Dreams of great undertakings, however unlikely, flourish in all the locales of the "little man." And new entrepreneurial fortunes piled up beginning in the postwar years. But they did not necessarily carry with them political access or social prestige. This stoked resentment among many midsized businesspeople, who in style, language, and emotional tone were much closer to their plebeian roots than they were to the transatlantic mores of the Establishment. These new men of the free market hated the snobbish exclusivity, the air of eastern sophistication, and the gratuitous, self-serving, tax-laden sympathies for the lower orders evinced by these mandarins of change.

One thing seems clear: the tumultuous evolution of capitalism over the past hundred years has repeatedly offered fresh possibilities to its family variety—including, in its most grandiose dynastic form, that embodied by the Koch brothers, Sam Walton, or Sheldon Adelson (casino magnate, CEO of Las Vegas Sands Corporation, and the fifth richest American). So it may live on even while the more respectable centers of power and wealth are being concentrated elsewhere. This world can't be consigned to some museum of early capitalist curiosities just yet.

The Political Economy of Business Insurgency

Is the Tea Party the latest iteration of family capitalism at the barricades? Its preoccupation with fiscal probity and especially its niggardly obsession with minimizing its own tax burden and starving the welfare state are certainly suggestive. Surveys demonstrate the presence of many small business owners in party ranks. They tend to be wealthier than average and driven as much by their sense of moral and cultural exile as by their economic circumstances. By the election of 2010, 40 percent of elected Republicans came from the world of small business, and of those newly elected that year, 74 percent hailed from that world.[26]

Plenty of others, however, are drawn from the ranks of hard-pressed lower-middle-class and working-class people who drive cabs, do work as subcontractors, take care of children, fix cars, paint houses, and live on two credit cards and second mortgages. Many struggling workers imagine escaping hard times through a bootstrap start-up and sometimes even manage to do so. This desire is practically a primordial part of the New World, present there at least as long ago as Lincoln's vision of self-employment as the promised relief from the tedium, dependency, and material deprivation of wage labor.

When they get their dander up about the Wall Street bailout, Tea Party partisans seem angrier about the government's interfering with the remorseless but just operations of the free market than they are with the felonious greed of financiers. They can turn against not only the government but also unionized workers and especially public employees paid out of tax revenues. For people caught in these straits, the market Leninism of Grover Norquist, the founder of Americans for Tax Reform, which holds that first, last, and always taxes must be cut, rings true.[27]

Moreover, it is noteworthy that heavyweight funders of Tea Party organizations tend to come from the ranks of newly minted robber baron family dynasties like the Coors family or the Koch brothers. Dynastic outsiders may sound like an oxymoron, but the cases of Henry Ford and the ardently anti–New Dealer William Randolph Hearst suggest otherwise. Nourished especially in the newer economies of the Sun Belt, privately held enterprises in oil, natural gas, real estate, regional finance, and service businesses outside the orbit of eastern corporate capitalism retained a traditional Protestant piety averse to the cosmopolitans of the old order. Dynastic capitalism can confront the world like small business on steroids. Nixon's visceral hatred of the Establishment, although he had to deal with it, meant his administrations were increasingly peopled by Babbitts from Main Street and country-club deal makers. Their road to wealth and power was the dynastic one. It did not depend on climbing the morally indifferent hierarchies of corporate America. They carried with them instead old prejudices, a provincialism, and patriarchal passions that set them apart from the world of the limousine liberal.[28]

Reagan's court was like that only more so. The novelist V. S. Naipaul, himself a conservative, attended the 1984 Republican national convention. He described its intellectual vacancy and mawkish sentimentality about the church and nation. Hope, vision, even piety, was crushed under by the brute pursuit of money and power. It was in his eyes arid terrain, mean, sleazy, and boring. It comprised "a ruling class of Rotary Club nihilists, Right-wing degenerates."[29]

But things are messier than that. The movement is too protean, chaotic, and fed by too many cultural and social and religious subcurrents to be reduced to family capitalism redux.

Still, the remarkable ascendancy of free market ideology over the last generation strongly implies that those ideas must have found fertile soil in which to root. "Shareholder democracy" and the "ownership society" were admittedly more public relations slogans than anything tangible. Nevertheless, half of all American families have become investors in the stock market. Dentists and engineers, midlevel bureaucrats and college professors, storekeepers and medical technicians—people, that is, from the broad spectrum of middle-class life—jumped headfirst into the marketplace, carrying with them all the febrile hopes for social elevation. Perversely, one tangible form of the ownership society that became real—some might say all too real—was the explosion of home ownership set off by the FIRE sector. Whatever its ultimate fallout, it would be a mistake to underestimate how the democratization of credit shored up the notion of an egalitarian, democratic capitalism.

Flexible capitalism, the term used to describe the new system of decentered corporations and casual labor markets, did in fact open up new frontiers of petty entrepreneurship; indeed, the era's lean-and-mean business machine demanded it. Megacorporations downloaded a range of functions once performed internally. Outsourcing, subcontracting, and licensing production, communication, distribution, marketing, and other activities to outside concerns meant that the universe of small and medium-sized businesses expanded considerably. Think Joe the Plumber and all those who bought into the dream of free agent self-employment. The military's insatiable appetite continued to jump-start ancillary businesses, especially throughout the Sun Belt. With the booming of the financial sector itself, all sorts of boutique consulting, accounting, legal, research, software, and other essential undertakings nourished entrepreneurial ambitions and ideology. So too, the worlds of retailing and service/entertainment opened up space for specialty small-scale niche businesses and franchises. New business formations doubled and self-employment rose nearly 25 percent alongside the downsizing of American industry, in part because of it. As noted earlier, corporations found it increasingly easy to off-load functions once performed internally, thanks in part to the information/communications technical revolution, which facilitated the coordination of far-flung operations. Modern and "archaic" labor systems and firms lived in side-by-side symbiosis.

According to a Small Business Administration report at the turn of the millennium, nearly six million new businesses were created during Bill Clinton's eight years in office, and nonfarm proprietorships rose 34 percent between 1992 and 2000. Moreover, small business received 23 percent of all federal contracts, not to mention loan guarantees.[30]

Still, however, this remains a precarious economic zone. The failure rate among small business during the period 2002–2006 (a prosperous time) was frighteningly high, especially among start-ups, whether in construction, retail, or wholesale trade, or even in the finance sector. Core corporations continue to deploy enormous power, enough to drive entrepreneurs and independent professionals under, perhaps even more than they once did, thanks to the near extinction of antitrust prosecutions. In Silicon Valley, for example, the biggest concerns vacuumed up hundreds of smaller ones. Google all by itself swallowed one hundred. But in a sign of the changing times, the vanquished don't complain nearly as much. For some defeat was sweetened by hefty buyouts. (Some-times the whole point was to be bought out.)[31]

Every time somebody opens a small business they don't apply for membership in the Tea Party. Many remain politically in the main-stream, or don't enter the political waters at all. However, the mythos of producer populism envelops multitudes. A shift in the zeitgeist has worked to dampen down hostility to business generally. Management-think as a pervasive cultural persuasion has permeated life way beyond the corporate sphere. Take, for example, debates over public education. At one time, conservatives mounted a frontal assault on multiculturalism in defense of the core curriculum and Western civilization. Nowadays, advocates of vouchers and charter schools emphasize market choice as the best way to invest in "human capital."[32]

Indeed, an older entrepreneurial romance survives even within the dense networks of corporate bureaucracy. The manager was once invis-ible behind the featureless façade of the smoothly functioning organiza-tional machine. Now he or she is encouraged to reimagine himself as a kind of mini-venture capitalist, a source of innovation inside his or her specialized realm. The expectation makes him or her more than a face-less functionary but rather a distinctly special individual. Management-speak talks of "commitment," "drive," "ambition," "leadership," and "control"—making managers miniaturized captains of industry.[33]

Speaking more candidly, however, for the country's Fortune 500, free market ideology and the conflation of freedom with limited government is a tactic, not a philosophy of life. That elite circle depends heavily on government assistance, including contracts, tax abatement, subsidies, publicly funded research, and above all a robust "bailout state."

Nevertheless, further down the food chain, among men and women who've struggled to create their own businesses (or dream of doing so) and whose success at doing just that is an affirmation of their self-reliance, ingenuity, discipline, and moral stamina, conflating the free market with individual freedom is instinctive. Collusion between big business and big government infuriates the world of the little man. But enthusiasm for capitalism is something the Tea Party shares with the bipartisan power elite.

Yet there are genuine areas of serious acrimony. How else can one explain the nasty exchanges within the Republican Party over the last several years about such matters as NAFTA and immigration? What about the brinkmanship of Tea Party politicians in debates over resolving the debt ceiling, which pitted zealots on the right against the Chamber of Commerce and otherwise powerful business and financial lobbies? When Tea Party favorite Texas senator Ted Cruz tells *The Wall Street Journal*, "One of the biggest lies in politics is the lie that Republicans are the party of big business. Big business does great with big government. Big business is very happy to climb in bed with big government. Republicans are and should be the party of small business and of entrepreneurs," he's not lying and he's not entirely wrong. The denunciation of the lifesaving billions received by the titans of finance by Glenn Beck and others can't be welcome on Wall Street. (Beck may be an unscrupulous liar and paranoid demagogue, but when he blames the Federal Reserve for collapsing the economy and calls for its extinction, he can't be helping those "too big to fail" banks for whom the Fed is a favorite watering hole.)

Hostility of that depth naturally cuts both ways. Often enough, peak corporations and business institutions don't trust the Tea Party, finding its slogans dangerous, too ideological, and apt to invite too many bad feelings about big business. Meanwhile, a survey of small business owners found a healthy majority favorably disposed toward the Tea Party. A party blogger advised, "Treating small business owners better than we treat real estate and Wall Street investors is an idea whose time has come." Such fighting words convey that indigenous will to "light out for the territories," to refresh an endless frontier of heroic self-creation— especially in the face of modern bureaucratic society, which is so debilitating and rule-bound. It eats away at the vigorous life, makes people craven seekers of security. A genuine idealism, a part Christian, part

secular version of frontier mythology, supplies the nuclear fuel for entrepreneurial radicalism.[34]

The Last Utopia

Utopian thinking has been banished from most precincts by horrific
twentieth-century history, and more intentionally by elites who have a
special interest in ensuring stability and good order, which utopian
yearnings disturb. And it is considered disreputable and woolly-headed
not only by these circles but also by much of the left and the labor movement. But utopias have risen again among true believers in the free market (even if they claim otherwise); they see in this "stark utopia" a
wondrous mechanism giving forth self-fulfillment, democracy, law and
order, and peace and justice so long as it is left alone to work its magic.

That utopian visions continue to smolder and flare up in these regions
and not elsewhere is telling. The handicraftsman is extinct. The yeoman
farmer is gone. The peasant-proletarian immigrant from the Old World
has been digested by the New. Slaves got free, got re-enserfed, and
finally got dispossessed and warehoused. What lives on clinging to life at
one moment, reproducing like a rabbit the next, is this breed of family
capitalist and all its managerial and blue-collar relations. A utopian capitalism in league with and at odds with really existing capitalism endures.[35]

Here the entrepreneurial romance remains very much alive and at the
same time anchored in an imagined past, one of a particular racial and
ethnic purity, where small towns husband the best in human nature.
Newt Gingrich called it the "great adventure" in a course he taught at
Reinhardt College, "Rescuing American Civilization." It marries the
heroics of cowboy conquest and the steadfastness of the Christian pioneer settler, "a moral undertaking and an inherent part of the makeup of
human beings." A Tea Party website put it like this: "Small business is
important for freedom.... Every American should be a small business
owner.... No job, unless you own your own business, is safe."

Note the sense of impending danger. That faith and desire feels also imperiled. This is in part due to the demographic and moral makeover the country is going through. But more earthbound worries contribute. How not to feel like you might be losing a grip when the portion of Americans living in middle-income neighborhoods dropped from 65 percent in 1970 to 44 percent in 2011?[36]

Sliding downward is routinely blamed by this milieu on the government. Yet these rugged, self-reliant pathfinders, like their corporate cousins, are deeply dependent on an array of local, state, and federal government programs and bureaucracies. But these ground-level realities may escape their notice and don't enter into their calculus. Tea Party partisans in the Boston area see themselves as producers, as productive citizens living in a moral universe—a universe far away from that of the "freeloader," what used to be called back in the Gilded Age "the undeserving poor," especially illegal immigrants living off the government (that is, taxpayers).[37]

Nor can they any longer face up to the disorienting fact that the permissiveness they condemn originates, first of all, in the corporate boardroom, the headquarters of consumer capitalism. And the denizens of Tea Party America are hardly immune to its seductions. Moreover, that same corporate economic engine can minister to the special needs of these reactionary rebels. Clouds of nostalgia hover over the Tea Party, hankering after days gone by. In part, this is because the present and future seem so anchorless. Consumer capitalism retrofits the past into saleable nostalgia: retro or vintage clothing, Disneyland, paddle steamboat excursions, resurrected antique railroad rides to nowhere, three-cornered hats. History for all of us—and most of all, for family capitalism—becomes less a resource than a sedative. In the fabulist imagination, all those real-world indictments of the family capitalist idyll—the family sweatshop, the private brothel, the emotional straitjacket—go to die.[38]

If, however, the sedative wears off, as it must, instead Tea Party Partisans scout the landscape for enemies that threaten their way of life. But the censure their political ancestors once directed at plunderers, "Molochs," "Judases," plutocrats, and Pharaohs is no longer an option.

Instead, the brunt of their fury is aimed at the lowly. The lowly and the resented are many: illegal immigrants perhaps, or the morally dissolute, or those living on the dole. A CNBC market correspondent captured the mean-spiritedness. In an outraged Wall Street state of mind, he declaimed: "This is America. How many of you want to pay for your neighbor's mortgage that has an extra bathroom and can't pay the bills." Soon enough this piece of social Darwinism became a recurring feature of Tea Party signage: "Your mortgage is not my problem." All of these "losers" and more may be enlisted in the army captained by limousine liberals. And to that foe, before all others, Glenn Beck says, "Don't tread on me."[39]

Our native taste for populist insouciance has soured and grown perverse. Tea Party insurgents remind us that the moral self-righteousness, sense of dispossession, anti-elitism, revanchist patriotism, and racial purity that were always present in populism's house of contradictions are alive and kicking. For all the fantastical paranoia that often accompanies such emotional stances, they speak to real experiences—for some of economic anxiety, insecurity, and loss; for others, deep feelings of personal, cultural, political, and even national decline and moral disorientation. For a half century now, Republican strategists have connived to deflect these feelings away from the understructures of power and wealth in America. One might say of this new cultural populism with its angry belligerence that it is hardly acquiescent, but it nonetheless serves the larger purposes of our own Age of Acquiescence.

14

Conclusion: Exit by the Rear Doors

All that is solid melts into air" is even truer about the hyperflux of everyday life today than it was when those words first appeared in *The Communist Manifesto* well more than a century and a half ago. Even adherents of the Tea Party—indeed, especially Tea Party partisans— might agree. In the realms of business and technology as well as in the evanescent fancies and fads of popular culture, we are fixated on now and tomorrow. But if Marx's aperçu is truer nowadays than anything he could have imagined, there is one major exception: in our political life we are fixated on the past, forever looking backward.

Arguably, national politics over the last half century has polarized between efforts to defend and restore the New Deal order, and relentless attempts to repeal it and replace it with something even older.

The liberal left has fought to extend or at least protect what has been dismantled and weakened since the days of Franklin Roosevelt and Lyndon Johnson. Its advances in the realms of individual rights for women and minorities are of profound historical significance. Jim Crow and patriarchy no longer can rely on the institutional and legal supports that empowered them for generations. Together with the earlier triumph over industrial autocracy, these breakthroughs are fairly seen as the lasting and last achievements of that long nineteenth-century age of resistance.

Indeed, the civil rights movement was steeped in folk Afro-Christianity as much as it was in the Declaration of Independence. It drew on that ancient reservoir of perseverance and translated its injunctions to wait on the Lord to "be free" into the here-and-now bravery it took to crush apartheid. Today the movement is inscribed in searing images we're all familiar with, in the sorrows and exaltations of its music, in the lingua franca of political speechifying, and in the iconography of a national holiday. If ever in the national experience there was evidence of the capacity of people to move out from under long generations of oppression, exploitation, and submission, out of the perennial midnight of all-sided coercions and fears and demeaning condescension, to free themselves of self-contempt, fatalism, and a sense of helplessness, this was that testimony.

Nonetheless, civil rights, like the rights of labor, were soon incorporated within the framework of civilized capitalism first erected by the New Deal. What began as collective shout-outs for liberation has ended in what the country's first African American president calls a "race to the top." Is there a more perfect way to express the metamorphosis of solidarity into self-advancement?

Still, the breakdown of old hierarchies rankles many. Seeking to restore the time before all that collapsed is the conceit of the conservative right. No one in those ranks (except for marginal cranks) actually imagines it possible or even desires to repost "colored" signs on water fountains or move people back to the back of the bus or repeal the Equal Opportunity Employment Act of 1972 or reestablish the sexual caste system. What they do yearn for is a time before the collectivism of the 1930s and the antic antiauthoritarianism of the 1960s despoiled the country. The right stands on that rock-of-ages flinty individualism of the free market, the disciplinary regime of the work ethic, the preeminence of business, and the reassurances of old-time patriarchal morality.

Two golden ages, two mythic moments, locked up in memory. While everything else about modern life accelerates the passage of time, political gridlock freezes it.

Efforts to stop the melting, to return the world to some solid state, do evince pathos. True, they also produce episodes of political burlesque, lots of adolescent noisemaking, gnashing of teeth, and mugging for the cameras, but not much else. Yet no one can deny the anguish trailing in the wake of neoliberal flexible capitalism. It has spread the liquidation of society and the psyche far afield and deeply into the tissues of social life. When Marx first spied it, the dynamic was as exhilarating as it was unnerving. It still is for those pioneering on the frontiers of advanced technology (although they tend to forget that the wonders invented in their homely garages would have been inconceivable without decades of government investment in military-related science, technology, and development). For many others, however, it is more apt to bring on queasiness, a sense of a free-falling, unmoored individual descending into the abyss, desperate for a grip.

More resonant even than "all that is solid melts into air" was another telling bit of social psychological insight by a man who, in his bones, couldn't have been less a Marxist. "The only thing we have to fear is fear itself," was FDR's legendary caution to a nation on the brink of the anti-capitalist end time. One measure of how the temper of our times has changed since the long nineteenth century drew to a close in the Roosevelt era is that today we might aptly inverse what the president recommended: the only thing we have to fear nowadays is not being afraid enough.

Neoliberalism didn't invent fear. Nor did FDR mean to minimize all that there was to be afraid of amid the calamity of the Great Depression. Losing a job, falling into debt, getting evicted, falling even further down the social pyramid, feeling degraded or helpless or abandoned, racial or ethnic threats to positions of relative privilege, moral vertigo, and phobias induced by deviations from norms of sexual behavior, and much more are not new. And FDR no doubt had his own reasons for cautioning against fear, including the overriding need to get the wheels of commerce and industry, paralyzed by the panic and collapse of confidence, moving again. What the president could count on — even if he didn't actually count on it and would not have invoked if he could—was a multifaceted and long-lived culture of resistance that was not afraid to venture onto new terrain, to question the given.

Since then, much has happened to wither away the courage and power to imagine a future fundamentally at odds with what we are familiar with or long to return to. In our times what at first seemed liberating sometimes ended up incapacitating.

The ubiquity of market thinking has transformed combative political instincts into commercial or personalized ones or both. Environmental despoiling arouses righteous eating; cultural decay inspires charter schools; rebellion against work becomes work as a form of rebellion; old-form anticlericalism morphs into the piety of the secular; the break with convention ends up as the politics of style; the cri de coeur against alienation surrenders to the triumph of the solitary; the marriage of political and cultural radicalism ends in divorce. Like a deadly plague, irony spreads everywhere.

What lends this thinking and behavior such tensile strength is its subterranean connection to the sense of personal liberation. One of the great discoveries of the feminist movement was that "the personal is political." This undermined axiomatic assumptions about female inferiority and subordination from which patriarchy will never recover.

However, personalizing of the political also carried with it unforeseen consequences as the aperçu migrated into the wider world, carried there by the tidal flows of consumer culture. Nowadays we live in a political universe preoccupied with gossip, rumor, insinuations, and innuendo. Personal transgressions, scandals, outré behavior, and secrets have become the pulp fiction of politics. Our times didn't invent that. Grover Cleveland was regularly raked over the coals for having an illegitimate child. Warren Harding's sexual adventures were notorious. This is to cite two of many possible examples. Nonetheless, this kind of inquisitorial and, let's be frank, voyeuristic pursuit, of venial sins as *the* way of sizing up political life, has reached heights undreamed of. And this can be entertaining—indeed, it may be intended by the media to be so, as it is eye- and ear-catching. It displays a kinship with the inherent sensation-alism of consumer culture more generally. It is also, often, if not always, stupendously trivial or only marginally relevant, but is treated in exactly the opposite way. We have grown accustomed to examine all sorts of personal foibles as if they were political MRIs lighting up the interior of the most sequestered political motivations.

Credit this hyperpersonalizing of political life with keeping interest alive, even if it's a kind of morbid interest in the fall of the mighty or the wannabe mighty. Otherwise, for many millions of citizens, cynicism (and only cynicism) prevails. The system seems transparently to have become an arena for gaming the system. Cycles of corruption and insid-erism repeat with numbing frequency and in a nonpartisan distribution, verging on kleptocracy.

Arguably, "the personal is political" has morphed into something far more debilitating than liberating: namely, that only the personal is polit-ical. Just how disarming this is can be fully appreciated only when mea-sured against the relentless growth of a leviathan state.

Government did not always arouse an instinctive suspicion. When first constructed, the administrative-regulatory-welfare state seemed a life-saver. And for a while it was. But it has become a grotesque caricature of its former self. Its presumptions of expertise and dirigisme emasculate rather than empower. A mandarinate of experts bearing Olympian pretensions, rationalized by social science and psycho-medical portfolios, instills a sense of incapacity in some, in others a subcutaneous resentment.

Meanwhile the security and protections the state once offered have grown frail or were killed. Under the regime of neoliberal finance, the government's inveiglement with commanding business institutions (trace elements of which were there at its creation under the New Deal) erodes its bona fides as an instrument of democratic will, not to mention the general welfare.

While the ranks of labor and its putative allies do vigorously complain about the undernourishment of social services and the like, little if any-thing is said about the nature of the state apparatus itself. Yet one epoch ago the rise of the bureaucratic state and the bureaucratic corporation were perceived by many as twin pillars of a new managerial capitalism. When anticapitalist urges still roiled the waters of public life, social reengineering aimed at restoring political stability and socializing the costs of capitalist production did not get a free pass. Critics saw it as a dead end or if not it seemed likely to create a new dependency and cut off pathways to class independence.

Now, even when all the boats sank in the recent financial tsunami, the labor movement and many of its progressive friends rushed into the arms of the government, cheering on the bailout state, cowed by the politics of fear into believing that without rescuing the banks the end of the world was nigh. Now the whole notion of rebelling against the state is a foreign instinct where it was once a birthright. It lives on ironically in the ranks of the populist right.[1]

Unlike the welfare state, what has not grown frail or inept, what instead has become ever more self-aggrandizing and worth fearing, is the national security state. It is easy and perhaps convenient to forget that it too originated in those golden years after World War II so often celebrated by progressives. Recovery from the Great Depression and the global war that followed seemed to demand the metastasis of the state. It facilitated the triumph of America as the superpower of the free world and as its economic locomotive. Security was promised in a double sense: economic and geopolitical stability, resting on each other.

It is impossible to pry apart these two kinds of security, to divorce the American garrison state from the global New Deal. They grew up together and helped prescribe an "end to history" long before that terminology became fashionable. Today this remains the case, only more so. The delectables of home consumption originate in a global system of industry and finance watched over by the political and military institutions of the world's sole superpower.

Neoliberal global capitalism is known for its antipathy to the state. It does not, however, deserve that reputation. It may in any particular instance be for or against government monitoring of commercial relations. But as a world order it depends completely on national and international political (and sometimes military) institutions to keep things humming: trade treaties, IMF loans, World Bank grants, mechanisms of debt enforcement or default, property law, a global necklace of military bases, state regulations monitoring the transmigration of labor, international concords assuring the unimpeded flows of liquid capital, oil, gas, and rare earth metals across national borders, and much more. A dense network of laws, sanctions, and government negotiations facilitate and defend flexible capitalism. As the regnant order, it naturally requires a thick and pervasive armature (cultural as well as coercive) to get its way.

However, we are not afraid of this state. This is not some Stalinist secret-police apparatus sending people off to the gulag. Instead, we fear what it fears, what it tells us to fear. There are real terrorists out there. They have slaughtered thousands of innocents. Around these acts of mayhem, however, there has grown up a demonology that persuades us to live in permanent fear, in a state not so much of total war (after all, more and more of the actual fighting is done with remote-control robotic weaponry) but of endless war.

State-sponsored paranoia exacerbates an already pronounced penchant to man up to the fear, to flex muscles not only at aliens overseas but at domestic strangers in our midst. What we are instructed to fear above all is that we are not fearful enough, not vigilant enough, not on the ready to detect and defend against each and every imputation against our way of life. We are incessantly reminded that indeed a way of life is in jeopardy. And that is true. What we are called upon to guard is global free market democracy, which incontestably is a way of life.

Presumably in this view the global market and democracy are joined at the hip. But as Iraq and the other Iraqs before and since suggest, or as the displacement or neutering of democratically elected governments in Europe behind in their debts indicates, or as our own "dollar democracy" here at home reminds us, what matters is the market. The United States has lived in harmony with corrupt military dictators, death squads, feudal sheikhs and plantation owners, kleptocrats and warlords — and with virtually every variety of autocracy and tyranny. The main point is to allow the state to do its work to keep fearsome enemies — any one of innumerable foes who might challenge the suzerainty of global capitalism run out of Washington — at bay.

Hence the dark matter of a para-state has grown up around us. It operates outside the law, or ad libs or reinvents the law, arrogating to itself powers undreamed of by the founders of democracy, but always on behalf of democracy. The smug self-assurance of these state mandarins is appalling. Still, there are no tanks in the streets (although now and then we do witness mass arrests or a drone takedown of a citizen). Rather persuasion, not force, does much of the heavy lifting. Many blame the media, which is so intertwined with the power blocs of politics and business, and is itself an increasingly concentrated planetary business. Now and then, it does indeed function like a propaganda machine and a censor.

But most of the time it operates more insidiously than that, narrowly circumscribing what is allowable and thereby what is verboten in public debate, what is legitimate and what is outré, what is to be taken seriously and what is to be coolly dismissed. It invokes the sounds of silence without gagging anyone.

Mainstream media instinctively mimic the version of events offered up by the empowered. Its elemental obligation as a "fourth estate" to interrogate and to keep its skeptical distance — something that happened with far greater frequency in past centuries — gets sacrificed on the altar of "insiderism." The run-up to the Iraq war is perhaps the most lurid instance of this pathology. Mea culpas surfaced only long after it mattered. This manufacturing of or flight from reality is not a conspiracy to deceive but a closing down of the cultural frontier.

When it came to the near terminal crisis of flexible finance capitalism itself during the Great Recession, ideas outside the box were locked out by fear and persuasion in equal measure. A culture that had learned to mythologize big moneymakers so extravagantly and without reservation as seers, saviors, prophets, and warriors was ill prepared to treat these heroes and the institutions they captained differently when they burned the house down.

After noting that a lot of people were ready to haul Wall Street out into the middle of New York harbor and drown it, the media picked up the more appropriate echo emanating from political and economic elites. We faced, all were tutored, a slim menu for how to get out of the mess: we could compress the social wage through austerity; we could use government largesse to seduce those corporate "job creators" and financiers who hadn't yet felt inclined to create many; we could resort to that out-of-favor Keynesian remedy of deficit spending to haul the economy out of the muck. What we could not do, what was not even speakable, was to tamper with the basic institutions of financial capitalism. So, as for the banks themselves, they were to be bailed out, "too big to fail." *Après* the banks *le déluge*, an article of faith even a large segment of the progressive community was too buffaloed to challenge.

Indeed, neoliberalism as a way of thinking about the world has been profoundly disempowering precisely because it conveys a techno-determinism about the way things are. It presents itself as a kind of Marxism of the ruling classes, suggesting that the telos of history and the relentless logic of economic science lead inevitably not where Marx thought they were heading, but rather to just where we are now. Defying that invites crushing irrelevance at best.

Naturally, under stress, the capacity of the neoliberal imagination to torture language has become Orwellian. Take the notion of economic "recovery," which after all is so essential if the system is to right itself and reinforce the hard-wiring of acquiescence. Almost before the Great Recession had hit bottom, the media filled up with astrological-like sightings of recovery. Recovery beckoned; it was about to start; it had already started; the crisis was over. People in charge, especially President Obama and his inner circle of savants like Ben Bernanke and Timothy Geithner and Lawrence Summers, were quoted to that effect. Evidence accumulated albeit mainly in the financial sector, where big banks found themselves so flush with cash they were patriotically (and loudly) paying back their bailout money or were begging to do so. Profits in the FIRE sector were back, lavish bonuses were back.

But then there was the other kind of story, the one about the spreading misery of joblessness, foreclosures, homelessness, wage cuts, firings, amputations of social services, repossessions, bankruptcies, defaults— the dispossession of dreams. This story was told, not censored. What is therefore most astonishing and telling about our Age of Acquiescence is that amid the gloom of this dark tale the sun kept shining.

It might be seen as appalling, arrogant, callous, myopic, credulous, and maybe most of all morally embarrassing to talk with a straight face about recovery amid all this. What could that word possibly mean? Who exactly was recovering? What, after all, is the whole point of economic recovery if it doesn't first mean some improvement in general well-being? What is it that licenses this official complacency that advises a sort of tough-love patience, but then again looks at the bottom line of Goldman Sachs and takes heart?

That is, however, the nub of the neoliberal persuasion. It also is the nub of our current dilemma. Recovery may indeed happen; it is already happening, but perhaps not in the way we might assume. As Keynes among others observed, there may be some absolute bottom to any severe downturn. But that does not mean that once reached, recovery will return the economy to its previous high point or move past it.

Something quite different may happen. Economic life may reproduce itself at some considerably lower level for a long time. That may be emphatically the case here at home, where long before the Great Recession hit, the financial sector was already cannibalizing what most people think of as the real economy. There have been sightings of the textile industry returning from the global South because the shipping costs to customers are lower, the quality control higher, and the wages in our native Dixie and even in the rust belt are now closing in on where they are in China. Flexible, neoliberal capitalism after all, was always, from one standpoint, not much different than regular capitalism minus the opposition that had made the long nineteenth century so fraught.[2]

More of that same toxic "recovery" medicine is on order for the future. The social inequities and iniquities and the cultural brutalization this will entail have been in plain sight for a generation now. Dispossession and loss are tough enough to bear. How much sorrier is it when a culture is so coarsened that it looks at legions of casualties and without batting an eye dismisses them as "losers."

Our political universe may indeed be locked in the past. It looks backward because that's just where we're headed.

Looking Forward

Is this all inevitable? No one can know. Decline is no more predestined than Progress was once thought to be. Occupy Wall Street seemed to erupt out of nowhere. It turned lower Manhattan into a Grand Guignol of long dormant resistance to the Street's overlordship. And it sparked fraternal eruptions all around the world. Then it dwindled away. But most would acknowledge it did, as the saying goes, change the conversation.

Perhaps it did more than that. Not long afterward, Bill de Blasio was elected mayor of New York in a wholly unanticipated landslide of populist sentiment that seemed to repudiate an era of Wall Street/real estate domination which had cast the city in the role of "Capitol City" of a Hunger Games country. This was a rare political spectacle in our Age of Acquiescence. Pundits quickly began prophesying a "new populism" led by mainstream politicians like Senator Elizabeth Warren of Massachusetts. The Democratic Party seemed to be rediscovering disquiet about inequality as a vendible political commodity. Pressure to raise the minimum wage spread from municipalities to the White House. A socialist actually got elected to municipal office in Seattle, and another one nearly did in Minneapolis.

Maybe there is a lesson or two to be learned. On the one hand, techno-determinism reigns. One of its pathologies is emotional evisceration, a creeping incapacity to feel; the danger it presents is not the old science-fiction one about machines taking on human qualities and taking over, but rather the scarier one about humans becoming increasingly machinelike and proud of it. Numbing like this may sedate. And it is antipathetic to the instinct to act politically in the world. Plenty of skepticism about just what New York's new mayor could or even would try to do to undo the gross inequalities of power and wealth that had characterized the city for a generation emerged even before the ballots were counted. The "new populism" of the Democratic Party may be a momentary aberration. Skepticism of that sort could turn out to be a gloomily accurate forecast of what lies ahead.

On the other hand, however, this realism or resignation or fatalism or whatever one chooses to call it may suffer from its own timidity as well as a fateful forgetfulness. It becomes itself an accomplice of decline in an era of auto-cannibalism.

What is forgotten in a prematurely mature standpoint is that the capacity to envision something generically new, however improbable, has always supplied the intellectual, emotional, and political energy that made an advance in civilized life, no matter how truncated, possible. To be grown up in the Age of Acquiescence may be a sign of early-onset senescence.

Had someone painted a picture or taken a photograph of the collective psyche of America in 1930, it would have been a grim one: demoralized, fatalistic, full of cynicism and fear, inert. Painted again just four years later, that portrait would have captured the eruption as if out of nowhere of combative resistance and fellow feeling, a transfiguration conjured up not by the councils of government, but by the social energy and creativity of ordinary people that no one knew existed.

New populists may fail to live up to expectations and may soon be forgotten—or be a straw in the wind. The uprisings of the working poor at fast-food chains, at car washes, inside Fortress Walmart, and at dozens of other sites may die away—or they may break through the ossified remains of the old trade union apparatus and seed the growth of wholly new organizations of the invisibles. An economy that sometimes seems like it wants to reinvent debt slavery has aroused passions not seen for a century among college students, home owners, and supplicants of the credit card. Is debt likely to become the Achilles' heel of the new capitalist order of things? Will the experience of mass downward mobility, the disappearing of the middle class so much talked about, shatter those cherished dreams of "making it" that have for generations renewed the will to believe? Mother earth grows sickly and dangerous. The environmental movement can count few victories in its struggle to save the planet. Yet that movement has sustained itself for decades and continues to grow, the only mass movement to accomplish that feat in the Age of Acquiescence. Is there some tipping point—an analog to the one global warming is fast approaching—when the convergence of auto-cannibalism and the ravaging of the earth open up a new era of rebellion and transformation?

Might we reimagine a future, as our ancestors once did, different than the mere extrapolation of the here and now? The myopia bred by short-term financial rewards and insatiable cravings for novelty cramps the future. It is a perspective about progress already grown stale by the stupefying, essential sameness of what's on offer. Under the guise of individual freedom, the commodification of everything expels like so much waste matter coherent social relations, replacing them with anomic behavior, antisocial criminal behavior, and the nihilist liberation of Dostoyevsky's "everything is permitted." Is there some natural limit to this?[3]

Money talks. That is an axiom all agree with. Even those moved to question the inequalities of our times tend to frame their response in these terms. But all the great social upheavals of the long nineteenth century, including the passionate, moral outburst of the civil rights movement, always originated in a realm before money and looked for gratification in a realm beyond money. To be sure they were rooted in material need and not shy about saying what they needed to live in a civilized way. However, intermingled with those material wants and desires, affixed to them like emblems of the spirit, were ineffable yearnings to redefine what it meant to be human together.

Perhaps that is the enduring legacy the long nineteenth century bequeaths to our own.

Acknowledgments

This book has mutated several times. It began as an attempt to write a history of America's first Gilded Age, the one Mark Twain memorably named shortly after the Civil War ended. Then, as what many now refer to as the country's second Gilded Age gathered steam, I was struck not only by the clear similarities between these two epochs, separated by a century, but also by how different they were. So I decided to write a comparative history of our two gilded ages. As I began, I realized that what I found most mysterious was why the first Gilded Age elicited such broad and multifaceted resistance to economic, political, and social inequities, while our own modern Gilded Age hardly did. That's how I came to write *The Age of Acquiescence*.

In writing a book that's gone through so many transformations, I have naturally accumulated a great many intellectual debts. First of all, this book would be inconceivable without the prior research and writing and insights of numerous scholars and writers—historians, social scientists, social theorists, economists, political scientists, journalists, and others—who have provided the book's understructure. Many of their works appear in the notes, but those citations hardly do justice to what this book owes to their creative labors.

I am lucky to have had Geoff Shandler as my editor, and I want to thank Steve Wasserman (once my agent, now an editor at Yale University Press) for bringing us together. Geoff is a skilled practitioner of a craft I was once employed at myself (and still undertake now and then). His edits were invariably smart, attentive, and carefully thought out. I appreciate as well his conviction that it was worth publishing a book that is as much an argument as it is an account of how the American past has shaped the dilemmas of the present. Thanks too to Geoff's assistant, Allie Sommer, for answering an avalanche of questions always with good humor and speed and to Victoria Matsui and Peggy Freudenthal at Little, Brown. Elena Cordova provided crucial research help.

Before the manuscript made its way to Geoff Shandler's desk, it was read by a number of astute critics. I want to thank Josh Freeman, Rochelle Gurstein, Jackson Lears, and Paul Milkman for their detailed critical comments and for cheering me on. I tried my best to follow their suggestions for revision. Some of what they wanted me to do was beyond my ability, but the book is immeasurably better than it would have been without their help and friendship. Over the years it took to put this project together, conversations with Eli Sagan, Tom Engelhardt, Joel Kaye, and Edmund Leites kept me plugging away. I owe a special debt to Michael Aronoff, whom I got to know just when doing this book or any book seemed too difficult to manage.

Jill Fraser read the manuscript several times and made one valuable suggestion after another, large and small, to make it better. But that's the least of what she did. She has managed to live with me through a number of books when I wasn't great company. Somehow, she has maintained her inherent warmth and happiness through it all. And she has lent me enough of her spirit to see me through the rough times. Jill; our two now grown children, Max and Emma; and my brother, Jon, and his husband, Marco, are my personal safety net.

This book explores the extraordinary capacity of people, at certain times and under certain circumstances, to collectively stand up against the most intimidating forms of power and prejudice and to overcome internalized forms of social deprecation that can be so disabling. In my own lifetime I have been extremely fortunate to know and work with such people, to experience firsthand that miracle. Mohawk was a young black man living in Starkville, Mississippi, when I arrived there as an eighteen-year-old naïf from the suburban north in the summer of 1964.

We became comrades in the struggle to dismantle American apartheid. Without Mohawk, and without the dozens and dozens of Mohawks I got to know that summer and in the years that followed, much more than this book would have been lost to me. I salute them and write to honor Mohawk's memory.

Notes

Introduction

1. James Carville, *Time*, November 16, 1994.

Part I

1. J. A. Dacus, *Annals of the Great Strikes in the United States: A Reliable History and Graphic Description of the Causes and Thrilling Events of the Labor Strikes and Riots of 1877—Illustrated* (New York, 1877), 430.
2. Carl Smith, *Urban Disorder and the Shape of Belief: The Great Chicago Fire, the Haymarket Bomb, and the Model Town of Pullman* (Chicago: University of Chicago Press, 1995), 103, 107–8, 125, 139, 239–40.
3. Justice Harlan quoted in Steven Pearlstein, "Too Much," November 14, 2007, www.Cipa-apex.org/too much/weeklies 2007/November 19, 2007.html.
4. Henry George quoted in John L. Thomas, *Alternative America: Henry George, Edward Bellamy, Henry Demarest Lloyd and the Adversary Tradition* (Cambridge, MA: Belknap/Harvard University Press, 1983), 3, 14; George quoted by Smith, *Urban Disorder*, 213.
5. Adam Smith, The *Wealth of Nations, Book V, Chapter One, Part II on the Expense of Justice* (New York, 2000).

Chapter 1: Progress

1. Steve Fraser, *Every Man a Speculator: A History of Wall Street in American Life* (New York: HarperCollins, 2005), 43.
2. Walter A. McDougall, *Throes of Democracy: The American Civil War Era, 1829–1877* (New York: Harper, 2008), 578–83; Charles R. Morris, *The Tycoons: How Andrew Carnegie, John D. Rockefeller, Jay Gould, and J. P. Morgan Invented the American Super-economy* (New York: Henry Holt, 2005), 119–20; William H. Rideing, "At the Exhibit," *Appleton Journal*, 1876; Alan Trachtenberg, *The Incorporation of America: Culture and Society in the Gilded Age* (New York: Hill and Wang, 1982), 41, 47; David McCullough, *The Great Bridge* (New York: Simon and Schuster, 1972), 351–52.
3. T. J. Stiles, *The First Tycoon: The Epic Life of Cornelius Vanderbilt* (New York: Knopf, 2009), 403; Rebecca Edwards, *New Spirits: Americans in the Gilded Age, 1865–1905* (New York: Oxford University Press, 2006), 40; Richard Bensel, *The Political Economy of American Industrialization, 1877–1900* (New York: Cambridge University Press, 2000), 293–95; Jack Beatty, *Age of Betrayal: The Triumph of Money in America, 1865–1900* (New York: Knopf, 2007), 14, 20; Maury Klein, *The Genesis of Industrial*

America, 1870–1920 (New York: Cambridge University Press, 2007), 42, 62; David Nasaw, *Andrew Carnegie* (New York: Penguin Press, 2006), 99.

4. Nasaw, *Andrew Carnegie*, 99.

5. Bensel, *Political Economy of American Industrialization*, 222; Giovanni Arrighi, *The Long Twentieth Century: Money, Power, and the Origins of Our Times* (New York: Verso, 1994), 300.

6. Matthew Josephson, *The Politicos, 1865–1896* (1938; reprint, New York: Commons, 2008), 436; Klein, *Genesis of Industrial America*, 24, 40–42, 62, 76, 83, 85, 92; Morris, *The Tycoons*, 109, 113; Worth Robert Miller, "Farmers and Third-Party Politics," in *The Gilded Age: Essays on the Origins of Modern America*, ed. Charles W. Calhoun (Wilmington, DE: Scholarly Resources, 1996); Edwards, *New Spirits*, 96.

7. Klein, *Genesis of Industrial America*, 29.

8. Ibid., 53, 92.

9. Edwards, *New Spirits*, 96.

10. Klein, *Genesis of Industrial America*, 177; Nell Irvin Painter, *Standing at Armageddon: The United States, 1877–1919* (New York: Norton, 1987); Edward Kirkland, "The Economics of the Gilded Age: An Appraisal," in Calhoun, ed., *The Gilded Age*; Edward C. Kirkland, "Multiplication, Division, Materialism," in *The Gilded Age: America, 1865–1900*, ed. Richard A. Bartlett (Reading, MA: Addison-Wesley, 1969); Kevin Phillips, *The Politics of Rich and Poor: Wealth and the American Electorate in the Reagan Aftermath* (New York: Random House, 1990), 104–5; S. J. Kleinberg, *The Shadow of the Mills: Working-Class Families in Pittsburgh, 1877–1907* (Pittsburgh: University of Pittsburgh Press, 1989), 8.

11. Painter, *Standing at Armageddon*, introduction; Douglas Steeples and David O. Whitten, *Democracy in Desperation: The Depression of 1893* (Westport, CT: Greenwood, 1998); Joyce Appleby, *The Relentless Revolution: A History of Capitalism* (New York: Norton, 2010), 167; David Brooks, *On Paradise Drive: How We Live Now (and Always Have) in the Future Tense* (New York: Simon and Schuster, 2004), 258–59; Thomas Cochran and William Miller, *The Age of Enterprise: A Social History of Industrial America* (New York: Harper, 1961).

12. Alexis de Tocqueville quoted in Klein, *Genesis of Industrial America*, 34.

13. Martin Sklar quoted in Arrighi, *Long Twentieth Century*, 294–95.

Chapter 2: Progress, Poverty, and Primitive Accumulation

1. George quoted in Stephen Pimpare, *The New Victorians: Poverty, Politics, and Propaganda in Two Gilded Ages* (New York: The New Press, 2004), 20.

2. Carnegie quoted in Rebecca Edwards, *New Spirits: Americans in the Gilded Age, 1865–1905* (New York: Oxford University Press, 2006), 81; Centers for Disease Control, National Center for Health Statistics.

3. Edwards, *New Spirits*, 37.

4. John A. Strong, *The Montaukett Indians of Eastern Long Island* (Syracuse, NY: Syracuse University Press, 2001).

5. Ibid.; Susie J. Pak, *Gentlemen Bankers: The World of J. P. Morgan* (Cambridge, MA: Harvard University Press, 2013), 92.

6. Marx quoted in Michael Perelman, *The Invention of Capitalism: Classical Political Economy and the Secret History of Primitive Accumulation* (Durham, NC: Duke University Press, 2000), 13.

7. Jefferson quoted in ibid., 270.

8. Perry Anderson, *The Origins of Postmodernity* (London: Verso, 1998) and quoting Rosa Luxemburg, *The Accumulation of Capital*; Karl Marx, *Pre-Capitalist Economic Formations*, ed. Eric Hobsbawn (London: Lawrence & Wishart, 1964); David Harvey, *The Enigma of Capital and the Crisis of Capitalism* (New York: Oxford University Press, 2010).

9. Perelman, *Invention of Capitalism*, 93–95, 104; Jack Beatty, *Age of Betrayal: The Triumph of Money in America, 1865–1900* (New York: Knopf, 2007), 85, 89, 92, 105, 106; Richard Bensel, *The Political Economy of American Industrialization, 1877–1900* (New York: Cambridge University Press, 2000), 293, 295; Thomas Cochran and William Miller, *The Age of Enterprise: A Social History of Industrial America* (New York: Harper, 1961).

10. Douglas Steeples and David O. Whitten, *Democracy in Desperation: The Depression of 1893* (Westport, CT: Greenwood, 1998), 15–16; Worth Robert Miller, "Farmers and Third Party Politics" in *The Gilded Age: Essays on the Origins of Modern America,* ed. Charles W. Calhoun (Wilmington, DE: Scholarly Resources, 1996); Beatty, *Age of Betrayal*, 314.

11. Steven L. Piott, *The Anti-Monopoly Persuasion: Popular Resistance to the Rise of Big Business in the Midwest* (Westport, CT: Greenwood, 1985), 14–16; Jonathan Levy, "The Mortgage Worked the Hardest: The Fate of Landed Independence in Nineteenth-Century America," in *Capitalism Takes Command: The Social Transformation of Nineteenth-Century America*, eds. Michael Zakim and Gary Kornblith (Chicago: University of Chicago Press, 2012), 49, 60.

12. Lawrence Goodwyn, *Democratic Promise: The Populist Moment in America* (New York: Oxford University Press, 1976), 15, 113.

13. Rebecca M. McLennan, *The Crisis of Imprisonment: Protest, Politics, and the Making of the American Penal State, 1776–1941* (New York: Cambridge University Press, 2008).

14. Douglas Blackmon, *Slavery by Another Name: The Re-enslavement of Black Americans from the Civil War to World War II* (New York: Anchor, 2009), 71, 88–90, 98, 99, 108–9, 131, 174, 189; Alexander Lichtenstein, *Twice the Work of Free Labor: The Political Economy of Convict Labor in the New South* (New York: Verso, 1996).

15. Blackmon, *Slavery by Another Name*, 300; Beatty, *Age of Betrayal*, 79, 85, 295, 314; Edwards, *New Spirits*, 67; Eric Arnesen, "American Workers and the Labor Movement in the Late Nineteenth Century," in Calhoun, ed., *The Gilded Age*; Steeples and Whitten, *Democracy in Desperation*, 16, 22.

16. Alan Trachtenberg, *The Incorporation of America: Culture and Society in the Gilded Age* (New York: Hill and Wang, 1982); Calhoun, ed., *The Gilded Age*, introduction; David Montgomery, "Epilogue," in *The Pullman Strike and the Crisis of the 1890s*, eds. Richard Schneirov, Shelton Stromquist, and Nick Salvatore (Urbana: University of Illinois Press, 1999); James Green, *Death in the Haymarket: A Story of Chicago, the First Labor Movement, and the Bombing That Divided Gilded Age America* (New York: Pantheon, 2006), 59, 63.

17. Nell Irvin Painter, *Standing at Armageddon: The United States, 1877–1919* (New York: Norton, 1987); U.S. Senate, *Report of the Committee of the Senate Upon the Relations Between Labor and Capital*, 1185, vol. 1: xxxv; James Livingston, "The Social Analysis of Economic History and Theory: Conjectures of Late Nineteenth Century American Development," *American History Review* 92 (February 1987); David Nasaw,

Andrew Carnegie (New York: Penguin Press, 2006), 179; Kim Voss, *The Making of American Exceptionalism: The Knights of Labor and Class Formation in the Nineteenth Century City* (Ithaca, NY: Cornell University Press, 1993).

18. Steve Fraser, "The Misunderstood Robber Baron," *The Nation*, November 30, 2009; Beatty, *Age of Betrayal*, 17, 350; Edwards, *New Spirits*, 61; Charles W. Calhoun, "Political Economy in the Gilded Age: The Republican Party's Industrial Policy," *Journal of Policy History* 8 (1996); Painter, *Standing at Armageddon*, 39; Janette Thomas Greenwood, *The Gilded Age: A History in Documents* (New York: Oxford University Press, 2000), 59; Maury Klein, *The Genesis of Industrial America, 1870–1920* (New York: Cambridge University Press, 2007), 140.

19. Greenwood, *Gilded Age*, 62; Beatty, *Age of Betrayal*, 298–99; S. J. Kleinberg, *The Shadow of the Mills: Working-Class Families in Pittsburgh:* (Pittsburgh: University of Pittsburgh Press, 1989), 174–75; Painter, *Standing at Armageddon,* xix–xxiii; Klein, *Genesis of Industrial America*, 140.

20. Klein, *Genesis of Industrial America*, 140.

21. Beatty, *Age of Betrayal*, 269–70; Klein, *Genesis of Industrial America*, ch. 6; Piott, *Anti-Monopoly Persuasion*, 14, 19, 58–59, 106, 112, 123; Samuel Rezneck, "Patterns of Thought and Action in an American Depression, 1882–86," *American Historical Review* 61 (January 1956); Livingston, "The Social Analysis."

22. Beatty, *Age of Betrayal*, 257; Cochran and Miller, *Age of Enterprise*, ch. 7.

23. Charles R. Morris, *The Tycoons: How Andrew Carnegie, John D. Rockefeller, Jay Gould, and J. P. Morgan Invented the American Supereconomy* (New York: Henry Holt, 2005), 236; Steeples and Whitten, *Democracy in Desperation*, 42, 50, 53; Charles Hoffman, "The Depression of the 1890s," *Journal of Economic History*, 16 (June 1956).

24. David Cannadine, *Mellon: An American Life* (New York: Knopf, 2006), ch. 2.

25. Drew R. McCoy, *The Elusive Republic: Political Economy in Jeffersonian America* (Chapel Hill: University of North Carolina Press, 1980), 116–17.

26. Alexander Keyssar, *Out of Work: The First Century of Unemployment in Massachusetts* (New York: Cambridge University Press, 1986); Pimpare, *New Victorians*, 172; Matthew Josephson, *The Politicos, 1865–1896* (1938; reprint, New York: Commons, 2008), 235–36; Paul Avrich, *The Haymarket Tragedy* (Princeton, NJ: Princeton University Press, 1984), 16–18, 79; Robert V. Bruce, *1877: Year of Violence* (Indianapolis: Bobbs-Merrill, 1959), 22; Rezneck, "Patterns of Thought and Action."

27. Painter, *Standing at Armageddon*, 116–18, 120–21; Green, *Death in the Haymarket*, 112–13; Samuel Rezneck, "Unemployment, Unrest, and Relief in the U.S. During the Depression of 1893–97," *Journal of Political Economy* 61 (August 1953); J. A. Dacus, *Annals of the Great Strikes in the United States: A Reliable History and Graphic Description of the Causes and Thrilling Events of the Labor Strikes and Riots of 1877— Illustrated* (New York, 1877).

28. Klein, *Genesis of Industrial America,* 143, 177; Livingston, "The Social Analysis"; Beatty, *Age of Betrayal*, 348; Edward C. Kirkland, "Multiplication, Division, Materialism," in *The Gilded Age: America, 1865–1900,* ed. Richard A. Bartlett (Reading, MA: Addison-Wesley, 1969).

29. Painter, *Standing at Armageddon*, xix–xx; Edwards, *New Spirits*, 100; Steeples and Whitten, *Democracy in Desperation*, 17, 20.

30. Richard Harvey Brown, *Culture, Capitalism, and Democracy in the New America* (New Haven: Yale University Press, 2005), citing *Marx and Engels on Britain* (1892; reprint, Moscow: Foreign Language Publishing House, 1953), 48–49.

Chapter 3: Premonitions

 1. Howells quoted in Douglas Steeples and David O. Whitten, *Democracy in Desperation: The Depression of 1893* (Westport, CT: Greenwood, 1998), 133.
 2. Stephen Innes, "Fulfilling John Smith's Vision: Work and Labor in Early America," in *Work and Labor in Early America*, ed. Stephen Innes (Chapel Hill: University of North Carolina Press, 1988).
 3. Gary B. Nash, *The Urban Crucible: The Northern Seaports and the Origins of the American Revolution* (Cambridge, MA: Harvard University Press, 1986), 6–7, 28.
 4. Marcus Rediker, *Between the Devil and the Deep Blue Sea: Merchant Seamen, Pirates, and the Anglo-American Maritime World, 1700–1750* (New York: Cambridge University Press, 1987).
 5. Drew R. McCoy, *The Elusive Republic: Political Economy in Jeffersonian America* (Chapel Hill: University of North Carolina Press, 1980), 51, 55, 63.
 6. Adams quoted in Richard Parker, *The Myth of the Middle Class* (New York: Liveright, 1972), 59; *Federalist Paper No. 10* quoted in Martin J. Burke, *The Conundrum of Class: Public Discourse on the Social Order in America* (Chicago: University of Chicago Press, 1995).
 7. Burke, *Conundrum of Class*, 42; Madison quoted in McCoy, *Elusive Republic*, 129; Hamilton quoted in Parker, *Myth of the Middle Class,* 61.
 8. Bruce Laurie, *Artisans into Workers: Labor in Nineteenth-Century America* (New York: Hill and Wang, 1989).
 9. Ibid., 35, 64, 71.
10. Eric Foner, "Abolition and the Labor Movement in Ante-Bellum America," in Eric Foner, *Politics and Ideology in the Age of the Civil War* (New York: Oxford University Press, 1980); Laurie, *Artisans into Workers*, 63; Peter George Buckley, "To the Opera House: Culture and Society in New York City, 1820–1860" (PhD diss., SUNY, Stony Brook, 1984); Alexander Keyssar, *Out of Work: The First Century of Unemployment in Massachusetts* (New York: Cambridge University Press, 1986).
11. Lawrence Goodwyn, *Democratic Promise: The Populist Moment in America* (New York: Oxford University Press, 1976), 16.
12. Stuart M. Blumin, *The Emergence of the Middle Class: Social Experience in the American City, 1760–1900* (New York: Cambridge University Press, 1989), 117–19, 120, 122–27; George Foster, *New York by Gas-light and Other Urban Sketches* (Berkeley: University of California Press, 1990), 234.
13. Blumin, *Emergence of the Middle Class*, 134, 145; Buckley, "To the Opera House."
14. Laurie, *Artisans into Workers*, 31; Melville quoted in Nicholas K. Bromell, *By the Sweat of the Brow: Literature and Labor in Antebellum America* (Chicago: University of Chicago Press, 1993), 67; Melville quoted in Robert Shulman, *Social Criticism and Nineteenth-Century American Fictions* (Columbia: University of Missouri Press, 1987), 204; Herman Melville, "The Paradise of Bachelors the Tartarus of Maids," in *The Great Short Works of Herman Melville*, ed. Warner Berthoff, (New York: Harper and Row, 1969).
15. Theophilus Fisk, "Capital Against Labor," address delivered at Julian Hall before the mechanics of Boston, May 5, 1835, reprinted in *New York Evening Post*, May 6, 1835.

16. Orestes Augustus Brownson, "The Laboring Classes," *The Boston Quarterly Review*, 1840; Brownson quoted in Oscar and Lilian Handlin, *Liberty in America*, vol. 2, *Liberty in Expansion, 1760–1850* (New York: Harper and Row, 1989), 68.

17. John C. Calhoun, speech in the Senate on the "Report of the Secretary of the Treasury," July 21, 1841, in *The Works of John C. Calhoun*, vols. 5–6, *Reports and Public Letters*, ed. Richard K. Crallé (New York: Appleton, 1854–1857); "Speculation and Trade," *Southern Quarterly Review*, February 1857; George Fitzhugh, "Wealth of the North and the South," *De Bow's Review*, November 1857; "The Times Are Out of Joint," *De Bow's Review*, December 1857; James L. Huston, *The Panic of 1857 and the Coming of the Civil War* (Baton Rouge: Louisiana State University Press, 1987), 16.

18. Jeffrey Sklansky, "William Leggett and the Melodrama of the Market," in *Capitalism Takes Command: The Social Transformation of Nineteenth-Century America*, eds. Michael Zakim and Gary Kornblith (Chicago: University of Chicago Press, 2012); Emerson quoted in Robert V. Bruce, *1877: Year of Violence* (Indianapolis: Bobbs-Merrill, 1959), 18.

19. Laurie, *Artisans into Workers*, 21, 28.

20. Ibid., 57; Abraham Lincoln, "Address to the Wisconsin State Agricultural Society," Milwaukee, September 9, 1859; Lincoln's First Annual Message to Congress, December 3, 1861; Christopher Lasch, *The Revolt of the Elites: And the Betrayal of Democracy* (New York: Norton, 1995), 71–72; Walt Whitman quoted in Ray Ginger, *Altgeld's America: The Lincoln Ideal Versus Changing Realities* (Chicago: Quadrangle, 1965), 339.

21. Laurie, *Artisans into Workers*, 58–59.

Chapter 4: The Second Civil War: In the Countryside

1. Michael Zakim and Gary Kornblith, "Introduction: An American Revolutionary Tradition," in *Capitalism Takes Command: The Social Transformation of Nineteenth-Century America*, eds. Michael Zakim and Gary Kornblith (Chicago: University of Chicago Press, 2012), 8; Jonathan Levy, "The Mortgage Worked the Hardest: The Fate of Landed Independence in Nineteenth-Century America," in ibid., 41, 45.

2. Richard Bensel, *The Political Economy of American Industrialization, 1877–1900* (New York: Cambridge University Press, 2000), 99, 222, 228.

3. Douglas Steeples and David O. Whitten, *Democracy in Desperation: The Depression of 1893* (Westport, CT: Greenwood, 1998), 148; Jack Beatty, *Age of Betrayal: The Triumph of Money in America, 1865–1900* (New York: Knopf, 2007), 92, 96, 102–3.

4. Rebecca Edwards, *New Spirits: Americans in the Gilded Age, 1865–1905* (New York: Oxford University Press, 2006), 67; Nell Irvin Painter, *Standing at Armageddon: The United States, 1877–1919* (New York: Norton, 1987), xxi–xxii; Charles R. Morris, *The Tycoons: How Andrew Carnegie, John D. Rockefeller, Jay Gould, and J. P. Morgan Invented the American Supereconomy* (New York: Henry Holt, 2005), 109–10.

5. Levy, "Mortgage Worked the Hardest," 57; Ambrose Bierce, *The Devil's Dictionary* (New York: Oxford University Press, 1999), 34.

6. Charles McArthur Destler, *American Radicalism, 1865–1901: Essays and Documents* (New London, CT: Connecticut College, 1946), 66; Lawrence Goodwyn, *Democratic Promise: The Populist Moment in America* (New York: Oxford University Press, 1976), xvii, 115–17, 361; Robert C. McMath Jr., *American Populism: A Social History, 1877–1898* (New York: Hill and Wang, 1993), 46.

7. Giovanni Arrighi, *The Long Twentieth Century: Money, Power, and the Origins of Our Times* (New York: Verso, 1994).

8. Destler, *American Radicalism;* Goodwyn, *Democratic Promise,* 32; McMath, *American Populism,* 46.

9. Bruce Palmer, *"Man over Money": The Southern Populist Critique of American Capitalism* (Chapel Hill: University of North Carolina Press, 1980), 134.

10. Ibid., 14, 16; James H. Davis quoted in Norman Pollack, ed., *The Populist Mind* (Indianopolis: Bobbs-Merrill, 1967), 220.

11. Honorable William P. Fishback, "Railway Financeering as a Fine Art," *Arena,* June 1897; Palmer, *"Man over Money,"* 14; Michael Kazin, *The Populist Persuasion: An American History* (New York: Basic Books, 1995), 31–32, 35, 44; George McKenna, ed., *American Populism* (New York: Putnam, 1974), 96, 110–11.

12. Destler, *American Radicalism,* 17, 19, 27; Goodwyn, *Democratic Promise,* 230.

13. Stump orator quoted in Pollack, *Populist Mind,* 222; Alabama congressman quoted in ibid., 229; Governor Nugent quoted in ibid., 286–87; Lloyd quoted in Destler, *American Radicalism,* 219.

14. James B. Weaver, "A Call to Action," in Pollack, *Populist Mind,* 131; Thomas E. Watson, *The People's Party Campaign Book* (1892; reprint, New York: Arno, 1975), 19–23.

15. Sean Dennis Cashman, *America in the Gilded Age: From the Death of Lincoln to the Rise of Theodore Roosevelt,* 2d ed. (New York: New York University Press, 1988), 202; Michael Denning, *Mechanic Accents: Dime Novels and Working-Class Culture in America* (New York: Verso, 1987), 153.

16. William A. Peffer, "The Farmers Side: His Troubles and Their Remedy," in Pollack, *Populist Mind,* 98–105.

17. George quoted in John L. Thomas, *Alternative America: Henry George, Edward Bellamy, Henry Demarest Lloyd and the Adversary Tradition* (Cambridge, MA: Belknap /Harvard University Press, 1983), 128–29.

18. *New York World,* January 1, 1888; Sioux Falls *Daily Argus* quoted in Sigmund Diamond, *The Reputation of the American Businessman* (Cambridge, MA: Harvard University Press, 1955), 89; Watson, *People's Campaign Book,* 219; Thomas Watson, "Wall Street Conspiracies Against the Nation," in Pollack, *Populist Mind,* 32–36; Peffer, "The Farmers Side"; "In the Mirror of the Present," *The Arena,* October 1905; John Clark Ridpath, "The True Inwardness of Wall Street," *The Arena* 19 (1898).

19. Pollack, *Populist Mind,* 10–11; Watson, *People's Campaign Book,* 222; "In the Mirror of the Present"; Thomas, *Alternative America,* 141, 309–12; Kazin, *Populist Persuasion,* 31–32.

20. Frederick Jackson Turner, "The Significance of the Frontier in American History," address to the American Historical Association, July 12, 1893; Christopher Lasch, *The Revolt of the Elites: And the Betrayal of Democracy* (New York: Norton, 1995), 72.

Chapter 5: The Second Civil War: On the Industrial Frontier

1. President Wilson quoted in John Milton Cooper, *The Warrior and the Priest: Woodrow Wilson and Theodore Roosevelt* (Cambridge, MA: Belknap/Harvard University Press, 1983), 264.

2. Herbert G. Gutman, "The Tompkins Square Riot in New York City on January 13, 1874: A Re-examination of Its Causes and Its Aftermath," *Labor History,* Winter 1965.

3. Ibid.

4. Ibid. Stephen Pimpare, *The New Victorians: Poverty, Policy, and Propaganda in Two Gilded Ages* (New York: The New Press, 2004), 109.

5. Carl Smith, *Urban Disorder and the Shape of Belief: The Great Chicago Fire, the Haymarket Bomb, and the Model Town of Pullman* (Chicago: University of Chicago Press, 1995), 148–53.

6. Richard Boyer and Herbert Morais, *Labor's Untold Story* (New York: United Electrical, Radio and Machine Workers of America, 1972), 45, 52; William Cahn, *A Pictoral History of American Labor* (New York: Crown, 1972), 126; Michael Denning, *Mechanic Accents: Dime Novels and Working-Class Culture in America* (New York: Verso, 1987), 54, 101–2, 120; Eric Foner, *Reconstruction: America's Unfinished Revolution, 1863–1877* (New York: Harper and Row, 1988), 483–84, 490.

7. Martin J. Burke, *The Conundrum of Class: Public Discourse on the Social Order in America* (Chicago: University of Chicago Press, 1995), 141, 144–45.

8. Wendell Phillips quoted in David T. Burbank, *Reign of the Rabble: The St. Louis General Strike of 1877* (New York: A. M. Kelley, 1966), 6; Gutman, "Tompkins Square Riot"; Charles Loring Brace, *The Dangerous Classes of New York and Twenty Years' Work Among Them*, 3d ed. (1880; reprint, Montclair, NJ: P. Smith, 1967), ii, 27, 29, 34–35.

9. Robert V. Bruce, *1877: Year of Violence* (Indianapolis: Bobbs–Merrill, 1959), 164, 175–76, 225–26, 313; J. A. Dacus, *Annals of the Great Strikes in the United States: A Reliable History and Graphic Description of the Causes and Thrilling Events of the Labor Strikes and Riots of 1877—Illustrated* (New York, 1877), 23, 70, 74, 75, 89, 95; Paul Boyer, *Urban Masses and Moral Order in America, 1820–1920* (Cambridge, MA: Harvard University Press, 1978), 126, 127, 128.

10. Burbank, *Reign of the Rabble*, 26; Bruce, *1877*, 89; Charles R. Morris, *The Tycoons: How Andrew Carnegie, John D. Rockefeller, Jay Gould, and J. P. Morgan Invented the American Supereconomy* (New York: Henry Holt, 2005), 97.

11. Bruce, *1877*, 22, 135–36.

12. Burbank, *Reign of the Rabble*, 13–14, 41, 43, 45–46, 55, 58; Boyer, *Urban Masses*, 176–77; Dacus, *Annals*, 385.

13. Burbank, *Reign of the Rabble*, 10.

14. Ibid., 169, 187.

15. Ray Ginger, *Altgeld's America: The Lincoln Ideal Versus Changing Realities* (Chicago: Quadrangle, 1965), 235; Smith, *Urban Disorder*, 154, 157, 161, 162, 163; James Green, *Death in the Haymarket: A Story of Chicago, the First Labor Movement, and the Bombing That Divided Gilded Age America* (New York: Pantheon, 2006), 252.

16. Smith, *Urban Disorder*, 143–44; "Address to the Court," in *Haymarket Scrapbook*, eds. David Roediger and Franklin Rosemont (Chicago: CH Kerr Publishing Company, 1986), 46–47.

17. Green, *Death in the Haymarket;* Dacus, *Annals*, 30, 33, 34, 36, 40, 47–48, 54–55, 57.

18. Herbert Gutman, "The Workers Search for Power: Labor in the Gilded Age," in *The Gilded Age: A Reappraisal*, ed. H. Wayne Morgan (Syracuse: Syracuse University Press, 1965); Dacus, *Annals*, 57, 89, 96, 98, 101, 121, 125, 126, 137, 210, 235, 296.

19. Dacus, *Annals*, 125.

20. Eric Arnesen, "American Workers and the Labor Movement in the Late Nineteenth Century," in *The Gilded Age: Perspectives on the Origins of Modern America*, 2d ed., ed.

Charles W. Calhoun (Lanham, MD: Rowman and Littlefield, 2007); Robert E. Weir, "Dress Rehearsal for Pullman: The Knights of Labor and the 1890 New York Central Strike," in *The Pullman Strike and the Crisis of the 1890s*, eds. Richard Schneirov, Shelton Stromquist, and Nick Salvatore (Urbana: University of Illinois Press, 1999); Kim Voss, *The Making of American Exceptionalism: The Knights of Labor and Class Formation in the Nineteenth Century* (Ithaca, NY: Cornell University Press, 1993).

21. Song quoted in Green, *Death in the Haymarket*, 153.

22. Jesse Jones quoted by Eugene Debs in Dan McKanan, *Prophetic Encounters: Religion and the American Radical Tradition* (Boston: Beacon, 2011); Edward Bellamy, *Looking Backward 2000–1887* (New York, 1888), 49.

23. Christopher Clark, "The Agrarian Context of American Capitalist Development," in *Capitalism Takes Command: The Social Transformation of Nineteenth-Century America*, eds. Michael Zakim and Gary Kornblith (Chicago: University of Chicago Press, 2012), 35; Ginger, *Altgeld's America*, 284, 288, 341; John L. Thomas, *Alternative America: Henry George, Edward Bellamy, Henry Demarest Lloyd and the Adversary Tradition* (Cambridge, MA: Belknap/Harvard University Press, 1983), 118, 127, 209, 214.

24. Nick Salvatore, *Eugene V. Debs: Citizen and Socialist* (Urbana: University of Illinois Press, 1982), 239–40.

25. David Scobey, "Boycotting the Politics Factory: Labor Radicalism and the New York City Mayoral Election of 1886," *Radical History Review*, September 1984.

26. Nell Irvin Painter, *Standing at Armageddon: The United States, 1877–1919* (New York: Norton, 1987), 33; Scobey, "Boycotting the Politics Factory"; Thomas, *Alternative America*, 107, 112, 214, 222, 225, 228, 232.

27. Richard Harvey Brown, *Culture, Capitalism, and Democracy in the New America* (New Haven: Yale University Press, 2005), 51–52.

28. Hamlin Garland, "Homestead and Its Perilous Trades," *McClure's Magazine* 3 (June 1894); David P. Demarest Jr., ed., *"The River Ran Red": Homestead 1892* (Pittsburgh: University of Pittsburgh Press, 1992), citing all of the following: *New York Herald*, July 7 and July 11, 1892; *New York World*, July 7 and July 11, 1892; *St. Louis Post-Dispatch*, July 8, 1892; *Frank Leslie's Illustrated Weekly*, July 14, 1892; *The New York Times*, July 12, 1892.

29. Demarest, *"The River Ran Red,"* citing *The New York Times*, July 12, 1892, and *St. Louis Post-Dispatch*, July 17, 1892; Morris, *The Tycoons*, 202–3, 205, 206.

30. Melvyn Dubofsky, "The Federal Judiciary, Free Labor and Equal Rights," in Schneirov, Stromquist, and Salvatore, eds., *The Pullman Strike;* Shelton Stromquist, "The Crisis of 1894 and the Legacies of Producerism," in ibid.; Richard Schneirov, "Labor and the New Liberalism in the Wake of the Pullman Strike," in ibid.; Smith, *Urban Disorder*, 235, 237–38, 241–44.

31. Ginger, *Altgeld's America*, 161, 164–66, 186, 341; Richard Schneirov, Shelton Stromquist, and Nick Salvatore, "Introduction" in Schneirov, Stromquist, and Salvatore, eds., *The Pullman Strike*; Stromquist, "The Crisis of 1894"; Richard T. Ely, "Pullman: A Social Study," *Harper's Monthly*, February 1885.

32. Harold R. Kerbo and Richard A. Schaffer, "Lower Class Insurgency and the Political Process: The Response of the Unemployed," *Social Problems* 39 (May 1992); Alexander Keyssar, *Out of Work: The First Century of Unemployment in Massachusetts* (New York: Cambridge University Press, 1986); Douglas Steeples and David O. Whitten,

Democracy in Desperation: The Depression of 1893 (Westport, CT: Greenwood, 1998), 88–89.

33. Robert Weir, "Dress Rehearsal for Pullman: The Knights of Labor and the 1890 New York Central Strike" in Schneirov, Stromquist, and Salvatore, eds., *The Pullman Strike*; David Montgomery, "Epilogue," in ibid.; Schneirov, "Labor and the New Liberalism"; Colston E. Warner, *The Pullman Boycott of 1894: The Problem of Federal Intervention* (Boston: D. C. Heath, 1955).

34. James Weinstein, *The Corporate Ideal in the Liberal State, 1900–1918* (Boston: Beacon, 1968); Robert A. Rosenstone, *Romantic Revolutionary: A Biography of John Reed* (New York: Knopf, 1975), 172–73.

35. James Gray Pope, "Labor's Constitution of Freedom," *Yale Law Journal* 106 (1997); Debs quoted in J. Anthony Lukas, *The Big Trouble* (New York: Simon and Schuster, 1997), 361, 450.

36. Wilson quoted in Richard Hofstadter, "Woodrow Wilson: The Conservative Liberal," in Richard Hofstadter, *The American Political Tradition and the Men Who Made It* (New York: Knopf, 1948).

37. Rick Beard and Leslie Cohen Berlowitz, eds., *Greenwich Village: Culture and Counterculture* (New Brunswick, NJ: Rutgers University Press, 1993).

Chapter 6: Myth and History

1. James Green, *Death in the Haymarket: A Story of Chicago, the First Labor Movement, and the Bombing That Divided Gilded Age America* (New York: Pantheon, 2006), 309.

2. Werner Sombart, *Why Is There No Socialism in the United States* (London: Macmillan, 1976); Richard Schneirov, "Labor and the New Liberalism in the Wake of the Pullman Strike," in *The Pullman Strike and the Crisis of the 1890s: Essays on Labor and Politics*, eds. Richard Schneirov, Shelton Stromquist, and Nick Salvatore (Urbana: University of Illinois Press, 1999).

3. Carl Smith, *Urban Disorder and the Shape of Belief: The Great Chicago Fire, the Haymarket Bomb, and the Model Town of Pullman* (Chicago: University of Chicago Press, 1995), 213–14.

4. Marx quoted in Samuel Rezneck, "Patterns of Thought and Action in an American Depression, 1882–86," *American Historical Review* 61 (January 1956).

5. Rezneck, "Patterns of Thought and Action."

6. Josiah Strong, *Our Country* (1891; reprint, Cambridge, MA: Belknap/Harvard University Press, 1963), 87, 88, 104, 105.

7. Paul Boyer, *Urban Masses and Moral Order in America, 1820–1920* (Cambridge, MA: Harvard University Press, 1978), 131.

8. Smith, *Urban Disorder*, 237; Laurence Gronlund, *The Cooperative Commonwealth* (1884; reprint, Cambridge, MA: Belknap/Harvard University Press, 1965), 45, 98.

9. Edward Bellamy, *Looking Backward, 2000–1887* (New York: New American Library, 1960); Ignatius Donnelly, *Caesar's Column: A Story of the Twentieth Century* (1890; reprint, Cambridge, MA: Belknap/Harvard University Press, 1960).

10. Douglas Steeples and David O. Whitten, *Democracy in Desperation: The Depression of 1893* (Westport, CT: Greenwood, 1998), 137–38; Alexander Saxton, "Caesar's Column: The Dialogue of Utopia and Catastrophe," *American Quarterly* 19 (Summer 1967); Robert S. Fogarty, "American Communes, 1865–1914," *American Studies* 27

(August 1975); William Dean Howells, *A Traveler from Altruria* (1894; reprint, New York: Sagamore, 1957), 147; Rezneck, "Patterns of Thought and Action."

11. Lloyd quoted in Smith, *Urban Disorder*, 216; Henry Demarest Lloyd, *Wealth Against Commonwealth* (1894; reprint, Englewood Cliffs, NJ: Prentice-Hall, 1963); Richard Hofstadter and Beatrice Hofstadter, "Wealth Against Commonwealth," in Richard Hofstadter and Beatrice Hofstadter, eds., *Great Issues in American History* (New York: Vintage, 1982), 3: 92–99.

12. Charles R. Morris, *The Tycoons: How Andrew Carnegie, John D. Rockefeller, Jay Gould, and J. P. Morgan Invented the American Supereconomy* (New York: Henry Holt, 2005), 216.

13. Stephen Pimpare, *The New Victorians: Poverty, Policy, and Propaganda in Two Gilded Ages* (New York: The New Press, 2004), 22, 24, 26, 28, 33, 49.

14. Boyer, *Urban Masses*, 172; Rezneck, "Patterns of Thought and Action."

15. Walter R. Rauschenbusch, *Christianity and the Social Crisis* (New York: Macmillan, 1910), 369, 372.

16. Donald E. Winter, *The Soul of the Wobblies: The I.W.W., Religion, and American Culture in the Progressive Era, 1905–1917* (Westport, CT: Greenwood, 1985); Kevin Christiano, "Religion and Radical Labor Unions," *Journal for the Study of Religion*, 1988; Melvyn Dubofsky, *"Big Bill" Haywood* (New York: St. Martin's, 1987), 34, 66–67.

17. Dorothy Day, *The Long Loneliness* (New York: Harper, 1952), 96; Jarod Roll, *Spirit of Rebellion: Labor and Religion in the New Cotton South* (Urbana: University of Illinois Press, 2010).

18. Smith, *Urban Disorder*, 225–27, 230; William Carwardine, *The Pullman Strike* (Chicago, 1894); Stanley Buder, *Pullman: An Experiment in Industrial Order and Community Planning, 1880–1930* (New York: Oxford University Press, 1967).

19. Smith, *Urban Disorder*, 184, 200.

20. Richard Newman, "From Love's Canal to Love Canal," in *Beyond the Ruins: The Meaning of Deindustrialization*, eds. Jefferson Cowie and Joseph Heathcott (Ithaca, NY: ILR Press, 2003).

21. Kathleen D. McCarthy, *Noblesse Oblige: Charity and Cultural Philanthropy in Chicago, 1849–1929* (Chicago: University of Chicago Press, 1982), 95, 103, 117–18; Smith, *Urban Disorder*, 61, 203–4, 206, 222.

22. Hanna quoted in Andrew Kroll, "The Dark History of Money," *Mother Jones*, July/August 2012; Morgan quoted in Eric Homberger, *Mrs. Astor's New York: Money and Social Power in a Gilded Age* (New Haven: Yale University Press, 2002).

23. Robert Stewart, "Clubs and Club Life in New York," *Munsey's Magazine*, October 1899; Paul R. Cleveland, "The Millionaires of New York," *The Cosmopolitan*, September–October 1888; Christopher Lasch, *The World of Nations: Reflections on American History, Politics, and Culture* (New York: Knopf, 1973), ch. 7; E. L. Godkin, "The Expenditures of Rich Men," *Scribner's*, October 1896; Justin Kaplan, *When the Astors Owned New York: Blue Bloods and Grand Hotels in a Gilded Age* (New York: Plume, 2007), 6, 29, 34–35, 51–53, 59, 71; Anonymous, "Is America Developing an Aristocracy?" *Everybody's Magazine*, June 1904; "American Aristocracy in Wall Street," *The Epoch*, November 1887.

24. Herman Melville to Nathaniel Parker Willis, 1849, cited in Jay Leyda, *The Melville Log: A Documentary Life of Herman Melville, 1819–1891* (New York: Harcourt Brace, 1951), 1: 347.

25. Homberger, *Mrs. Astor's New York*, 224; Kaplan, *When the Astors Owned New York*, 6, 29, 31.

26. Homberger, *Mrs. Astor's New York*, 212.

27. Dixon Wecter, *The Saga of Society: A Record of Social Aspiration, 1607–1937* (New York: Scribner's, 1937), 1, 2.

28. Ibid., 2–3; Albert Jay Nock, *Memoirs of a Superfluous Man* (New York: Harper and Brothers, 1943), 112, 120; William Graham Sumner, *What Social Classes Owe to Each Other* (1883; reprint, New York: Arno, 1972), 31; Richard Sennett, *Authority* (New York: Knopf, 1980), 46.

29. Kaplan, *When the Astors Owned New York*, 41; Thorstein Veblen, *The Theory of the Leisure Class* (1899; reprint, New York: New American Library, 1953); Wecter, *Saga of Society*, 481.

30. Wecter, *Saga of Society*, 3–4, 148, 155.

31. David Montgomery, "Strikes in Nineteenth Century America," *Social Science History* 4 (1980); Phillip English McKey, "Law and Order, 1877: Philadelphia's Response to the Railroad Riots," *Pennsylvania Magazine of History and Biography* 96 (April 1972); Smith, *Urban Disorder*, 221; Baer quoted in James O. Castagnera, "Workers Don't Suffer," *The Progressive Populist*, 2003.

32. Adams quoted in Lewis H. Lapham, *Money and Class in America: Notes and Observations on Our Civil Religion* (New York: Weidenfeld and Nicolson, 1988), 154.

Chapter 7: The End of Socialism

1. Hillman quoted in Steve Fraser, *Labor Will Rule: Sidney Hillman and the Rise of American Labor* (New York: Free Press, 1991).

2. Robert K. Murray, *Red Scare: A Study in National Hysteria,1919–1920* (Minneapolis: University of Minnesota Press, 1955); Cameron McWhirter, *Red Summer: The Summer of 1919 and the Awakening of Black America* (New York: Henry Holt, 2011); Richard Harvey Brown, *Culture, Capitalism, and Democracy in the New America* (New Haven: Yale University Press, 2005), 44–45; Margaret McMillan, *Paris 1919: Six Months That Changed the World* (New York: Random House, 2002); David Brody, *Steelworkers in America: The Non-Union Era* (Cambridge, MA: Harvard University Press, 1960).

3. Candace Falk, ed., *Emma Goldman: A Documentary History of the American Years* (Urbana: University of Illinois Press, 2008); Emma Goldman, *Living My Life* (1931; reprint, New York: Arno, 1970), 2: 716–17.

4. Murray, *Red Scare*; Melvyn Dubofsky, *"Big Bill" Haywood* (New York: St. Martin's, 1987); Mother Jones, *Autobiography of Mother Jones* (1925; reprint, New York: Arno, 1969), ch. 24; *The New York Times*, October 24, 1919; *Chicago Tribune*, October 24, 1919.

5. Murray, *Red Scare*; Beverly Gage, *The Day Wall Street Exploded: A Story of America in the First Age of Terror* (New York: Oxford University Press, 2010); General Wood quoted in *The American Schoolmaster*, Michigan State Normal College, January 1920; Palmer quoted in "The Post-war Red Scare," Digital History, 2013; Billy Sunday quoted in William E. Leuchtenburg, *The Perils of Prosperity, 1914–32* (Chicago: University of Chicago Press, 1958), 66.

6. McWhirter, *Red Summer*; William M. Tuttle, *Race Riot: Chicago in the Red Summer of 1919* (New York: Atheneum, 1970).

7. Fraser, *Labor Will Rule*, 94, 96, 198, 239.

8. Mellon quoted in Herbert Hoover, *Memoirs of Herbert Hoover*, vol. 3, *The Great Depression, 1929–1941* (1952; reprint, New York: Garland, 1979).

9. Susie J. Pak, *Gentlemen Bankers: The World of J. P. Morgan* (Cambridge, MA: Harvard University Press, 2013), 213.

10. Henry Kraus, *The Many and the Few: A Chronicle of the Dynamic Auto Workers*, 2d ed. (Urbana: University of Illinois Press, 1985), 288–90, 293.

11. Judith Stein, *Pivotal Decade: How the United States Traded Factories for Finance in the Seventies* (New Haven: Yale University Press, 2010), 1–2.

12. Nelson Lichtenstein, *The Most Dangerous Man in Detroit: Walter Reuther and the Fate of American Labor* (New York: Basic Books, 1995); Robert M. Collins, *More: The Politics of Economic Growth in Postwar America* (New York: Oxford University Press, 2000), 23, 41, 53; Lauren Berlant, *Cruel Optimism* (Durham, NC: Duke University Press, 2011), 193–94.

13. Collins, *More*; Berlant, *Cruel Optimism*.

14. Alan Brinkley, *The End of Reform: New Deal Liberalism in Recession and War* (New York: Knopf, 1995); Robert Griffith, "Dwight D. Eisenhower and the Corporate Commonwealth," *American Historical Review* 87 (February 1982).

15. Mirra Komarovsky, *Blue-Collar Marriage* (New York: Vintage, 1967); John C. Leggett, *Class, Race, and Labor: Working-Class Consciousness in Detroit* (New York: Oxford University Press, 1968); E. E. LeMasters, *Blue-Collar Aristocrats: Life-Styles at a Working-Class Tavern* (Madison: University of Wisconsin Press, 1975); Christopher Lasch, *The True and Only Heaven: Progress and Its Critics* (New York: Norton, 1991), 460.

16. Brown, *Culture, Capitalism, and Democracy*.

Part II: Introduction

1. Steven Lukes, *Power: A Radical View* (New York: Macmillan, 1974), 137.

2. David Morris Potter, *People of Plenty: Economic Abundance and the American Character* (Chicago: University of Chicago Press, 1954).

3. Jonathan Glickstein, *Concepts of Free Labor in Antebellum America* (New Haven: Yale University Press, 1991).

4. Margaret Thatcher quoted in Douglas Keay, *Woman's Own,* October 1987.

5. Christopher Lasch, *The True and Only Heaven: Progress and Its Critics* (New York: Norton, 1991), 146.

Chapter 8: Back to the Future: The Political Economy of Auto-cannibalism

1. Bruce J. Schulman, *The Seventies: The Great Shift in American Culture, Society, and Politics* (New York: Free Press, 2001), 107.

2. Howard Gillette Jr., "The Wages of Divestment: How Money and Politics Aided in the Decline of Camden, New Jersey," in *Beyond the Ruins: The Meanings of Deindustrialization,* eds. Jefferson Cowie and Joseph Heathcott (Ithaca, NY: ILR Press, 2003), 147.

3. John Russo and Sherry Lee Linkon, "Collateral Damage: Deindustrialization and the Uses of Youngstown," in Cowie and Healthcott, eds., *Beyond the Ruins,* 205.

4. S. Paul O'Hara, "Envisioning the Steel City: The Legend and Legacy of Gary, Indiana," in Cowie and Healthcott, eds., *Beyond the Ruins,* 225–28.

5. James Cypher, "The Double Economy: Bubbles of the Twenty First Century" (unpublished manuscript); Christopher Phelps, "American Idle," *The Nation,* February 2010; Jefferson Cowie, *Stayin' Alive: The 1970s and the Last Days of the Working Class* (New York: The New Press, 2010), 240.

6. Marj Charlier, "Quiet Crisis: Small-Town America Battles a Deep Gloom as Its Economy Sinks," *The Wall Street Journal,* August 4, 1988.

7. John Russo and Sherry Lee Linkon, "The Social Costs of Deindustrialization," in *Manufacturing a Better Future for America,* ed. Richard McCormack (Washington, D.C.: Alliance for American Manufacturing, 2009), 183–217.

8. Harold Meyerson, "Business Is Booming," *The American Prospect,* March 2011; Jeffrey G. Madrick, *Age of Greed: The Triumph of Finance and the Decline of America, 1970 to the Present* (New York: Knopf, 2011), 195–200; Steven Greenhouse, *The Big Squeeze: Tough Times for the American Worker* (New York: Knopf, 2008), 85.

9. Greenhouse, *Big Squeeze,* 18.

10. Dale Maharidge, *Journey to Nowhere: The Saga of the New Underclass* (Garden City, NY: Dial, 1985), 22, 34–35.

11. Barry Bluestone and Bennett Harrison, *The Deindustrialization of America: Plant Closings, Community Abandonment, and the Dismantling of Basic Industry* (New York: Basic Books, 1982), 10; Steve May and Laura Morrison, "Making Sense of Restructuring: Narratives of Accommodation of Downsized Workers," in Cowie and Heathcott, eds., *Beyond the Ruins,* 277; Russo and Linkon, "Social Costs of Deindustrialization," 183–85.

12. Thomas Byrne Edsall, *The Age of Austerity: How Scarcity Will Remake American Politics* (New York: Doubleday, 2012), 19; Nick Turse, "Econoside," *The Huffington Post,* June 4, 2009; Nick Turse, "Tough Times in Troubled Towns," *The Huffington Post,* February 25, 2009.

13. Kevin Sack, "A City's Wrenching Budget Choices," *The New York Times,* July 4, 2011; Rick Lyman and Mary Williams Walsh, "Struggling San Jose Tests a Way to Cut Benefits," *The New York Times,* September 23, 2013.

14. Douglas McIntyre, "America's Ten Dying Cities: From Detroit to New Orleans," *The Wall Street Journal,* August 23, 2010.

15. Paul Harris, "How Detroit, the Motor City, Turned into a Ghost Town," *The Observer,* October 31, 2009; Terrance Heath, "What Does Deindustrialization Look Like?" *Campaign for America's Future* (www.ourfuture.org), March 24, 2011; Paul Clemens, *Punching Out: One Year in a Closing Auto Plant* (New York: Doubleday, 2011), 7.

16. Heath, "What Does Deindustrialization Look Like?"; Clemens, *Punching Out,* 34–37.

17. Sabrina Tavernise, "Life Span Shrinks for Least-Educated Whites in the U.S.," *The New York Times,* September 20, 2012; Sabrina Tavernise, "For Americans Under 50, Stark Findings on Health," *The New York Times,* January 9, 2013.

18. Jason DeParle, "Harder for Americans to Move from Lower Rungs," *The New York Times,* January 4, 2013.

19. Harold Meyerson, "If Labor Dies, What's Next?" *The American Prospect,* September 13, 2012; Eduardo Porter, "America's Sinking Middle Class," *The New York Times,*

September 18, 2013; Barbara Garson, *Down the Up Escalator: How the 99 Percent Live in the Great Recession* (New York: Doubleday, 2013).

20. David Harvey, *The Enigma of Capital and the Crisis of Capitalism* (New York: Oxford University Press, 2010).

21. Louis Uchitelle, "Once Made in the U.S.A.," *The American Prospect*, June 9, 2011; Greenhouse, *Big Squeeze;* James Gustave Speth, *America the Possible: Manifesto for a New Economy* (New Haven: Yale University Press, 2012); Bluestone and Harrison, *Deindustrialization of America,* 9; Stephanie Clifford, "U.S. Textile Plant Returns, with Floors Largely Empty of People," *The New York Times,* September 20, 2013.

22. Richard McCormick, "The Plight of American Manufacturing," *The American Prospect,* December 21, 2009; Clemens, *Punching Out,* 7; Bennett Harrison, *Lean and Mean: The Changing Landscape of Corporate Power in the Age of Flexibility* (New York: Basic Books, 1994), 385.

23. Simon Johnson and James Kwak, *Thirteen Bankers: The Wall Street Takeover and the Next Financial Meltdown* (New York: Pantheon, 2010), 70–74.

24. Kevin Phillips, *Bad Money: Reckless Finance, Failed Politics, and the Global Crises of American Capitalism* (New York: Viking, 2008), 5–29; Gerald F. Davis, *Managed by the Markets: How Finance Reshaped America* (New York: Oxford University Press, 2009), 144; Summers quoted in Mark Levinson, "The Broken Economy," *Dissent* 54, no. 4 (2010): 53–57.

25. Bluestone and Harrison, *The Deindustrialization of America*.

26. B. Mark Smith, *Toward Rational Exuberance: The Evolution of the Modern Stock Market* (New York: Farrar Straus Giroux, 2001), 223; Kevin Phillips, *Wealth and Democracy: A Political History of the American Rich* (New York: Broadway, 2002), 83–88; John B. Judis, *The Paradox of American Democracy: Elites, Special Interests, and the Betrayal of the Public Trust* (New York: Pantheon, 2000); Robert Brenner, *The Boom and the Bubble: The U.S. in the World Economy* (New York: Verso, 2000); Robert M. Collins, *More: The Politics of Economic Growth in Postwar America* (New York: Oxford University Press, 2000), 117–23; Harrison, *Lean and Mean,* 39; Judith Stein, *Pivotal Decade: How the United States Traded Factories for Finance in the Seventies* (New Haven: Yale University Press, 2010), 155–56, 248; Robert M. Collins, *Transforming America: Politics and Culture in the Reagan Years* (New York: Columbia University Press, 2007), 8–10; David Harvey, *The Conditions of Postmodernity: An Enquiry into the Origins of Cultural Change* (Cambridge, MA: Blackwell, 1990), 164–66.

27. Peter L. Bernstein, *Capital Ideas: The Improbable Origins of Modern Wall Street* (New York: Free Press, 1992), 2–3; Phillips, *Wealth and Democracy,* 83–88; Susan Strange, *Casino Capitalism* (Oxford and New York: Blackwell, 1986), 4; Haynes Johnson, *Sleepwalking Through History: America in the Reagan Years* (New York: Norton, 1991), 118.

28. Kevin Phillips, *The Politics of Rich and Poor: Wealth and the American Electorate in the Reagan Aftermath* (New York: Random House, 1990), 110–11; Paul Krugman, *The Age of Diminished Expectations: U.S. Economic Policy in the 1990s* (Cambridge, MA: MIT Press, 1990), 21–23.

29. Collins, *Transforming America,* 77; Phillips, *Politics of Rich and Poor,* 70–71; James Livingston, "Their Great Depression and Ours," in *The Great Credit Crash,* ed. Martijn Konings (London: Verso, 2010), 45–46.

30. Madrick, *Age of Greed,* 312; Collins, *Transforming America,* 86; David Johnston, *Free Lunch: How the Wealthiest Americans Enrich Themselves at Government Expense (and Stick You with the Bill)* (New York: Portfolio, 2007).

31. Phillips, *Politics of Rich and Poor,* 114; Johnson and Kwak, *Thirteen Bankers,* 74–85.

32. Johnston, *Free Lunch,* 170–86.

33. Roger Lowenstein, "Gambling with the Economy," *The New York Times,* April 20, 2010.

34. Richard Dienst, *The Bonds of Debt: Borrowing Against the Common Good* (New York: Verso, 2011), 59–63; Karl Marx, *Capital, vol. 3, A Critique of Political Economy* (London: Encyclopedia Britannica, 1991).

35. Phillips, *Politics of Rich and Poor,* 103–4.

36. Steven Pearlstein, "Time for Washington to Pay," *The Washington Post,* September 20, 2008.

37. Chris Harman, *Zombie Capitalism: Global Crisis and the Relevance of Marx* (Chicago: Haymarket, 2010), 295, 332–33; Greenhouse, *Big Squeeze,* 85–87; Nelson D. Schwartz, "Industries Find Surging Profits in Deeper Cuts," *The New York Times,* July 25, 2010; Madrick, *Age of Greed,* 199; Johnston, *Free Lunch,* 182; Davis, *Managed by the Markets,* 125–30.

38. Harrison, *Lean and Mean,* 186; Davis, *Managed by the Markets,* 21, 84.

39. Madrick, *Age of Greed,* 74–85, 332; Karen Ho, *Liquidated: An Ethnography of Wall Street* (Durham, NC: Duke University Press, 2009), 155–56; Randy Martin, *Financialization of Daily Life* (Philadelphia: Temple University Press, 2002); Davis, *Managed by the Markets.*

40. Madrick, *Age of Greed,* 395; Matt Stoller, "Towards a Creditor State: One in Seven Pursued by a Debt Collector," *Naked Capitalism* (www.nakedcapitalism.com), February 28, 2012; Edsall, *Age of Austerity,* 14; Benedict Carey, "Life in the Red," *The New York Times,* January 14, 2013.

41. Ho, *Liquidated,* 151.

42. Phillip Augar, *The Greed Merchants: How the Investment Banks Played the Free-Market Game* (New York: Portfolio, 2005), 23–24.

43. Alan Blinder, "How Many U.S. Jobs Might Be Offshorable?" CEPS Working Paper, No. 142, March 2007; Greenhouse, *Big Squeeze,* 194–204; Steven Greenhouse, "More Workers Face Pay Cuts, Not Furloughs," *The New York Times,* August 10, 2010.

44. Isaiah Poole, "Employment Report Shows Job Creation Stuck in Traffic," *Campaign for America's Future* (www.ourfuture.org), July 8, 2011; John Schwartz, "Small Infrastructure Gains Are Observed in Infrastructure Report," *The New York Times,* March 19, 2013; Bob Herbert, "That Can't-Do Spirit," *The New York Times,* February 3, 2009; Felix G. Rohatyn and Everett Ehrlich, "A New Bank to Save Our Infrastructure," *The New York Review of Books,* October 9, 2008.

45. Dienst, *Bonds of Debt,* 63; James Glassman, "Primitive Accumulation, Accumulation by Dispossession, Accumulation by 'Extra-Economic' Means," *Progress in Human Geography* 30, no. 5 (2006): 608–25.

46. Phillips, *Politics of Rich and Poor,* 200–201; Bob Herbert, "They Still Don't Get It," *The New York Times,* January 22, 2010; Stephen Pimpare, "Why No Fire This Time: From the Mass Strike to No Strike," *New Labor Forum* 20, no. 1 (Winter 2011): 16;

Sabrina Tavernise, "Soaring Poverty Casts Light on 'Lost Decade,'" *The New York Times,* September 13, 2011.

47. Collins, *Transforming America,* 124; Phillips, *Politics of Rich and Poor,* 200.

48. Richard Harvey Brown, *Culture, Capitalism, and Democracy in New America* (New Haven: Yale University Press, 2005), 55; Collins, *Transforming America,* 130; Edsall, *Age of Austerity;* Speth, *America the Possible,* 23–24; Nick Turse, "Tomgram: Nick Turse, Younger and Hungrier in America," *TomDispatch.com,* March 8, 2009; Erik Ekholm, "Recession Raises Poverty Rate to Fifteen-Year High," *The New York Times,* September 16, 2010; Tavernise, "Soaring Poverty Casts Light on 'Lost Decade'"; Stephen Pimpare, *The New Victorians: Poverty, Politics, and Propaganda in Two Gilded Ages* (New York: The New Press, 2004), 177–78; Andy Kroll, "How the McEconomy Bombed the American Worker: The Hollowing Out of the Middle Class," *TomDispatch.com,* May 9, 2011; Greenhouse, *Big Squeeze,* 267.

49. Greenhouse, *Big Squeeze,* 226; Duff McDonald, "The Catastrophist View," *New York,* October 8, 2007.

50. Steve Fraser and Joshua Freeman, "Tomgram, Fraser and Freeman: Creating a Prison-Corporate Complex," *TomDispatch.com,* April 19, 2012; Brown, *Culture, Capitalism and Democracy,* 31; Rania Khalek, "Twenty-First Century Slaves: How Corporations Exploit Prison Labor," *AlterNet (www.alternet.org),* July 21, 2011.

51. Sabrina Tavernise, "Middle Class Shrinks as Income Gap Grows, New Report Finds," *The New York Times,* November 15, 2011.

52. Peter Goodman, "After Training, Still Scrambling for Employment," *The New York Times,* July 18, 2010; Michael Luo, "New Job Means Lower Wages for Many," *The New York Times,* August 31, 2010; Levinson, "The Broken Economy"; Michael Luo, "99 Weeks Later, Jobless Only Have Desperation," *The New York Times,* August 2, 2010; Louis Uchitelle, "The Wage That Meant Middle Class," *The New York Times,* April 20, 2008.

53. Greenhouse, *Big Squeeze,* 185–95.

54. Henri Simon, "Crisis in the U.S.: Social and Economic Effects, Restructuring and Methods of Adapting," *Insurgent Notes,* January 19, 2010; Robert E. Parker, *Flesh Peddlers and Warm Bodies: The Temporary Help Industry and Its Workers* (New Brunswick, NJ: Rutgers University Press, 1994), 11; Michelle Rodino-Colocino, "High-Tech Workers of the World, Unionize! A Case Study for WashTech's 'New Model of Unionism,'" in *Knowledge Workers in the Information Society,* eds. Catherine McKercher and Vincent Mosco (Lanham, MD: Lexington, 2007), 209–28.

55. Greenhouse, *Big Squeeze,* 129–30; Vanessa Williamson, Theda Skocpol, and John Coggin, "The Tea Party and the Remaking of Republican Conservatism," *Perspectives on Politics* 9, no. 1 (March 2011): 25–43.

56. Ibid.

57. David Shipler, *The Working Poor: The Invisible in America* (New York: Knopf, 2004), ch. 3.

58. Ibid., ch. 2 and 3.

59. Davis, *Managed by the Market,* 26.

60. Harman, *Zombie Capitalism,* 280; Martin, *Financialization of Daily Life,* 31, 161–62; Emma Rothschild, "Can We Transform an Industrial Society," *The New York Review of Books,* February 26, 2009; Johnna Montgomerie, "Neoliberalism and the Making

of the Subprime Borrower," in Konings, ed., *Great Credit Crash*, 105; Speth, *America the Possible*, 23–24.

61. Speth, *America the Possible*, 25.
62. Thomas Bryne Edsall with Mary D. Edsall, *Chain Reaction: The Impact of Race, Rights and Taxes on American Politics* (New York: Norton, 1991), 11–25.
63. Dick Bryan, Michael Rafferty, and Scott MacWilliam, "The Global Financial Crisis: Foreclosing or Leveraging Labor's Future," in Konings, *Great Credit Crash,* 367; Larry Bartels, *Unequal Democracy: The Political Economy of the New Gilded Age* (Princeton, NJ: Princeton University Press, 2008), 224–28.
64. Daniel H. Pink, *Free Agent Nation: How America's New Independent Workers Are Transforming the Way We Live* (New York: Warner Books, 2001), 241; David Harvey, *A Brief History of Neoliberalism* (Oxford: Oxford University Press, 2005), 26; Pimpare, *New Victorians,* 136–37; Mark Brenner, "Pensions: The Next Casualty of Wall Street," *Labor Notes* (www.labornotes.org), September 29, 200; Greenhouse, *Big Squeeze,* 43–44.
65. Timothy Pratt, "The New Faces of Day Labor," *Las Vegas Sun,* November 2, 2009; Don Peck, "How the New Jobless Era Will Transform America," *The Atlantic,* March 2010; Luo, "99 Weeks Later"; Eduardo Porter, "At the Polls, Choose Your Capitalism," *The New York Times,* October 30, 2012.
66. Steve May and Laura Morrison, "Making Sense of Restructuring," in Cowie and Heathcott, eds., *Beyond the Ruins,* 262; Pimpare, *New Victorians,* 121–31; George Will, "No One Blushes Anymore," *The Washington Post,* September 15, 1988.

Chapter 9: Fables of Acquiescence: The Businessman as Populist Hero

1. T. J. Stiles, *The First Tycoon: The Epic Life of Cornelius Vanderbilt* (New York: Knopf, 2009).
2. C. Wright Mills, *The Power Elite* (New York: Oxford University Press, 1956), 6–10.
3. Kai Bird, *The Chairman: John J. McCloy, the Making of the American Establishment* (New York: Simon and Schuster, 1992), 663.
4. Stanley A. Deetz, *Democracy in an Age of Corporate Colonization: Developments in Communication and the Politics of American Life* (Albany: SUNY Press, 1992), 3–20.
5. Mills, *Power Elite,* 329; John Kenneth Galbraith, *The New Industrial State,* 2d ed. (Boston: Houghton Mifflin, 1971).
6. Joshua B. Freeman, *Working-Class New York: Life and Labor Since World War II* (New York: The New Press, 2000), 50–51.
7. Karen Ho, *Liquidated: An Ethnology of Wall Street* (Durham, NC: Duke University Press, 2009), 149–50; Gerald F. Davis, *Managed by the Markets: How Finance Reshaped America* (New York: Oxford University Press, 2009), 125.
8. Judith Stein, *Pivotal Decade: How the United States Traded Factories for Finance in the Seventies* (New Haven: Yale University Press, 2010), 26.
9. Tom Engelhardt, *The End of Victory Culture: Cold War America and the Disillusioning of a Generation* (New York: Basic Books, 1995).
10. Peter Schrag, *The Decline of the WASP* (New York: Simon and Schuster, 1971), 120–39; Robert C. Christopher, *Crashing the Gates: The De-WASPing of America's Power Elite* (New York: Simon and Schuster, 1989), 111–12.
11. Roger Lowenstein, *The End of Wall Street* (New York: Penguin Press, 2010), 56; John B. Judis, *The Paradox of American Democracy: Elites, Special Interests, and the Betrayal of*

the Public Trust (New York: Pantheon, 2000), 158 and passim; Kevin Phillips, *Wealth and Democracy: A Political History of the American Rich* (New York: Broadway, 2002), 230–32; Connie Bruck, *The Predators' Ball: The Junk-Bond Raiders and the Man Who Staked Them* (New York: Simon and Schuster, 1988), 153, 171, 185, and passim.

12. George Gilder quoted in Kevin Phillips, *The Politics of Rich and Poor: Wealth and the American Electorate in the Reagan Aftermath* (New York: Random House, 1990), 62.

13. Richard Dorman quoted in Lewis H. Lapham, *Money and Class in America: Notes and Observations on Our Civil Religion* (New York: Weidenfeld and Nicolson, 1988), 231.

14. Ho, *Liquidated,* 133–37; Milken admirer quoted in Bruck, *Predators' Ball,* 84, see also 19, 84–85, 93, 95, 270; Michael Oriard, *Sporting with the Gods: The Rhetoric of Play and Game in American Culture* (New York: Cambridge University Press, 1991), 351–52; Phillips, *Wealth and Democracy,* 366; Ken Auletta, *Greed and Glory on Wall Street: The Fall of the House of Lehman* (New York: Random House, 1986); Christopher, *Crashing the Gates,* 111–12.

15. Ho, *Liquidated,* 27–28.

16. *Newsweek,* September 15, 1980; Jerry Falwell quoted in Haynes Johnson, *Sleepwalking Through History: America in the Reagan Years* (New York: Norton, 1991), 198, see also 199; *Institutional Investor* and *Forbes* as quoted in Bruck, *Predators' Ball,* 270; Michael M. Thomas, "The Eyes Still Have It," *Manhattan Inc.,* April 1985; Michael M. Thomas, "Deals," *Manhattan Inc.,* March 1985; David Remnick, *Manhattan Inc.,* April 1985; Barry Rehfeld, "The Liquidator," *Manhattan Inc.,* September 1985; John Taylor, "Baby Tycoon," *Manhattan Inc.,* November 1985; Michael Thomas, "The New Tycoonery," *Manhattan Inc.,* December 1985; "Corporate Culture," *Manhattan Inc.,* February 1986; Ron Rosenbaum, "Society's Dissidents," *Manhattan Inc.,* April 1986; Hope Lampert, "Society Steps Out," *Manhattan Inc.,* October 1985; Brad Gooch, "The New Gilded Age," *Manhattan Inc.,* October 1986; Paul Cowen, "The Merger Maestro," *Esquire,* May 1984; Jesse Kornblath, "The Working Rich: The Real Slaves of New York," *New York,* November 24, 1986; "Making It by Doing Good," *The New York Times,* July 3, 1983; Gwen Kincaid, "Ivan Boesky, Money Machine," *Fortune,* August 6, 1984.

17. Steve Fraser, *Every Man a Speculator: A History of Wall Street in American Life* (New York: Harper Collins, 2005), 586–87; David Brooks, *Bobos in Paradise: The New Upper Class and How They Got There* (New York: Simon and Schuster, 2000), 110–11; Matthew Klam, "Riding the Mo in the Lime Green Glow," *The New York Times Sunday Magazine,* November 21, 1999; Ron Chernow, "Hard Charging Bulls and Red Flags," *The New York Times,* September 2, 1998; Chris Smith, "How the Stock Market Swallowed New York," *New York,* October 3, 1998.

18. Fraser, *Every Man a Speculator,* 189–90; B. Mark Smith, *Toward Rational Exuberance: The Evolution of the Modern Stock Market* (New York: Farrar Straus Giroux, 2001), 255.

19. Connecticut billboard quoted in Robert J. Shiller, *Irrational Exuberance* (Princeton, NJ: Princeton University Press, 2000), 42; Jane Bryant Quinn, "Investment Clubs: What Makes Them Work?" *Good Housekeeping,* September 1997; Barzou Daragahi, "How to Start an Online Stock Club," *Money.com,* August 1999; Grace W. Weinstein, "Club Clout," *Ms.,* September 1989; Barnard Rascho, "Investor Illiteracy," *American Prospect,* March/April 1999; Smith, "How the Stock Market Swallowed New York"; Michael Peter Gagne, "Wall Street: Symbol of American Culture" (PhD diss., University of Hawaii, 1996), 168–70; Jean Sherman Chatsky, "Money

Talk," *Money Magazine,* May 1998; Amy Dickinson, "Kids and the Dow," *Time,* October 30, 2000; "Turning Kids into Investors," *U.S. News and World Report,* October 17, 1988.

20. Peter L. Berger, *The Capitalist Revolution: Fifty Propositions About Prosperity, Equality, and Liberty* (New York: Basic Books, 1986).

21. Christopher Lasch, *The Revolt of the Elites: And the Betrayal of Democracy* (New York: Norton, 1995), ch. 2; Chrystia Freeland, "The Rise of the New Global Elite," in *The Best Business Writing 2012,* eds. Dean Starkman et. al. (New York: Columbia University Press, 2012), 236; Felix Salmon, "The Wall Street Mind: Oblivious," *New York,* April 10, 2011; Simon Johnson and James Kwak, *Thirteen Bankers: The Wall Street Takeover and the Next Financial Meltdown* (New York: Pantheon, 2010), 182; Ronald Reagan, State of the Union address, February 6, 1985.

22. John Duka, "A New Opulence Triumphs in the Capital," *The New York Times,* January 22, 1981; Phillips, *Wealth and Democracy,* 333.

23. NewsHour with Paul Solomon, "Living Large," *NewsHour,* May, 20, 1999, www.pbs.org/newshour/bb/business/Jan-June99/living_large_5.20.html.

24. Phillips, *Politics of Rich and Poor,* 44; Lapham, *Money and Class in America,* 40, 54–60.

25. Lapham, *Money and Class in America,* 198.

26. Ibid., 204–9.

27. Phillips, *Politics of Rich and Poor,* 180.

28. Jonathan Chait, *The Big Con: The True Story of How Washington Got Hoodwinked and Hijacked by Crackpot Economics* (Boston: Houghton Mifflin, 2007), 56–58; David Johnston, *Free Lunch: How the Wealthiest Americans Enrich Themselves at Government Expense (and Stick You with the Bill)* (New York: Portfolio, 2007); Johnson, *Sleepwalking Through History,* ch. 2; Phillips, *Wealth and Democracy,* ch. 2; Harvey, *A Brief History of Neoliberalism* (Oxford: Oxford University Press, 2005).

29. Haynes Johnson, *The Best of Times: America in the Clinton Years* (New York: Harcourt, 2001), 20–43.

30. Harvey, *Brief History of Neoliberalism,* 15; David Carr, "Business Is a Beat Deflated," *The New York Times,* November 1, 2009.

31. Robert M. Collins, *Transforming America: Politics and Culture in the Reagan Years* (New York: Columbia University Press, 2007), 94; *Wall Street,* DVD, directed by Oliver Stone (Twentieth Century–Fox, 1987); Robert Frank, *Richistan: A Journey Through the American Wealth Boom and the Lives of the New Rich* (New York: Crown, 2007), ch. 2.

32. Lapham, *Money in America,* 63.

33. Christopher Lasch, *The Culture of Narcissism: American Life in an Age of Diminishing Expectations* (New York: Norton, 1978), 218; Thorstein Veblen, *The Theory of the Leisure Class: An Economic Study of Institutions* (1899; reprint, New York: New America Library, 1953).

34. Robert M. Collins, *More: The Politics of Economic Growth in Postwar America* (New York: Oxford University Press, 2000), 123.

35. Bruce J. Schulman, *The Seventies: The Great Shift in American Culture, Society, and Politics* (New York: Free Press, 2001), 37–39; Jefferson Cowie, *Stayin' Alive: The 1970s and the Last Days of the Working Class* (New York: The New Press, 2010), 134, ch. 4 and 5.

36. Daniel T. Rodgers, *Age of Fracture* (Cambridge, MA: Belknap/Harvard University Press, 2011), 75; Doug Marlette, *Faux Bubba: Bill and Hillary Go to Washington* (New York: Times Books, 1993), 1–36.
37. Damien Cave and Michael Luo, "More of the Rich Run as Populist Outsiders," *The New York Times,* July 23, 2010.
38. Chait, *Big Con,* 120–21, 135.
39. Thomas C. Cochran and William Miller, *The Age of Enterprise: A Social History of Industrial America* (New York: Harper, 1961), ch. 7; Christopher, *Crashing the Gates;* Perry Anderson, *The Origins of Postmodernity* (London: Verso, 1998), 62–63.

Chapter 10: Fables of Freedom: Brand X

1. Elaine Tyler May, *Homeward Bound: American Families in the Cold War Era* (New York: Basic Books, 2008), 20–21.
2. Terry Eagleton, *The Illusions of Postmodernism* (London: Oxford, 1996), 88; Richard Harvey Brown, *Culture, Capitalism, and Democracy in the New America* (New Haven: Yale University Press, 2005), 139–40, 150, 153; David Brooks, *On Paradise Drive: How We Live Now (and Always Have) in the Future Tense* (New York: Simon and Schuster, 2004), 196, 209–10.
3. John Kenneth Galbraith, *The Affluent Society* (Boston: Houghton Mifflin, 1958); Vance Packard, *The Hidden Persuaders* (New York: D. McKay, 1957); David Riesman, *The Lonely Crowd: A Study of the Changing American Character* (New Haven: Yale University Press, 1950); Daniel Bell, *The End of Ideology: On the Exhaustion of Political Ideas in the Fifties* (Glencoe, IL: Free Press, 1960); Herbert Marcuse, *One-Dimensional Man* (Boston: Beacon, 1964).
4. Randy Martin, *Financialization of Daily Life* (Philadelphia: Temple University Press, 2002), 30–31; Lizabeth Cohen, *A Consumers' Republic: The Politics of Mass Consumption in Postwar America* (New York: Knopf, 2003); James Gustave Speth, *America the Possible: Manifesto for a New Economy* (New Haven: Yale University Press, 2012), 23–24, 135; Christopher Lasch, *The True and Only Heaven: Progress and Its Critics* (New York: Norton, 1991), 521–22.
5. Stephen Lukes, *Power: A Radical View* (New York: Macmillan, 1974); Martin, *Financialization of Daily Life*, 31, 38; David Harvey, *The Enigma of Capital and the Crisis of Capitalism* (New York: Oxford University Press, 2010).
6. David Shipler, *The Working Poor: The Invisible in America* (New York: Knopf, 2004); Cohen, *Consumers' Republic*, 373, 377.
7. Franklin quoted in Christopher Lasch, *The Culture of Narcissism: American Life in the Age of Diminishing Expectations* (New York: Norton, 1978), 54.
8. Victor Lebow, "Price Competition in 1955," *Journal of Retailing*, Spring 1955.
9. Quoted in Bell, *End of Ideology*, 254.
10. Marx quoted in Perry Anderson, *The Origins of Postmodernity* (London: Verso, 1998), 114; Kristin Wartman, "The One-Two Punch: Big Food Gets Kids Hooked Early and Often," *Huffington Post*, October 18, 2012.
11. Bruce J. Schulman, *The Seventies: The Great Shift in American Culture, Society, and Politics* (New York: Free Press, 2001), 72–80; *Business Week*, October 17, 1970.
12. Tom Wolfe, "The Me Decade and the Third Great Awakening," *New York,* August 23, 1976; Thomas Frank, *The Conquest of Cool: Business Culture, Counterculture, and the*

Rise of Hip Consumerism (Chicago: University of Chicago Press, 1997); Wolfgang Steeck, "Citizens as Consumers," *New Left Review*, March–April, 2012.

13. Brown, *Culture, Capitalism, and Democracy*.

14. Martha Rosler, "Culture Class: Art, Creativity, Urbanism," *E-Flux*, September 2013; Chris Lehmann, *Rich People Things* (New York: OR Books, 2010), 132; Richard Sennett, *The Culture of the New Capitalism* (New Haven: Yale University Press, 2006); Neil Postman, *Amusing Ourselves to Death: Public Discourse in the Age of Show Business* (New York: Viking, 1985).

15. Schulman, *Seventies*, 249.

16. Rosler, "Culture Class"; Eagleton, *Illusions of Postmodernism*, 24, 61; Garry Wills, *Reagan's America: Innocents at Home* (Garden City, NY: Doubleday, 1987), 446–47, 452, 456.

17. Linda Kintz, *Between Jesus and the Market: The Emotions That Matter in Right-Wing America* (Durham, NC: Duke University Press, 1997), 195–97, 199, 205; Kathryn Lofton, "The Sigh of the Oppressed," *New Labor Forum* 3 (Fall 2012); Kevin Phillips, *Bad Money: Reckless Finance, Failed Politics, and the Global Crises of American Capitalism* (New York: Viking, 2008), 92–93.

18. Phillips, *Bad Money*, 92–93; Postman, *Amusing Ourselves to Death*, 92–93, 114; Lehmann, *Rich People Things*, 76–77; Brown, *Culture, Capitalism, and Democracy*, 150.

19. Haynes Johnson, *Sleepwalking Through History: America in the Reagan Years* (New York: Norton, 1991), ch. 16; Kintz, *Between Jesus and the Market*; Wills, *Reagan's America*, 456; Pat Robertson quoted in David Graeber, *Debt: The First 5000 Years* (Brooklyn: Melville House, 2011), 376.

20. Russell Conwell, *Acres of Diamonds* (Philadelphia: Temple University Press, 1966); Brooks, *On Paradise Drive*, 91, 95, 104.

21. Arlie Russell Hochschild, *The Outsourced Self: Intimate Life in Market Times* (New York: Metropolitan/Henry Holt, 2012), 13; Brown, *Culture, Capitalism, and Democracy*, 32, 183; Gerald F. Davis, *Managed by the Markets: How Finance Reshaped America* (New York: Oxford University Press, 2009).

22. Robert M. Collins, *Transforming America: Politics and Culture in the Reagan Years* (New York: Columbia University Press, 2007), 155–57; Brown, *Culture, Capitalism, and Democracy*, 153; Lasch, *Culture of Narcissism*, xvi–xvii, 6, 10, 57, 63, 69, 71, 83, 92; Lauren Berlant, *Cruel Optimism* (Durham, NC: Duke University Press, 2011), 193–94.

Chapter 11: Wages of Freedom: The Fable of the Free Agent

1. Michelle Rodino-Colocino, "Technomadic Work: From Practical Vision to WashTech's Opposition," *Work Organization, Labour, and Globalization* 2 (Spring 2008).

2. Peter S. Goodman, "After Job Training, Still Scrambling for a Job," *The New York Times*, July 19, 2010.

3. Steven Greenhouse, *The Big Squeeze: Tough Times for the American Worker* (New York: Knopf, 2008), 112, 117–18, 120.

4. Steven Greenhouse, "Low Wage Workers Are Often Cheated," *The New York Times*, September 1, 2009; Ruth Milkman, A. Gonzales, and V. Navarro, "Wage Theft and Workplace Violations in Los Angeles," UCLA Institute for Research on Labor and Employment, 2010.

5. Robert E. Parker, *Flesh Peddlers and Warm Bodies: The Temporary Help Industry and Its Workers* (New Brunswick, NJ: Rutgers University Press, 1994), 2–3, 7, 8, 11, 145; Greenhouse, *Big Squeeze*, 117–18; Miriam Ching Yoon Louie, *Sweatshop Warriors: Immigrant Women Workers Take On the Global Factory* (Cambridge, MA: South End, 2001), 3, 5.

6. Daniel T. Rodgers, *Age of Fracture* (Cambridge, MA: Belknap/Harvard University Press, 2011), 83–84; Gerald F. Davis, *Managed by the Markets: How Finance Reshaped America* (New York: Oxford University Press, 2009), 198, 201.

7. Chris Lehmann, *Rich People Things* (New York: OR Books, 2010), 90; Richard Sennett, *The Corrosion of Character* (New York: Norton, 1998), 10.

8. Management text quoted in Rodino-Colocino, "Technomadic Work"; Daniel H. Pink, *Free Agent Nation: How America's New Independent Workers Are Transforming the Way We Live* (New York: Warner Books, 2001), 116.

9. Christopher Lasch, *The Culture of Narcissism: American Life in an Age of Diminishing Expectations* (New York: Norton, 1978), 26–27, 47.

10. Kathi Weeks, *The Problem with Work: Feminism, Marxism, Antiwork Politics, and Postwork Imaginaries* (Durham, NC: Duke University Press, 2011), 70; Arlie Russell Hochschild, *The Outsourced Self: Intimate Life in Market Times* (New York: Metropolitan/Henry Holt, 2012), 70–72.

11. Rodino-Colocino, "Technomadic Work"; Pink, *Free Agent Nation*, 3, 14, 16–17; Sennett, *Corrosion of Character*, 10; Lasch, *Culture of Narcissism*, 49; Rodgers, *Age of Fracture*, 83–84.

12. Peter Frase, "The Politics of Getting a Life," *Jacobin*, Spring 2012.

13. Andrew Ross, *Nice Work If You Can Get It: Life and Labor in Precarious Times* (New York: New York University Press, 2009), 74.

14. Pink, *Free Agent Nation*, 46.

15. Ibid., 215; Sennett, *Corrosion of Character*, 56; American Management Association, "Workplace Monitoring and Surveillance Report," 2001; *USA Today*, October 18, 2001; Eric J. Sinrod at Law.Com, "The Latest Workplace Monitoring and Surveillance," HumanResources.about.com; Michael Levy, "Electronic Monitoring in the Workplace: Power Through the Panopticon," besser.tsoa.nyu.edu/impact/s94/students/mike/mike_paper.html; *CNN Money*, October 4, 1991.

16. *The New York Times*, February 11, 2014.

17. Vicki Mayer, *Below the Line: Producers and Production Studies in the New Television Economy* (Durham, NC: Duke University Press, 2011).

18. Pink, *Free Agent Nation*, 24, 55, 84, 102, 158–59, 195, 241; Durkheim quoted in Richard Harvey Brown, *Culture, Capitalism, and Democracy in the New America* (New Haven: Yale University Press, 2005), 166.

19. Eli Cook, "The Pricing of Everyday Life," *Raritan*, Winter 2013; Lasch, *Culture of Narcissism*, 92.

20. Pink, *Free Agent Nation*, 285; *InternetNews.Com*, March 5, 1999.

21. Ross Perlin, *Intern Nation: How to Earn Nothing and Learn Little in the Brave New Economy* (Brooklyn: Verso, 2011); Gavin Mueller, "Reality TV and the Flexible Future," *Jacobin*, Spring 2012.

22. Michelle Rodino-Calocino, "High-Tech Workers of the World, Unionize: A Case Study of WashTech's 'New Model Unionism,'" in *Knowledge Workers in the Information*

Society, eds. Catherine McKercher and Vincent Mosco (Lanham, MD: Lexington, 2007).

23. Lehmann, *Rich People Things,* 29–30; Christopher Lasch, *The Revolt of the Elites: And the Betrayal of Democracy* (New York: Norton, 1995), introduction; Fredric Jameson, *The Seeds of Time* (New York: Columbia University Press, 1994), 60, 63.

24. Ibid.

25. Garry Wills, *Reagan's America: Innocents at Home* (Garden City, NY: Doubleday, 1987), 452.

26. Martijn Konings, "Rethinking Neoliberalism and the Crisis: Beyond the Re-Regulation Agenda," in *The Great Credit Crash,* ed. Martijn Konings (London: Verso, 2010); Lasch, *Culture of Narcissism,* 26–30.

Chapter 12: Journey to Nowhere: The Eclipse of the Labor Movement

1. Jefferson Cowie, *Stayin' Alive: The 1970s and the Last Days of the Working Class* (New York: The New Press, 2010), 236–38 and ch. 5.

2. Cal Winslow, "Overview: The Rebellion from Below, 1965–81," in *Rebel Rank and File: Labor Militancy and Revolt from Below During the Long 1970s,* eds. Aaron Brenner, Robert Brenner, and Cal Winslow (New York: Verso, 2010); Kim Moody, "Understanding the Rank and File Rebellion in the Long 1970s," in Brenner, Brenner, and Winslow, eds., *Rebel Rank and File;* Judith Stein, *Pivotal Decade: How the United States Traded Factories for Finance in the Seventies* (New Haven: Yale University Press, 2010), 117–18.

3. Cowie, *Stayin' Alive,* 8, 45–50; Winslow, "Overview"; Moody, "Understanding the Rank and File Rebellion."

4. Cowie, *Stayin' Alive,* 2, 8, 45–50.

5. Robert M. Collins, *Transforming America: Politics and Culture in the Reagan Years* (New York: Columbia University Press, 2007), 8–10; Kevin Phillips, *The Politics of Rich and Poor: Wealth and the American Electorate in the Reagan Aftermath* (New York: Random House, 1990), 14–21; Garry Wills, *Reagan's America: Innocents at Home* (Garden City, NY: Doubleday, 1987), 437; Stein, *Pivotal Decade,* 115, 127; Robert Brenner, "The Political Economy of Rank and File Rebellion," in Brenner, Brenner, and Winslow, eds., *Rebel Rank and File.*

6. Brenner, "Political Economy"; Cowie, *Stayin' Alive,* 363.

7. John Schmitt, "Minimum Wage: Catching Up to Productivity," *Portside,* June 17, 2013, https://portside.org/2013-06-17/minimum-wage-catching-productivity; Barry Bluestone and Bennett Harrison, *The Deindustrialization of America: Plant Closings, Community Abandonment, and the Dismantling of Basic Industry* (New York: Basic Books, 1982), 10; Christopher Lasch, *The True and Only Heaven: Progress and Its Critics* (New York: Norton, 1991), 481, 486.

8. Meany quoted in Stanley A. Deetz, *Democracy in an Age of Corporate Colonialization: Developments in Communication and the Politics of American Life* (Albany: SUNY Press, 1992), 236.

9. Richard McCormack, "The Flight of American Manufacturing," *The American Prospect,* January–February 2010; Collins, *Transforming America,* 8–10, 72–76; Phillips, *Politics of Rich and Poor,* 14–21; Wills, *Reagan's America,* 437 and quoting Stockman on 438; Volcker quoted in Stein, *Pivotal Decade,* 267, see also 8–12, 215–20, 259; Elizabeth Tandy Shermer, *Sunbelt Capitalism: Phoenix and the Transformation of American*

Politics (Philadelphia: University of Pennsylvania Press, 2013); Moody, "Understanding the Rank and File Rebellion"; David Harvey, *The Condition of Postmodernity: An Enquiry into the Origins of Cultural Change* (Cambridge, MA: Blackwell, 1990); Johnna Montgomerie, "Neoliberalism and the Making of Sub Prime Borrowers," in *The Great Credit Crash*, ed. Martijn Konings (London: Verso, 2010).

10. Michelle Rodino-Calocino, "High Tech Workers of the World, Unionize! A Case Study of WashTech's 'New Model Unionism,'" in *Knowledge Workers in the Information Society*, eds. Catherine McKercher and Vincent Mosco (Lanham, MD: Lexington, 2007); Michelle Rodino-Calocino, "Technomadic Work: From Practical Vision to WashTech's Opposition," *Work Organization, Labour, and Globalization* 2 (Spring 2008); Cowie, *Stayin' Alive*, ch. 5.

11. Daniel T. Rodgers, *Age of Fracture* (Cambridge, MA: Belknap/Harvard University Press, 2011), 95–96, 122–23, 205–6.

12. Steven Greenhouse, *The Big Squeeze: Tough Times for the American Worker* (New York: Knopf, 2008), 82–85, 87–89, 90–91; Steven Greenhouse, "More Workers Face Pay Cuts, Not Furloughs," *The New York Times*, August, 4, 2010.

13. Greenhouse, *Big Squeeze*, 83.

14. Louis Uchitelle, "Diminishing Expectations," *The Nation*, February 25, 2013; Phillips, *Politics of Rich and Poor*, 21.

15. Greenhouse, *Big Squeeze*, 409; David Shipler, *The Working Poor: The Invisible in America* (New York: Knopf, 2004), introduction, ch. 1 and 2; Stephen Pimpare, "Why No Fire This Time? In Search of a Modern Progressivism," *New Labor Forum*, Spring 2010.

16. Daniel H. Pink, *Free Agent Nation: How America's New Independent Workers Are Transforming the Way We Live* (New York: Warner Books, 2001), 215–17; Richard Sennett, *The Corrosion of Character* (New York: Norton, 1998), 49, 50, 56; Tamara Draut, *Strapped: Why America's 20- and 30-Somethings Can't Get Ahead* (New York: Doubleday, 2006); American Management Association, "Work Place Monitoring and Surveillance Report," 2001; *USA Today*, October 18, 2001; Eric J. Sinrod at Law.Com, "The Latest Workplace Monitoring and Surveillance," HumanResources.about.com; Michael Levy, "Electronic Monitoring in the Workplace: Power Through the Panopticon," besser.tsoa.nyu.edu/impact/s94/students/mike/mike_paper.html; *CNN Money*, October 4, 1991; Simon Head, *The New Ruthless Economy: Work and Power in the Digital Age* (New York: Oxford University Press, 2003); Tom Juravich, *At the Altar of the Bottom Line: The Degradation of Work in the Twenty-First Century* (Amherst: University of Massachusetts Press, 2009); Greenhouse, *Big Squeeze*, 12–13; Phillips, *Politics of Rich and Poor*, 21; Robert E. Parker, *Flesh Peddlers and Warm Bodies: The Temporary Help Industry and Its Workers* (New Brunswick, NJ: Rutgers University Press, 1994), 146.

17. Lauren Berlant, *Cruel Optimism* (Durham, NC: Duke University Press, 2011), 211, 217–18; Richard Harvey Brown, *Culture, Capitalism, and Democracy in the New America* (New Haven: Yale University Press, 2005), 215; John Schmitt, "Inequality as Policy: The U.S. Since 1979," Center for Economic Policy Research, October 2009.

18. Greenhouse, *Big Squeeze*, 10–12; Shipler, *Working Poor*, ch. 1 and 2; Bruce J. Schulman, *The Seventies: The Great Shift in American Culture, Society, and Politics* (New York: Free Press, 2001), 231–34; Collins, *Transforming America*, 76–77; Haynes Johnson, *Sleepwalking Through History: America in the Reagan Years* (New York: Norton, 1991), ch. 14.

19. Cowie, *Stayin' Alive*, 257; Timothy Noah, "The Great Divergence and the Death of Organized Labor," *Slate*, September 12, 2010; Schulman, *Seventies*, 234; Wills, *Reagan's America*, xix.

20. Powell quoted in Stephen Pimpare, *The New Victorians: Poverty, Politics, and Propaganda in Two Gilded Ages* (New York: The New Press, 2004), 56.

21. Susan Feiner, "GOP Attack on Child Labor Threatens Our Daughers," *WeNews* (www.womensenews.org), April 12, 2011; Benjamin C. Waterhouse, "Mobilizing a Lobby for Capital: The Rise of the Business Roundtable in the 1970s," paper delivered at conference on Power and the History of Capitalism, April 15, 2001; Alan Pell Crawford, *Thunder on the Right: The "New Right" and the Politics of Resentment* (New York: Pantheon, 1980), 11, 29; Jonathan Chait, *The Big Con: The True Story of How Washington Got Hoodwinked and Highjacked by Crackpot Economics* (Boston: Houghton Mifflin, 2007), ch. 2; Stein, *Pivotal Decade*, ch. 8.

22. Michelle Chen, "States Attempt to Instill Work Ethic by Rolling Back Child Labor Protections," *The Nation*, January 1, 2012.

23. Greenhouse, *Big Squeeze*, 39, 40; David Harvey, *A Brief History of Neoliberalism* (Oxford: Oxford University Press, 2005), 26; Collins, *Transforming America*, 77; Pimpare, *New Victorians*, 117–21; Larry Bartels, *Unequal Democracy: The Political Economy of the New Gilded Age* (Princeton, NJ: Princeton University Press, 2008), 222–26; Shipler, *Working Poor*, introduction; Federal Reserve Bank of New York, "Quarterly Report on Household Debt and Credit," February 2003.

24. Stein, *Pivotal Decade*, 120–21, 239; Robert M. Collins, *More: The Politics of Economic Growth in Postwar America* (New York: Oxford University Press, 2000), 168, 170, 173.

25. Schulman, *Seventies*, 92; Thomas Bryne Edsall with Mary D. Edsall, *Chain Reaction: The Impact of Race, Rights, and Taxes on American Politics* (New York: Norton, 1991), 1–4; Stein, *Pivotal Decade*, ch. 3; Lizabeth Cohen, *A Consumers' Republic: The Politics of Mass Consumption in Postwar America* (New York: Knopf, 2003), 312–13.

26. Cowie, *Stayin' Alive*, 12–13; Chris Hedges, "The World Liberal Opportunists Made," *Truthdig* (www.truthdig.com), October 25, 2010.

27. Lasch, *True and Only Heaven*, 439; Stein, *Pivotal Decade*, 174, 200, 244, and see ch. 6, 8, 11; Collins, *Transforming America*, ch. 5; Phillips, *Politics of Rich and Poor*, 91, 93–96; Randy Martin, *Financialization of Daily Life* (Philadelphia: Temple University Press, 2002), 124; Hedges, "World Liberal Opportunists Made"; Collins, *More*, 157, 170, 173; Rodgers, *Age of Fracture*, 62; Thomas Bryne Edsall, "The Changing Shape of Power: A Realignment in Public Policy," in *The Rise and Fall of the New Deal Order, 1930–1980*, eds. Steve Fraser and Gary Gerstle (Princeton, NJ: Princeton University Press, 1989).

28. Greenhouse, *Big Squeeze*, 7–8.

29. Shipler, *Working Poor*, ch. 2 and 3.

30. Kathi Weeks, *The Problem with Work: Feminism, Marxism, Antiwork Politics, and Postwork Imaginaries* (Durham, NC: Duke University Press, 2011), 58.

31. Ibid.; Ruskin quoted in Lasch, *True and Only Heaven*, 137; Jay L. Hart and Tracy E. Meyer, "Work, Memory, and Narrative: Personal Stories of Deindustrialization in Louisville, Kentucky," in *Beyond the Ruins: The Meaning of Deindustrialization*, eds. Jefferson Cowie and Joseph Heathcott (Ithaca NY: ILR Press, 2003); Parker, *Flesh Peddlers*, 145.

32. Pimpare, *New Victorians*, 121.

33. Parker, *Flesh Peddlers;* E. E. LeMasters, *Blue-Collar Aristocrats: Life-Styles at a Working-Class Tavern* (Madison: University of Wisconsin Press, 1975), 6, 18, 30; William Deresiewicz, "The Dispossessed," *American Scholar* 75 (Winter 2006).

34. Cohen, *Consumers' Republic,* 312; Deresiewicz, "The Dispossessed"; Gramm and Snow quoted in Chait, *Big Con,* 126–27; Shipler, *Working Poor,* ch. 1; Steven Lukes, *Power: A Radical View* (New York: Macmillan, 1974); Thatcher quoted in Martin, *Financialization of Daily Life,* 177.

35. Cowie, *Stayin' Alive,* ch. 5.

36. Stein, *Pivotal Decade,* ch. 6.

37. Rodgers, *Age of Fracture*; Peter Schrag, *The Decline of the WASP* (New York: Simon and Schuster, 1971).

38. Pete Hamill, "The Revolt of the White Lower Middle Class," *New York,* April 4, 1969; Cowie, *Stayin' Alive,* 128, 134, 162, and ch. 3.

39. Deresiewicz, "The Dispossessed"; Terry Eagleton, *Why Marx Was Right* (New Haven: Yale University Press, 2011), 163, 170; Rodino-Calocino, "High-Tech Workers".

40. Linda Kintz, *Between Jesus and the Market: The Emotions That Matter in Right-Wing America* (Durham, NC: Duke University Press, 1997), 247 and ch. 7; Cowie, *Stayin' Alive,* part I and 15, 18, ch. 1, and 168–71; Roger Shattuck, "The Reddening of America," *The New York Review of Books,* March 30, 1989; James C. Scott, *Weapons of the Weak: Everyday Forms of Peasant Resistance* (New Haven: Yale University Press, 1985); Weeks, *Problem with Work,* 51, 57; preacher quoted in Ric Locke, "Recovery," Ric's Rulez, warlocketx.wordpress.com, September 17, 2009.

Chapter 13: Improbable Rebels: The Folklore of Limousine Liberalism

1. Mario Procaccino quoted in Steve Fraser, "The Limousine Liberal's Family Tree," *Raritan* 3, no. 1 (Summer 2011), 138–55; Glenn Beck, "American Progressivism," GlennBeck.com, April 16, 2009; Glenn Beck and St. Louis Tea Party leader quoted in Fraser, "Limousine Liberal's Family Tree."

2. Garry Wills, *Reagan's America: Innocents at Home* (Garden City, NY: Doubleday, 1987), 446–47; John Maynard Keynes, *The Collected Writings of John Maynard Keynes,* vol. 9, *Essays in Persuasion,* eds. Austin Robinson, Elizabeth Johnson, and Donald Moggridge (London: Macmillan, 1972), 294.

3. Daniel Bell, *The End of Ideology: On the Exhaustion of Political Ideas in the Fifties* (Glencoe, IL: Free Press, 1960), ch. 2; Stefan Link, "Transitional Fordism: Ford Motor Company, Nazi Germany and the Soviet Union in the Interwar Years" (PhD diss., Harvard University), ch. 2; *The International Jew* (Dearborn, 1922), originally a series of articles published in the *Dearborn Independent* between 1920 and 1922 under the title "The Jewish Question," see particularly articles published on June 12, September 4, October 2, November 13, November 20, December 4, 1920, and February 19, June 25, July 2, July 23, 1921; Albert Lee, *Henry Ford and the Jews* (New York: Stein and Day, 1980), 7–8, 14, 16, 45, 47, 49, 59; Leo P. Ribuffo, "Henry Ford and the 'International Jew,' " *American Jewish History* 69 (June 1980); David L. Lewis, "Henry Ford's Anti-Semitism and Its Repercussions," *Michigan Journal of History* 24 (January 1984); Edmund Wilson, *The American Jitters: A Year of the Slump* (New York: Scribner's, 1932), 79; Michael N. Dobkowski, *The Tarnished Dream: The Basis of American Anti-Semitism* (Westport, CT: Greenwood, 1979), 196–200.

4. Chip Berlet and Matthew N. Lyons, *Right-Wing Populism in America: Too Close for Comfort* (New York: Guilford, 2000), 140–43; Coughlin quoted in David H. Bennett, *Demagogues in the Depression: American Radicals and the Union Party, 1932–1936* (New Brunswick, NJ: Rutgers University Press, 1969), 230.
5. Robert Taft quoted in John Nichols, "Why Do GOP Bosses Fear Ron Paul?" *The Nation,* December 21, 2011; McCarthy on Acheson quoted in Robert J. McMahon, *Dean Acheson and the Creation of the American World Order* (Washington, D.C.: Potomac, 2009), 114; McCarthy on John McCloy in *Panama City News Herald,* October 29, 1953.
6. Robert Britt Horwitz, *America's Right: Anti-Establishment Conservatism from Goldwater to the Tea Party* (Cambridge: Polity, 2013), 50.
7. Matthew D. Lassiter, *The Silent Majority: Suburban Politics in the Sunbelt South* (Princeton, NJ: Princeton University Press, 2006); Elizabeth Tandy Shermer, *Sunbelt Capitalism: Phoenix and the Transformation of American Politics* (Philadelphia: University of Pennsylvania Press, 2013); Horwitz, *America's Right,* 50.
8. Bruce J. Schulman, *The Seventies: The Great Shift in American Culture, Society, and Politics* (New York: Free Press, 2001), 200–207; Joseph E. Lowndes, *From the New Deal to the New Right: Race and the Southern Origins of Modern Conservatism* (New Haven: Yale University Press, 2008), 80; Wallace quoted in Michael Kazin, *The Populist Persuasion: An American History* (New York: Basic Books, 1995), 221; Dan T. Carter, *The Politics of Rage: George Wallace, the Origins of the New Conservatism, and the Transformation of American Politics* (New York: Simon and Schuster, 1995), 315–16.
9. Alan Pell Crawford, *Thunder on the Right: The "New Right" and the Politics of Resentment* (New York: Pantheon, 1980), 1–10, 126; Berlet and Lyons, *Right-Wing Populism in America,* 218–22.
10. Wallace quoted in Crawford, *Thunder on the Right,* p. 82.
11. Carter, *Politics of Rage,* 314, 352; Lowndes, *From the New Deal to the New Right,* 83, 92, 101; Crawford, *Thunder on the Right,* 126.
12. Arno Mayer, "The Lower Middle Class as a Historical Problem," *Journal of Modern History* 47 (September 1975).
13. Lassiter, *Silent Majority,* 18.
14. Hicks and Procaccino quoted in Christopher Lasch, *The True and Only Heaven: Progress and Its Critics* (New York: Norton, 1991), 478, 486, 505–6.
15. Rusher, Weyrich, and Laxalt quoted in Crawford, *Thunder on the Right,* 168, 213–14, 218–19; Berlet and Lyons, *Right-Wing Populism,* 201, 202, 222; Thomas Frank, *Pity the Billionaire: The Hard Times Swindle and the Unlikely Comeback of the Right* (New York: Metropolitan/Henry Holt, 2012), 93–95.
16. *Right Woman* quoted by Crawford, *Thunder on the Right,* 147; Berlet and Lyons, *Right-Wing Populism,* 209–10.
17. Daniel T. Rodgers, *Age of Fracture* (Cambridge, MA: Belknap/Harvard University Press, 2011), 169, 171.
18. Berlet and Lyons, *Right-Wing Populism,* 236; Terry Eagleton, *The Illusions of Postmodernism* (London: Oxford, 1996), 70.
19. Paul Boyer, *When Time Shall Be No More: Prophecy Belief in Modern American Culture* (Cambridge, MA: Belknap/Harvard University Press, 1992), 254–55, 263, 270, 288–89.
20. Ibid., 265–66.

21. Schulman, *Seventies*, 212; Thomas Bryne Edsall with Mary D. Edsall, *Chain Reaction: The Impact of Race, Rights, and Taxes on American Politics* (New York: Norton, 1991), 1–4.

22. Richard Harvey Brown, *Culture, Capitalism, and Democracy in the New America* (New Haven: Yale University Press, 2005), 26, 96; Richard Parker, *The Myth of the Middle Class* (New York: Liveright, 1972), 43, 201–2.

23. Michael Novak, *The Rise of the Unmeltable Ethnics: Politics and Culture in the Seventies* (New York: Macmillan, 1972), 7, 16, 142–43; Dave Barry, "One Nation, Slightly Divisible," *The Atlantic Monthly*, December 2001; Mayer, "The Lower Middle Class."

24. Shermer, *Sunbelt Capitalism*; Schulman, *Seventies*.

25. F. Bechhofer and B. Elliott, "The Petite Bourgeoisie in Late Capitalism," *Annual Review of Sociology*, 1985; Frank, *Pity the Billionaire*, ch. 6.

26. Frank, *Pity the Billionaire*, 93–95, 97; Anthony Dimaggio, *The Rise of the Tea Party: Political Discontent and the Corporate Media in the Age of Obama* (New York: Monthly Review Press, 2011).

27. Parker, *Myth of the Middle Class*; Jonathan Chait, *The Big Con: The True Story of How Washington Got Hoodwinked and Hijacked by Crackpot Economics* (Boston: Houghton Mifflin, 2007), 96.

28. Lassiter, *Silent Majority*; Berlet and Lyons, *Right-Wing Populism*, 218; Schulman, *Seventies*, 37–40; Robert C. Christopher, *Crashing the Gates: The De-WASPing of America's Power Elite* (New York: Simon and Schuster, 1989), 111–12.

29. Mark Ames, "V. S. Naipaul and the American Right," *Jacobin*, Spring 2012.

30. Bechhofer and Elliott, "The Petite Bourgeoisie"; Scott Shane, "Why Small Business Owners Trust the Tea Party," *The American*, October 17, 2010; Judson Phillips, "The Party of Killing Small Business," Tea Party Nation (www.teapartynation.com /forum), May 9, 2011; U.S. Small Business Administration, Report #3, "The Facts About Small Business, 1999" and "The State of Small Business: A Report of the President, 1997," Small Business Administration, Office of Government Contracting: Fiscal Year 1999 Report on Annual Procurement Preference, April 4, 2000; David Harvey, *The Conditions of Postmodernity: An Enquiry into the Origins of Cultural Change* (Cambridge, MA: Blackwell, 1990), 192, 194.

31. Parker, *Myth of the Middle Class*; Barry C. Lynn, "Killing the Corporation," *Harper's*, February 2012.

32. Rodgers, *Age of Fracture*, 218–19.

33. Stanley A. Deetz, *Democracy in an Age of Corporate Colonialization: Developments in Communication and the Politics of American Life* (Albany: SUNY Press, 1992), 2–5.

34. "Ted Cruz Interview: On Obama, the GOP, and Big Business," *The Wall Street Journal*, May 20, 2012; Jeffrey R. Cornwall, "Small Business Turns to the Tea Party," *Christian Science Monitor*, June 17, 2010; "Why Business Doesn't Trust the Tea Party," *Bloomberg Business Week*, October 13, 2010; Shane, "Why Small Business Owners Trust the Tea Party"; Morgan Warstler, "Pssst—Super-Congress...Cut the Tea Party Taxes," *Breitbart News Network* (www.breitbart.com), August 3, 2011; Mark Naison, "Small Business Nation—Understanding the Social Base of Tea Party America," New Black Man (in Exile), newblackman.blogspot.com/2011/04/small -business-nation, April 11, 2011; Linda Kintz, *Between Jesus and the Market: The Emotions That Matter in Right-Wing America* (Durham, NC: Duke University Press, 1997), ch. 6.

35. Fredric Jameson, *The Seeds of Time* (New York: Columbia University Press, 1994), 60; Vanessa Williamson, Theda Skocpol, and John Coggin, "The Tea Party and the Remaking of Republican Conservatism," *Perspectives on Politics* 9 (March, 2011).

36. Gingrich quoted in Kintz, *Between Jesus and the Market*, 195; Phillips, "The Party Killing Small Business"; Sabrina Tavernise, "Middle Class Areas Shrink as Income Gap Grows," *The New York Times*, October 16, 2011.

37. Williamson, Skocpol, and Coggin, "The Tea Party."

38. Brown, *Culture, Capitalism, and Democracy.*

39. CNBC quoted in Chris Lehmann, "How We Learned to Stop Worrying and Love the Robber Barons," *Mother Jones*, October 18, 2010.

Chapter 14: Conclusion: Exit by the Rear Doors

1. Christopher Lasch, *The Culture of Narcissism: American Life in an Age of Diminishing Expectations* (New York: Norton, 1978), 234; Joseph E. Lowndes, *From the New Deal to the New Right: Race and the Southern Origins of Modern Conservatism* (New Haven: Yale University Press, 2008), 148; Stephen Pimpare, *The New Victorians: Poverty, Politics, and Propaganda in Two Gilded Ages* (New York: The New Press, 2004), 106.

2. Barbara Garson, *Down the Up Escalator: How the 99 Percent Live in the Great Recession* (New York: Doubleday, 2013); George Packer, "Don't Look Down," *The New Yorker*, April 29, 2013.

3. Jefferson Cowie, *Stayin' Alive: The 1970s and the Last Days of the Working Class* (New York: The New Press, 2010); Kathi Weeks, *The Problem with Work: Feminism, Marxism, Antiwork Politics, and the Postwork Imaginaries* (Durham, NC: Duke University Press, 2011); Jennifer Senior, "Recession Culture," *The New York Times Magazine*, May 18, 2009; David Harvey, *A Brief History of Neoliberalism* (Oxford: Oxford University Press, 2005); Randy Martin, *Financialization of Daily Life* (Philadelphia: Temple University Press, 2002), 34–35, 125, 133.

Index

Index

American Socialist Party, 126, 136
American Society of Civil Engineers, 249
American Woolen Company, 142
Americans for Tax Reform, 400
anarchy/anarchists, 145, 146, 184, 211; and anti-monopoly movement, 162; and armed forces, 137; and labor, 118, 119, 124, 133, 143, 151, 183, 185; and Lloyd (H. D.), 160; Strong (Josiah) on, 154–155
Anthracite Coal Commission, 177
anticapitalism, 106, 142, 151, 163, 178, 191, 195, 197, 201, 213, 346, 368, 370; and Ford (Henry), 380; and Great Depression, 187; and limousine liberalism, 379, 384, 385; and New Deal, 304
antimonopolists, 19, 126, 128, 130, 155, 161–162
anti-semitism, 380
antitrust movement, 379, 397
Apple (company), 236, 333
aristocracy, 69–70, 97, 99, 155, 169–178, 208, 264, 284, 294, 296, 338, 377, 384
Arizona, 159, 229
armories, 181
Armour, Philip, 18, 36, 61, 119
Arnold, Matthew, 172
Art of War, The (Sun-tzu), 280
artillery of commodities, 312
Aston Martin, 288
Astor, John Jacob, IV, 171
Astor, Mrs., 170–171
Astor Place Opera House, 78
Astor Place riot (1849), 78–79
Atlantic, The, 397
auto industry, 197, 347, 351, 380
auto-cannibalism, 234, 259, 262, 419, 420

Bachman, Michele, 377
Baer, George, 176–177
Bain Capital, 299
Bakker, Jim, 280
Bakker, Tammy Faye, 280
Bakunin, Mikhail, 124
Baltimore and Ohio Railroad, 114, 120
Baltimore, Maryland, 231, 251
Bank of America, 259
Bank of the United States, 93

bankruptcies, 259, 308, 309, 348
banks, 6, 82, 95–96, 150, 208, 219, 234, 242, 248, 266, 268–273, 359; and agriculture, 77, 89, 91, 93; and aristocracy, 69; and convict labor, 51; and Coughlin (Father Charles), 383; and deindustrialization, 228; and Democratic Party, 5, 93; and economic depressions, 62, 188; failure of, 241; and financial meltdown (2008), 413; and FIRE sector, 236, 237; and Ford (Henry), 380–381, 382; and Goldwater (Barry), 386; and Great Recession, 416, 417; and homesteading, 47; and Jackson (Andrew), 76; jobs at, 253; and Leggett (William), 83; and limousine liberalism, 390, 394, 398; and McCarthy (Joseph), 384; and modern corporations, 270; and Morgan (J. P.), 134, 169; and populist politics, 98, 105; and progress, 41; during Reagan era, 347–348; relationship vs. transactional banking, 278–279; and Wall Street, 275; zombie, 241
barter, 84, 265
Baum, Frank, 158
Beard, Charles, 183
Beardstown Ladies' Common Sense Investment Guide, The, 283–284
Beck, Glenn, 375, 377–379, 394, 404, 407
Become a Better You (Osteen), 319
Beecher, Henry Ward, 116
Bell, Alexander Graham, 26
Bell, Daniel, 306–307
Bellamy, Edward, 118–119, 125, 156–157, 165, 231
Belmont, August, 169
Benjamin, Walter, 307
Benson, Arthur, 44–45
Bentham, Jeremy, 45, 353
Berger, Peter, 284
Bergerac, Michel, 276
Berkeley Light Guard and Infantry, 120
Berkman, Alexander, 133–134
Bernanke, Ben, 416
Beyond the Bourne (Fiske), 160
"Bible of Currency Reformers, The," 77
Biddle, Nicholas, 69, 76
Bierce, Ambrose, 92

Index

Index

JILL ANDRESKY FRASER

STEVE FRASER is the author of *Every Man a Speculator, Wall Street*, and *Labor Will Rule*, which won the Philip Taft Award for the best book in labor history. He also is the co-editor of *The Rise and Fall of the New Deal Order*. His work has appeared in the *Los Angeles Times*, the *New York Times*, *The Nation*, *The American Prospect, Raritan*, and the *London Review of Books*. He has written for the online site tomdispatch.com, and his work has appeared on the Huffington Post, Salon, Truthout, and Alternet, among others. He lives in New York City.